THE SCOTTISH LION ON PATROL

To those gallant seventy-three
of the
15th Scottish Reconnaissance Regiment
whose lives ended young because they fought between
Arromanches and Elmenhorst

(27 June 1944 - 8 May 1945)

The
Scottish Lion on Patrol

Being the story of the
15th Scottish Reconnaissance Regiment

1943-1946

original book by

CAPTAIN W. KEMSLEY

and

CAPTAIN M.R. RIESCO

Walter Kemsley

Michael R. Riesco

1950
THE WHITE SWAN PRESS LTD
BRISTOL 8

This version by

TIM CHAMBERLIN

2010

Pen & Sword
MILITARY

First published in Great Britain in 2011 by
Pen & Sword MILITARY
an imprint of
Pen & Sword Books Ltd,
47 Church Street,
Barnsley,
South Yorkshire.
S70 2AS

A CIP record for this book is available from the British Library.

ISBN 978184 884 5695

Typeset by S Keeling, typeset-design@hotmail.com

Printed and bound by CPI

Pen & Sword Books Ltd incorporates the Imprints of
Pen & Sword Aviation, Pen & Sword Maritime, Pen & Sword Military,
Wharncliffe Local History, Pen & Sword Select, Pen & Sword Military
Classics, Leo Cooper, remember when, Seaforth Publishing and
Frontline Publishing.

For a complete list of Pen & Sword titles please contact
Pen & Sword Books Limited
47 Church Street, Barnsley, South Yorkshire, S70 2AS, england
e-mail: enquiries@pen-and-sword.co.uk
website: www.pen-and-sword.co.uk

Contents

List of illustrations

* These photographs appeared in the original edition (1950) by courtesy of the Imperial War Museum.

Photographs H34493 and B11272 are reproduced by kind permission of the Imperial War Museum.

Many of the photographs are previously unpublished and are from the private collections of Regimental Association members and their inclusion is acknowledged with grateful thanks

ACKNOWLEDGEMENTS

The production of this book is another example of the team spirit which took the 15th Scottish Reconnaissance Regiment through France, Belgium and Holland and far into Germany. Finding that even the formidable pile of the Regimental War Diary left unrecorded much that was worthy of recording, the authors sought the help of many old comrades in arms, and from many corners of the British Isles help came. Even now, time has buried deeds which should have found a place in these pages, and the names mentioned are by no means all the names which should have been mentioned, but the bare bones of the War Diary have been covered with the flesh and blood of personal anecdote, and many gaps have been filled.

The following contributed accounts of the actions in which the regiment took part: G. R. Blount MC, J. Bosch, J. K. Boynton MC, A. Buck MC, J. Connor, G. T. B. Dalton, P. R. Dobson, A. E. Gillings, J. Kay, P. C. Kerridge MC, J. Kirman MM, W. B. Liddell MC, A. Little, M. B. McFall, R. W. Parker, P. D. Peterson, C. W. Ridge, E. A. Royle MC, K. B. M. Shirley, D. C. Waters and J. Wheeler.

Many more went to great trouble to supply important details to fill gaps in the text: A. Gilbert and R. Davidson typed, drew maps and made valuable suggestions; and the original draft of the story was greatly improved by the amendments of Colonel J. A. Grant Peterkin DSO, Lieut Col K. C. C. Smith DSO, W. B. Liddell MC, and G. R. Blount MC Photographs have been included by permission of the Imperial War Museum.

Not the least important contribution to the writing of this story has been the tolerance with which the compilers' wives have borne the disruption of domestic routine which it has entailed.

W.K.
M.R.R.

ACKNOWLEDGEMENTS

I count myself fortunate to have known many of the men who took the 'Scottish Lion on Patrol'. Walter Kemsley and Michael Riesco were fully supportive of my intention to write an updated version of the Regiment's history. Their children Sarah Kemsley and Jane and Philip Riesco have continued with their encouragement. The members of the Regimental Association who contributed new material are identified and it is cause for regret that so many of them are now dead. All of them shared a determination to ensure that important events were recorded accurately, and not forgotten. Throughout the course of production they continued to cajole, encourage and inspire me to completion.

Major Victor Sadgrove was fulsome in his praise of Captain C. G. Lawton and his work *The Path of the Lion* from which a quote is taken.

Former members of the Regiment George Blount M.C., 'Gilly', Bill Howlett, Bill Mincedorf, John Kay and Edwin Reetham continue to help and ensure accuracy. Many of the photographs are from private collections and have never been previously published; their inclusion is acknowledged with grateful thanks.

Armand Deknudt-Montbaliu in Belgium has been a great supporter of the Regimental Association and a most valuable source of information.

A former Captain in the Dutch Army, Hans Steenmetz, helped in many of our visits to Holland and has an encyclopaedic knowledge of the area over which the Regiment fought.

In Tilburg Leon Timmermans and his 'Orange Committee', overwhelmed the veterans with kindness and care on several visits to the town to commemorate its long awaited liberation in late 1944.

I am especially indebted to Major General Peter Grant Peterkin CB, OBE for writing the foreword to this new edition.

Writing, researching and checking the material has been challenging over a long period of time; I could not have achieved it without unceasing help from my wife, Gail, and my sons, Douglas and Scott, for practical assistance.

Tim Chamberlin
October 2010

FOREWORD

This is the simple story of a very happy family, brought together for more than three years by war. Its members' aims were to hasten victory, retain freedom for their country, and then return to their homes and jobs.

This story has been written for the members of that family, who will always cherish and maintain their pride in the good name of their regiment, and it will refresh the many pleasant associations and friendships within both regiment and division and with the many members of Second Army with whom we had the honour to work.. In addition, it will recall the kindness shown to the members of the regiment by so many men, women and children of France, Belgium and Holland.

It is, perhaps above all else, our one means of acknowledging our great debt to those who did not live to see the fulfilment of our ambitions or the days of peace.

In no way do we claim special distinction; we were but one of the many, all doing their utmost to defeat the enemy. Fate decreed that some were to have great chances, others little or none, to make history.

These pages will bring to life again memories of people with whom we are proud to have been associated and incidents and actions in which we are proud to have shared. How great was our good fortune to be part of the 15th Scottish Division cannot be told in mere words—its commanders, staff and 'Jocks' were our friends, and could not have done more to help us. Nor can we exaggerate the debt we owe to the officers and men of the infantry battalions— so nobly supported by our gunners and sappers—who fought under far worse conditions than we did, and whose gallantry and devotion to duty made our task possible. We can only hope that they still feel that the Recce made their task easier at times, and that we helped them to uphold the glorious traditions of the 15th Scottish Division.

We would like to place on record our thanks to Capt Michael Riesco (C Squadron and Adjutant) and Capt Walter Kemsley (Regimental Signals Officer) for their great work in bringing out this book, and to congratulate them on so successful an outcome. We know, too, that they would be the first to acknowledge their debt to Sergeant Gilbert (Orderly Room Sergeant) for his part in typing, drawing and generally being helpful.

These alone have made possible the appearance of this our story. Starting with little material except the Regimental War Diary, full of dull details of exercises, moves and locations in Europe, they have given an accurate account of the life of the regiment, full of live interest to the whole family. It will be a highly esteemed and lasting memorial to the name of the regiment now, officially, no more.

Foreword

This newly revised edition of *The Scottish Lion on Patrol* is the history of a Regiment which played a significant part in the campaign in North West Europe. This book, covering the three years of the 15th Scottish Reconnaissance Regiment's existence, gives a fascinating insight into the raising of a regiment in a new role and the realities of prolonged fighting in the van of the Allied advance. Landing soon after D Day they went straight into battle near Caen; and from that day until the German surrender near the Baltic, the Regiment was always in the thick of the fighting.

This book is an important addition to the history of the Reconnaissance Corps. The art of reconnaissance in the Second World War has not been well documented in most Divisional and general histories of the period. Reinforcing the truism that 'time spent in reconnaissance is never wasted', this book reminds us that, unlike today with all its airborne surveillance assets, the eyes and ears of every formation were their recce: bravely probing enemy lines and reporting back so that commanders could make a plan based on the latest dispositions. Others have written interestingly enough about other capabilities but the reconnaissance role, both highly specialist and demanding great courage, has not been fully appreciated.

We are fortunate to have in Tim Chamberlin an acknowledged expert with a real feel for his subject matter. His interviews with those who fought bravely with the Regiment have brought a fresh and well-informed insight into the story. This must be one of the last books about the War that includes so many interesting eye witness accounts of the fighting. This helps capture the fierce loyalty and pride in the Reconnaissance Corps, an organization whose esprit de corps was second to none, despite their short history.

My father in his foreword described the original edition as 'the simple story of a very happy family'. Now the revised edition can be seen as very much more than this; it is a masterly description of the realities of reconnaissance at unit level with many pertinent lessons for the soldier and military historian of today.

Major General Peter Grant Peterkin CB OBE
October 2010

Dedication

To two thoroughly good men:
Len Watson and Bryan White

CHAPTER I

THE BEGINNING

The 15th Scottish Reconnaissance Regiment was formed in the fourth year of the Second World War and disbanded in Germany at the end of March 1946. It landed in North-West Europe for the Battle of Normandy as part of the 15th Scottish Division in the last days of June 1944, fought throughout the rest of the campaign against Germany—for one brief but memorable period under the command of the 6th Airborne Division—and when Germany surrendered was at Elmenhorst, within an hour's drive of the Baltic port of Lubeck.

Seven of the regiment's officers and sixty-six of its other ranks lost their lives. Many others were wounded.

The two men who commanded it in action were each awarded the Distinguished Service Order, and to other members of the regiment were made twelve awards of the Military Cross, two of the Distinguished Conduct Medal, fourteen of the Military Medal and three of the Croix de Guerre. Ten officers and seven other ranks were Mentioned in Despatches, two officers and seven other ranks received the Commander-in-Chief's certificate for gallantry, and one officer and eighteen other ranks received the Commander-in-Chief's certificate for good service.

The 15th Scottish Division was one of the drafting divisions chosen, late in 1942, to go on to the Higher Establishment and to become part of the ultimate Second Army, then being formed. This decision meant that the division was entitled to a reconnaissance regiment in place of the independent reconnaissance squadron of a division on the Lower Establishment. Thus, to form a regiment as the 15th Reconnaissance Regiment at Felton, Northumberland, on 15 February 1943, the powers decreed that the 15th, 45th and 54th Independent Reconnaissance Squadrons be amalgamated. They were the tangible ingredients in the make-up of the new unit. Intangible ingredients were the traditions of the 15th Scottish Division and experience of the teething troubles of the Reconnaissance Corps.

The 15th Scottish Division, not a regular division, was formed in the 1914-18 war. It fought many battles of the Western Front, including Loos (September, 1915), the Somme (August, 1916), Arras (April, 1917), Ypres (1917 and March, 1918) and on the Marne-Buzancy (July, 1918), where the French 17th Division erected a monument in homage to the Scottish Division. The 15th Scottish Division, although still untested by its second war, was one in which a soldier could take pride. Soon the regiment expressed that pride by putting Scottish into its title and by wearing the Balmoral until it had to be replaced for action by the more practical black beret of the Royal Armoured Corps.

The regiment was not the first reconnaissance unit to be part of the division. The Reconnaissance Corps had been founded two years earlier to do in the war of the internal combustion engine the work which had been done by the old horsed divisional cavalry in the wars of marching men—to look and to listen, to find out and report back, to be a screen against surprise, to see that the division was forearmed by being forewarned, to seize and to hold. Reconnaissance battalions grew mainly from the brigade anti-tank companies, and the battalions' part in the armies of liberation was evolved in training by a process of trial and error and—in those days of shortage—improvisation. With motor-cycles of civilian origin, a few ungainly armoured trucks called 'meatsafes' (which is what they would have been in action), anti-tank rifles and wireless sets lamentably insufficient in power and numbers, infantrymen began to learn the job which they were to do as mechanised cavalry with fast and powerful armoured cars and reconnaissance cars, an impressive assortment of tracked and half-tracked vehicles, a wireless system which could give communications over many miles and a regiment's fire power equal to that of an infantry brigade.

The unit which went through the early training adventures with the 15th Scottish Division was formed at Kirkee Barracks, Colchester, on 13 January 1941, and became the 15th Battalion, Reconnaissance Corps. Officers and other ranks were drawn from the brigade anti-tank companies and from all the infantry regiments then in the division: the 6th and 7th King's Own Scottish Borderers, the 8th Royal Scots, the 9th and 10th Cameronians, the 6th Royal Scots Fusiliers, the 2nd Glasgow Highlanders, and the 10th and 11th Highland Light Infantry. The battalion was first commanded by Lieut Colonel Sandeman, and Major N. C. Hendricks was second-in-command.

It was, however, a short-lived 15th Battalion, through no fault of its own. Army reorganization made it necessary for the 15th Scottish Division and several other formations to revert to Lower War Establishment, under which the divisional reconnaissance strength was reduced to a company, whose chief job, it seemed often, was to supply men for units nearer in time to the line of battle. The battalion, commanded by Lieut Colonel Hendricks with Major J. I. Faircloth as second-in-command, was broken up at Consett, County Durham, on the first day of 1942 to form the 15th, 48th and 77th Independent Reconnaissance Companies. Later the Reconnaissance Corps took cavalry names, and the companies became squadrons.

The 48th and 77th Companies left the division and they pass from the pages of this history. The 15th remained and thirteen months later became A Squadron of the 15th Scottish Reconnaissance Regiment in a division which returned to full strength in preparation for what was to be an important part in the invasion of Europe. The 15th Independent Reconnaissance Company was commanded first by Major Faircloth with Captain J. Roberts as second-in-command and CSM D. Dobbin as company sergeant major. In March 1942, Major P. T. I. MacDiarmid took over command, with Captain O.W. Butler as second-in-command. The unit was stationed at Black Hill, County Durham, Throckley, Northumberland, and Brunton Hall, Northumberland, before going to Felton Hall.

It was fitting that the 15th Scottish Reconnaissance Regiment was formed so close to the border between Scotland and England, for there was much of both countries in its make-up. The 15th Independent Reconnaissance Squadron had always been part of the Scottish Division and had drawn its men in the first place from Scottish units. The 45th and 54th Independent Reconnaissance Squadrons, which went to Northumberland from Essex and Suffolk to become parts of the new regiment, brought with them a strong English strain. Their ties were with the infantry regiments of London and the counties round about.

These two squadrons were old friends: at Felton they resumed an association which had been interrupted by the breaking up of the 54th Battalion, Reconnaissance Corps, a little more than a year before. The 54th Battalion was formed under the command of Lieut Colonel E. L. Ricketts OBE, at Faringdon, Berkshire, in July 1941, from the 21st Battalion, The Royal Fusiliers, and the anti-tank companies of the 54th Division. In January 1942, that division, like the 15th Scottish, was placed on Lower War Establishment, and the battalion ended its brief life at Rendlesham Hall in Suffolk. From the ashes, however, rose the Phoenix of the 45th, 54th and 76th Independent Reconnaissance Companies. The 45th, commanded first by Major L. Nash and later by Major Adam Gordon, Scotsman and regular soldier, went south to Danbury in Essex. The 54th, under the command of Major L. H. Mills, spent its year of independence in the remote and pleasant Suffolk coast village of Orford, where it survived a bomb on its officers' mess and the loss of its MT stores by fire.

In the welding of Scot and Cockney at Felton Hall the 45th Independent Reconnaissance Squadron became the 15th Scottish Reconnaissance Regiment's B Squadron, still commanded with the care of a hen watching over her brood by Adam Gordon—a man with a great belief in a notebook, a rather slight figure to be seen walking the path from mess to squadron office with head thrust forward and hands clasped behind back. The 54th Independent Reconnaissance Squadron emerged from the transformation as C Squadron, still following the pipe smoke and ready laughter of Harry Mills.

To make a regiment out of three independent squadrons, whose stories had been of struggles against shortages of men and equipment, the War Office sent Lieut Colonel J. A. Grant Peterkin, a tall Scotsman from Forres, a regular soldier of the Queen's Own Cameron Highlanders. He had been an adjutant at the outbreak of war. He had been brigade major to the 4 Infantry Brigade in the British Expeditionary Force in 1940, and afterwards a 'teacher' at Camberley and on staff duty with V Corps. Next he had formed and commanded the Reconnaissance Training Centre at Scarborough with an energy which had already gained him a reputation in the Reconnaissance Corps. He brought with him to Felton Hall a tremendous capacity for work, definite ideas on training, a determination to make a crack regiment, a blackened pipe and a habit of brushing his hair as an antidote to fatigue and stress in exercise and action. Working harder and longer than anybody else in the regiment, he was to dominate its life in preparation for battle and in battle for nineteen months and in three countries.

Major Peter MacDiarmid became the regiment's second-in-command, and his first successor in the command of A Squadron was Major Brian Crowder. As RSM the regiment had Mr W. H. Eardley, a Grenadier Guardsman by trade, who had been squadron sergeant major of the 54th Independent Squadron.

Some of the newly formed regiment were already veterans, having survived the Dunkirk evacuation. Three of them were:

George Blount was a Staff Sergeant in the RAMC on leave from the BEF when recalled back to France. On his return he was issued with a rifle, fifty rounds and told that he was now an infantryman. George recalls being close to Waterloo in the hectic days of the retreat; eventually with only another non swimming companion he found himself on the wrong side of a stretch of water over which the bridge had been destroyed. An RE Sergeant with a squad appeared and stated that he had no intention of getting wet and began with salvaged timbers to build a crossing linked to the remaining pillars of the bridge. Eventually a relatively safe cellar in Bray les Dunes was reached. George almost boarded HMS *Ivanhoe* which was severely bombed, disabled and had to be towed back to England. On 1 June 1940 George boarded HMS *Whitehall* from the Mole at Dunkirk and reached England safely.

Later he was selected for promotion and attended an OCTU at Lanark joining 15th Independent Recce in June 1942.

Bryan White served with the Worcestershire Regiment and was evacuated from Dunkirk. Attended OCTU at Sandhurst and was commissioned into the Royal Fusiliers and then to 54th Independent Reconnaissance Squadron. He was stationed at Orford, which was bombed on 22 October 1942, eleven civilians losing their lives. Bryan married Betty on 31 October 1942; 'Stinker' Gray was best man and, suffering badly from the previous night's festivities forgot the licence which had to be sent by despatch rider to enable the marriage to take place on the Isle of Wight.

Ken Jenkins a native of Wolverhampton went to France with the 1/6th Battalion South Staffordshire Regiment in 1940. He saw his first German (in anger) close to the Menin Gate in Ypres in late May 1940. 'We could only put up token resistance, and we were so short of equipment, that my little mob was only allocated the Bren gun every fourth day.' Jenks was eventually evacuated from the beaches of Dunkirk. Commissioned in 1943 and posted to the regiment where he joined B Squadron sharing the responsibility of 6 Troop with Lieut Nick Carey and much enjoyed working with the carrier section.

*   *   *   *   *

King George VI signed a royal warrant on 14 January 1941 authorising the formation of the Reconnaissance Corps.

*   *   *   *   *

George Blount:- Scottish Regiments retained a high proportion of Scots within their ranks often linked to their traditional areas of recruitment. The formation of 15th Scottish Reconnaissance Regiment from the 15th, 45th and 54th Independent Reconnaissance Companies meant that the Scottish element averaged between 25-35 per cent of the establishment throughout its lifespan. A Squadron had a higher proportion of Scottish members than B or C.

The 15th (Ind) Squadron was based at Brunton Hall, Embleton near the Northumberland coast. Within the grounds of the large house were Nissen huts. The short cut to the 'local' was to cross the river that bordered the grounds of the Hall by way of two steel cables anchored to trees on either side of the river, thirty feet above the water.

"THE SCOTTISH LION ON PATROL"

being the story of

15TH SCOTTISH RECONNAISSANCE REGIMENT
1943-1946

On behalf of Colonel J. A. Grant Peterkin, D.S.O., our first Commanding Officer and President of our Old Comrades' Association, I am writing to let you know that the book telling the story of the 15th Scottish Reconnaissance Regiment is now available. It is entitled "The Scottish Lion On Patrol," and may be obtained (price 15s.) from M. R. Riesco, 70, Coombe Road, Croydon, Surrey.

The text, illustrated with photographs and maps, covers the Regiment's antecedents; its formation in 1943; its days in Northumberland, Yorkshire and Sussex; the part it played in the battles in France, Belgium, Holland and Germany; and the many duties which it undertook as part of the British Army of the Rhine until the Regiment was disbanded in 1946. Many of those who fought in the Regiment have written of their experiences.

In his foreword Colonel Grant Peterkin says that the book is "the simple story of a very happy family . . . it will refresh the many pleasant associations and friendships within both Regiment and (15th Scottish) Division and with many members of Second Army with whom we had the honour to work." These included The 6th Guards Tank Brigade, The 6th Airborne Division and The Special Air Service.

Now, four years after disbandment, we have lost touch with many of "the family" and those whom we like to think were our close relations. They are scattered far and wide in civilian life and in the Regular Army, for our Regiment was composed not only of men from Scottish Infantry Regiments but also from Southern Regiments such as The Royal Fusiliers and The Queen's Own Royal West Kent, and from R.A.C. training centres.

We shall have to rely, therefore, on sending out this letter to as many of our members and friends, whose addresses are known to us, and to a chosen number of Libraries—both civil and military—hoping they will help us achieve our object of distributing copies to where they rightfully belong.

Should there remain a balance in our History Fund after all expenses have been met, it will be placed towards the cost of our Regimental Book of Remembrance.

The object in view when producing the story of our Regiment is contained in the foreword of the book, "It is, perhaps above all else, our one means of acknowledging our great debt to those who did not live to see the fulfilment of our ambitions or the days of peace."

M. R. RIESCO,
Hon. Secretary, Regimental Association.

70, COOMBE ROAD,
CROYDON, SURREY.

Original *Scottish Lion on Patrol* notification sent by Michael Riesco to all members in 1950

The Scottish Lion still patrols

Card from W. Kemsley - Christmas 2002

Bryan White and Ken Jenkins - Dunkirk Veterans

CHAPTER II

FELTON HALL

Felton Hall, the regiment's first home, was a large, rambling house set high above the village in grounds which sloped steeply to the dark and tumbling waters of the Coquet. War had dotted the grounds with Nissen huts, which shared with the hall the housing of the regiment. The townsman would agree that it was a pleasant place on a fine day; to the countryman it was good on any day. And it was a place which contained little to distract the soldier from his training, for the nearest towns—Alnwick to the north and Morpeth to the south—were ten miles away, and the more extensive urban refinements of Newcastle far enough to be almost a mirage. Liberty trucks ran at the weekend to Alnwick, Morpeth and Ashington, where the pace of a dog meant for some the difference between a week of affluence and one of poverty. For the rest of the week there was work, the camp NAAFI, the camp dance (with WAAF partners), football, cricket on a wicket which called for brave batsmen, and darts and dominoes in Felton's two inns. At the end of a hard day's training thirst for village beer had to be weighed against the steep climb back to camp.

Most of that training was done in the wild Border country which was almost on the regiment's doorstep— ideal country in which to learn to fight and live rough.

The three squadrons which assembled at Felton Hall in that February seemed a motley collection: vehicles and uniforms bearing different signs, khaki berets, inadequate equipment and too few men, except for masses of young officers, all regretting that they appeared to have lost their independence. The memories of those early days are strange now to those who stayed to see the regiment welded, tested and proved. Imperceptibly, the transition from three entities to one regiment with very high esprit de corps and great morale began within hours of the squadrons' arrival. It was a transition due to the avowed intention which men of all ranks shared with their commanding officer: to make the 15th Scottish Division's youngest unit its best.

As early as 12 April Brigadier H. D. K. Money DSO, Commander of 44 Lowland Infantry Brigade, who carried out an administrative inspection, was able to say: 'It was a great joy to see the obvious pride the regiment had already got in itself.' This was the first time the regiment paraded as a regiment, being drawn up with fixed bayonets to salute the inspecting officer. The inspection was a great success and a most auspicious start to the unit's career. Other visits to Felton Hall were paid by the GOC, 15th Scottish Division, Major General G. H. A. MacMillan CBE, DSO, MC, who met his reconnaissance troops for the first time on 26 April, shortly after taking over from Major General D. C. Bullen Smith MC; by Lieutenant General G. C. Bucknall MC, Commander of I Corps; and by the GOC, Northern Command, Lieutenant General Ralph Eastwood KCB, DSO, MC.

The unit they saw was bigger than it had been when the 15th, 45th and 54th Independent Squadrons came together. That amalgamation was not itself sufficient to produce a complete regiment, and it was followed in two days by the arrival at Felton of about three hundred young men—soldiers for only six weeks—sent from Infantry Training Centres and Primary Training Wings. Later reinforcements were received from Royal Armoured Corps training units, principally 162nd Regiment, RAC, which had sprung from the Royal West Kents.

The training of the three hundred, known at first as 'the intake,' was the regiment's first big job, tackled by the best instructors from squadrons under the direction of Major MacDiarmid. One end of the camp became a 'sausage machine' into which went three hundred recruits and out of which—after an almost incredibly short time—came three hundred men shaped to be gunners, drivers, mechanics, wireless operators and assault troopers. They had entered their intensive training with an enthusiasm that was a pleasure to see, and they were to become the backbone of the regiment. To the intake and its early instructors the regiment owed a great debt.

While the intake was being prepared in cadres to fit into the pattern of a reconnaissance unit the pattern of the unit's training and tactics was being worked out under the colonel's guidance on cloth model, in lectures and in TEWTs—tactical exercises without troops. Training was no haphazard, happy-go-lucky affair. Before the men, the armoured cars, the carriers and the weapons went out on their manoeuvres the lines on which they were to practise fighting had been decided by directive and discussion. After the routine of the day, officers and NCOs went to night school in the little hall outside Felton Park to study problems on the cloth models constructed by the I men, and to hear talks by the technical adjutant and other specialists. Sundays were days for officers and NCOs to be up and out with sandwich packets for TEWTs on the moors. The young officer, lost in contemplation of the charms of his partner at the Alnwick Saturday night dance, would be recalled sharply to the serious present by Major Gordon, flinging himself to the ground, saying: 'Shots from the ridge on your right. What are you doing about it?' In such ways the manifold problems of a regiment in action were considered, including those of harbouring for the night, disposing of casualties and obtaining replenishments of food, petrol and ammunition. By the time that the men of the intake—no longer the intake but fully-fledged members of the regiment—were ready to take their places in the armoured cars and carriers everything was ready for the theory of cloth model and TEWT to be tested in exercises with men and vehicles.

What can be said, in retrospect, about military exercises that will not cause the reader, after a brief glance, to skip a couple of pages, then look again to discover whether another subject has been reached? They require much preparation. They are a mixture of excitement, boredom, humour, discomfort, fatigue and argument. They stand somewhere between the business of war and the Cowboy and Indian games of childhood. In the chill of breaking camp amid the dews of early morning they test the best of tempers. They prove that warrant officers have a sixth sense which reveals when and where tea is being brewed (only the soldier in war can know more than the soldier on an exercise the sweetness of tea). They teach the value of a shave. No matter how differently they are planned, some things about them are constant, such as the extreme caution and reluctance with which the signals officer rode his exercise motor-cycle. They are controlled by umpires, who are invariably distinguished by white arm bands and a complete blindness to the brilliance of one's own military tactics. A 'Punch' humorist can make amusing reading of exercises.

But fundamentally they are serious things, which can teach lessons that win battles and save lives. And recalled seriously they make rather dull reading in detail, being battles only in make-believe and lacking the full-bloodedness of a campaign.

In the green days of spring and in the golden days of summer the regiment went forth from Felton upon its exercises. North it went to Wooller and west toward Carlisle. Names on maps became places seen from armoured car turrets—Hexham, Humshaugh, Harper's Town. The regiment learned to move in disciplined convoy, smart, alert, making sure of the roadworthiness of its vehicles during halts, reaching appointed places at appointed times. (Woe to the sleeper in convoy, and to the covert smoker.) It learned to set up its headquarters in the field, making an orderly business of its maps, its telephones, its wireless sets, its offices, its cookhouses, its rest areas, its latrines. With the arrival of that marvel of science, the No. 19 wireless set, it learned to use its communications between points many miles apart. It practised discovering, compiling and sending back—from car patrol through squadron and regimental headquarters to divisional headquarters —the information on which battle decisions are made: where the enemy is, how strong he is, what he is doing, whether there is a way round him, or perhaps whether a bridge is standing or demolished, a river fordable, a road cratered or usable. Time and again the sequence of the encounter was rehearsed: the contact by armoured cars, the use of carriers, assault troopers, mortars and anti-tank guns to 'winkle' the enemy out of his position, or, the position being too strong, the keeping of observation until the task was handed over to the following infantry brigade.

The colonel would disappear after dinner, and in his room the light would burn late. A day or two days later Sergeant Gilbert and his colleagues would despatch from the remoteness of the orderly room the typewritten details of another battle to be fought and the lessons to be learned. Each exercise was followed by its inquest, with the colonel, equipped with pointer and large map, as coroner in front of the assembled regiment, sifting the reports of umpires, pointing out mistakes, praising the successful, weighing suggestions. The mistakes were many in those early days, but the lessons were being learned. Gradually, on 'Peter', on 'Patience', on 'Zulu', the text book of the regiment's tactics was compiled.

Exercises were the 'star turns of the regiment's programme. Between the upheaval of their comings and goings was the very necessary "chorus work": the PT before breakfast; the weapon exercises after dinner; the cross-country runs down through the woods and back beside the Coquet; Officers' Week; the assault course and its precarious crossing of the river (known also as the back door to camp); the days on the ranges and of field firing on Longframlington moors; the driving, gunnery and wireless cadres.

B Squadron, discovering the great stride of Shackleton, won the sports on a ground laid out with great pains by Sergeant Instructor Tyler, APTC. On Rothbury moors 10 Troop of C Squadron, commanded by Lieut Bryan White, won the tactical competition in which reconnaissance troops had to meet and eliminate a pocket of enemy and advance through a minefield. Sergeant J. Cattanach, of A Squadron, enriched himself with many prizes, and the padre, the Revd E. Bradbrooke, showed what seemed almost an unholy proficiency, at the rifle meeting at Ponteland. L/Cpl Johnstone won the highland dancing at the division's assault-at-arms, a day of games and tests of military prowess in a bowl in the Northumberland hills, where even English breasts were stirred as the massed pipes of the division played the old Scottish airs in this land of border foray.

Perhaps the men of the three reconnaissance squadrons and the anti-tank and mortar troops remember most vividly their days of camping and training in lonely places near North Charleton or Rothbury or amid the rocky rises which bear the lovely name of Shaftoe Crag. Anyone who has been a troop commander or NCO will know only too well how difficult it is to keep a full troop together for training in barracks or anything resembling them. So many men must go to the quartermaster to fetch stores from the station; so many to the RSM for regimental guard; so many to the cookhouse. How many battles have troop officers, anxious to carry out a programme, fought and lost against the insatiable demands of barrack routine! When the standards of training had been propounded, the colonel solved those problems by sending squadrons to live, to toughen and to learn in their own camps on the moors. Food and letters were sent to them daily. Sometimes, brown and fit, they paid hurried visits to Felton

Hall for baths and changes of clothing. The policy was that the farther troops and squadrons got from their squadron and regimental commanders the better. Living together under active service conditions, troop officers really began to know their men, and the confidence which grew between them, and the training done during this period, were to pay a high dividend in action.

While the squadrons were 'living out' an aeroplane crashed in A Squadron's area and burst into flames. The pilot, flight officer and navigator were rescued by Sergt T. Fraser, L/Cpl E. Fifield and Troopers J. Arnold, W. Charlton, A. Conyer, B. Mellors and H. Witherall. Their action was commended in a letter from 416 Fighter Squadron.

There were incidents less exciting but memorable to those who knew Felton. The I section is not likely to forget the enthusiast who decided that the steep slopes to the Coquet were ideal for its first lesson in motor-cycling. Eyes blurred with perspiration saw indelibly the tall figure of the colonel, watch in hand, at the finish of the cross-country runs, awaiting the laggards. Nobody will dance an eightsome reel without recalling the major who insisted that to do this he must wear spurs. Nobody will hear 'Allouette' without thinking of how tremendously it was sung when Canadian, French, Belgian, Czech and Polish airmen came to see how the regiment worked. To tread the Great North Road may be to remember a long walk in the moonlight after missing the returning liberty truck. The crack of bat against ball will bring to mind the zest with which that enthusiast, Jack Lane, imagining bat and ball, hurled himself into the bowling of Bradmans, the clouting of Grimmetts and the catching of Ponsfords in the brief intervals between Officers' Week parades.

By 10 September, when the regiment moved south to Yorkshire, the division and brigades had 'accepted' it and were beginning to show signs of wanting to know what the 'Recce' could do. Close liaison was established, and each reconnaissance squadron was affiliated to a brigade—affiliations which endured to be tried and proved in battle a year later. The co-operation between 44 Lowland Brigade and C Squadron was particularly close, while A and B Squadrons were both pupils and teachers in their relations with 46 and 227 Highland Brigades respectively.

The regiment was lucky in many ways. At one time there were sixty-one officers on the books, and when the call for drafts for units already trained and in action came it was not necessary to cripple the 'first eleven' to find the bodies. The greatest help was always given by HQ, 15th Scottish Division, and particularly by the GSO1, Lieut Colonel J. D. Tyler RA, the A/Q, Lieut Colonel Kingsford Lethbridge, and ADOS - that well known and beneficent figure, Lieut Colonel Sid Walker, who had a warm corner in his heart for the 'Recce'.

There were few clues to indicate how long there would be for training and when the regiment would be called upon to fight. Determined not to be caught unprepared, it worked at full pressure throughout the summer, and the response to the demands of training was enough to enable the unit to feel worthy of its place in a division that was to make a great name for itself in action. It is easy to look back and remember all that was fine and successful, but, as is the case with all new units, there were teething troubles. Like the building of Rome, getting to know everyone and putting him in his best place took more than a day. One small incident may recall early troubles—who took the truck on the night of the Felton dance and dumped it in a ditch on the Great North Road?

However, at Felton the regiment got off to a very good start.

This staff table shows the major appointments in the regiment between 15 February and 10 September 1943:-

Commanding Officer: Lieut Colonel J. A. Grant Peterkin. Second-in-Command: Major P. T. I. MacDiarmid. Adjutant: Capt E. A. S. Sole. Technical Adjutant: Capt T. J. Bryson. Anti-Tank Officer: Capt E. A. Hutchings. Signals Officer: Lieut W. Kemsley. Lieut and Quartermaster: Lieut H. E. Hughes. Intelligence Officer: Lieut W. B. Liddell. M. T. Officer: Lieut W. H. Rogers. Mortar Officer: Lieut C. J. McCathie. Medical Officer: Capt T. S. Chalmers, RAMC. LAD Commander: Lieut P. A. Todd, REME. Padre: the Revd F. Ockenden. Regimental Sergeant Major: RSM W. H. Eardley. Regimental Quartermaster Sergeant: R.Q.M.S. D. W. Dobbin.

A Squadron.—Officer Commanding: Major B. C Crowder. Second-in-Command: Capt O. W. Butler Squadron Sergeant Major: SSM W. McMinn. Squadron Quartermaster Sergeant: SQMS J. Waddell.

B Squadron.—Officer Commanding: Major A Gordon. Second-in-Command: Capt T. G. Fordyce. Squadron Sergeant Major: SSM A. Franks. Squadron Quartermaster Sergeant: SQMS L. Piper.

C Squadron.—Officer Commanding: Major L. H. Mills. Second-in-Command: Capt J. K. Boynton. Squadron Sergeant Major: SSM A. Ward. Squadron Quartermaster Sergeant: SQMS C. G. Reeder.

Headquarter Squadron.—Officer Commanding: Capt M. C. K. Halford. Second-in-Command: Capt A. C. Davies. Squadron Sergeant Major: SSM L. A. Evans. Squadron Quartermaster Sergeant: SQMS W. R. Leadbetter.

May.—Major W. L. Rowlands was posted to the regiment and assumed command of Headquarter Squadron. Capt Butler was posted to the 80th Reconnaissance Regiment. Capt Davies became Second-in-Command of A Squadron.

June.—Capt Halford was posted from the regiment. Capt L. T. Ford became Second-in-Command of Headquarter Squadron.

July.—Major Crowder was posted to the 80th Reconnaissance Regiment. Major Rowlands became commander of A Squadron.

August.—Major G. W. T. Norton was posted from the 51st Training Regiment, RAC, assumed command of Headquarter Squadron and was posted to the 3rd Reconnaissance Regiment. Major C. K. Kemp was posted from the 162nd Regiment, RAC (RWK), and became commander of Headquarter Squadron. The Rev F. Ockenden was posted to the 119th L.A.A. Regiment. The Revd E. Bradbrooke was posted to the regiment.

George Blount:- On Saturdays, off duty ORs went into Ashington by 'Liberty Truck'. This truck would be driven by John "Bomber" Donnelly, who took many liberties. On his return from Ashington one Saturday night, he swerved through a hedge into a field. It was claimed that some stray animals had run across the road ahead of him! A LAD was commissioned to recover the truck and no injuries were reported.

It was here that Lieut Colonel Grant Peterkin authorised the manufacture and issue to officers of the Regimental badge with the Lion of Scotland on a yellowed enamel disc, this on a white O (15th letter in the alphabet). Today these badges are extremely rare and are eagerly sought by collectors. Vehicles were identified with the number 41, white numbers on a square halved green over blue together with the 15th Scottish Lion Rampant Divisional sign.

Gordon Nursaw:- The Regiment was brought up to strength with intakes from various sources, Graham Nicklin and myself came from the Green Howards, based at Richmond, Yorks where we had completed six weeks initial training.

Felton being a small village possessed two pubs one on each side of the bridge over a river, the first closed at 10.30pm and the other at 11.00pm. With the Regiment at full strength the two pubs could not adequately cope with the powerful thirst of some 800 men!

A number of us left Felton for Barnard Castle where we were to take part in a film called 'Battle Encounter'. I drove my Bren carrier into a field and executed a few manoeuvres, an armoured car also performed. The completed film was later shown at a cinema in Pontefract.

Len Watson:- In early 1942 I received a letter from King George VI saying 'Welcome to his Majesty's Service. You are about to become a soldier. This will mean a big change in your life'. How right they were! I was posted to Cornwall for six weeks intensive training, two of us were sent to Scarborough to join 15th Recce. When in Scarborough we had a morning dip in the sea and then ran around the town prior to breakfast. Rather than run around in wet trunks we dropped them off just prior to entering the water. The local landladies objected to this practice and it was stopped! At Felton we took part in many schemes and were commando trained over demanding assault courses.

Ben Howe:- Returning from London after a period of leave the train was two hours late on arrival at Newcastle and the liberty bus had departed. Unable to hitch a lift I walked the twenty-four Miles to Felton, my arrival at camp was nine hours 'overdue'. I was given seven days CB. The 'Red Caps' later confirmed that the bus had indeed departed and on appeal my punishment was quashed.

We were on exercise with small boats on a river; small tins filled with ammonal were thrown close to us. The tins with a lit fuse normally sank before exploding, on this occasion the tin ignited on the surface of the water close to me injuring my leg. I was hospitalised for six weeks and was treated with the new wonder cure penicillin.

Sgt Jimmy Cattanach. 1 Troop A Squadron

CHAPTER III

PONTEFRACT

From Felton to the Pontefract area of Yorkshire was a wet day's drive down the Great North Road and the difference between two worlds. Instead of a sweep of bare moor against a smokeless sky the regiment's horizon was the slag heaps and tall chimneys of a mining district in which one town straggles grimily into another. The clean air of Felton was changed for the smell by which Castleford first makes itself known to the traveller from the north. The compactness of Felton camp was succeeded by a web of billets —houses, church halls, shops, offices, cafes and a race course—spread at first over two towns and a village and later over a still wider compass. In these aspects the move to Yorkshire might be counted to the regiment's loss. But for many of its members the balance was redressed by the cinemas, dance halls, public houses (Pontefract alone had fifty-three) and clubs with which they were surrounded, and not least by the engulfing hospitality of the Yorkshire people. Nobody, for instance, could have done more for the regiment's wellbeing than Mrs C. W. Thompson, head of the WVS in Pontefract.

Regimental Headquarters set itself up in first-floor offices above one of Pontefract's main streets, and most of Headquarter Squadron was scattered over this town, distinguished from others of the Black North by a touch of Newmarket and evidence in its architecture, spaciousness and ruins that it was associated with England's history before the dark onrush of the Industrial Revolution. The Anti-Tank and Mortar Troops had their own small world in and about the long-fronted hall in the village of Darrington, B and C Squadrons occupied the racecourse and A Squadron moved into Castleford. Pontefract was one of the few places where wartime racing was still allowed. It introduced the regiment to the riding artistry of Billy Nevett, to Lady Electra—swift daughter of Fairway and Eclair—and other winners, to Fair Tor, which stood unmoving at the start, and to the many which started yet managed to lose. Before each meeting the two squadrons experienced the upheaval of moving beds and belongings out of the grandstand and Tote huts. After each meeting came the chore of restoring tidiness to a scene resembling Hampstead Heath after a Bank Holiday. Compensations were the free passes which enabled members of the regiment to go even to enclosures where winners are whispered, and the substantial contribution which the racecourse authorities made to the regiment's funds. Over these funds Major Cyril Kemp, the PRI, presided cheerfully and energetically in a small office invariably stacked with oranges, razor blades and dance tickets, which he would sell expertly to the unwary, lulling them with reminiscences of his days in the Royal West Kents.

The move to Yorkshire had been preceded by much speculation about Castleford. Castleford's look was blacker, less inviting than Pontefract's but occupation of Castleford carried with it an aura of independence. When the choice fell upon A Squadron, already a squadron of rather independent air, there was some surprise, and grumbles rumbled from that squadron's office. The grumbles stopped under the impact of Castleford's kindness and good billets in cafe and club, and the men of A Squadron moved with the greatest reluctance when changes in January switched them to the open hills near Shipley, the Anti-Tank Troop to Castleford and C Squadron to Crofton Hall, close to the many attractions of Wakefield. It seemed, too, that the people of Castleford were sorry to see A Squadron go, in spite of the way in which it had disrupted their road traffic with its Wednesday runs and their canal traffic with the scrambling nets which were hung from the bridge on Saturday mornings.

Other scrambling nets hung from the indicator board on the racecourse, and on the racecourse, too, a concrete ramp was built to provide practice in driving vehicles on to and off landing craft, with hand signals to guide the driver by day and torch signals by night. In these and many other ways training outlined ever more clearly the shape of things to come. French was studied in that enlightening book *Bill et Tommy en France*. Once a week regimental orders—translated by the adjutant, Capt W. B. Liddell—appeared in French. French names were given to places in cloth model exercises, and the less fluent officers went down with colours flying and 'I'll bibe tout beer' and 'Ma pere est dans la jardin' on their papers in a French examination. A series of lectures by Captain S. Rosdol, the division's intelligence officer and always a welcome visitor, widened the regiment's knowledge of the enemy waiting on the soil of France.

Early in December the preparation for disembarking vehicles off shore was begun with the first of a long series of waterproofing cadres directed by Lieut W. H. Rogers, and in the same month a regimental party, under Lieut G. R. Blount, took Humber armoured cars to Weymouth for wading trials, in which the Inns of Court and the Household Cavalry joined. Sgt Gartland, REME, was in charge of the regiment's fitters. The vehicles were loaded at Portland Bill on to two tank landing craft and disembarked at Weymouth into about four feet of choppy water. The trial was a failure in that all the vehicles were 'drowned'. But the information gained helped to make a success of the disembarkation off the Normandy coast. Another preparation for days of action, or, more accurately, for the days of inaction mingled with them, was the filling of the troop comfort boxes with writing paper, ink, playing cards, draughts, chess, cigarettes, books, liver pills and a variety of other odds and ends which varied from troop to troop.

Exercises took the regiment through miles of smoky streets to the fresh, sharp air, the mud and the ice of the moors and wolds, and Captain Lane and his battery travelled the width of England with their six-pounders to fire them on the Harlech ranges. It was from Pontefract that the regiment went on its first really large-scale manoeuvres—the great wolds exercises, Blackcock and Eagle, on which tactics for the Normandy bridgehead were tried. On Blackcock the unit moved, lightless, on a September night, through Wetwang and Fridaythorpe to a forward area, broke out of the bridgehead, seized and held crossings of the Derwent and led the advance towards York. When Eagle spread its wings over miles of February mud the regiment practised being traffic policeman on a minefield (a role which it was to undertake a year later before the Siegfried Line near Cleve). Forty-six Highland Brigade secured the bridgehead on the far side of the Eagle minefield, and while A and B Squadrons, under Major MacDiarmid, exploited this advance the rest of the regiment made sure that the clattering, roaring columns of the 11th Armoured Division and the Guards Armoured Division passed safely and without congestion through the lanes which had been cleared of mines. This was a vast and complicated process involving march tables and serials, REME recovery parties, RAMC ambulances, the Provost and Royal Signals line parties. Each end of each lane was controlled by an officer of the regiment, in communication with the colonel at gap control headquarters by wireless from an armoured car, and, when the tanks' rough tracks chanced to spare the patient work of the signallers, by field telephone. One of the minor crises of this operation arose over the lavatory at gap control headquarters. The regiment took a modest pride in its field hygiene, and portable lavatory seats were part of its battle equipment. In consequence, the news that the general himself intended to make use of gap control headquarters was received without alarm—until it was discovered that on this occasion of all occasions the lavatory seat had been forgotten. Hasty improvisation with an upturned ration box solved the problem and saved the good name of the unit!

While training indicated the nature of the regiment's future, a series of inspections and visits suggested that it was a future not very far ahead. In the February and March of 1944 the unit, parading as part of the 15th Scottish Division, was inspected at Leeds by General Sir Bernard Montgomery and by the King, who was accompanied by the Queen and Princess Elizabeth, and at Harrogate by the Prime Minister, Winston Churchill. Lieut General Sir Richard O'Connor, KCB, DSO, MC, who had taken command of VIII Corps after his escape from Italy, addressed officers of the division on 2 March, and a fortnight later visited the regiment and inspected a representative squadron at Darrington Hall.

In spirit Pontefract was the regiment's 'Eve of Waterloo'. When Byron wrote his famous line 'There was a sound of revelry by night' he might have been describing Pontefract, Castleford and Wakefield in a later war instead of the Brussels of 1815. Days of arduous training for a hazardous task not far away were followed by nights of revelry at Pontefract Town Hall and at the barracks on the hill. At the Town Hall Ronnie Regan, known on parade as Cpl Thomas, conducted the regiment's own dance band, 'The Recce Rascals', and for those who were not taking part in the shoulder-to-shoulder dancing there was the endless fascination of watching to see if the tall, flame-headed Hudson would ever drop his whirling drumsticks. At the barracks the regiment joined gladly in the dances of the ATS Training Centre. At Christmas time the ATS produced 'Aladdin' and sent a party of helpers to the party which the regiment gave 650 Pontefract children.

This party was organized by Lieut A. V. Sadgrove who had taken Pontefract very much to his warm heart, and who was prepared to lavish his shining enthusiasm and boundless energy upon the causes of the unit and those of the town. He wrote to the barracks for the help of one ATS NCO and eleven other ranks, using the Army abbreviation 'one and eleven'. The first feminine response, erring on the side of generosity, was a postal order for two shillings. But the help arrived. Among the guests were the Mayor of Pontefract, Councillor F. W. Lane, the chairman Education Committee, Alderman Frain, and the matron of Pontefract Hospital. The RSM assumed unusual benevolence as Father Christmas, and at the end of the party the colonel solved the problem of allocating 650 children to 650 coats by holding up each coat in the manner of an auctioneer. At a similar party A Squadron entertained 150 Castleford children. Such events provided copy for the 'Racecourse Rag', a wall newspaper published by L/Cpl McFarlane and Tpr Kingsbury, of B Squadron.

The regiment's rugby football match on Boxing Day against the Home Guard of Castleford was of sufficient importance to be copy for the local newspaper. The Home Guard team, including J. Croston, the international, and other Rugby League players, had not been beaten in its annual match against the unit stationed in the district. The regiment's team, captained by Michael Blair, who had played sturdily in the jersey of university and country, was one of the best in the division. This time the regiment won. Later in the season the Home Guard had its revenge.

The teams for the Boxing Day encounter were:- Reconnaissance Regiment: Tpr McShane; Lieut Royle (Worksop), Tpr Kenefick (Cardiff), Lieut Gray (Haileybury), Sgt John; Capt Liddell (Glasgow University), Lieut Blair (Oxford University and Scotland); Lieut Arundel (Brigade of Guards), SSM Franks (King's Liverpool Rgt), Sgt Holland (Burton), Lieut Shirley (Repton), Lieut Dalton (Worksop), Capt Ford (Torquay), 2/Lieut Green (Eastern Counties), Capt Bryson (Blairhill). Home Guard: Pte K. Place (Headingley OB); Cpl Norfolk (Knottingley and Selby), Pte Womersley (Headingley O.B.), Lieut J. Croston (Castleford and England), Capt H. L. Donovan (Blackrock

College and Selby); Cpl K. Brooks (Castleford), Lieut F. Ablett; Cpl Hodgson (Pontefract), Pte J. H. Hill (Castleford), Pte Hall (Knottingley), Pte J. Frost (Knottingley), Sgt H. Hale (Castleford), Sgt E. Bailey (Selby), Pte Thornton (Castleford), Cpl J. Walker (Wakefield OB). The referee was L. Tune (County Durham).

This is what the newspaper said about the match: 'Before about 2,500 spectators on Sunday afternoon on the Wheldon Road ground, Castleford, Army and Home Guard fifteens met in a Rugby Union encounter which was fairly even until the last ten minutes, when Lieut Croston, who with Pte K. Place, full back, had played an outstanding game, was injured and had to go on the wing, thus weakening the centre. The Home Guard were the better side in the first half, but the Reconnaissance men were fitter and stayed the course better. They were best represented by Lieut Blair. Early in the game Lieut Croston kicked a lovely penalty goal and then made the opening for Capt Donovan to score a fine try, which was not converted. Pte Womersley scored in the second half, and Lieut Croston converted. The Recces ran in a couple of tries in the last few minutes to win by 16 points to 11. Their scorers were Lieut Blair (2), Capt Liddell and Sgt John with tries, two of which were improved. A Scottish regimental pipe band played before the match and during the interval. The match was for the benefit of the local Prisoners of War Fund, and cleared about £70.'

In the semi-final of the division's rugby championship the regiment lost to the 190 the Field Regt, RA. There were, in addition, the unit's own sports championships, fiercely contested. A Squadron had a notable season, winning the seven-a-side rugby, the six-a-side hockey and, with 1 Troop, the six-a-side football, and reaching the final of the football championship, in which Headquarter Squadron gained a victory that was unexpected but well deserved. The unofficial sport was cycling. Because the regiment was so scattered, the colonel borrowed about forty bicycles from the Glasgow Highlanders, and by day they took officers soberly and sedately from mess to office, and messages from headquarters to headquarters. Their more interesting journeys were made under the cloak of darkness. This mercifully hid the erratic progress of the officer who returned from the barracks with the inner tube of the rear wheel entwined in the spokes, and complained thickly about the steering when picked up from the gutter. No night, however, was long enough to hide the beautiful black eye of the officer (fairly senior) who rode at the post at the racecourse entrance with the valour of Don Quixote charging his windmill.

In the later days of the regiment's stay in Yorkshire came the two clearest indications that the time of training was drawing to its close. Officers began the nightly labour of censoring mail, and on 5 April all leave was cancelled. Squadrons went in turn to Spaunton ranges, bivouacking for five days each in the village of Lastingham. Armoured cars carried out exercises on the field firing ranges at Fylingdales Moor, north of Scarborough. The wireless vehicles of the command net—the links between regimental and squadron headquarters—ranged north and south in a final test of long-range communications.

On 21 April the regiment moved south again. Many friends were left among the Yorkshire smoke, many happy memories taken to the Channel shore. The people of Pontefract could not have been kinder, and the regiment was sorry that security reasons compelled it to slip away without being able to express its thanks in some visible way. As the next best thing, a letter, addressed to the Mayor, was sent to the local paper, and a very warm acknowledgement was received.

There had been changes since the regiment left its first home. Captain Sole, posted to HQ, 15th Scottish Division as a staff captain, Lieut McCathie, Capt Chalmers, RAMC, and Lieut Todd, REME, had gone; Captain Boynton was appointed to command first-line reinforcements; and Captain Bryson joined first line reinforcements. Capt Liddell became adjutant; Lieut J. A. Isaac succeeded him as intelligence officer; Capt Lane assumed command of the anti-tank battery; Capt G. E. Pearce became technical adjutant, and Lieut A. R. Rencher MTO. Lieut J. M. B. Pooley, RAMC, came to the regiment as medical officer, and Lieut F. Sharman, REME, assumed command of the LAD. In February 1944, Major K. C. C. Smith (12th Lancers) was posted from GSO 1, VIII Corps, to be second-in-command of the regiment, and as a result of this appointment Major MacDiarmid became officer commanding Headquarter Squadron, and Major Kemp second-in-command of that squadron. Capt Ford succeeded Capt Boynton as second-in-command of C Squadron.

Capt Sole's departure to divisional headquarters was made after he had completed the difficult task of forming the administration of the unit, a task to which, unflagging, he had devoted many hours a day. The regiment's reputation for its administration was a sufficient measure of his success.

Gordon Nursaw:- I was delighted with the move to Pontefract because I was only thirty minutes away from my home in Leeds. B and C Squadrons were billeted on the racecourse and the first night out resulted in many cases of over indulgence after the restriction of supply at Felton! Next day the Sergeant Major marched us some distance from the racecourse buildings where we received a stern rebuke for our conduct of the previous evening.

Len Watson:- Pontefract was the longest racecourse in Britain and we ran round it several times a week. We participated in many training schemes on the Yorkshire Moors. I was in bed in the racecourse stand when one of our Corporals dashed in and grabbed his neatly folded blankets and disappeared. I think he spent the night with his girlfriend in the judge's box; he was wounded in action shortly after landing in Normandy.

Clive Ridge:- During my stays at Pontefract we at HQ were stationed in pubs in the town, and I found myself constantly on wireless courses in a room above the 'Green Dragon'. I had been trained as a Driver Operator at Staindrop near Barnard Castle. No doubt as a result of all this training in operating I found myself the CO's Driver Operator code 15. We had a Dingo for the purpose but the Colonel soon opted for a jeep instead, this was fitted with a high power 19 set similar to the one in the HQ command vehicle. This increased the power of the set and the range to double the standard 19 set.

John Stevenson:- While we were stationed in Pontefract the Colonel's jeep was with the signal section and I was the designated driver. It was only used by the Colonel when the staff car was unavailable. This was the case when the Colonel requested the jeep to enable him to attend the dentist in the barracks at Pontefract. I took the Colonel and while I was waiting outside, an ATS sergeant came to look at the jeep which was in pristine condition. She asked if she could bring some of her section to look it over. As they looked admiringly at the condition of the vehicle I showed them the engine compartment and said in a self assured manner 'Now that is what I want our transport to look like'. They had virtually finished their examination when the Colonel emerged from his treatment and so I hurriedly closed everything down. We were to visit a unit in Crofton near Wakefield and the Colonel always drove if he was in a hurry. As we sped down the hill to Featherstone the bonnet flew up and covered the windscreen; fortunately he brought the jeep to a halt without mishap. He didn't criticise me but it was clearly my fault for not fastening the bonnet securely; he carried on as though nothing untoward had happened. I respected him for being a very fair man in all his dealings with the troops.

Ben Howe:- We were on exercise when our enthusiastic 2/Lieut pointed to a bird some distance away and said that he would give five Woodbines if we could shoot it. I promptly fired five rounds from my Bren held at the waist and the bird disappeared in a flurry of feathers! The officer then refused to hand over my prize, a Major came over to see what the fuss was about and declared that I should have my reward as I had done what was asked of me. Being a city boy I had never seen a pheasant before and didn't realise it was intended for the pot!

*   *   *   *   *

The Regiment organised a Christmas party for 650 Servicemen's children at the Assembly Rooms, Pontefract on Thursday 23 December 1943. This was much enjoyed by the children and a huge file is testimony to the effort Lieut Victor Sadgrove as Entertainments Officer put in to ensuring the success and safety of the event.

*   *   *   *   *

Fire at the Horse and Jockey Hotel, Castleford 16 January 1944.

This information was in Gordon Dalton's papers.

Lieut Gordon Dalton stated that on the night of Sunday thick fog necessitated an overnight stop. Corporal Dickie James and L/Cpl 'Bomber' Donnelly arranged to stay at the Horse and Jockey. At about 05.30 hrs on Monday morning he was informed by a member of the National Fire Service that a fire had occurred on the premises and that L/Cpl Donnelly had been burned and removed to hospital.

Corporal Richard James stated 'about 22.45hrs on Sunday the 16th January, I arranged to spend the night at the Horse and Jockey Hotel, Castleford. I was accommodated in a bedroom with a relative of the landlady of the hotel. About 03.30hrs on the following morning one of the landlady's daughters woke me up and said that one of the rooms was on fire. I found that the sitting room on the same floor on which I was sleeping was on fire. I knew that one of the members of my Squadron L/Cpl Donnelly was sleeping in this room. And in company with a police constable I tried to get into his room but I could not owing to the heat and fumes. He was eventually got out by a member of the NFS. I have no idea how this fire originated as I was in the next room to which the fire occurred.'

The Column Officer of the NFS stated that the fire was reported to the police via telephone at 03.16hrs and the first appliance arrived at 03.18hrs (quick in those days!) The fire had originated in an upstairs dining room and flames were then through the windows. On enquiry it was found that the licensee, Mrs Fowler, and her daughter had escaped but a soldier of the 15(S)Recce Regt. Home Forces, Cpl James stated that another soldier L/Cpl Donnelly was in the room on fire. Attempts had already been made by the police to find him and had failed but after further examination he was eventually discovered behind an armchair in the corner of the room. He was removed and was then unconscious, artificial respiration was applied and a resuscitating set was used and he came round sufficiently to be removed to hospital by ambulance. It can only be assumed that L/Cpl Donnelly was smoking on the settee on which he was sleeping and dropped his cigarette which caused the fire to start.

*   *   *   *   *

Bomber Donnelly did suffer from burns but he always regarded Dickie James as his saviour from then onwards and hopefully the experience cured him of smoking in bed. We do not know what effect the incident had on Dickie's relationship with the proprietor's family!

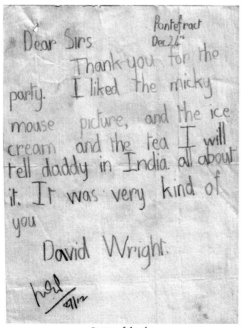

The Commanding Officer & All Ranks
of the Reconnaissance Regiment
request the pleasure of the company of

at a
CHRISTMAS PARTY,

given to all Servicemen's Children, whose ages
are between 5 and 12, at the Assembly Rooms,
Pontefract, on Thursday, 23rd December, 1943.

Children at School on this date
will be escorted by men of the
Regiment at 4 p.m.

Party begins at 4-15.   Party ends
at 7-0.   Parents may use
Balcony after 6 p.m.

ADMISSION STRICTLY LIMITED TO TICKET HOLDERS.

Invite to Christmas party

Pontefract
Dec 24th
Dear Sirs.
Thank you for the
party. I liked the micky
mouse picture, and the ice
cream and the tea I will
tell daddy in India all about
it. It was very kind of
you

David Wright.

Letter of thanks

9 Troop C Squadron, 15th (S) Reconnaissance Regiment - Spring 1944, Crofton Hall, Near Wakefield, Yorkshire
Back row (L to R): G. Masi; G. Nursaw; E. Lewis; S. Evans; J. Neville*; J.C. Lloyd; A. Maddy
Second row (L to R): G.D. Green; B. Jackson; G. Nicklin; O. Thomas; J. Bunker; P.R. Dobson; R. Penfold; H. Higginson*
Third row (L to R): J. Southall; N. Jones; J. Hoolachan; J. Lawrie; J. Butterfield; D. Berresford; H. Dove; J. Mills
Fourth row (L to R): J. Songhurst; W. McMinn; R. Tilby; J. Wheeler; C.T. Royle; W. Jennings; S. Kirrage; J. Pearson

10 Troop C Squadron - Wakefield 1944
Front row (L to R): Tpr Wilkinson; Sgt Cameron*; Sgt Rainbow; Lt Riesco; Lt White; Sgt Collins; Sgt Knight; Tpr?
Second row (L to R): Cpl Hartley*; Cpl Hubbard; Cpl Watson; Tpr Fowler; Tpr Coburn MM; Tpr Beard*; Tpr Mills; Tpr Catt; Tpr Cudmore*; Cpl Lavery; Cpl Little
Third row (L to R): Tpr Bateman; Tpr ?; Tpr Rowlands; Tpr Holmes; Tpr Bolton MM; Tpr Ireland; Tpr Whiting; Tpr Baird; Cpl Birch
Rear row (L to R): L/Cpl King; Tpr Watson; Tpr Smith; Tpr Mincedorf; Tpr Gurney*; Tpr Martin; Tpr Harris
* killed

C Squadron, 15th (S) Reconnaissance Regiment
Spring 1944, Crofton Hall, Near Wakefield, Yorkshire

A Squadron Officers - Pontefract May 1944
Seated (L to R): George Blount; William Rowlands; Chris Davies
Standing (L to R): Michael Blair*; R. Parker (arm in sling); John Arundel*; Ron Rencher; Peter Kerridge
* killed

Rugby team
Back row: Lt Shirley; Lt Dalton; Lt Arundel; Sgt Holland; Lt Todd
Middle row: Tune (ref); 2/Lt Green; Capt Liddell; Lt Blair (Capt); SSM Franks; Capt Ford; Lt Gray
Kneeling: Tpr Kenefick; Tpr McShane; Cpl John; Capt Bryson
Lt Royle did not play - Lt Todd took his place

Game played before 2,500 spectators at Castleford - £70 was raised for the Prisoner of War Fund.
Final score: Recce Regt 16   Home Guard 11

This Humber armoured car left an LCT to wade ashore onto Weymouth beach. All vehicles involved in the trials 'drowned'. Photo taken Christmas Day, 1943 (Imperial War Museum - H 34493)

A Squadron - April 1944, Pontefract

CHAPTER IV

ANGMERING-ON-SEA

The regiment's last days in England were days by the sea in the sun and in surroundings which might have been created to provide the greatest contrast with the life in the field which was to follow. At Angmering-on-Sea, set between the sparkle of the Channel and the dapple of the Downs, houses built expensively for those who could afford seaside holiday homes became the unit's billets. It was indeed life with every modern convenience—labour-saving kitchens, gleaming bathrooms, bedrooms with hot and cold water, parquet floors, balconies, french windows opening on to smooth lawns. Part of A Squadron, occupying the house of a famous man of theatres at Kingston Gorse, lived among stained glass, a shining cocktail bar, sunken baths and garden fountains. Other people of the stage whose homes were here became the regiment's friends, notably Nervo and Knox, who renewed old acquaintance months later, when they were making the Second Army laugh in Holland.

The soldier waking in his Angmering bedroom, seeing from his window the pleasant houses with their dewy lawns and flower borders and beyond them the sea glinting in the early sunshine, needed the presence of folded battledress, kitbag and rifle leaning against the wall to remind him that this was indeed the prelude to battle. The lengthening day, however, brought with it other reminders. There was a sense of finality about things now. Vehicles were being made waterproof, ready for landing on a foreign beach. They were loaded as for embarkation and weighed to make sure that they did not exceed the weight permitted on board ship. Loading lists were completed, and equipment marked with its serial number. Packing for a holiday and even moving a home were as nothing compared with this preparation for fighting and living for an unknown period in foreign lands.

Waterproofing in itself was a major operation of war. Scientists and engineers had spent months devising materials and means to enable motor vehicles to be driven through the narrow strip of sea between ship's ramp and shore. There had been many trials to test and improve the results. Many weeks and many courses had been devoted to teaching how the materials must be used. Now many hours of hard and dirty work were necessary before the cars, the carriers and the trucks, engines sealed and exhausts pointing like chimneys to the sky, were ready. The waterproofers, directed by Lieutenants R. H. Fleet, P. C. Kerridge and Rogers, were the hardest worked men in the regiment in these weeks. Two representatives of Humber Ltd, Mr F. W. Kennington and

Mr R. J. Harter, lived with the regiment for a month while they supervised the waterproofing of the Humber armoured cars.

Bereft of its vehicles by these preparations, the unit took to its feet and for four days marched by squadrons eighty miles over the Sussex Downs, finishing with a forced march back from Amberley. Weapons were given their final tests on Kithurst and Seaford ranges and by firing out to sea. Troop commanders and troop sergeants visited infantry battalions with which they were to work, and the foot soldiers were given a final demonstration to show what could be expected of a reconnaissance unit.

Planning proceeded in secret. The regiment learned with regret that because of the demands on shipping it could not go abroad as one body, but must leave one squadron to sail later with parts left by other units. These were called the divisional residue, and Major Smith was appointed to command them, Major MacDiarmid becoming acting second-in-command of the regiment. A toss of the coin, lost by Major Gordon, ordained that B Squadron would be the one left.

One tragedy came upon the regiment at this time. Returning to Kingston Gorse from Worthing by way of a short cut, two members of 1 Troop in A Squadron, Troopers Simmonds and Hancox, were killed by a beach mine.

On 17 May Lieut General Sir Richard O'Connor addressed officers in a Worthing cinema, and on 4 June Major General MacMillan spoke to each squadron about the forthcoming operations.

Drake played bowls on the eve of battle. The regiment ran and jumped, and played cricket. The padre, the Revd E. Bradbrooke, an old Oxford and England jumper, cleared 5 feet 6 inches, and Cpl Williams, of A Squadron, established himself as the regiment's best long distance runner, but B Squadron again won the regimental sports. The 1st Middlesex athletes were beaten in a match at Brighton, held to choose the team to represent the two units in partnership in the division's highland games at Brighton Stadium. The joint team came third of six, and L/Cpl Johnstone again won the highland dancing. At the end of the games the divisional commander remarked 'Today the highland games have been won by the Lowland Brigade, the dancing by the Reconnaissance Regiment and the throwing the hammer by a Sapper.'

The regiment's representatives in the games were:- 100 Yards Relay: Sgt Carmichael, Sgt Campbell, Capt Liddell, Tpr Holmden. 440 Yards Relay: Lieut Blair, Craftsman Lovell, Tpr Wolfenden, Cpl Williams. 880 Yards Relay: Lieut Blair, Tpr Shackleton, Cpl Williams, Tpr Hart. High Jump: Padre and Tpr Slaughter. Throwing the Hammer and Putting the Weight: Sgt Holland.

The hospitality of the Home Guard, who allowed unrestricted use of ground and kit, brought the regiment's cricketers together for a brief but glorious season on the field between the tall trees and the long grey barn at East Preston. To those who enjoyed those games in the blaze of afternoon and the lengthening shadows of evening the one matter for regret was the certainty that a side which seemed made for the Saturdays of peaceful summers would be scattered when those days returned. No captain would hesitate to lead on to club ground or village green a team which could produce the venom of Lane's bowling, the wholeheartedness of Abbott's, the graceful strokes of Hudson and Gray, the smites of padre and adjutant, the zest of Green and the all-round worth of the colonel and Sgt Harrison. Squadron played squadron. The RSM ran between the wickets with unquestioned daring but questionable wisdom. Littlehampton and Divisional Signals were met and beaten, and, no matter how steadily Wiggins bowled for them, the Home Guard came off second best in a series of duels.

The arrival of Major Mills on horseback for the match in which RHQ and C Squadron played the rest of the regiment created both precedent and problem. There was a place at fine leg for the major, but none for the horse, whose presence would have given RHQ and C an unfair advantage in numbers. When, however, the horse departed, the major was still in the saddle, which gave undue advantage to the Rest. Eventually Major was retrieved minus horse, and he occupied his place in the field with a mixture of the energetic and the recumbent until the fingers of shade stretched out to the pitch and, Jack Lane having led the Rest to a one-wicket victory, stumps were drawn for the last time. Already the wings of towed gliders had shadowed the field, and the broadcast voice of General Eisenhower had confirmed what the regiment had guessed on seeing the armada of the air fade over the Channel on a clear June night—the invasion of Normandy had begun.

The 'Three Crowns' at Angmering was adopted as the regimental pub although one diary notes rather plaintively that on the 22nd of May all pubs had sold out of beer!

On 23 May the Regiment adopted the wearing of black berets.

Thirty ATS girls had arrived in Worthing from Pontefract and four were killed in a 'hit and run' attack on the 28 May.

Troopers Simmonds and Hancox took an ill-advised short cut across a beach and were both killed on 27 May when they detonated a mine.

*   *   *   *   *

Gordon Nursaw:- Pontefract to Denmead (Portsmouth) May 1944.
The big drive to Angmering on Sea near Littlehampton took place mostly during

the hours of darkness. On arrival we were billeted in houses, I wondered where the residents had gone! I recall one of our number became very friendly with the local vicar's daughter.

Quite a lot of men in C Squadron came from London, and as we were close some of them made a quick visit home. I don't know how they got away with it, as we were not supposed to leave the area.

Then onto Denmead, where we parked in the streets, and slept on the pavements, next to our vehicles; local people made us cups of tea, together with some buns, fortunately the weather was fine.

Our next move was to Portsmouth to board an LST, I was down near the engines, the smell they gave off was overpowering and I felt sick but managed to control it. We remained below until we were ready to disembark; we drove down the ramp into the sea and onto the beach, moving a short distance inland. I regret not going up on deck during the crossing, it must have been quite a sight!

5 Troop B Squadron
Angmering-on-Sea, May 1944
Back row: Tpr Ritchie; Tpr Peters; Tpr Smith; Tpr Bayley; Tpr Russel; Tpr Miggins*; Tpr Hay
3rd row: Cpl Gurney; Tpr Burke*; L/Cpl Jenkinson; Cpl Harris; Tpr Roberts; Tpr Sarll; Tpr Greenhough; Cpl Finnerty
2nd row: Tpr Reetham; Tpr White; Tpr Homes; Cpl Rees; Tpr McManus; Tpr Briggs; Tpr Swann
Bottom row: Sgt Clark; Sgt Knibb; Sgt Litton; Lt Leppard; Lt Rogers; Sgt Maxfield; Sgt Dobson; Sgt Holland
*killed

B Squadron - June 10th 1944
Taken at Angmering-on-Sea just prior to Normandy

6 Troop B Squadron 15th Scottish Reconnaissance Regt. May 1944
Back row: Haynes*; Watson; Bodsworth*; Armstrong; Feany; Lawn*; Unknown; Gilbertson; Unknown
Middle row: Willoughby; Hanson; Sharp; Connor; Fosdyke; Gaskell; Baxter; Frost; Border*; Griffiths
Bottom row: Unknown; Raymond; Short; Thompson*; Trim; Carey*; Jenkins; Moss; Chapman; Carlyon
Quail with Recce the dog

7 Troop B Squadron 15th Scottish Reconnaissance Regt. June 1944
Back row: Tredinnick; Coomber; Quirk; Foster; Bates*; Oliver; Taylor*; Hart
3rd row: Jamerson; Hickman; Mee; Spencer; Stones; Moffatt; Simmons; Harvey; Shackleton
2nd row: Richardson; Grice; King; Eaton*; Dynnock; Ward*; Ritson
Bottom row: Bonner; McKean; Jarrett; Falloon; Fleet, Vranch; Baldwin; Berrill

*Killed

CHAPTER V

TO NORMANDY

Everybody in the regiment knew—training alone had been enough to show it—that if all went well with the Normandy assault he would soon be taking part in operations by the 15th Scottish Division to prise gaps in the enemy forces being pressed back from the bridgehead. In experience of battle the regiment lacked much, for few in it had been under fire. In preparation and equipment, it lacked little. Its great fire power, the variety of its weapons, its mobility and its long-range communications made it suitable for many roles.

Its 270 vehicles included twenty-eight armoured cars, twenty-four light reconnaissance cars, sixty-nine carriers, fifty-five motor-cycles (some of which were later discarded), armoured half-tracks, jeeps and 3-ton and 15 cwt trucks. In addition to the 37 mm gun and Besa machine gun mounted in the turret of each Humber armoured car, the regiment was armed with 151 Bren guns, thirty-six PIATs, eight six-pounder anti-tank guns, six three-inch mortars, twenty-five two-inch mortars, 410 rifles, 223 Sten guns and eighty-eight pistols.

It had well over a hundred wireless stations, each combining transmitter and receiver. Most of them were the No. 19, which had three parts—the A set for long range communication; the B set for short range communication, as between cars on a patrol; and a 'house telephone' which enabled members of a vehicle crew to talk to each other without removing their headsets.

The regiment had trained to be a Jack of many trades, and a Jack of many trades it was to be in the dust of Normandy, the green Bocage, swiftly covered miles of Northern France, Belgium and Germany, and the mud of a Dutch winter and the Siegfried Line. But above all, in training and in action, its name was its purpose, and for most of the campaign the basis of its reconnaissance was the Humber car—the bulky armoured car and the long-nosed light reconnaissance car with its Bren. Both carried commander, driver and gunner-wireless operator. Each of the three reconnaissance squadrons had three car troops (each of three armoured cars and two light cars), three tracked carrier troops (each of seven carriers) and an assault troop (four sections equipped as infantry and carried in half tracks). At first car and carrier troops were combined, and the numbering of the troops was altered when the carriers were granted their independence in the course of the campaign.

The regiment's wireless communications were so arranged that regimental headquarters was in touch with the squadrons on a forward link and with divisional headquarters and the headquarters of the brigades on a rear link operated by a Royal Signals detachment; and each reconnaissance squadron headquarters was in touch with all its cars and with its carrier and assault troop headquarters. The regiment and the squadrons were commanded from half-tracks, fitted in a variety of ingenious ways with wireless, shelves, map boards, tables and seats, and bristling outside with aerials. Light reconnaissance cars or jeeps, equipped with wireless and called 'rovers', enabled the colonel and squadron commanders to tour their commands without losing touch with the general progress of the battle.

Thus equipped, and waterproofed, prepared by fifteen months' hard training and tensed by the news of D Day, the regiment awaited its own D Day like the batsman who has proved his eye and strokes at the nets, yet has a certain feeling of the stomach mingled with his impatience and his curiosity about the bowling as he awaits his innings. Channel gales were to prolong the wait. The day after D Day was a day of prayer for the invasion troops, and at each squadron location the padre held a service, which was followed by a talk by the colonel. On 11 June the advance party—Lieut Isaac, Sgt J. Millroy and Cpl J. Kay—left to join 227 Highland Brigade, with which they were to cross the Channel. They had to secure a concentration area for the regiment in Normandy. On 15 June French francs were drawn on pay parade—two hundred a man—and two days later the regiment, leaving B Squadron behind, drove through Arundel, Chichester, Midhurst and Petersfield to a marshalling area in the woods of Denmead, near Portsmouth. On arrival there was chaos. Ship sheets had not been sent by Movement Control, and it was not until midnight that vehicles and their crews were arranged in five shiploads; LST 1107, commanded by the colonel; LST 1108, commanded by Major Mills; LST 1109, commanded by Major Rowlands; LCT 997, commanded by Lieut H. A. Green; and LCT 998, commanded by Capt Lane. Vehicles were parked on Denmead's roads; men moved into tents behind barbed wire in the woods. Next morning lifebelts, embarkation rations and bags, vomit, were issued, and by one o'clock in the afternoon everybody and everything had been made ready to sail. The move to the boats was expected to be on that night, but the wind whipped the Channel, and eight days of waiting went by. They were days of hanging about, expecting that everyone of the many calls of 'Attention please, attention please, calling Serial 36115' on the camp loudspeakers would be marching orders. But day succeeded day and no marching orders came. The camp cinema and NAAFI were visited, letters were written and none received. On 24 June the colonel organised a section stalk in the fields and woods round the camp, and pent-up energies were released in glorious rough-and-tumbles. Money ran short, and Major Smith and Major Gordon, paying a visit from the division's residue at Worthing, brought welcome financial aid.

Having waited for more than a week, Craft Load 1107 received orders in the typical army manner to move in fifteen minutes at eleven o'clock on the night of Sunday 25 June. This party reached Gosport early the following morning. The other craft loads arrived later in the day, and everybody sat by his vehicle in Gosport's streets until seven in the evening, when orders to move to 'the hards' were received. From ten o'clock that night until two in the morning the vehicles were driven up the ramps into the gaping jaws of the landing ships. The past twenty-four hours had been wearisome waiting tempered with movement and excitement There had been little sleep. It was a tired regiment which turned in on board the long, grey, blunt-nosed ships in Gosport harbour.

The passengers woke up to find their ships lying in convoy off the Isle of Wight, and at ten o'clock that morning, 27 June, the convoy rolled, rose and dipped into a Channel gale. Many were sick.. The final stage of waterproofing was carried out in the tossing ships. 'Boat drill' and 'Action stations' were rehearsed, but apart from the individual trials of the stomach the crossing was uneventful. In the early evening the convoy nosed its way through a grey armada to the beaches between le Hamel and Arromanches les Bains, and the blurr of distant coastline sharpened into the regiment's first close view of Normandy: a line of prisoners in green uniforms on the wet, smooth sand; one or two landing craft stranded with broken backs; seaside bungalows awry; a white fountain where a mine exploded; and, behind all this a green country fading to the blue of distance, where, three weeks after D Day, the rest of the 15th Scottish Division was already locked in its first battle about the River Odon.

At seven in the evening the craft beached on a falling tide, and the first vehicles went down the lowered ramps, plunged their bonnets into four feet of water and made for the shore. All went well until the signals office half-track disappeared in a crater between ship and shore, and Trooper Templeman and his passengers had to scramble out through the top. After this misadventure, for which nobody could be blamed, the beachmaster ordered that the remaining vehicles should be unloaded on the following morning, when they disembarked into one and a half feet of water. The half-track was the only casualty in the landing of more than 150 vehicles.

One after another the cars, carriers, jeeps, half-tracks and trucks sped across the sands and headed inland. Trusting an unseen organization rather than knowing what they were about, the drivers found their way to a transit area a mile away, where part of the trappings of waterproofing, was left with the discarded waterproofing already littering the fields. The vehicles formed up on the Bayeux road and moved off in groups of ten for the regiment's concentration area—St Gabriel.

As the vehicles passed slowly along roads busy with military traffic drivers reminded themselves repeatedly that they must keep to the right, and commanders looked anxiously from map to land, realising that finding the way, with these maps of smaller scale, was harder over here. The painting of a picture of Normandy was beginning—a picture that was to be framed in the memory around dusty roads scalloped by shell-bursts; fields crowded with men and trucks and guns; grim 'Minen' notices; dead animals, swollen and with stiff legs pointing skyward; trampled hedges and crumpled buildings; route signs which first seemed hopeless in their very profusion; reddened, knocked-out tanks; and the French country people, inevitably dressed in black, somehow surviving it all.

The Regiment was landed on Nan section of Juno beach; it was transported in the *Robert Henry*, an American Liberty ship.

The 43rd Wessex Reconnaissance Regiment suffered almost 200 casualties when their ship, the *Derrycunihy* was sunk by a mine on 24 June off Sword Beach. Their disembarkation had been seriously delayed by bad weather.

*   *   *   *   *

Alan Westby:- The Landing Craft Tank grounded on 28 June, after an uneventful crossing, quite unlike the previous day, when the craft had been secured to another flat bottomed LCT with its complement of vehicles and men because it was so rough in Gosport harbour. The pills, dispensed to combat the effect of sea travel had, in some cases, proved effective but in others, they had not. The crew of the LCT was well aware that several meals had not been eaten and asked if there was any 'gash', the naval term for 'buckshee.' They were not disappointed! The vessel remained grounded for ages and ages. We were not to know that the OC Anti-tank Troop and the ship's captain had agreed to wait for the tide to recede. At last the ramp was lowered and the two Carden Lloyd carriers, each towing a 6-pounder anti-tank gun, and the third carrier with its load of ammunition rattled down into the water. Our many months of lectures, wading trials and demonstrations showing how to enable vehicles to function efficiently even under water, had more than prepared us for this moment. The drive through a mere six inches of sea water and then over the sand dunes to a temporary harbour was successfully accomplished. On then to a more permanent resting place where a meal was enjoyed and letters written home from the 'British Liberation Army in France'.

The Anti-Tank battery was part of HQ Squadron, but once we were in Normandy the CO decided that we would be more effective split into Troops and attached to the Squadrons. Two anti-tank guns with their towing carriers and one ammunition carrier were dispatched to A, B and C Squadrons. Many unkind comments have been made about the Carden Lloyd carrier. In its defence it must be said that C Squadron's ammunition carrier, was driven by me from Normandy to a certain place just over the German border without very serious trouble. It wasn't a pretty thing with its canvas top and radiator at the rear. It did not possess the delicacy of steering of the Bren gun carrier, with the bowing of track for small changes of direction. The Carden Lloyd was steered entirely by applying the brakes on one side to slew in the required direction by means of two tillers each controlling the brakes on different sides of the vehicle. On icy roads the Carden Lloyd came into its own, for the links of the Bren-gun tracks acted like miniature skis allowing the carrier to slide sideways on any surface having a camber. It isn't known why this phenomenon only applied to the Bren-gun carrier since both vehicles were fitted with identical tracks. However, in winter weather, the Carden Lloyd did have a serious shortcoming. Its carburettor, sitting on top of the Ford V8 engine, did have a tendency to freeze up when ice particles formed on the outside and the engine failed. There was nothing for it but to wait for the heat of the engine to thaw out the carburettor when the engine could be restarted. The whole convoy had to wait for this process to take effect in fifteen to twenty minutes. Fortunately we operated through only one winter campaign.

Clive Ridge:- upon landing in Normandy the Colonel, Grant Peterkin, drove the jeep and I operated the wireless, and this we did everyday until his leaving the Regiment. In addition to operating the wireless I was supposed to read the map. The Colonel would show me where we were going, fold up the map, and put it under his seat. So much for my map reading! We would leave RHQ in the morning to visit the Squadron HQ's, keep in touch with RHQ and end up in the evening at Div HQ for our orders for the following day. We would then go to each Squadron's HQ with the next day's orders which meant that we would arrive back at RHQ next day usually around 1.00 or 2.00 in the morning.

During the day RHQ would have moved on and we returned to a new harbour; fortunately Captain Kemsley usually found somewhere for me to put my bed roll. On one occasion, on returning late, the Colonel said we were to go and get something to eat. We went to the cookhouse in HQ and saw Sgt Peeny the cook in charge. 'Now Sir,' said Sgt Peeny, 'what can I get you?' I thought something good was going here and was looking forward to a good meal. 'Nothing fancy Sergeant. We will have some bully beef and a couple of slices of bread, that will do us fine' said the Colonel, 'Won't it Ridge,' 'Yes sir' I said, and so we left with three slices of bully beef and the bread. 'Good night, see you in the morning Ridge' and so much for the good meal!

George Bunn:- We met an English lady married to a Frenchman who had assured her family and friends that following Dunkirk she knew the British would return! She had saved a quarter-pound packet of Brooke Bond tea in anticipation to share with British soldiers; Arthur Watkins, myself and two others enjoyed that special brew.

Gordon Nursaw:- After landing in Normandy we were harboured in an orchard, ordered to dig slit trenches which was not very successful as the perimeter was very stony. An officer instructed us to go across an adjoining field where there was a burnt out German tank, he said it was for 'Battle Inoculation', and we were to move over in small groups.

We climbed up onto the tank to have a look inside, and there before our eyes, the tank crew still occupying their positions but burnt black, they just looked like waxwork figures.

Later on an injured cow wandered into the orchard and someone was told to put it out of its misery, without success. I had farming experience and told them to aim in the forehead not for the heart.

A friend of mine, at the end of his guard duty, was climbing out of the slit trench when he accidentally knocked over the Bren gun, a stone became caught in the trigger guard and a round was discharged lodging in his foot; fortunately the weapon was not on automatic. The wound healed and he returned to us where later in April of '45 he was wounded at Nettlekamp and sent back to England. His foot continued to cause pain and yet X-Rays detected nothing. An enterprising surgeon decided to open up the foot and discovered a piece of leather left in from the incident in the Normandy orchard.

CHAPTER VI

THREE MEN IN A CAR

At St Gabriel the three members of the advance party were waiting to welcome the regiment with the air of seasoned campaigners, which, indeed, was what that old cavalryman Sergeant Millroy was. This is the story of their adventures and misadventures:

We left Angmering on that dull Sunday evening, 11 June, in a light reconnaissance car so humped with its equipment, our equipment, unit signs, extra petrol and 'Compo' rations that it might have been mistaken for an overburdened camel. In other characteristics, however, it was to bear greater resemblance to a mule. We expected to find 227 Brigade in its hotel on the front at Worthing, and eventually traced it to a park by the Horsham road, where the car was put in convoy with a large board strapped to its front and we were put to bed until 3.30 a.m. That morning was cold but splendidly fine. We drove through a sleeping countryside, and stopped at Sutton for 'char' and 'wads'. North-east of Clapham Common we stopped again, but only the car knew why. No fault could be found in the petrol system, and the plugs were sparking. More petrol was poured in and stirred violently, a whim of the driver which was presumably successful, for the engine started and ran well enough for Kay to maintain a terrifying pursuit of the convoy, guided by the route boards 'S' and 'T' over Waterloo Bridge, through central London and out on to Lea Bridge Flats. Oxford Street was crossed against the red light and at fifty miles an hour while a policeman held up other traffic. At Lea Bridge Flats we caught up the convoy, and again the engine died out. Unfortunately, after persuasion and blowing, we arrived at the old Territorial camp at Purfleet in such good running order that it seemed silly to take the car to the overworked REME, and two days later Kay, on his way to the unknown dock at the end of route 'M', found himself in the middle of Dagenham with an unresponsive vehicle. Three hours passed, the car was towed to the City of London Workshops, the wrong dock party was notified, and in the evening Kay and car arrived in Millwall, where his irate crew waited, and whence the MTS had sailed. The night was passed in the customs sheds and the next day in awaiting the arrival of an LST, on to which we drove the only 'funny-looking' vehicle among a cargo of RASC three-tonners and staff cars. The voyage was down the Thames, through the Straits of Dover at night, along the coast to

Portsmouth—a magnificent day of lazing on deck, listening to the news of the battle, writing and reading—and across to France. Our introduction to Normandy was a smoke screen and a solitary attempt at low-level bombing, at which everybody stood gaping on deck. We drove in darkness across the sands and on and on, following the shape in front, until morning found us in the middle of nowhere and certainly at the wrong report point. However, by mid-morning we had reached divisional headquarters, which already displayed signs about not raising dust.

The regimental area—never used by the regiment—was a few hundred yards away, across two or three fields, but owing to the traffic system the journey was more than a mile by road. It was a farm which was unapproachable for half the day because it was beyond the one spring in the area and therefore the rendezvous, it seemed, of every water truck east of Bayeux. The first night we slept in a field, and woke wet. Thereafter we shared an outhouse with the cattle. There we stayed for seven days—unitless, midway between the coast and the Battle of Cheux.

Having a splendid ration system (it allowed a fair surplus), and ability to speak the tongue, and three sets of earphones through which the farm people and an increasing number of their friends could listen to the news in French, we were soon properly 'feet under' with the farm, the laundry girl and the barber. Our days consisted of searching for ammunition that had been left about by the Germans; driving down to the beach to see whether the regiment had arrived on the tide; visiting divisional, corps and army headquarters (in chateaux of increasing magnificence); being constipated; and fetching mail until we were surrounded by it. In the evenings we had the company of the people of Vienne en Bessin from 9.15 ('*Ici Londres*') until midnight, at which time the bombing of the coast was deemed to have ended and Madame la Fermiere would order '*Au lit*' in such a military fashion that none refused. The two most vivid memories of these days are of digging the car out of an immense dung pit, into which Kay had tactlessly backed it, and of listening to the peculiar gurgle of the large shells fired from the battleships in Arromanches Bay at Germans fifteen miles away. In spite of the sound of the shells and the sight of the Allies' big bombing raids, this life was altogether too much like an exercise to last. We were ousted by a mapmaking unit and relegated to a ditch outside St Gabriel. The next day, unannounced, the regiment arrived. The holiday in France was over.

CHAPTER VII

INTO BATTLE (CAEN FRONT)
Map No.1

The fields of St Gabriel were a quiet introduction to life in a Normandy of war, and the slit trenches that were dug were only a little deeper than the token slit trenches of exercises. It was not easy to realise that only a few miles away the rest of the15th Scottish Division, having landed more than a week earlier, was fighting the battle which has been called—in its honour—the Battle of the Scottish Corridor. Its official title was more prosaic—Operation Epsom. The regiment had arrived just in time to join in its closing stages, unspectacularly but not without loss. The division's attack, supported by the 7th and 9th Royal Tanks and 320 guns, started from le Mesnil-Patry and Norrey en Bessin on the morning of 26 June. Now the maps showed a long finger jabbed into the German lines, a finger which covered Cheux and had its tip beyond the Odon at Mondrainville, where the 2nd Argyll and Sutherland Highlanders had captured the bridge intact. The ground won, nearly six miles forward and in places only 2,500 yards wide, was being held against counter-attacks by men and tanks of seven panzer divisions. On the evening of 29 June the regiment received orders to move from St Gabriel to Putot en Bessin on the following day to become divisional reserve, and long before light on 30 June the harbour parties, with Major MacDiarmid in charge, were groping their way forward by torchlight and the flashes of the guns astride the main Caen-Bayeux road. There was much traffic in the darkness. There was much when the main body of the regiment moved soon after dawn. So many vehicles and guns had been poured into the bridgehead that the roads were nearly always crowded. The distance to Putot en Bessin, through Coulombs, le Parc and along the Bayeux-Caen road, was only about seven miles, but the journey took several hours. As soon as the regiment had reached its place among the barking guns in the fields just west of Putot en Bessin C Squadron was given a warning order to move forward and take up a position under the command of 44 Brigade. Major Mills left for brigade headquarters, and troop commanders for an RV at Cheux.

The close fighting of the Caen front, in which armies were locked like wrestlers straining toe to toe, gave no scope for the employment of the regiment as a whole in the type of reconnaissance for which it was best equipped. Until the opportunity for this occurred the unit was used piecemeal as the division's odd job man—occupied variously as infantryman, traffic policeman, messenger, chauffeur, ambulance man. The one essay in squadron reconnaissance on this sector brought out the difficulties which attended such a venture if it started while the infantry were already closely engaged with an obstinate enemy. But that had no place in this first battle. The first task, which had fallen to C Squadron, was to assume the role of infantry and fill a gap on the boundary between VIII Corps and XXX Corps, which was on the right. The position was about a mile south of le Haut du Bosq. Just before noon that day, 30 June, the squadron started from Putot en Bessin on its first slow, bumpy, dusty, unforgettable journey to the front. The roads were tracks. Maps were useful only to give the general direction; the important thing was to have sharp eyes for, and blind faith in, the signs 'Ship Route Up'. The way was between fields where tanks were scattered while their crews re-equipped them after battle, brewed tea and rested. From the top of a rise the country looked so full of 25-pounders that it seemed impossible that room could be found for even one more. Groups of infantry trudged forward, glancing enviously at the vehicles which made the dust clouds that enveloped them. Other groups were coming back, escorting a few wretched-looking prisoners. At the men tramping back, at the men beside the tanks, C Squadron stared curiously. They were men who were different, for all the sameness of battledress; they were men who had been in battle. Faith in 'Ship Route Up' was not misplaced, and in the rubble and smell of Cheux the squadron found its troop commanders waiting.

In the early afternoon the squadron took up a position which was—of necessity—very different from the positions advised in military text books. The area was thickly wooded, and the field of fire was not more than two hundred yards. Vehicles were lined along a hedge on a front of nearly four hundred yards. There were no anti-tank guns, as they had landed only that morning. Wondering what was in the wood in front, straining to identify among the many noises those which betokened danger, the squadron dug furiously, and hoped. Shortly after midnight the positions were heavily mortared, and C Squadron suffered the regiment's first casualties. Sgt Cameron was killed and Tpr Beard was fatally wounded. Lieut White, Sgt Collins, L/Cpl King, L/Cpl Mincedorf and Tpr Bateman also were wounded. They were sent back through the infantry under difficulties and later the regiment learned that Lieut White, one of its ablest and best liked troop commanders, who had served unscathed in the BEF, had to lose a leg and two fingers. That morning some of the laughter had gone from C Squadron's world. But there was not much time to dwell on the loss of comrades. At eight o'clock the air shook with a louder thunder of artillery; the Germans had counter-attacked to the south. For more than two hours armoured car crews at their guns and carrier crews in slit trenches stared anxiously at the wood, where a section of the assault troop was posted to give the alarm. But the German attack did not spread to those four hundred yards, and by noon the situation had become calm enough for the squadron to dig deeper.

Back at Putot en Bessin RHQ had become the first part of the regiment to experience enemy shellfire—somewhat to its own surprise and certainly to the loss of some of its dignity. This happened not long after C Squadron had left on 30 June. Everybody was becoming accustomed to the shriek of shells which followed the crack of the guns in the neighbouring fields, and the dinner queue at the cook's truck did not realise until two shells had burst that this time the crack followed the whine. The awful truth seemed to explode in every mind at once. In a few moments the only people who remained above the ground were the colonel, sitting at his wireless and calling for a 'shellrep', his wireless operator, and those who lay prone under the cook's truck, having been slow starters in the race to the slit trenches. In the rush a plate of rice pudding, borne in the second 'wave', spread itself over the head of one of the swift starters who had already reached the comforting depths of a trench. That was the only direct hit, although twenty-five shrapnel shells exploded over the area and there were casualties nearby. RHQ's sharpened perception of war was summed up by the action of the trooper who did not emerge from his trench when the shelling stopped, but groped over the edge for a spade and pick. In the evening RHQ and A Squadron watched a stream of Lancasters and Halifaxes fly relentlessly through a curtain of anti-aircraft shells and drop 1,500 tons of bombs on Villers Bocage, eight miles to the south, where an armoured counter-attack was believed to be gathering. The dust and smoke from the flattened town spread over the area like a fog.

On the morning of 1 July, while C Squadron was anxiously scanning the wood to its front, A Squadron was ordered to move forward and fill another gap in the Haut du Bosq area, where C Squadron and the King's Own Scottish Borderers, of 44 Brigade, were out of contact with the 49th Reconnaissance Regiment, the XXX Corps' unit on the right of them. The gap was so wide that A Squadron, deployed as infantry, never got into touch with the troops on the right. Only one platoon of the Borderers could be spared to cover the squadron as it took up position and dug. At first there were no anti-tank weapons available, except the PIAT, but a few tanks from 34 Tank Brigade arrived in time to ward off an attack by German tanks, some of which were hit. Digging was punctuated by the groan and crump of German mortar bombs, and there were casualties in 4 Troop. Sgt D. Heath and Tpr Milligan were wounded.

In the afternoon the regiment's anti-tank guns, their waterproofing hurriedly removed after their later landing, reached the forward area, and were quickly sited on both squadron fronts. The gun crews regarded their field of fire— only two hundred yards—with pained surprise, but, whatever their private misgivings on this score, their presence gave a feeling of greater security to the two squadrons throughout an uneventful night and a day that was quieter than the one before. That day, 2 July, 44 Brigade was relieved by 160 Brigade of the 53rd Welsh Division, and in the evening A and C Squadrons, their places taken by squadrons of the 53rd Reconnaissance Regiment, were able to go from the smell of dead cows and horses to the purer air of Secqueville en Bessin, where the regiment was concentrated in reserve. The 15th Scottish Division's first battle was over. The regiment's part had been the smallest, and the pride with which it read the praises that followed was the pride of one member of a family in the achievements of his brothers. Special Orders of the Day were issued by Major-General MacMillan ('I am proud indeed of all officers and men in this division . . .') and Sir Richard O'Connor ('Your courage, tenacity and general fighting qualities have confirmed in battle the high opinion I have always held of you'). 'Scotland can well feel proud of the 15th Scottish Division,' wrote Montgomery, and Sir Miles Dempsey, the army commander: 'It has been a great start, and you have every right to be proud of yourselves.'

Somehow war's rough hand had brushed lightly over Secqueville en Bessin, a pale village clinging to the skirts of its old church, cupped among low green hills. Large guns still spoke loudly from the hollow, and at night the red balls of tracer floated lazily up to an inquisitive German plane, but the village had already become the sanctuary of cattle that had survived bullet and bomb, mine and shell. They crowded a large field, lowing and forlorn, but not so forlorn as the stiff legs and swollen bodies in the fields of Cheux. The regiment made itself comfortable on hillside and in hollow, stretching tarpaulins from the sides of vehicles to make tents over the shallow trenches. Weapons were cleaned, batteries charged, vehicles maintained and experiments carried out with baths which ranged from a petrol tin for each leg to a tarpaulin lining a hole. The results of the latter method surprised those who had not realised that the sheet was heavily tarred. Peasant girls going to milking stood agape. A brief entry in Lieut Sadgrove's diary is eloquent of another important activity of those days: '4 July—rained all day. Not a good drying day.' Parties marched to Cully, a little more than a mile away, to visit the mobile cinema. A football match in which there were three balls, three referees and 240 players was won by A Squadron, and a basketball tournament by C Squadron's 10 Troop.

While the regiment played and rested, maps displayed at RHQ and squadron headquarters showed the changing line of battle, and welfare wireless sets boomed the news from London of what was happening within half an hour's drive of Secqueville en Bessin. On 7 July the hill above the village became a grandstand from which to watch the RAF drop two thousand tons of bombs on the industrial district of Caen as a prelude to the attack in which the 3rd British, 3rd Canadian and 59th Divisions occupied the whole of the town north and west of the Orne. On 8 July A Squadron was warned to be ready to move. It was to be placed under the command of 46 Brigade with the object of helping to mop up the area west of Caen and Carpiquet.

On 9 July A Squadron moved off, flying the pennants which distinguished troop from troop. The sign of 1 Troop was a flying pig, while 2 Troop paid a compliment to its commander, Michael Blair, by flying a bulldog astride a rugby ball. Billie the Bun, by which 3 Troop was known, was inspired by a little rabbit which travelled in a car turret but always kept out of the way in action. Less inventive, 4 Troop paraded its number. After threading its way through the traffic on roads and tracks, the squadron halted in a cornfield near Verson, dug deeply and slept fitfully. Its orders for 10 July were to reconnoitre in front of the brigade in the direction of Verson, Eterville and Maltot with the intention of reaching the Orne about half a mile beyond Maltot. It was thought that the area was fairly clear of Germans. In fact, they were in great strength on the reverse slopes behind Eterville. Approaching Eterville, the squadron was attacked by enemy fighter planes, and Sgt Robinson, of 1 Troop firing a Bren, shot one down in flames.

The operation was planned to begin with the capture of Eterville by a battalion of the 43rd Division, after which the 9th Cameronians were to pass through, with A Squadron unleashed in front of them, to gain the high ground dominating the river. The Wessex battalion, however, was unable to capture the village, and, instead of passing through, the Cameronians had to take over and clear it. They were already fighting when the three reconnaissance troops of A Squadron were sent forward: 2 Troop (Lieut Blair) leading, 3 Troop (Lieut J. M. Arundel) next and 1 Troop (Lieut G. R. Blount) last. The road through the village was blocked by burning vehicles and the village church, which had collapsed across it. Lieut Blair's troop found a way round, through a field and a farmyard, and made good progress to the area of Louvigny, where it came upon German infantry and shot some of them.

After crossing the main Caen-Eterville road, 3 Troop, heading for Maltot, also met enemy infantry, who disappeared into the cornfields. Lieut Arundel called his carriers forward to support the armoured cars, with which he intended to cut through the enemy and reach the river. Tpr J. Connor, who was in a carrier, has given this account of what happened:

The situation was extremely tricky, as the whole troop was perched on the top of a hill, from which we could see the opposite bank of the river. The Brens in the carriers and the Besas in the armoured cars were firing at the enemy snipers, who would pop up, fire and dive back into the corn. My carrier commander, Sgt Munton, told me to keep their heads down with bursts from my Bren. I did. I saw two Jerries rise at once and had a go at them, but I do not know whether I got them. My gun slipped from its resting place and fired through the front of the carrier above the driver's head; my head was bleeding slightly, and for a moment I thought that the holes in the carrier had been caused by German bullets.

A smoke screen on the right flank cleared, and five German tanks, which had been hidden behind it, opened fire, dispersing the troop and knocking out the two leading armoured cars. Sgt Ireland and his crew escaped from one, but in the other big, bluff, kind John Arundel and his driver and friend, Tpr Griffiths, were killed, although it was ten days before the regiment could find out what had happened to them.

Because the battle was not what had been planned, the enemy resistance being fiercer than had been expected, 1 Troop was ordered to abandon its original task and to consolidate on the left flank of the Cameronians and prevent the enemy from infiltrating back into Eterville. It came under heavy fire. Major Rowlands, the squadron commander, was in his reconnaissance car when it was hit by a shell, and for twenty-four hours nobody knew what had happened to him. Then it was found that he had been seriously wounded, and his driver, Tpr C. H. G. Ballard, killed. In the meantime Capt Davies, the second-in-command, was directing the squadron. Lieut Blair's troop, having met the Canadians near Caen, found its return route blocked, and reconnoitred another, thus adding to valuable information which the squadron was able to give 46 Brigade at a cost that day of twenty casualties. L/Cpl J. R. Hutchinson was killed, and Cpl J. Innes was fatally wounded.

That evening the squadron harboured just south of Verson, but found little rest. This section of the front was mortared repeatedly, and a German plane dropped a stick of bombs in the harbour. During the night the squadron was lent to 214 Brigade and ordered to dig itself into position before dawn on an exposed flank of the brigade, which was trying to establish itself on Point 112. This was high ground which dominated the area, and in the fighting for it many infantrymen of both armies lost their lives. It had been captured by 129 Brigade on 10 July, but counter-attacks in the evening drove the brigade to the west. To obtain exact information about a confused situation 214 Brigade sent officer patrols from A Squadron to the forward battalions on 11 July. After these patrols had made their reports the squadron was given permission to return to Secqueville en Bessin.

The interlude of Secqueville en Bessin was ended by Operation Greenline, an attack on the far side of the Odon towards Evrecy. Its object was twofold: to deepen the bridgehead, and to draw German forces away from the First United States Army on the right. The regiment's part was to have been fourfold, but owing to lack of opportunity C Squadron was not called upon to go into action with 227 Brigade, under whose command it was placed. Light cars driven by Tpr Yount and Tpr Flavell were lent to the commanders of 44 and 227 Brigades as 'chargers'; A Squadron's carriers, commanded by Lieut Gordon Dalton, brought wounded over ground which ambulances could not cover; and RHQ, part of A Squadron and part of Headquarter Squadron became an organisation for controlling the traffic approaching and crossing the Odon. Traffic points were set up on five routes, called Hereford, Dundee, Quarry 2, Coal 1 and Coal 2. RHQ, the control headquarters, established itself in an orchard where Quarry route turned off the main Verson road. 'Doc' Watson, the regiment's genial new medical officer, had his post among the disordered contents of the house on the opposite side of the Verson road. C Squadron moved into fields near Verson on the night of 13 July, and on 15 July the traffic control organisation took up its positions, which were linked by lines laid and courageously maintained in the face of dangers and difficulties by signallers of the 11th Armoured Division.

The attack opened on the night of 15 July in artificial moonlight supplied by batteries of searchlights. The crossroads le Bon Repos, within a thousand yards of Esquay, and the high road to the west were secured by 227 Brigade, whose commander, Brigadier J. R. Mackintosh-Walker, was killed by a mortar bomb. Next day 44 Brigade captured Gavrus and Bougy, but counter-attacks and mortaring prevented further advances. C Squadron went forward to an orchard between Baron and Gournay, but after waiting under shellfire was sent back to harbour.

Mortar bombs and shells burst frequently on the roads to the Odon and the crossings of the river. One of the casualties was Lieut Blair, who was fatally wounded by a mortar bomb at his traffic point. This was a blow to his troop, his squadron and the regiment. Everybody liked this stocky, dark-haired Scottish rugby footballer, and everybody respected his soldierly qualities. Tpr G. J. Grant was killed, and when C Squadron's harbour was mortared; Tpr D. B. Torrance was fatally wounded.

On the night of 16 July low-flying planes bombed the Verson road, where a long line of tanks was waiting. Sgt Millroy, bringing despatches to RHQ, swore his way from ditch to ditch along this unpleasant stretch of road after Tpr Merryman's jeep, in which he had been riding, had collided with a carrier in the darkness near Verson. On the night of 17 July the Scottish Division was relieved by the Welsh, and the 53rd Reconnaissance Regiment took over traffic control. Lieut Colonel Grant Peterkin had a lucky escape when a shell burst close to him in the orchard.

The traffic control parties made their way back to the rest of the regiment, now harboured near Fontenay le Pesnel, south of Cheux, under the long black barrels of 155 mm guns—Long Toms. That night flares lit the harbour, and German planes attacked. Cpl H. A. Ward, a professional footballer and a mainstay of the A Squadron team, was killed. So was Tpr R. Forster, another member of A Squadron. Seven vehicles, including two ammunition trucks, were set on fire, and a party quickly organised by Lieut Blount drove the other vehicles clear of the blaze and the exploding ammunition. The fire burned for several hours, but no more planes came. Next day C Squadron found the explosive from a German Beetle tank in the middle of its area, and, thinking on the night's events, moved to another field.

B Squadron, the residue, arrived on 19 July, full of enthusiasm, eager to hear what the regiment had done and learned, and remarkably forbearing in the face of 'old soldier' airs and tall stories. Rain fell heavily on the dusty fields for several days. Umbrellas appeared—whence, nobody knew—and Capt Kemp, the PRI, produced the first liquor ration with the air of one consciously performing a great public service. On 21 July the three assault troops, commanded by Lieut R. W. Parker (A Squadron), Lieut G. J. Harvey (B) and Lieut K. B. M. Shirley (C), were combined to form Macforce and sent under Major MacDiarmid's command to help the 7th Seaforth, who were holding positions in the area of Le Baltru. What life was like there has been described by one of Macforce:

The position was high ground, with a valley and high ground in front of us—a lousy place that stank to high heaven. It rained like hell for the first two days, and we were mortared. The infantry were down to eight men to a platoon and were very tired. They rested while we manned forward posts and patrolled. One of the posts, right down in the wooded valley, was periodically cut off. We had German patrols coming and looking at us. A patrol of three men from each troop was sent out on reconnaissance, down through the valley and up the other side, and as it was crossing a field it saw that the hedge in front was lined with German machine guns. These opened up when the patrol was backing out, but everybody except Tpr W. J. Pugh, of C Squadron, who was killed, managed to get back. Another patrol, looking for the Germans in the blackness of a rainy night, was nearly shelled by our guns. During a burst of German gunfire one member of Macforce mistook a latrine for a slit trench in his dive to avoid a shell which killed two infantrymen in a slit trench nearby.

James Ferrier:- Peter Kerridge took over command of 3 Troop upon Lieut. Arundel's death and the disaster of our first action in Normandy, the loss being two killed and four wounded when a Tiger tank knocked out two heavy armoured cars. The whole troop was shooting up German infantry in a field. The carriers and light recce cars were hidden by the tall corn but the three heavies stuck out like sore thumbs! The two cars had been dealt with and the shell fired at my heavy arrived just when the car dropped into a pothole or rut and the shot bounced on the two turret doors and took away both wireless masts.

I met Peter Kerridge that night when he was re-organising the troop and promoted me to Lance Corporal. I wanted to refuse the rank but he made it an order and I continued as gunner in the only heavy car in the troop.

Bryan White:- Looking back fifty years to le Haut du Bosq.

It was 30 June, my vehicle led my troop and C Squadron to Cheux deep in the bocage country and at that time the only village where approach road and tracks enabled the massive build up of supplies and ammunition to reach the infantry and armour in the Scottish corridor. We were attempting to force the crossing of the river Odon and cut off the city of Caen. The role of the Squadron was to act as infantry filling a gap at le Haut du Bosq between VIII and XXX Corps. The troop position was on a wooded slope overlooking a hedgerow with a limited field of fire of 200 yards. I requested the Squadron Commander for permission to move the troop further up the hill with, in my opinion, a better field of fire and a less exposed position. Understandingly he refused, wishing to maintain his original plan of defence!

We found a dead Scottish soldier by the hedge, the area stank of dead cows and some poor beasts were wandering around with their guts protruding from their stomachs until mercifully dispatched by a sten-gun burst. Mortar and machine-gun fire were very evident to our right front where a Scottish infantry company was under intense and accurate bombardment. When liaising with a Battalion on our left I heard the Colonel telling the gunnery liaison officer that many of his soldiers had been killed by our own artillery fire that morning. The warships lying off the beachhead were heavily shelling the German lines, and in the early evening a mass of Allied bombers passed overhead to attack Villers Bocage, a suspected assembly point for German armour.

The Hitler Youth had occupied the spot where my Bren gun carrier was positioned and I and my crew enlarged one of their slit trenches for our own use, and all around us the sections dug in. As darkness fell we posted sentries and the soldiers were told to get what sleep they could as a major German counter-attack was expected at dawn. I recall sleeping fitfully and getting up probably around midnight to check my troop pickets. I had covered only a few yards when I felt an immense pain in my left thigh rather as if someone had swung hard at my leg with an axe. A second or so later without pain in my right hand two fingers were whisked off rather like a knife slicing an onion. One then heard the whistle of more mortar bombs.

I discovered later that Sgt Cameron had been killed outright, and that my Troop Sgt Collins had been wounded, also, Troopers Bateman and Beard and my crew

L/Cpls Mincedorf and King. Apart from Beard, who was desperately wounded, I believe these men did much to sort out the fires and chaos that resulted from the Nebelwerfer stonk.

I knew from the first impact that my leg or that which remained of it would inevitably have to be amputated and my career as a Regular Army Officer (I had passed a WOSB for a Regular commission in recent times) and my capability of serving my Regiment were now completely kaput. I worried for my soldiers but after struggling and failing to pull my field dressing from my battle-dress pocket, I passed out. I regained consciousness to find my chest smouldering and little whisps and puffs of fire were going up from the carrier, where obviously mortar bombs had exploded our stock of phosphorous grenades spraying, hissing and spitting segments on to my chest. Again there was not much pain; possibly the initial shock of the mortars' impact was so intense that it had given me immunity for a period. Eventually the Squadron medical corporal and medical orderly arrived and attended to the badly wounded.

Predictably I said to the corporal who was applying a much needed tourniquet, 'I am saying goodbye to that bloody leg', and equally predictably he replied 'We'll get you out of here Sir, and you will be fine.' Stretcher bearers carried me and Trooper Beard across the fields to the Regimental Aid Post of one of the neighbouring Scottish infantry battalions.

Inevitably German mortar bombs were falling in clusters round about, and the MO rushed out of his bunker, stuck morphine needles into us both and sensibly disappeared underground. Our bearers then carried us some way to the nearest track where a military ambulance picked us up and bumped along the lanes to the nearest casualty clearing station. There were other wounded in that vehicle but Trooper Beard was on the bunk above me and as he was dying he became incoherent. I think he was calling for his mother and his hand gripped my nose with incredible strength and I had difficulty in freeing myself from his dying grasp. He was dead on arrival at the CCS.

I knew I was taken for surgery involving amputation. I believe I came to in the middle of the operation but went off again. On regaining consciousness in a bed with clean sheets (I had not slept in sheets for years except on occasional leave) I knew the leg had gone but predictably asked the nurse for some of the mortar fragments. She dutifully went off and returned minutes later to say, 'Sorry the surgeon has disposed of such waste material and is pretty busy on the next operation.'

A nice Padre arrived and asked me if I required 'the last sacrament.' On my polite (I hope) refusal, he dished out a boiled sweet for the future and a cigarette for the present. My memory of that place is hazy; I was always thirsty and never received water but always some foul fruit juice. The food, which I couldn't eat, consisted of pack rations. A nurse was constantly making me take M and B tablets (I think they were called).

I was moved to the 79th General Hospital at Bayeux after a few days and in this tented establishment the facilities were good and the care with the Queen Alexandra Nursing Sisters, the RAMC surgeons and the medical orderlies was of a high standard. Some RAMC staff appeared to be sleeping in hammocks slung under the trees, and French civilians seemed to be wandering among the tents. On one occasion I was in the open on a stretcher laid on the ground on my own when an enormous black dog came and licked my face. Perhaps this was all fantasy! Gradually I was able to take more notice. My burns irritated, my stump stank as gangrene had set in but those fine ladies of the QARANC were most professional. They came in all shapes and sizes and their battle-dress trousers did nothing to enhance their feminine appeal. They were all good and in the daytime were rushed off their feet as more wounded from the various battle areas came flooding in, but at night when the occasional German bomber ventured out and the Ack-Ack thundered forth, a night nurse would stop by the bed and talk for a minute or so. Such little things are precious to a man who is not certain whether or not he is going to make it.

I was twenty-four at the time with a wife Betty and a new born baby son at home. Sometimes I thought I was going off and would not recover, and I was rather surprised on one occasion to find myself in the ward with the orderly dispensing that awful sweet cordial and the usual stink of the gangrenous stump, and the pus oozing out of the chest burns. I have a blurred memory of some death threshold incidents, not seeing a bright light in a tunnel, but more like turning back one step away from the edge of a precipice. There was a little nurse, rather plain but a lovely person to me and others, who would sit on the end of the bed and fiddle with my ankle where a little bone would appear to flit about like pressing on a tiddly wink. (A rugger injury, nothing to do with the war). In fact she reset the bone which clever doctors had failed to do.

There was a plump nurse who seemed to be in charge, always gentle and considerate. When the stretcher came to load me on the way back to England, she said to the orderly in a whisper, 'Be careful, he has only one leg,' and as they carried me into the sunshine, the orderly winked and I knew I was back in the world again.

Len Watson:- We drew alongside a very well made artificial hedge. Sgt Armstrong was soon off the carrier and shot out the two protruding glasses in a large 'V' type telescope in an immaculate slit trench. We took five German prisoners, the confrontation between our Titch Quail was really something (Titch being the smallest man in our troop) his huge opponent who eventually threw his rifle away. The German Officer dropped to his knees in tears; he thought we were going to shoot him. Our sergeant turned him round and relieved him of his gold pocket watch. We handed the prisoners over to members of our infantry.

I was examining a German rifle when I was knocked flat to the ground; surprised and shaken I felt the back of my head, no blood – thank God for that, so I dashed for the cover of a nearby hedge. Sgt Knibbs called out to Titch Quail instructing him to crawl as he had been taught, lying flat on the ground with the Bren across his arms. Titch had fired a burst towards the sniper's position, it seemed ages before he got to me. It was only when I took my helmet off that I realized that a bullet had struck the rim of my helmet and part of it remained imbedded. Fortunately we wore the tank type helmet which afforded slightly more protection to the back of the head than the regular infantry issue. If the bullet had struck another half inch lower I would have joined comrades in Bayeux war cemetery. Snipers, if captured, rarely made it back to the safety of a POW camp!

George Blount:- The aircraft that was shot down by Sgt Jack Robinson was in fact a Messerschmitt 109. Some of my troop salvaged the clock from the wreck and presented it to me. It accurately ticked away the years in Dumfries and when Jack died in 2002 it pleased me to be able to present the clock to his son John who was a serving officer in the Royal Armoured Corps.

Bill Thomas:- Our Troop was on flank protection supporting the Canadians who were attempting the capture of Carpiquet aerodrome on the outskirts of Caen. We had endured two noisy nights as the Luftwaffe had attempted to bomb the 25-pounders situated in the next field to us, so we were happy to receive orders to relocate our position. Our new location was two miles away but even closer to a battery of Canadian 5.5s. We camouflaged our vehicles and settled down in a slit trench courtesy of the Canadian infantry who had previously occupied it.

Standing in the middle of the field was the usual latrine 'soldiers for the use of', very imposing in its hessian surround. I had just finished writing a letter when Nick (Graham Nicklin) informed me he was going to pay a visit, I knew what he meant. About ten minutes later, and, hearing the sound of aircraft, I popped my head out of the slit trench. Overhead were a couple of enemy aircraft dropping flares in an attempt to locate the guns, one flare directly over the latrine. Through the light of the flames was a figure minus his trousers making a determined and courageous effort to break the four minute mile. When a breathless Nick composed himself, his words were 'they can bomb my bloody trousers but not when I am in them!' Suffice it to say his trousers were recovered later; we still laugh over this episode!

Bernie Higham:- On Friday 30 June we went into the line for the first time at Cheux. We were ordered to dig in; after completing our slit trenches we were then instructed to move forward to the next location. Lofty Higgs using colourfully descriptive trooper's language stated 'that's the first and last time I dig a hole.' Mortared and shelled for most of the night, one killed and six wounded, Lofty survived the night. I had no idea where he had taken cover. He did not dig a trench during the next ten months as we advanced from France through Belgium and Holland to Germany; Lofty was never seen with a spade or pick in his hand. He was the most courageous man I had the honour to serve with; sadly he was killed in a RTA shortly after the war had ended.

Ernie Clarke:- I can add a personal word to the incident of our first experience of shell-fire. I was first into one of the slit trenches! Someone landed on my back and there was a nearby shell burst. Somebody gave a jump and shouted out 'I'm hit, I'm hit!' I was thinking – crikey, what do I do now – when a voice from the side of the trench said 'shut up you fool, it's my rice.' Actually, the rice had gone down the back of his neck.

Bill Howlett:- the night patrol was led by Lieut. Shirley C Squadron Assault Troop, to establish the reason for sudden quiet on the front. Members of the patrol were Monty Solomons, Johnny Wagg, Curly Herriot, myself and three others I cannot recall. Object was to 'probe' the German lines and capture a prisoner(s). All went well until suddenly our searchlights lit up the front and we were caught exposed in the open ground. We hit the deck and made for nearby hedges in a hail of machine-gun fire. We tried to re-group but could not find Pugh or Solomons; after a lot of crawling we reached our own lines. Pugh was never found, Solomons turned up later and was granted early leave from which he never returned.

Alan Westby:- Enemy mortaring was a problem and the order came that no one should sleep above ground. Slit trenches were dug and, in some cases these were covered with tree branches to support petrol cans (square sectioned before jerrycans replaced them) filled with earth as protection from air-bursts. This system was fine except when it rained. The whole troop awoke one morning to discover the bottom of their trench awash and clothing wet through. It was decided to light a fire and rig up a clothes line round it, strip off and dry our uniforms. Unfortunately, the smoke from this fire attracted a German fighter, which strafed our position with guns blazing. It would be interesting to know what the pilot thought as he witnessed white bottoms heading at full speed for the hedges surrounding the field. Fortunately the only wounds were to our dignity.

In the absence of a slit trench at the start of a mortar attack, it was permissible to dive under the nearest vehicle. On such occasions, time is short to select which, and during one such event, it chanced to be the ammunition wagon, which I chose; this could have proved to be a fatal mistake. When the attack ceased we discovered that a jagged hole had been torn in the side of the carrier by a piece of shrapnel. Closer examination revealed that the fragment had penetrated the container of six anti-tank rounds and that it had also entered the cartridge case of a shell, lodging in the explosive but without any ignition thereby failing to blow the lot to smithereens.

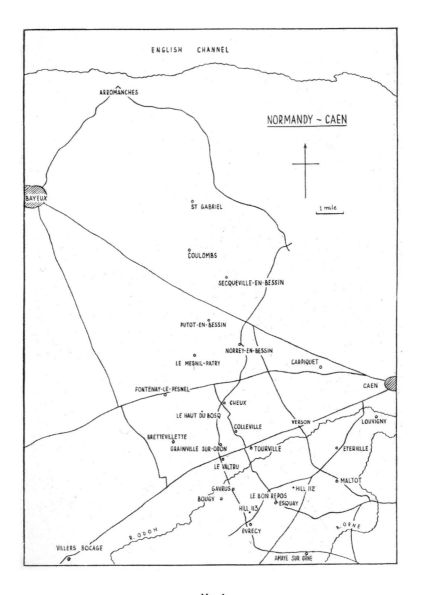

Map 1

On patrol in Normandy

The clock salvaged from
the Messerschmitt Bf 109
shot down by Sgt Jack
Robinson

Lieut. James Michael Blair,
Reconnaissance Regiment,

James M. Blair

Whose death from wounds in Normandy was reported on
Thursday.

Lieut. Blair, who was 21, had played for Scotland in three services rugby internationals since the outbreak of war.

The only son of Mr and Mrs James Blair, residing at 12, St
Ninian's Terrace, Edinburgh, he was educated at Edinburgh
Academy. He captained the Academy XV in 1939-40, and afterwards played for Oxford University and was captain in the
1941 match against Cambridge.

NOTHING is to be written on this side except the date
and signature of the sender. Sentences not required may
be erased. If anything else is added the post card will
be destroyed.

[Postage must be prepaid on any letter or post card
addressed to the sender of this card.]

~~I am quite well.~~

I have been admitted into hospital

{ ~~sick~~ } and am going on well.

{ wounded } ~~and hope to be discharged soon.~~

I am being sent down to the base.

~~I have received~~ { ~~letter dated~~ ....

~~your~~ { telegram , ...

{ ~~parcel~~ ,, ...

Letter follows at first opportunity.

I have received no letter from you

{ lately

{ ~~for a long time.~~

Signature } BRIAN.
only }

Date 3rd July 1944 ...

Forms/A2042/7.
Wt. 18709/314. 45,000M. 7/41 W. & S. Ld. 51-725. 192326F.

Half a sixpence removed from Bryan White's left thigh. No indication of the severity of his wounds on the card
home and clearly not signed by Bryan but the padre

Beard and Cameron - the Regiment's first two casualties

Bryan and Betty White at Sgt Cameron's graveside

CHAPTER VIII

ADVANCE FROM CAUMONT

Map No.2

On 23 July the 15th Scottish Division moved secretly to the extreme right of the Second Army front, relieving the 5th United States Division south of Balleroy in the Caumont sector. It was like going from the bustle of Oxford Street into the tranquility of Hyde Park, this journey which began in the dust and smell and clatter of the country around Caen and ended in an unscarred land of little fields. C Squadron went straight into the line some miles from Balleroy. The rest of the regiment drove down Balleroy's wide street (between houses that might have been part of a Utrillo painting), turned right and right again, climbed a steep lane and found a home in green meadows. Here Major MacDiarmid took command of A Squadron. Major G. A. Gaddum joined the regiment to command Headquarter Squadron.

Relieving an American reconnaissance unit in the area la Chavetiere—le Bisson, C Squadron became the link between first 44 Brigade and later 46 Brigade and the Americans on the right. Squadron headquarters were in a lonely grey farm, already equipped with excellent dug-outs. Over the whole of the Caumont front was the buzzing stillness of high summer, disturbed only by the stealthy tread of patrols and outbursts of small arms and artillery fire that were as spasmodic as the convulsions of a drowsy animal irritated by flies. Behind Caumont, set on its ridge like a small English town on the North Downs, VIII Corps gathered its forces to plunge a mailed fist into the plain that stretched from the foot of the ridge like the 'distant, dim, blue goodness of the Weald'.

Operation Bluecoat began at seven o'clock on the morning of 30 July. There was no preliminary bombardment, but more than 1,500 planes bombed prearranged targets in two attacks that day. Advancing along the main road to St Martin des Besaces, 46 Brigade, with the tanks of the 4th Coldstream Guards, reached the Hervieux crossroads before noon. On the left 227 Brigade, with the tanks of the 3rd Scots Guards and two squadrons of the regiment (A and B) enveloped the Lutain Wood and went on to la Recussonniere and les Loges. The two squadrons, their carriers bumping along behind lumbering Churchills, mopped up enemy pockets. The going was not easy because of the many hedges and woods and many mines on the tracks. During the afternoon Capt Fordyce was bringing B Squadron headquarters forward to join Major Gordon when the light reconnaissance car in which Capt Fordyce was travelling ahead of the other vehicles 'brewed up' on a mine. He and his crew got out, but with only his pistol to engage the Germans who appeared on the other side of the road. Tpr P. Walker, the wireless operator, and Trooper A. Richardson, the driver, were killed, and Capt Fordyce, who tried to cover their withdrawal, was wounded.

By the end of the day a sharp wedge had been driven six miles into the enemy. The small town of St Martin, which lay across the main line of the advance, was still in German hands, but a mile and half to the east the 2nd Glasgow Highlanders, at the tip of the wedge, were established on Quarry Hill (Point 309), to which they had ridden the tanks of the Grenadier Guards behind the tanks of the Coldstream Guards.

While A and B Squadrons were in action the rest of the regiment, tensed by a warning to be ready to try to gain the high ground overlooking le Beny Bocage, followed the advance like a led horse waiting to be given its head. RHQ, C and HQ Squadrons, and parts of A and B Squadrons which had been left, drove out of Balleroy in the afternoon, paused at Mitrecaen, clattered through the empty, dishevelled streets of Caumont, and halted in the evening beside a burning copse at Hervieux on the straight road to St Martin. A and B Squadrons were waiting in fields beside the road. C Squadron was told that it was to lead the Second Army's break-out from the Normandy bridgehead; the day's advance had raised hopes so high that darkness, usually a shepherd who drove the regiment to the fold, was not to prevent immediate reconnaissance. An hour before nightfall Lieut E. A. Royle and Lieut K. W. Gray set out with their troops on unreconnoitred tracks to look for a way past St Martin over Quarry Hill. A Squadron's 1 Troop explored the main road to the town until halted by an anti-tank gun firing from the St Martin crossroads. These 1 Troop patrols then tried to get round on the right, but came under small arms fire on reaching the railway. When 11th Armoured Division tanks arrived an anti-tank gun opened fire, and one of the tanks was knocked out. After sending back this information, the A Squadron patrols were recalled to await the clearing of the town by the 11th Armoured Division. On the left flank the C Squadron patrols encountered many difficulties. Lanes were narrow and their banks high. In the darkness vehicles got stuck. It became obvious that the road through St Martin was the only way good enough to bear the advance. At dawn the patrols crossed Quarry Hill, but found the way barred at la Mancelliere. Typhoons fired rockets so close to them that they had to make yellow smoke signals to establish their identity. In the evening of 31 July C Squadron was withdrawn to a harbour north of St Martin.

The town had been cleared by the 11th Armoured Division in the afternoon.

Next day the regiment watched the Guards Armoured Division stream south and listened to the battle around Quarry Hill, where German counter-attacks were repulsed and 44 Brigade, clearing the Bois du Homme, made contact with the 43rd Wessex Division, which had advanced more slowly on the left. This action was fought on Minden Day, and the King's Own Scottish Borderers made their successful attack with roses in their hats, as the same regiment had done at the Battle of Minden.

In the evening B Squadron helped 46 Brigade to clear the area of Galet and la Mancelliere. Leading 6 Troop towards la Mancelliere, Cpl Raymond's car was fired on by a gun from the left. After reversing, the car went forward again to draw fire while Lieut G. H. L. Carey looked out for the gun from the top of a bank. The next shell landed almost underneath Cpl Raymond's vehicle, ricochetted and damaged the steering of Sgt Short's car. Lieut Carey saw the gun. It was a large one on the far side of a valley on the left of the road, and he led the men from his carriers across a cornfield on foot to attack it while an assault troop advanced on their left, up the valley. Reaching a hedge on the opposite side of the valley to the German gun, Lieut Carey's party came under heavy machine-gun fire, which killed Lieut Carey and Sgt E. P. Thompson and wounded others as they tried to make the best of scanty cover. Tpr Phillips was shot in the foot, and Sgt Austen Knibb, whose birthday it was, was hit in the wrist while attending to him with Cpl Chapman. Crawling to cover, Sgt Knibb was hit three times more. He ordered the rest of the party to withdraw, and, if possible to return for the wounded. Tpr Lawn covered the withdrawal and was shot in the stomach, but he was helped back to the carriers. Sgt Knibb lay where he was until midnight, when he began to crawl back to the British lines. He was wounded again, by fire from a house, as he crossed the cornfield, but he avoided a German patrol, and after going more than three miles reached the assault troop at four in the morning. Before being taken to hospital he gave the squadron commander a plan of the enemy position. Cpl Frost, Tpr Baxter and Tpr Johnson also were wounded in this action. Tpr Lawn was lost in the sinking of the hospital ship in which he was being taken to England.

On 2 August the regiment left its fields beside the Caumont-St Martin road, and, avoiding the dead horse in St Martin, went forward to protect the left flank of the Scottish Division, which was itself holding the corps left flank while the armour thrust towards Vire. There was a minor misunderstanding on this regimental move. The result was that the leading armoured cars, nosing cautiously forward, came upon RHQ established in 'uncharted' territory and blithely announcing its presence with the largest of signs. C Squadron, looking for the 43rd Division took up positions in the area of la Boulintere and Beaumont while the rest of the regiment, with A and B Squadrons in reserve, settled in le Bressi. This village in a valley had been free of Germans for only a few hours, and life there had its excitements. The French people brought out wine and calvados to celebrate *liberation*; the PMC, looking for eggs, came face-to-barrel with the Sten gun of the signals sergeant, Sgt Davidson, looking for snipers; and from the heights of Montamy the enemy fired shells which burst about one hundred yards from RHQ, tucked away behind a tall hedge on a hillside.

Next day A Squadron, lent to the Guards Armoured Division, was ordered to relieve the Grenadier Guards at St Pierre Tarentaine, but it was evident that this order was not based on a true appreciation of the situation. The Grenadier Guards were being shelled, mortared and counter-attacked, and relief by the squadron would have meant putting troop strengths in the place of companies and self-propelled guns. So the Guards stayed, and A Squadron stayed to help them repel more counter-attacks under heavy fire until evening, when the squadron went back to le Bressi. Tpr. D. Machen was killed.

C Squadron spent the day patrolling on the left in country where the high banks and hedges beside the roads made patrolling an extremely risky business, always liable to ambush. Overlooked by the German strongpoints on the Montamy heights, Lieut Gray took his patrol forward under shell and mortar fire, obtained valuable information and surprised an enemy patrol. He thus became the first member of the regiment to win the Military Cross. A patrol from 10 Troop came under enemy fire at close range, and Tpr F. McNeil, gunner in the leading car, was killed before the German party was dispersed.

Lieut Royle has described what happened when his patrol encountered a young Frenchwoman, running from the direction of the German positions:

She cried out to us not to shoot because there was somebody else coming, and a moment later we saw an old woman running down the road faster than I had ever seen an old woman run before. The old woman told me that there were about a hundred Germans in the wood round the house where she lived, and others in the house. She asked us to fire on them. We gave the information to the artillery, and as shells landed on her home she jumped for joy.

The same day, 3 August, Major General MacMillan, to whom the Scottish Division owed much, was wounded by a mortar bomb which fell near his jeep. Brigadier C. M. Barber DSO, commander of 46 Brigade, became the divisional commander.

On August 2nd Major General MacMillan had issued this Order of the Day:

I have received from the Army Commander today the following message, which will be given to all ranks in the 15th Scottish Division: 'It was the 15th Scottish Division which broke through the enemy's main defence line South of Caumont on July 30th and opened the way for the Armoured

Divisions to pass through. The result of your great action on that day can now be seen by everyone. You have set the very highest standard since the day you landed in Normandy, and I hope you are as proud of your achievements as I am to have you under my command. I am proud of the Division, and I wish to include in my congratulations and thanks the 6 Guards Armoured Brigade, whose splendid co-operation made our latest success possible.' - M. C. Dempsey.

On 3 August Sir Richard O'Connor issued an Order of the Day, congratulating the division on 'a magnificent achievement in the recent operations South of Caumont', and the Commander-in-Chief, talking to the divisional commander, praised the division for breaking right through the enemy defences without regard to the situation on its flanks.

Montchauvet (known to the regiment as Montcharivel) and Montchamp fell to the eastward attack of 44 Brigade and the tanks of the Welsh Guards on 4 August, and the same day the regiment's car patrols made contact with the 43rd Division at le Mesnil Auzouf. Advancing from the Montchauvet area on the following morning, 227 Brigade turned south down the main Vassy road and secured the important crossroads at la Caverie. The regiment moved to fields at Montchauvet, removed the carcass of a cow and considered its part in the next day's attack towards Vassy. The plan was based on information which suggested that the Germans were about to withdraw - they had already abandoned Esquay and Evrecy on the XII Corps front, and all that bombing had left of Villers Bocage (a mess of rubble) had been captured by XXX Corps.

The attack was opened on the misty morning 6 August by 46 Brigade and B Squadron, which advanced east from Au Cornu and took le Codmet without opposition. When, however, the advance was continued towards Gourney there was strong resistance.

B Squadron, contending also with bad tracks, was unable to reach Lassy. Two hours after the 46 Brigade attack opened, 227 Brigade, C Squadron and a squadron of tanks from the Grenadier Guards were due to cross a start line at la Caverie crossroads, but the start was delayed until the tanks had dealt with enemy tanks which broke through on the left to within a few hundred yards of the start line. On the Estry route Lieut Royle's troop found that Estry itself was strongly held and the main road to le Theil mined and covered by German tanks and machine guns. Patrols of the troop managed to enter Estry, but had to withdraw. They continued to harass the enemy, and obtained much information for the brigade, whose advance was halted by the resistance.

At Estry Cpl H. J. Higginson and Tpr H. L. Roberts were killed, and Sgt W. McMinn and Tpr J. Bunker won the Military Medal. Sgt McMinn, commanding a carrier section in support of the armoured cars, saw that the leading car had been knocked out, left his carrier and went forward on foot for about 250 yards under machine-gun fire to some houses, from which he could see the car and discover what was happening in the village. He climbed to the top of a house overlooking an enemy machine-gun post. The Germans shelled the building and it collapsed, but he extricated himself and reconnoitred the village street, discovering the positions of machine guns and a tank. This information he gave to the infantry.

Tpr Bunker was the driver of the car which was knocked out by the tank and set on fire. He was wounded by a shell. He could have left the vehicle and withdrawn to cover, but he waited for three Germans to approach, raised the car visor and shot them with his Sten gun. It was not until he was ordered to do so by his patrol commander that he left his vehicle, and then, in spite of his wounds, he sought out his troop commander and gave him a full account of the situation.

On the main Vassy road 10 Troop came upon an extensive minefield just over a mile from the start point. The Germans had the area well covered by fire, and two vehicles were knocked out. The crews, under Sgt Phillis, made their way back on foot. Throughout the day la Caverie crossroads were heavily shelled. In the evening B and C Squadrons returned to harbour, and the infantry, who had been able to make little progress, withdrew to better positions. Capt J. Watson and Sgt W. Ponting, who had moved the regimental aid post forward in support of 227 Brigade, were not warned of this withdrawal, and they spent several hours in no man's land.

These were the days of the beginning of the end in Normandy. General Patton's columns were on the move. Mount Pinçon, a natural fortress, fell to the Wessex Division, and the Americans captured Vire. But between them the 9th SS Panzer Division clung to its strongholds in and around Estry without a hint of withdrawal.

The regiment remained at Montchauvet while A and B Squadrons successively protected the left flank of 46 Brigade on the boundary between the Scottish and the Wessex Divisions. To do this A Squadron moved to high ground south of Linoudel, from which the mortars fired at enemy moving on the far slopes. A patrol of the 43rd Reconnaissance Regiment passed through A Squadron, and although given details of the 1 Troop positions fired on them by mistake when it came under machine-gun fire. A Squadron was shelled at night, but, having dug deeply, suffered lightly, whereas a squadron which had lately come from Britain to join the 43rd sustained considerable casualties because men were sleeping above ground. When B Squadron took over the position patrols reached the river line several hundred yards in front. On 10 August the Inns of Court Regiment relieved B Squadron. Tpr J. Burke was killed that day.

On 11 August Lieut Sadgrove was posted as a liaison officer to divisional headquarters, where he later became Major General Barber's ADC. At six o'clock on 12 August the regiment was ordered to move back to the Caen sector on the following day, but two hours later orders came over the wireless for Operation Estry to begin at once. This was the operation previously planned to follow up an enemy withdrawal from Estry. Swiftly the regiment prepared for the chase, and armoured cars moved out of harbour in the twilight. Then the order was cancelled; the enemy had not withdrawn.

Next day the regiment drove through the wreck of Villers Bocage and over old, bitter battlefields of the Caen front to Amaye sur Orne. The same day the carriers of the 8th Royal Scots entered Estry at last, and the Inns of Court began the dash that was to take them through Vassy to meet the Americans on the far side of the trap which was closing round a large part of the German forces in Normandy. That night the Scottish Division was relieved by the 11th Armoured Division.

Maurice Lawn was an accomplished all round sportsman and was on Leeds United's books. He was a big man and had complained about his difficulty in moving adroitly into and out of the armoured cars; his request for a transfer to the carriers had been agreed the morning of the 1 August.

* * * * *

George Bunn:- It was 1 August when George Carey was killed (2 on CWGC records) I think it was his birthday, mine is on the 2nd. I thought on that day I probably would not reach 21 years and it was inevitable that the third shot would hit us. It was quite close, my whole vision was filled with red fire and black smoke. As we came back, I had no option but to drive over two Germans lying on the track. After the shots the action took place by the carrier lads.

Oscar Thomas:- Corporal Henry Joseph Higginson, killed 6 August 1944.

On 6 August 1944 whilst on patrol, we came to a small village called Estry; in the outskirts there were two of our tanks which had been shelled. We were informed that there could be German Tiger tanks in the village.

My commander, Corporal Harry Higginson, was asked to try and get to the edge of the woods near the village and ascertain what the situation was. We drove there and Corporal Higginson jumped out of the vehicle to scout along the woods. He told Tpr Peter Dobson the gunner/wireless operator and myself (driver) to reverse back a few yards under some tall trees. He was thinking of the armoured car and us. The last time we saw him was as he walked towards the wood.

In the meantime there was a lot of firing coming from the village. After a short time Tpr Dobson became anxious and as the Corporal had not returned decided to look for him. He came back to report that he had found the Corporal's body; he had been killed by shrapnel from a mortar that had pierced his neck. We returned to the Squadron HQ, Peter reported the incident and other information regarding the village.

We did not know what happened at Estry afterwards, to us it was such a terrible shock to lose a great comrade, such a likeable experienced commander, always one of the boys. He was very particular with anything concerning the armoured car; should I miss the gears, I was rewarded with a swift knock on the head. He would say 'I have to rely on you, concentrate'.

After all the years I still remember the incident so clearly; 6 August is always my 'special remembrance day' for my gallant comrade Harry Higginson.

Major Adam Gordon wrote to Sgt Austen Knibb on 4 October 1944.

My dear Sgt Knibb,

We have all been wondering how you have been getting on. And in so wondering we were all pleased to get your letter of the 15/8/44. I agree that it seems an awful time to have waited before answering you. But as you will have gathered things have been moving rather fast and furious since you left. On the whole and considering the distances we have covered and the work we have had to do, our casualties have not been unduly heavy. Censorship Rules forbid exact figures, but they are encouraging. I have included herewith a complete list of the other casualties out of your troop on that day.

> Out of your own section
> Baxter (arm wound)
> Witmill (shoulder wound)

Neither of these was dangerous as far as I could make out from the Doctor. In fact I should not be surprised if they were about again.

Lt Carey was killed. Out of Sgt Thompsons section there were;

> Sgt Thompson (Killed)
> Cpl Frost (Tummy)
> Tpr Johnson (ankle)
> Tpr Lawn (chest)

It was a very sad business that Lawn was subsequently lost at sea (hospital ship struck a mine) he was a good man and a bad loss. Mr Carey and Sgt Thompson we buried side by side the next day. And I am glad to say that the tide of battle soon flowed past that spot. So that they are at peace again. I have written to Mrs Carey and to Mr Thompson.

Thank you so much for your very valuable advice on 1st Aid arrangements. All these points serve to help in the eventual smooth working of the machinery. 1st Aid is an ever present bother because no matter where you have the ambulance or the stretcher the casualty is always at the other end.

The matter that I feel really needs buttoning up is the question of getting casualties in out of an awkward spot such as you were in and as that changes with each set of circumstances; one had to deal differently with each case. Since you left, the Squadron, Regiment and Division have all earned extremely high names for themselves. We have had two or three really grand days that have gone better than the most perfectly conducted scheme. And of course every time we go out we learn something new. I hope we will meet again in the near future and I will be able to spin you 'Plenty big story'!! Unfortunately censors do not allow of us saying much in a letter. But already two or three bits have crept into the press. Master Connor and Mr Gillings, Sgt Lytton have all featured in their local papers.

Do write and let me know how you are getting on. The whole Sqd. is desperately anxious to know how their old friend fared. Maj. Smith is now looking after us all very well. The CO has gone off on other business which is a sad loss to us. Best of luck to you from the whole of the Sqd. old man Knibb - and keep smiling however difficult it may be.

Yours Aye
Adam Gordon

Len Watson:- We were on a hillside at Caumont and had been briefed the previous evening on our role; providing the weather was suitable, a huge bomber attack would take place. We changed from denim clothing into battledress in case of capture. Sergeant Knibb came round with his whisky flask and dispensed a welcome measure. A huge cheer went up when the first Lancasters appeared through a hole in the clouds, the aircraft were quite low and we could see the open bomb bays.

We set off driving through standing corn at a good speed thinking this is great, we will soon have the war won, unfortunately this progress did not last long when we ran into a mortar barrage. I saw a Highland Regiment Officer with his legs shredded supported by two members of his unit, he had been blown up on a mine; they were calling for stretcher bearers. The dreaded 'moaning minnies' were sending up spurts of dust in the distance and we soon realised how devastating they could be. Lt Jenkins was knocked out, his driver a good steady soldier, Dick Carlyon came by with a neck injury, sadly we never saw him again. Lt Jenkins came on our carrier complaining he had lost his bottle of whisky. Our carrier was set on fire from the camouflage netting and as I lay flat my boot heel was hit by shrapnel, we quickly realized we had to dig and get below ground level for protection.

Gordon Nursaw:- I was at Estry in the action when Tpr Bunker won his MM. There was a Tiger tank at the top of a hill, six Churchill tanks broke through the hedge at the foot of the incline and I saw each one hit by fire from the German machine.

Bill Ponting:- recalls how the RAP came to be left in no man's land at Estry. Captain Watson the MO said that we were ordered forward to help the RAP of the Highland Brigade who were fighting in Estry; they were suffering heavy casualties and were finding it difficult to cope. We set off late afternoon down a steep hill over the la Caverie crossroads towards Estry. We halted some distance from the village and Capt Watson went to find a suitable place to set up the RAP. I ordered everyone to take shelter in a deep ditch because we were under intense shell and mortar fire. Soon we had a German waiting to give himself up. Capt Watson soon returned and we set up the RAP in a farm house. The RAMC light ambulance attached to us was soon ferrying the wounded back, the driver was awarded the MM. We treated a large number of wounded from 227 Brigade and buried five dead.

Sergeant Fred (Nobby) Clarke:- was wounded when his Humber heavy was hit by an 88mm shell, the driver was also wounded but the gunner had a lucky escape. Nobby was from Southampton and his wife, Molly, managed to see him on the hospital train at Eastleigh. Despite losing both legs Nobby showed indomitable courage and lived a full and happy life.

Gordon Nursaw:- After sometime in action we were pulled out for a supposed rest! Time for a bath, rather a large hole, quite long and wide, about a foot deep into which had been placed a big tarpaulin. The hole had then been filled with hot water into which a number of men leapt. They sat down to cleanse themselves of the battle's dust. One with difficulty struggled to his feet and displayed a bottom completely black from the tar of the tarpaulin which had melted with the heat of the water, a lighter moment of the campaign.

Len Watson:- The Falaise Gap was a terrible place where dead horses and cows lay stinking in the sun. We hated having to halt beside the stinking carcasses. We had shot up a German horse-drawn convoy and civilians soon appeared to cut up the animals and load them onto their bicycles; we learnt that both the French and the Belgians ate a lot of horse meat.

*   *   *   *   *

Following the unveiling of the Divisional Memorial at Tourville in June of 1949, **Michael Riesco** wrote:

An expeditionary force of Bryan White, Tony Royle and myself, took this opportunity of being in Normandy to visit all the areas in which the Regiment fought and to seek out the cemeteries in which the graves of our Normandy casualties are now placed. In our former object, we succeeded in retracing the Regiment's movements almost exactly. The disembarkation area at le Hamel was soon recognised and what a mess that whole coastline still is. Offshore the remains of Port Winston remain as a grim memorial. On shore seaside villas are still mere shells, roads are still being remade and pillboxes are being demolished.

The peaceful atmosphere round the village of St Gabriel and the fields of Secqueville en Bessin made it difficult to recall the circumstances which took us there before. As we approached the Cheux area, however, the evidence of bygone days became more apparent, battered churches still being rebuilt, large empty spaces where houses or even villages had once stood now replaced mostly by wooden huts. Empty ammunition boxes filled with earth are built up to act as low walls between the new dwellings. There is a tangled and rusty pile of barbed wire at the spot where 'Ship Route' entered Cheux and the Route itself looks like a long disused farm track. From this point those terrible fields at le Haut du Bosq were not difficult to find. The field in front of 9 Troop is producing a nice crop of hay and the fields of 10 and 11 Troops are grazing grounds for a sleepy herd of cows (all alive and looking very contented!) The banks, which border the fields are still a network of slit trenches now overgrown with brambles. The only real sign that indicates the turmoil that once enveloped the area is the fact that not one of the many trees can be considered of normal proportions. Some stand dead and leafless, others are stunted with torn trunks and a large number stand erect, branchless, but with a tuft of newly formed branches at the very top. This state of the trees and woods is characteristic of the whole beachhead area and serves as an unpleasant reminder of the past.

Over the river Odon at Verson and on to the well known features of Operation Greenline - Baron, le Bon Repos, Hill 112 and down the long forward slope to a most pathetic sight - the village of Evrecy. The destruction in this whole area is terrible to see. All that remains of Evrecy is a few isolated houses and the rest of the area consists of stones and bricks where rows of houses once stood. Reconstruction is progressing as quickly as their very primitive methods allow. Full reconnaissance of the Caumont sector was in parts hampered by the state of the tracks, some of which are traversable only by horse and cart and sometimes not even by that. But by keeping to the reasonable looking roads we managed to see most of our positions. Balleroy could hardly look any different - the same undamaged and rather picturesque village.

A start was made down C Squadron's route to la Chavetiere - where we took over from the Americans – but beyond Sallen the road became non-existent and a detour had to be made in order to reach the two positions at le Bisson and le

Chavetiere. What 10 Troop and a Company of infantry could have seen from the latter position I now cannot imagine. But perhaps the trees have grown a little in the last few years. It was also here that the inevitable cider and calvados was produced by 'Madame'. Even Tony Royle could not cope with the large amount of very raw calvados that was poured out for each of us - it nearly singed our toe-nails!

Back into Caumont and down the main road to St Martin des Besaces, which we were lucky to negotiate without a puncture. At Hervieux crossroads, the wood on the right, from which snipers were being burnt out by flamethrowers, has once again taken on reasonable proportions. An even worse road to the left took us over Quarry Hill to the main St Martin – Villers road. From here we had to walk down the track towards Galet and la Manceliere. It appeared even more extraordinary how C Squadron managed to cruise down that very open-forward slope and suffer only slight shock to the nervous system. When the Regiment passed through St Martin des Besaces some may have noticed a damaged Café on the near right-hand side corner of the cross roads. It was here that we had lunch with our French driver, a wonderful character. We arrived at midday, allowing one hour's break from the timetable for the day's excursion. When we literally staggered to our feet at half past two, we thought that we could face no more food for that day, however, once back in Bayeux that evening, a fat juicy steak was not unwelcomed!

The car, considerably lower on its springs, took us on our way through areas of le Bressi, la Mateliere, Beaumont and St Pierre Tarentaine - except for the latter all very peaceful and undamaged. It was market day in Montcharivel, our next port of call, and in our Orchard Harbour beyond the village Tony Royle found a rusty old biscuit tin. He was convinced it was the very one in which his vehicle crew brewed tea during that last unsettled week's visit. Neither Bryan nor I were prepared to argue.

That group of trees on the cross roads at la Caverie – the Brigade start line for Operation Estry – still bears grim evidence of the days when it received the accurate attention of German shells. The road to Estry seemed so long that even Tony thought we had overrun the famous crossroads west of the village. When we did reach the village we saw what we may well have expected – a horrible sight of destruction. However, a very valiant job is being done in tidying up and rebuilding. A welcome refresher was taken at the Café on the crossroads and 'Madame' talked nonstop about the battle of Estry!

An interesting route was taken for our return to Bayeux, passing through the completely destroyed villages of Aunay Sur Odon and Villers Bocage. From the ruins of these two villages are springing new and modern buildings, which appeared to us of doubtful construction and in no way attractive. It was interesting to note that it was only in these two latter villages that any rebuilding on a large scale was seen. The smaller villages are plodding on with the task of reconstruction in their own sweet way – a task which will not be completed for years to come – are, I should imagine, glad that the tide of modern development has not overtaken them.

Tilly sur Seulles was never in the Regimental area but some may have passed over the main crossroads of that village. Those crossroads are now bordered by green fields. A few wooden 'pre-fabs' set in a still devastated scene is all that remains of Tilly. In this country we were used to seeing bomb damage cleared up within hours by bulldozers and other mechanical devices. In Normandy, the whole task of reconstruction is slowly being carried out with labour supplied only from the immediate locality, and with nothing to help them but the use of their own hands. One could not help thinking that if one could only lend them a road-mending machine or cement mixer, we could complete a job in days that would take them months or even years. The machine age is still far ahead of the times in which they live.

Those children in Normandy who are unable to remember what their coast and countryside looked like in pre-invasion days will probably never see the task of reconstruction completed. Theirs too is the permanent task of caring for the thousands of graves and the upkeep of many memorials. This task they accomplish now with a care that must be seen to be believed. The cheerfulness and kindness with which they greet visitors, most of whom took some part in the destruction of their land, seemed to us little short of miraculous. In our latter objective we managed to visit all the cemeteries in which our Normandy casualties are now placed, except for Banneville which unfortunately was too far off our route.

Lieut. Kingsley Gray - Citation for immediate award of Military Cross.

On 3 August, when overlooked by many enemy strongpoints on the MONTAGNY feature, this Officer was ordered to patrol forward to get more detailed information of the enemy's positions. He was under observation from the time that he started and immediately came under accurate mortar and artillery fire. Though he realised that the thick country he was to pass through was infested with enemy infantry posts, his determination to get the vital information was such that he succeeded in moving forward over two miles and keeping close observation on the enemy feature throughout the whole day. The very thick country through which he had to pass would have deterred all but the most resourceful Commander and he was liable to ambush at any moment, and was often in fact subjected to sniping from close quarters. He exposed himself to the enemy's accurate fire for long periods in order to obtain details of the enemy's movement. This he did without any regard to his own personal safety. In spite of the enemy infantry being aggressive throughout the day, his cunning and initiative enabled him to surprise and cause severe casualties to an enemy patrol. His reports, often given under most difficult conditions, were of the highest standard and a great encouragement and example to all, and were responsible for the saving of many lives when it came for the MONTAGNY feature to be occupied.

Signed Field Marshall B. L. Montgomery, C in C 21st Army Group

L to R: Michael Riesco; French driver; Bryan White, Tony Royle

Bryan White at le Haut du Bosq scene of C Squadron's first casualties

Le Caverie cross roads

Memorial to Brigadier Mackintosh-Walker

Bayeux - entrance to Lion d'or

Michael Riesco, Bryan White and Tony Royle prior to ceremony

General Sir Richard O'Connor unveils 15th Scottish Memorial, 26 June 1949

Humber armoured car believed to be that of Capt Fordyce, 30 June 1944

Sherman tank moves forward to battle past the disabled Humber

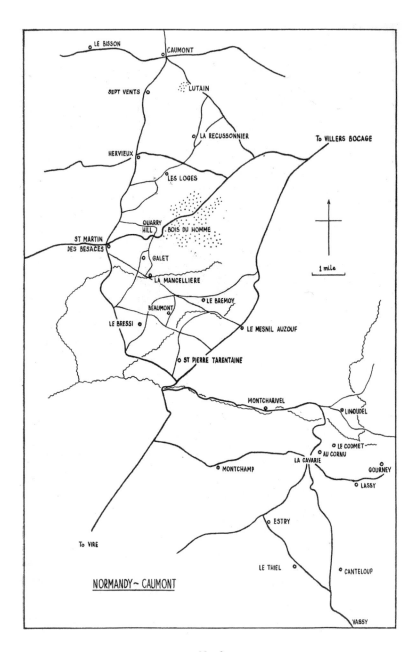

Map 2

A carrier patrol in the advance from Caumont

CHAPTER IX

TO THE SEINE—AND ON

Maps 3 and 4

For ten days the regiment rested, first at Amaye sur Orne, then at Fresney le Vieux, eight miles farther forward, while almost everything movable in the Second Army, including field bakeries, overtook it, and prisoners of many nationalities in German uniform streamed back from the 'pocket'. Amaye was one of those French villages whose natural air is one of elegant, shuttered decline. It suffered less destruction than many, but the passage of war had knocked the elegance awry, leaving bared rafters, a smell of death and muddled furniture which showed its coating of dust where probing fingers of sunlight found their way through the shutters into dark rooms. The regiment shared the village with the sun and a plague of insects. Parties wandered down through dusty fields to the Orne and bathed while tanks clattered by, or went to Hill 112, Evrecy and Esquay to study the positions in which the Germans had fought so stubbornly. A mobile canteen appeared, and an excellent ENSA show. There was a race meeting. The horses were wooden, fashioned by Cpl Maher, the carpenter, and their progress over taped squares was determined by the throw of large dice. The chief bookies were the colonel, Major MacDiarmid and the RSM, who was the most strident and the least fortunate. On 16 August Major General Barber came to Amaye and said that because senior commanders normally visited only the infantry brigades after the division had done well in battle he felt that perhaps the regiment was not always given credit for the work it did.

The move to the flat fields and industrious mosquitoes of Fresney le Vieux was on 18 August. Three days later A Squadron was placed under the command of the 1st Royal Dragoons and sent to Teprel, six miles west of Falaise, to be ready for a flying start in Operation Gallop—the name for the advance to the Seine. The squadron reverted to the regiment's command, but remained at Teprel. This is the War Diary record of the only 'action' in these days of waiting:

21 Aug. A report was received via various channels by A Squadron this afternoon that there were 40 enemy south-west of Falaise. This was investigated by OC, A Sqn, and it turned out that the location given was Tac HQ, Second Army, the first enemy to be seen being the Army Commander driving his jeep.

On 23 August the regiment drove through the shell of Falaise to La Hougette, and after a night in the rain broke camp at dawn on 24 August and began its unforgettable dash to the Seine through the stinking wreckage which littered the wake of a fleeing army. It was the first time in the campaign that the regiment had really been given its head. On 26 August its patrols were reconnoitring the Seine.

The chief task on the littered miles between the Falaise area and the river was route reconnaissance for the following brigades. C Squadron, in the north, was given Star route—Falaise, St Pierre sur Dives, St Foy de Montgomery, Vimoutiers, Orbec, Bernay, Beaumont le Roger, le Neubourg and Louviers. In the centre B Squadron travelled on Sun route—Trun, Vimoutiers, le Sap, Monnai, Broglie, Beaumont le Roger and Emanville. A Squadron, in the south, was allotted Moon route—Vignats, Coulances, Trun, north of Chambois, Neuville sur Touque, Heugon, Mesnil-Rousset, la Barre en Ouche, la Ferriers sur Risle and Emanville. The squadrons were accompanied by Royal Engineers, bulldozers, bridging equipment and recovery vehicles.

C Squadron found that Star route was impassable west of St Foy de Montgomery, and a diversion on to Sun route had to be made. That night the regiment occupied scattered harbours on the line Orbec-LeSap, but the armoured cars of 11 Troop, under Lieut Gray, had entered Bernay, about forty miles from Falaise. It had been hard going all day over narrow, muddy roads strewn with German tanks and trucks and wagons and guns, some the reddened victims of Typhoons, some just abandoned. The stench from the bodies of dead German soldiers and horses was so great in places that rags were soaked in petrol and held to the nose. From time to time debris had to be pushed aside. Some of the bad roads on Moon route collapsed under the heavy equipment with A Squadron, and the bulldozers had to be taken off their transporters and used to extricate the transporters. This difficulty and the presence of much Canadian transport in the early stages of the move made progress so slow that Major MacDiarmid decided to go ahead with the squadron's armoured cars, leaving the carriers to escort the other equipment. In spite of the dead horses, which had to be dragged out of the way, and mined bridges, which the RE officer de-fused, the car force got well in front, and in the evening was out of wireless touch with RHQ. In an attempt to get into contact with RHQ, Major MacDiarmid set out with L/Cpl Kay and Tpr Murray in a reconnaissance car after dark, but came into collision with a Canadian tank. Major MacDiarmid escaped injury, but both his crew received cuts. This is Kay's story of the incident:

We had arrived at the arbitrary line – Euston – at which we were to stop for the night. For us this turned out to be an attractive little village between high hedges, and for Squadron HQ a complete manor house with beautiful lawns and an abundance of chickens and the like. The welcome, being the first was overwhelming: wild roses for everyone, and, of course, the Commander—Major MacDiarmid—would sleep in the house. Well no, he would not, but perhaps his second-in-command—Capt Davies—would. As it turned out, neither of them slept until nearly next morning.

We were by now well out in the blue, in the region of Ommai, and quite out of radio touch; so in the middle of a belated supper, at about eleven o'clock, Major MacDiarmid decided to take the sergeant-major's reconnaissance car, with Murray as driver and myself as operator, to look for the regiment. We set off in the dark, finding an assault section with about twenty prisoners en route, and stopped from time to time to try to establish radio contact. At last we made Strength One on key. Major MacDiarmid decided to go on until we could be understood. There was no moon, and we had no lights. I heard Major MacDiarmid say 'Hard right', and received a mighty wallop on the left of my face as the side of the turret drove my civvy glasses up into my forehead. I was lifted down in a stupor. Canadian voices came from nowhere: 'Gees, but I'm pleased you're all alive.' Bill Murray was lying on the grass with a bleeding forehead, but his main complaint was that he had personally tuned this engine till it was the best in the squadron 'and now look at it'. He and I spent the night with a Canadian repair 'outfit'.

In the morning we were treated to breakfast with Canadian hospitality, mixed with a dissertation on 'those Jews' by the lieutenant in charge, and one on 'those Germans' by the farmer in whose yard we were. We were collected by one of the regiment's medical trucks. Bill Murray had two stitches and four days' rest. I had a trip back to the starting point near Falaise, to enter the hospital 'sausage machine'.

While Major MacDiarmid and his crew were trying to establish contact with RHQ a party from RHQ—Capt Kemsley, Cpl Stevenson and Tpr Yount—was out in a reconnaissance car trying to establish contact with A Squadron. These three also came to grief, the car going into a ditch in the darkness—fortunately near B Squadron's harbour.

The advance was continued at dawn, and B and C Squadrons reached Beaumont le Roger by the early afternoon. Here the Risle bridges were destroyed, but a wooden bridge on the outskirts of the town was still standing and was strong enough to bear most of the vehicles. On Moon route A Squadron's cars, still ahead of the rest of the squadron, were also confronted with blown bridges at the Risle. Going to inspect a ford, 1 Troop met some Royal Dragoons, who crossed the ford first. Their last vehicle was blown up, and six mines were lifted while another patrol report was awaited. This report was that a good bridge was still intact, and this bridge the squadron used.

That evening the regiment harboured on the line le Neubourg-Barquet, not far from the Seine. The day's drive had been free of many of the encumbrances of the previous day. The debris had thinned out, but the joy of the French people was evidence of the recent passage of the fleeing enemy. Whenever the regiment stopped near houses there were flowers, and calvados and wine.

Reconnaissance of the banks of the Seine was begun on 26 August by C Squadron, which went forward through Louviers and reached the high ground west of the river without incident. Patrols were sent to Tournedos sur Seine and Portejoie in the north, to St Pierre du Vauvray in the centre and to Heudebouville and Venables in the south. The country to the north was flat and wooded on the west bank, but steep hills rose from the river's edge on the German side. In the centre and south there were steep hills on the west side and rolling country across the river. Extensive patrolling did not draw any organised fire from across the Seine. That night reports giving details of the approaches to the river and the positions of OPs were sent to divisional headquarters.

Next day the regiment harboured just west of Louviers, where the division was concentrating before the assault on the river line. C Squadron continued its reconnaissance, and extended it to the opposite bank and to the island opposite Muids. Lieut John Wheeler and his small patrol became the first men in the division to cross the Seine when they rowed to Herqueville after finding a boat at Portejoie, as Lieut Wheeler has related:

After my patrol of four carriers had moved up and down the west bank without drawing fire, I got together a small patrol, and, taking one of the FFI with us, we rowed straight across the river in a boat which we had found on the bank. On reaching the other side I left the Bren gunner in the boat and the rest of us went off to explore. I saw a group of French women and children outside a farm. I managed to attract their attention, and they immediately put their fingers to their lips and pointed up the road. We took cover and I sent the French guide round the back of the farm to get information. When he came back he told us that three Germans had just left the farm and were only round the corner when we got there. One of them had just gone back to bring up reinforcements. I decided that we had all the information we needed and that it would be unwise to get involved in a fight, so we returned to our boat. Before we reached our side of the river again the Germans started firing single shots at us with a machine gun. As soon as we landed we made for what little cover there was, but Corporal Dove was wounded in the chest.

Lieut Shirley and some of his troop crossed in an assault boat to the island opposite Muids, where it was proposed to build a bridge. From the island they kept the village under observation, and obtained valuable information. That evening another long report was given to divisional headquarters. On the information which the regiment supplied it was decided that the river could be crossed without all the preparations originally intended, and soon after seven o'clock that evening 227 Brigade began the operation, the 10th Highland Light Infantry and the 2nd Gordon Highlanders crossing just south of St Pierre du Vauvray against stiff opposition, the enemy sinking the first three boats and inflicting heavy casualties on the Gordons. By midnight a bridgehead was well established; 44 Brigade crossed in the Portejoie area. At 9.15 the following morning, 28 August, 46 Brigade went across in the Muids area, encountering little opposition.

Armoured car patrols of A and B Squadrons were ferried across the river on rafts early in the morning. A Squadron's patrols were given the task of enlarging the 46 Brigade bridgehead, 2 Troop (Lieut Dalton) taking the road running parallel with the Seine in the direction of les Andelys, 1 Troop (Lieut Blount) going through the woods towards Fretteville, and 3 Troop (Lieut Kerridge) following 1 Troop, then branching towards le Thuit. On the outskirts of Fretteville 1 Troop's leading car, commanded by Cpl F. Whiting, came under heavy fire from machine guns and mortars. The fire from Cpl Whiting's car silenced some of the machine guns, and with his Bren he killed several attacking Germans while the patrol altered its course to the left flank. Here also the opposition was strong, and Cpl Whiting's car was blown up. It landed in a small quarry. Machine-gun bullets hit it repeatedly, and the corporal was given permission to abandon it, but, working for forty-five minutes under fire, he directed its recovery, and patrolled and fought in it for the remainder of the day, although the steering was damaged, the turret jammed and the gun mounting useless. Afterwards the car, almost shot to pieces, was written off as a complete loss. Cpl Whiting was awarded the Distinguished Conduct Medal. Lieut Blount, who received the Military Cross, went forward to help Cpl Whiting's car when it was disabled and, leading patrols in vehicle and on foot under steady fire, commanded the road between Fretteville and le Thuit, frustrated several German attempts to reinforce le Thuit, and so subdued an enemy company that it was unable to hinder the infantry who passed close to its positions. At least twenty Germans were killed by the 1 Troop cars.

Lieut Kerridge, too, was awarded the Military Cross. His patrol of three cars found the enemy strongly dug in at le Thuit, and fought them for eight hours, attacking them in their slit trenches at close range. Thirty Germans were taken prisoner by the patrol and many were killed. Manoeuvring so that the enemy should not realise that there were only three cars, the patrol formed a screen behind which infantry of the division were able to reach their positions without deploying and dig in without interference. During the day British guns bombarded the woods between the river and 1 and 3 Troops, although that area had been reported clear.

Lieut Dalton's troop found that the riverside road to les Andelys was dominated by the enemy positions on the cliffs above it and defended by anti-tank weapons. The Germans could fire down into the cars, and Tpr N. P. Ellis was mortally wounded at his post in the turret of one of them. It was on this road that Sgt T. Craig won the Military Medal by coolly taking his patrol, under fire from above, from the flank and from ahead, into what he knew must be almost an ambush. He obtained important information, destroyed enemy machine-gun posts, and got out of his own vehicle under fire to evacuate the wounded crew of the leading car after it had been knocked out by an anti-tank gun.

This road by the Seine was also the scene of The Charge of the Litton Brigade. The Litton Brigade consisted of two cars from B Squadron under the command of Sgt Litton. How they came to charge to within sight of les Andelys, while Germans to the left of them, Germans above them and Germans in front of them volleyed and thundered, has been described by Lieut P. D. Peterson:

B Squadron patrols had crossed the river to the left of A Squadron, and I was ordered to reconnoitre to the right with cars from 5 Troop and 7 Troop. It was believed at this time that A Squadron had not yet been able to cross, so I was told to investigate the road to les Andelys. The two cars from 5 Troop, under Sgt Litton, were to lead as far as the forward infantry on the far side of the bridgehead on the right. The plan was to halt there and glean information from the infantry before going on towards les Andelys.

Arriving at the forward infantry positions, I saw a Humber halted on a bend in the road ahead, and assumed that it was Sgt Litton's and that the other car was round the bend. The infantry told me that A Squadron patrols had already made determined efforts to explore the road to les Andelys, but had been forced back by the heavy opposition. Then I discovered that the stationary car was from A Squadron. The crew reported that the 5 Troop cars had gone by at a speed fast enough to have taken them to Paris by that time. Wireless messages to the two cars were unanswered, and we could not help fearing the worst, for A Squadron told us that the road ahead was covered at many points by machine guns and anti-tank guns from the high ground on the left.

B Squadron headquarters now knew that A Squadron patrols had crossed the river, and we were ordered to go back to be a wireless link between the other B Squadron patrols and squadron headquarters, still delayed on the other side of the river. Permission to make a search for the missing cars was refused. In most minds they were 'written off', but more than an hour later, when we were perched on high ground as the wireless link, we heard a faint message -' . . Report my signals.' Then came the good news -'Returned to brother Able's house.'

Owing to a slight error in map reading and the unexpected appearance of the A Squadron cars, Sgt Litton's party had failed to recognise the forward infantry positions, and, driving on, had realised too late that its support was no longer close behind. Soon the cars came under machine-gun and anti-tank fire, but their speed carried them through it. The road was too narrow for them to reverse out of danger or to turn round. There was only one way open—forward. Both cars increased speed.

Going round a bend in the road, the light reconnaissance car, leading, was confronted by a large anti-tank gun. One gunner was resting against the gun shield, the others were gathered round a stationary truck on the other side of the road. The Bren in the light reconnaissance car was fired at the truck and the gun crew, and a quick shot from the heavy car's 37mm hit the German gun. The crew dived underneath the truck, which, however, was driven off at high speed. In this chaos the two B Squadron cars were able to turn round and race for home, after looking down into les Andelys and seeing that the town was full of enemy.

The way back was under the heavy fire of Germans who were by now very much on the alert. The light car, with one of its front wheels shot off, wobbled the last hundred yards to A Squadron on three flat tyres and a brake drum, and the heavy lurched in with three flat tyres, all riddled. The crews were safe.

B Squadron's other car patrols that day—from 5 and 6 Troops—were commanded by Lieut M. H. Leppard and by Lieut A. E. Gillings, who was awarded the Croix de Guerre for his leadership in the advance from the Seine. The Germans had strong positions in the area of Connelles, and Lieut Leppard, going left from the bridgehead, soon met opposition. His cars fired so much ammunition that pistols, and even Verey pistols, had to be used.

Lieut Gillings went straight ahead after crossing the river, and about three miles from Heudebouville his car was hit by shots from a small anti-aircraft gun, which was being used as an anti-tank gun. Reversing, the vehicle went off the road, toppled down a bank and landed upside down. Lieut Gillings opened the door and tentatively put out a leg. This drew a hail of fire, and the leg was swiftly withdrawn.

Back at squadron headquarters Capt Boynton, the second-in-command, had chosen this moment to send a wireless message urging the patrol to greater speed.

'My car is stuck,' Gillings replied, after groping for the microphone.

'Then get another car,' said the second-in-command.

This brought the full, desperate explanation, delivered from among a jumble of upset kit while bullets beat a tattoo on the armour plate: 'I am upside down in my car in a ditch. There is a machine gun firing at us. I am trapped.'

Sgt F. Short organised the rescue. A smoke screen was laid, and he took his car forward under heavy fire and engaged the enemy while a light car drew up beside the overturned vehicle. Under cover of the smoke Tpr J. Connor dashed from the light car and helped the trapped crew to scramble to safety. Thanks largely to Sgt Short's efforts, the enemy post was destroyed, and a German captured. Sgt Short was awarded the Military Medal.

By the evening of 28 August the division's bridgehead across the Seine stretched from le Thuit to Connelles.

The regiment crossed the new Seine bridges early on 29 August, and A and B Squadrons continued to reconnoitre in front of the division. It was in these advances from the banks of the Seine that Major MacDiarmid won the Military Cross and a bottle of whisky. The Military Cross was the reward for leadership which achieved the destruction of the enemy at Fretteville and le Thuit and the early liberation of les Andelys. The squadron fought a successful action at Fretteville and le Thuit on the 29th, and beyond le Thuit learned from the driver of a French Red Cross ambulance that the enemy was withdrawing from les Andelys. Lieut Blount was sent there, and Major MacDiarmid was promised the whisky if his squadron raced the infantry, who were advancing along the riverside road, to the town. When Lieut Blount's cars drove into the town it was deserted; the FFI had made the inhabitants take refuge in the chalk cliffs along the Seine until liberation was accomplished. This was typical of the excellent organization of the FFI, whose members helped the regiment many times between Falaise and the Belgian border and often volunteered to ride with the leading patrols. On the high ground beyond les Andelys A Squadron met a patrol of the 43rd Reconnaissance Regiment and exchanged information. A patrol under Lieut Dalton was given a task which took it outside the division's boundary, and there was an exchange of fire—fortunately without casualties—when the cars crossed the line of advance of the 11th Armoured Division. To prevent further misunderstandings, the patrol was given an escort for its return.

On the left B Squadron reached Houville and Bacqueville during the morning, and soon after noon entered Ecouis, where stragglers were captured and where the squadron was later to be given a formal reception by the townspeople in honour of liberation. C Squadron, driving forward in convoy from the Seine ahead of RHQ, caught two German officers who were sufficiently 'out of the picture' to be going to inspect German positions which no longer existed. Later in the day C Squadron was ordered to pass through B Squadron and reconnoitre beyond Ecouis. About five miles east of Ecouis Lieut Gray's troop, leading, was halted by a strong rearguard with guns. At the first contact one car was knocked out, and Sgt W. C. Young, who had long served the squadron with quiet efficiency, was killed. Attempts to by-pass the German rearguard were unsuccessful, and that night the regiment concentrated in the area of Ecouis and Jean de Frenelle, where it waited while the 7th Armoured Division and the Welsh Division passed through the Scottish Division to carry the chase into Northern France.

In the fighting which followed the Seine crossing Tpr J. D. Roebuck was killed.

On 30 August the following Special Order of the Day was issued by Lieut Col Grant Peterkin:

Since 27 August when the Regiment for the first time was able to get on its proper role, 15(S) Division has advanced over 50 miles, crossed the major obstacle in France, the River Seine, and driven the enemy back much faster than he wished. It is an established fact that the speed of our advance has surprised him very much.

A great deal of the credit for this rapid advance is due to the excellent information obtained by the patrols of the Regiment.

Their initiative, and eagerness to get at the enemy and to get information back have been of the greatest value to our higher Commanders.

The Commanding Officer has received the following letter from Major General C. M. Barber DSO, GOC 15 (S) Inf Div:—

'I should like to congratulate you very much on the excellent work done by your Regiment during the past few days and on the excellent and valuable reports sent in. They have been highly commended to me verbally by the Corps Commander. Will you please convey to all ranks my appreciation of all their very good work done in foul roads for very long hours in pretty wet weather.'

The congratulations of the whole Regiment are due to the Patrol Commanders and their crews, particularly those whose reports hastened very materially the crossing of the River Seine, and the subsequent rapid advance of the British Second Army.

I congratulate all ranks on their excellent work which has raised even higher the good name of the Regiment, and through this Order would like to express my appreciation and thanks.

(Sgd) J. A. GRANT PETERKIN,
Lieut Colonel.
Comd 15th Scottish Reconnaissance Regt

30 Aug., '44.

On 1 September the regiment, placed under command of the Welsh Division to protect its flank, drove more than fifty miles north-east to Marlers by way of Fry, where the girls at the large farm sang 'Ma Normandie' so prettily and the PMC dutifully and successfully negotiated for eggs. So swift had been the British advance since the crossing of the Seine that the only Germans encountered were a party that had somehow got left behind between Fry and Marlers. The armoured cars of 11 Troop dealt with them, as Cpl D. C. Waters describes:

We were stopped by some FFI who told us that Germans were holding out in a farmhouse. Lieut Gray decided that this was just our meat, and under the guidance of the Frenchmen we were taken to within 300 yards of the house. Sgt Bradley's car was leading, and I was at the guns. We all studied the house carefully without seeing any sign of life inside, but the Frenchmen assured us that the Germans were there, so we let fly with a belt of Besa and six high explosive shells from the 37 mm. There was straw in the loft, and a glow showed us that the house was burning. Smoke began to pour from the windows. But still no sign of life. Only when the roof was ablaze from end to end did a white flag appear at the doorway. We stopped firing, and out came twenty Germans—a mixture of SS, paratroopers and infantry, with couple of medical orderlies. One of them told us that two were dead in the house. We handed the prisoners over to an infantry company.

The drive from Fry to Marlers showed that the left flank of the Welsh Division was already firmly held by Canadian echelon transport, and in the fields and orchards of Marlers the regiment spent three pleasant days—resting; working on its vehicles, which had had little rest since leaving Falaise; looking for useful things among the enemy equipment which littered the area; and going in armoured cars to answer the urgent pleas of the Maquis: 'Il y a quarante bosches bien armees dans un bois par plus que deux kilometres d'ici.' The results of these excursions proved so disappointing that a roster was kept to show who should turn out next. Other squadrons looked on with amazement and awe when the sedentary Headquarter Squadron puffed along behind the long stride of Major Gaddum on a cross-country run. On Sunday, 3 September, the fifth anniversary of the outbreak of war, the padre held a church parade in a field. At Marlers' Trooper Parker, who had been wounded while on traffic control on the Odon, rejoined A Squadron; he was the first casualty to come back.

When dawn broke on 5 September the regiment was on the road again, with many miles to go. The few days' rest had been enough to leave it far in the rear of the pursuit; the 7th Armoured Division was advancing on Ghent. That day the regiment crossed the Somme a few miles west of Amiens, went north through Doullens and reached Houvin, five miles south of St Pol and more than sixty miles by road from Marlers. The news was that German resistance between the Escaut and the Lys threatened the main axis of the 7th Armoured Division, and the regiment became part of a battlegroup formed from units of the Scottish Division and the 1st Royal Dragoons to clear the enemy from east and south of the Lys and advance north to the corps boundary at Ypres and Roulers. Most of the Scottish Division was still being ferried from the Seine in the limited number of troop carrying vehicles that could be spared.

Leaving Houvin before light on 6 September with provisional orders concerning an area seventy miles away, the regiment drove by cheering, waving people in industrial towns of Northern France—Arras, Lens, Carvin, Seclin and the southern outskirts of Lille and Roubaix. Whenever the vehicles halted girls and children chalked on them—the names of their towns, their own names, slogans. There were kisses and V signs, flowers and fruit, and 'Cigarette pour papa' (how many of the cigarettes ever found their way to papa's lips ?).

Soon after 10 o'clock the regiment, passing the southern outskirts of Roubaix, came across the characteristic square white building bearing the word 'DOUANE' in large block letters. Outside it the frontier barrier pointed skyward, and French and Belgian gendarmes cheered side by side while hundreds cheered around them. The regiment, having come about 300 miles through France in fourteen days, drove on beneath the red, yellow and black of many Belgian flags, through more cheering crowds, receiving more garlands. But marked on the talc of the mapboards were the blue circles which showed that not far ahead the enemy waited. RHQ and B Squadron went to Belleghen, A Squadron to Kerkhove and C Squadron to Avelghem.

George Blount:- As my wireless operator was back with the remainder of my troop at last, Sqd. HQ, answered my signal giving us a map reference of their location and assuring us that guides would be out to lead us in. Thus we returned to the fold where I had a lengthy report to prepare before getting a meal and then a well earned rest.

Next morning at 05.00 we were off again for another successful day; C Sqd., were first off the mark and made more rapid headway than the rest of the Regiment. They were duly rewarded for their efforts, in the early evening patrols from C Sqd. reached the banks of the River Seine, east of Louviers. One patrol borrowed a rowing boat and rowed out to an island in mid-stream which was found to be unoccupied by the enemy although enemy movement was observed on the far bank. So by nightfall the entire Regiment was in the area of the river awaiting the Division's arrival. Next day, 27th, was spent on maintenance and preparation for our next task, it was thought that it would take several days to 'work up' an assault crossing of the major water obstacle in France.

Whilst attending a Church service with our Padre, I was called to Sqd. HQ for an 'O' Group. The Divisional Commander had decided to exploit success and with the limited resources available, to make a crossing at first light the next morning (28 August). The Sqd. were to supply three patrols, 1 Trp three cars (myself in command); 2 Trp three cars (Lt Dalton), 3 Trp four cars (Lt Kerridge). So after last light we moved forward to a rallying point to await the erecting and launch of the rafts. At first light 227 Bde commenced to cross against only light opposition, the rafts were launched and chestnut paling laid on both banks to facilitate loading and unloading. We were called forward to load and, as my Troop was to lead, I loaded first. This was a crossing I would not forget, the rafts were equipped with an outboard motor at each corner for propulsion and steering, the Sappers were unfamiliar with the means of steering and coupled with a strong current our progress to the opposite bank was somewhat erratic to say the least. However, after what was surely under different circumstances some weird gyrations, we eventually made landfall some fifty yards downstream of the prepared landing. However, with the aid of some infantry we were dragged upstream and eventually drove ashore. The infantry had now penetrated 100 yards and were holding the village of Muids whilst in contact with pockets of the enemy, we moved into the village to await the arrival of my other armed cars. Once they joined up, we moved out on our allotted task which was to tap out and try to enlarge the bridgehead; meantime the Sappers were to attempt to construct a class 9 bridge.

Our route was through a very ominous looking wood to the north of the river; we reached the wood without contacting the enemy although heavy firing could be heard to our right. Three Troop followed us along our route and then to push along on our right flank, 2 Troop were given the unenviable task of following us out then to strike along the river line in the direction of les Andelys, the road here was dominated by high ground. Once the wood was reached we discovered the track shown so clearly on our maps (prepared from aerial photographs) was little more than a forest ride with trees almost down to the width of our cars and low hanging branches which necessitated closing the turret flaps on our cars. Progress was fairly slow and soon my problems were made ever greater as Sqd HQ ordered us to pull out as our artillery were to register on the wood in support of our infantry. Due to a high wire fence at this part, we were unable to turn our cars and to reverse with our very low gearing was impossible in the time allotted before the first shells were to fall.

In the circumstances, I ordered Cpl Whiting, commander in my leading car to press on regardless; by the time we emerged from the wood at the north side, shells from our Div Artillery were falling in the wood behind us. Before us when we emerged from the wood lay the village of Fretteville, a tiny village maybe, but to be long remembered by my Troop. We abandoned the track and moved across the fields in the direction of the village; we had almost reached an orchard which lay between us and the nearest houses when the enemy spotted us. Soon all hell was let loose, enemy mortar bombs began to explode amongst us. In spite of this I decided aggressive action would be best, so we attempted to enter the village. My objective was not to be fulfilled: with the enemy withdrawing from their forward position in confusion 'lady luck' deserted us – the Besa heavy machine guns on all three cars jammed almost simultaneously entailing stripping to correct the faults. This was not possible in our very exposed position so whilst engaging the enemy with Bren and Sten-gun fire from the roof and driving hatches, I decided to withdraw to the edge of the wood and carry out repairs to our guns.

Meanwhile 3 Troop moving up on our right flank came under fire from the area of the village and withdrew to try a further track leading to le Thuit. Two Troop were also having a rough time trying to progress along the river bank, several casualties had been sustained by enemy fire from the high ground overlooking the road, Lt Dalton's car had been hit and was on fire so this patrol also had to retire.

Having carried out the necessary repairs and with all guns now firing I decided to make a further attempt to enter the village. This time I moved from the high ground to the east of the village hoping to gain some element of surprise; however the enemy had made good use of the short respite. We were met with concentrated mortar and MG fire, the whistle of a high velocity shell warned us that an A/T gun was also in position. Misfortune was not yet finished with us; manoeuvring in the open Cpl Whiting's car slipped over the edge of a small quarry hole about twenty feet deep. On hearing of this Major 'Mac' ordered me to abandon this car and withdraw. Although this car had already been hit it was still fairly serviceable. Further if we abandoned the car it would mean the crew would have to be transported on the outside of my other cars; in the circumstances it would be virtual suicide for the crew. So I decided to attempt the recovery of Cpl Whiting's car to give my other car commander (Sgt John) a chance to get into a position to tow it.

I moved forward towards the village thus drawing the enemy attention to my car; this was quite successful drawing all the enemy fire on us. Meanwhile Cpl Whiting dismounted and hitched a tow to the other car; unfortunately it proved too much for the Humber, even in four-wheel drive it slipped on the grass. There appeared only one other chance to succeed and that was to anchor the slipping car with my own, so after manoeuvring into position I dismounted to hitch another tow. What a target we presented to the enemy which they took advantage of. However with all three cars joined, we were successful in pulling Cpl Whiting out of the hole and likewise got ourselves out of a hole. It was now apparent that with only three cars (nine persons) we were never going to be able to take and occupy the village.

I therefore decided that the best course of action was to keep the enemy subdued by intermittent fire from our cars thus preventing reinforcements reaching the village or the enemy in the village being able to reinforce le Thuit, the neighbouring village. Soon we were rewarded with a target of three armoured cars approaching the village from the west; we engaged same but were unable to prevent them reaching the village. Shortly afterwards, approximately fifty infantry moving in A/A formation appeared from the same direction; upon engaging same they scattered and withdrew.

So the hours dragged by, communications with Sqd. HQ were poor and messages had to be relayed through out-stations put out for this purpose. Throughout the day we made frequent sallies towards the village; this always brought down heavy fire on us but kept the enemy occupied. Meanwhile 3 Troop on our right, after taking a number of prisoners, was relieved by an infantry battalion in support, their objective being the capture of le Thuit village and surrounding high ground.

So, as darkness was falling, I received a message to withdraw to the river, where Lt Dalton met us with orders for our withdrawal across the river. We were once more ferried across the Seine and rejoined our Sqd in harbour. Here our hopes for a night's sleep were dashed as we were to recross the river this time by a bridge which was under construction, our estimated time to cross 24.00 hours. We formed up on the road and moved off in direction of the bridge; once more frustration that the bridge was not yet completed, thus we sat with crews dozing in their vehicles until we eventually crossed at 02.00 hours and laagered about a mile ahead of the bridge, outside the village of Muids. Just a couple of hours' sleep and we were getting orders for another task, we were to attempt to outflank les Andelys, a reported strong point in the enemy's defences. On this occasion I was limited to one patrol, as the patrol I left behind on the previous day under Sgt Robinson had met with misfortune. Sgt Robinson's car whilst approaching the river had slipped and overturned down a twenty foot embankment; all the crew were badly injured, Sgt Robinson's injuries being of such severity he was invalided out of the Army.

During the night a heavy rainstorm turned the tracks we were to use into a sea of mud and thus our initial progress was very slow indeed. Motorcycles were loaded onto carriers and few vehicles could make the gradients unassisted. In many cases it took three carriers to get the heavy armoured cars up the gradient even with four-wheel drive. After much sweating, swearing and wallowing in mud, we eventually hit the main road to les Andleys about four miles west of the town. Here we met a French civilian ambulance and with great difficulty I learned that they had just been in the town and that the enemy were preparing to withdraw. This information I passed on to Sqd HQ, and carried on with our task. Soon the voice of Major Mac sounded over the air with urgent orders for me. The Guards Tank Brigade had got tanks across the river and were advancing parallel to the river with les Andleys as their objective. I was to drop my task and to get into les Andelys first at all costs, it was worth a bottle of whisky or so Col Grant Peterkin thought.

Orders were issued to the patrol; we retraced our route back to the main road and leaving the carriers to follow in their own time, we set off. At first we made fairly slow progress but after a few words with Cpl Whiting leading the patrol in a new car, we started to crack on. Two or three miles from the town we observed the tanks advancing well to our right and over quite a wide front. By now the cars were racing ahead at 40 mph careering round the last corner to a halt in the edge of the town. We now proceeded with great caution.

This is one of my eeriest experiences, as we moved through the narrow streets with turrets closed, eyes glued to gun sights and periscopes. The only visible movement was the flapping of curtains at open windows and only sound that of the car engines. By now we were all tensed up, the leading car's guns covering the street ahead whilst the other two cars covered the buildings to our left and right especially watching the upper windows for an ambush. On previous patrols on attempting to enter a town or village we had been met by a hail of fire or jubilant civilians but here nothing, only this deathly silence, perhaps a burst of machine gun would have been welcome. Sqd HQ were informed that we were in the town and pressing on. Major MacDiarmid informed us the rest of the Squadron was being concentrated and would follow us up as quickly as possible. By now we had reached the square in front of the church in the town centre, I dismounted to have a look around when the first evidence of life appeared, two members of the 'Maquis' (French Resistance) one of whom was the local leader of the patriots and proved most helpful. He informed me that all the civilians had been concentrated in a disused quarry in the hills overlooking the town (1) to avoid casualties if the town was shelled before our advance (2) to avoid any looting during the transition period from the Bosche withdrawing and the arrival of the Allies. Having passed on this information I was ordered to make for a disused castle on the high ground dominating a bend in the river, where there had been a bridge, now demolished. The REs were already standing by ready to construct a Class 40 bridge on this site when the town was cleared. With three Maquis warriors as guides we made for our objective, en route we encountered a patrol of 43rd Recce Regiment.

This Troop had crossed the river further upstream and had been observing the town prior to attempting to enter. Armed with this further knowledge we pushed on towards the castle; half a mile short we left our cars with the drivers and pressed ahead on foot. Our Maquis friends were able to tell us all the positions occupied by the enemy and we were able to pinpoint these. The enemy however had pulled out completely without leaving a rearguard, so unlike the Bosche. From this position we pushed ahead to cover another road leading into the town where we halted in a farm to prepare a long overdue meal – eggs supplied by a grateful populace.

By now the remainder of the Sqd were in the town awaiting the arrival of the infantry Battalion who were to occupy the town, the Sqd now concentrated in the area of the farm we had occupied. At nightfall we gathered the Troop in the barn where, after a short reflection on the day's events, a short prayer was said for our fallen comrades, we had a quiet spell of singing. Other Troops were not so lucky and had to carry out patrols in the area on the following day whilst we had a rest day.

This we spent talking of our successes and preparing for our next move.

Orders came on 31 August that 15th Scottish Division were to rest whilst the 7th Armed Div passed through followed by 53rd(W) Div in transport, this force to follow up the now disorganised enemy. However, the Regiment were to go ahead of our Division to protect the flank of the force following up the enemy. Early next day (1 September) we pushed on and continued to do so for the next two days when orders from Div HQ ordered us to halt in the area of Marlers and await the Division catching us up. Now some eighty miles ahead, we were again pulled out of the chase much to our disgust. We remained in this position until first light 6 September when ordered to assist in the protection of 7th Div lines of maintenance; this Division was now in Ghent. This necessitated a long and hasty move into Belgium to join 4 Armoured Brigade our route took us by way of the battlefield of our fathers, Vimy, Arras etc.

Doug Peterson:- I was in charge of 7 Troop, B Squadron at the time of the Seine crossing and was still two months short of my 27th birthday. On 29 August 1944 with the Seine now behind us, 7 Troop were under orders to patrol to the small town of Ecouis.

From a distance there appeared to be no enemy there, indeed it seemed completely deserted. We entered with the usual caution but it was sometime before, at first just a bold few, and then many more inhabitants emerged to welcome us and confirm the very recent departure of enemy forces. We occupied an area in front of a building I believe was the Town Hall and, with the armoured cars strategically sited, paused to question the natives and to report back.

Within a few minutes and despite our obvious presence, there came from the far side of the square, an enemy solo motorcycle driven by a German soldier and carrying another, of officer rank, on the pillion seat. Fortunately no member of the troop opened fire and the machine was driven virtually into our midst and the two totally surprised riders became our prisoners. The officer was deprived of his map case and the contents, although appearing of no significance, were sent back for examination by Intelligence. The prisoners were escorted away in 'protective custody'. A little closer attention to the maps may have changed the course of their war for both of them. A closer inspection of the motorcycle, which was in good condition, revealed far more chromium plating than could be found on any machine produced for military use, but now concealed beneath the typical German camouflage. I had no difficulty in identifying it as a British machine and certainly originally intended for the civilian market. How it fell into enemy hands some five years after the start of the war could never be known. Obviously, after some repainting the machine could be a valuable additional means of transport for the troop and it was not too outrageous to think that in due course it might be returned home for personal use! It was not too easy to find a rider for the machine within the manpower of the troop, and the following day I arranged with Gerry Harvey that one member of his assault troop should use it and ensure its safe passage from base to base. Where necessary it might be carried in one of their half-tracks.

We had no further close contact with 8 Troop for a few days and it was somewhat later that I had the opportunity of asking about the health of 'my' motorcycle. To my horror Gerry admitted having given it to the Free French who, very naturally, were delighted to have it. Gerry's explanation was that there were ample volunteer riders of the machine during fine weather but on colder and wet days just none. The motorcycle then became a nuisance and a problem that Gerry quickly and decisively solved. I wonder what eventually happened to the thing.

Bernie Higham:- Trooper Ronald Packman. On 16 August, late afternoon I was preparing a meal when from the direction of our half-track a shot rang out. We found Ron slumped in the seat with the rifle muzzle pointed into his waist and the butt was in the well on the other side; there were ten unused bullets on the floor of the vehicle. The general opinion of what had occurred was that he was unloading his rifle with the bolt action removing ten rounds but had forgotten the round 'up the spout' and had inadvertently shot himself.

I visited his grave in 1993 and remember him as a good comrade.

Alan Westby:- Lost in France! The last vehicle in a convoy finds that it is quite easy to become detached from the others, especially if there is no despatch rider to act as a shepherd. This occurred in France and I believed it was prudent to wait for rescue rather than blunder about and probably run into trouble. At this time, 'Standing Orders' were that all vehicles, which are stationary for any considerable time, must be camouflaged on account of enemy air activity. The Carden Lloyd was driven into a field of perhaps one or two acres in size with high hedges surrounding it and was camouflaged using the net and branches taken from the hedges. We did not realise until much later what an efficient job we had made of our deception. We made friends with a Light Anti-Aircraft gun detachment in a corner of the field; there was nothing else to do but wait. It was not until the following day that I met our Transport Officer at the entrance to the field. He wanted to know where I had been and, more importantly, where was the vehicle. It transpired that he had passed the field several times the previous day and the carrier was so well hidden that he had not spotted it from the road. Eventually the officer led the way to the Squadron harbour where I made my report to the anti-tank troop commander and nothing more was heard of the incident.

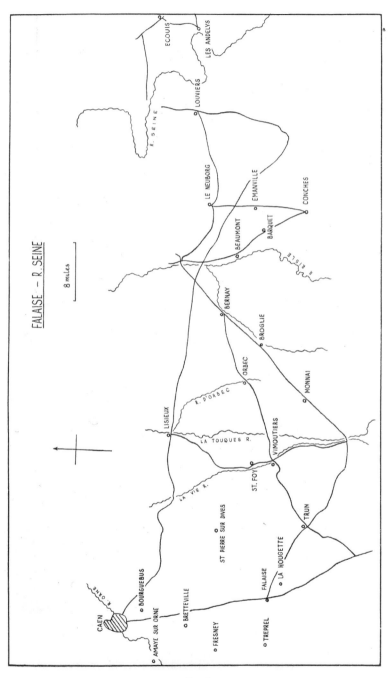

Map 3

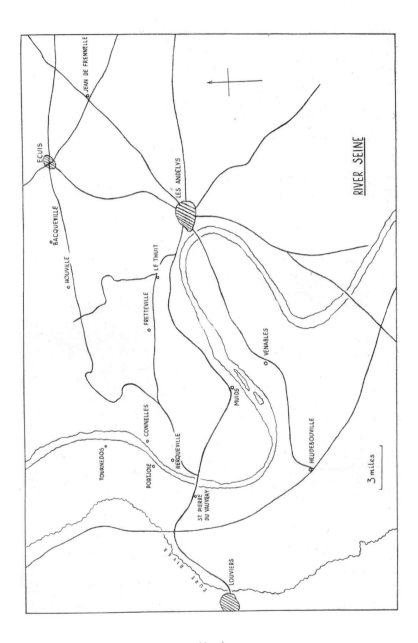

Map 4

Lieutenant K.W. Gray, 11 Troop, leads the C Squadron convoy through Northern France to the Belgian Frontier

CHAPTER X

BELGIUM, AND A FAREWELL
Maps 5 and 6

The regiment's new positions were on the edge of a 'pocket' in which were large, well-armed but disorganised, enemy groups, trapped by the swiftness of the armoured divisions' advances from the Seine and going this way and that in efforts to break out. The 7th Armoured Division had entered Ghent at six o'clock that morning, 6 September, and the enemy groups were a menace to one of its main supply routes, through Avelghem and Oudenarde. The regiment immediately sent patrols into the 'pocket'.

On the left B Squadron was joyfully welcomed in Courtrai, which was later taken over by the Seaforth. In the centre C Squadron reached the canal beyond Sweveghem and met opposition. Both 9 and 11 Troops were engaged in confusing fighting north and west of Vichte, and this is Sgt D. C. Waters's story of the 11 Troop patrol, carried out by three armoured cars, Lieut Gray's, Sgt Bradley's (with Tprs Waters and Crouch as crew) and Sgt Morrison's (with Tprs Wardle and Wiffen as crew):

We went to Vichte crossroads, where the assault troop was sitting, and went on carefully. After about three miles we were met with that deadly silence which always foretold trouble ahead. The civvies were in their houses, and only viewed us from the corners of windows and half-open doorways. A couple of braver lads came forward to tell us that a long line of Germans was moving along a road about half a mile away in the direction of Waerghem. We moved to a point of vantage, traversing our guns on to a gap in some houses on the enemy's route. All three cars opened fire at once. There was panic among the Germans. Our car moved to a better position, and Sgt Bradley bawled '37 mm fire'. I fired. There was a terrific crash and glass fell for several seconds; to our great relief we found that all that had happened was that the blast of the gun had broken a shop window. I looked down the road, and was surprised to see a German eyeing us through binoculars. When we traversed in his direction he disappeared behind a house. We set off down the road, and on passing the house Sgt Bradley screamed 'Fire'. I fired; the Besa jammed. Instantly I pressed the other trigger, as I knew the situation was desperate by the way in which the order was given. Two explosions occurred, followed by a third. The first was mine. The last was mine. The second was a Bazooka which had landed six inches from our rear wheel. We halted, and traversed to the rear. Our 37 mm had scored a direct hit. The steady knocking of Spandau bullets on the outside of the car told us that someone else was asking for trouble. We wirelessed the other two cars, telling them that they were surrounded and we weren't far from it. Their reply came quickly—'We will join you.' Only a few seconds later the first car tore round the corner about a hundred yards away with its guns firing into the ditch; the crew had spotted a Spandau position. The other car followed.

It was now getting late, and the order to withdraw came over the wireless, so we began to go back the way we had come, knowing that it had been clear of enemy. Sgt Morrison was leading, and to our amazement he suddenly stopped his car and began reversing. We followed his example. Over the air came 'Enemy 88 mm sitting Vichte crossroads.' We were cut off. Under cover of houses Lieut Gray studied the map and made a quick appreciation. 'Follow me' he said, and we drove after him down some lanes. A squadron of 11th Armoured Division tanks was firing in our direction from about 1,500 yards away. Not knowing what lay between us and them, we prepared to destroy our codes. It was now nearly dark. We suddenly hit a main road, turned left and went flat out so that very little could stop us except an anti-tank gun met head-on. We met one, but it was one of ours, and luckily it did not fire.

While 11 Troop was on this patrol 9 Troop ambushed and shot up a bus full of Germans. Lieut Royle's troop suffered several casualties during the day, losing an armoured car and two carriers. The car was knocked out with an 88 mm shell by Germans who had changed their minds after surrendering when taken by surprise. Sgt H. W. Hanby, the car commander and Tpr J. C. Neville, the driver, were killed, and Tpr Hoolachan, the wireless operator, was wounded. Two members of the troop were taken prisoner that day.

A Squadron, on the right, patrolled northward, in the direction of Gruyshautem, and captured about 130 prisoners. Under orders to reconnoitre to Waereghem from Kerkhove, Lieut Kerridge set out with his troop of three armoured cars and two carrier sections reinforced by a section of the assault troop with an half-track and 6-pounder. He has described what happened:

We passed through tanks and motorised infantry outside Kerkhove and mooched comfortably on for about eight miles. Then I called up my tracks under Lieut Roy Higgs to form a firm base two miles behind me on some high ground. Meanwhile Sgt Ramsay was gallantly taking his car by itself into Waereghem and out again, reporting the presence of many Germans with anti-tank guns. On the road he met and knocked out a German lorry. He also met two German ambulances, but those he did not molest. While he was away my car and that of Sgt T. Hughes came under mortar, shell and small arms fire.

Soon afterwards Roy Higgs arrived with the tracks, having overshot the proposed firm base, and the whole troop was immediately deployed and the 6-pounder brought into action to cover the road. The small arms and mortar fire was heavy, and a shell landed under the back axle of my car. A German OP was eliminated, but enemy infantry, plus what we presumed to be a self-propelled gun, attacked us from left and right, the gun bringing fire to bear on the rear of our 6-pounder. As the half-track was unable to manoeuvre quickly, a carrier was sent to recover the 6-pounder, but the carrier was hit and ditched. At the same time Sgt Hughes's car was put out of action by a small anti-tank gun and my own was hit in the radiator. Sgt Ramsay was ordered to retire towing Sgt Hughes's car while I covered him. This worked, and I retired to the carriers, which were being organised for withdrawal by Lieut Higgs and Sgt Bob Gillespie. Owing to the built-up nature of this area, the wide, deep ditches and two woods, our arcs of fire were narrow. The assault troop section and the carriers of Sgts Munton and Ladds were covering the left flank well, but our blind side was 'sticky'.

Wireless contact with squadron headquarters was regained through a step-up, and we were ordered to pull out instantly, as the Germans were reported to be behind us. The assault section and the cars went first, followed by the carriers. While retiring to his section an assault trooper was killed by machine gun fire. The 6-pounder—without its firing mechanism— and the damaged carrier had to be abandoned.

After going back five or six miles we met an advance troop of the Royal Tank Regiment who said that three tanks had been sent to help us and two of them had been knocked out five miles behind where we had been in action. We all returned to Kerkhove.

Other A Squadron vehicles patrolled the main road between Kerkhove and Avelghem, on which unescorted supply vehicles came under fire from an enemy machine gun. This was eventually traced to a factory on the outskirts of Avelghem. It was only after a gallant member of the White Brigade, the Belgian underground army, had lost his life that the post was overcome.

Throughout a drearily wet night patrols from the regiment guarded crossroads around the squadron harbours, and next day, 7 September, the 'pocket' was again explored while the Germans continued their frantic efforts to find a way out of it. The haphazard movements of these enemy groups meant that unless a patrol was on the spot it was never certain whether a town or village was clear of the enemy. The Belgians in the area found this bewildering, and became understandably cautious in the display of national flags, which were something of an embarrassment when Germans arrived. The sight of the Scots Greys' tanks going south through Avelghem to a night harbour made the inhabitants so anxious that hundreds of flags disappeared and an exodus began, in spite of the presence and reassurances of C Squadron, the Cameronians and the underground forces, which gave the squadron much help. After the war Major Mills returned to Avelghem at the invitation of the burgomaster and townspeople, and opened an avenue named Liberation Avenue (Major L. H. Mills) in honour of C Squadron.

Some of the regiment's hardest fighting at this time took place at Deerlyck, where Tpr A. A. D. Davies and Tpr B. T. Miggins were killed. L/Cpl L. Cole and Tpr H. Hoyle, too, lost their lives in the 'pocket'. B Squadron, obtaining information about the crossings of the Lys on 7 September, met stiff opposition in Deerlyck and Harlebeke, and the assault troop casualties in Deerlyck included the troop commander, Lieut Harvey. Wounded, he was removed by Belgians to a cellar, where they were celebrating liberation while the battle continued above. The 6th Royal Scots Fusiliers attacked and captured Deerlyck, taking nearly seventy prisoners.

C Squadron discovered a strong group of Germans in Kaphoek, only a mile north of Avelghem, and A Squadron, working with the tanks of 4 Armoured Brigade, met self-propelled guns and dug-in infantry in Caster, a mile north of Kerkhove. While the tanks were heavily engaged there the squadron shot up German transport and took forty prisoners.

At dusk 4 Armoured Brigade withdrew to the line of the Escaut canal, and A Squadron, with the 4th Royal Tank Regiment, formed a defensive ring round the Kerkhove bridge. In the night the bridge was attacked by about two thousand Germans. It was a night of noise and tension. A Squadron had crossed the canal at dusk and taken up positions covering the bridge, but as the bridge was wooden the tanks had to stay on the far side, and their crews made most of the noise by firing in all directions except to the rear. The attacks failed. It was the last coordinated effort to break out of the 'pocket'.

Next day, 8 September, 44 Brigade, with the regiment under its command, had the task of clearing from the line of the Courtrai-Bossuyt canal northward to the main Olsene-Oudenarde road. B Squadron went first. Squadron headquarters became worried by the slowness of the advance, but it was discovered that this slowness was caused by the hundreds of Germans coming from all sides to surrender. All semblance of order in the German ranks had vanished. Those who were not trying to surrender were trying, with anything that had wheels, to find a way back to the Fatherland by trial and error. They must have got tired of the errors. After a separate organisation had been set up to deal with the prisoners, B Squadron's patrols made good progress through this flat country, which seemed to be an unending mixture of market gardens and suburbs with garish brick houses. Armoured cars met the 7th Armoured Division near Ghent, but the B Squadron troop on the right encountered more resistance in Deerlyck, and Lieut L. Bray was wounded in a skirmish beyond Hadebeke. B Squadron reported that the bridges over the Lys between Courtrai and Dentze had been destroyed, and that enemy were seen at several places on the north bank.

C Squadron, on B Squadron's right, found British soldiers who had been taken along as prisoners in the German retreat. One of them was Trooper Dennis, a former member of the regiment. He had been captured while on patrol after being posted to another reconnaissance regiment. C Squadron had news of him when a patrol was stopped by a Belgian and led to a house in which two RASC men were hiding; after being marched for four days and nights with little rest they had escaped from their captors in the confusion of the retreat. Dennis, they said, had been with them, but they had had to leave him some miles away. Major Mills went to look for him. As he drove up to the house Dennis limped out. 'Hello, sir, I'm glad you've come. I've been here a week,' he said.

That night the regiment harboured at Oyke. On the way to Oyke—a drive through joyful crowds whose flags were now displayed without fear of a return of the enemy—Lieut Isaac, leading RHQ, looked down from his light reconnaissance car into a pair of eyes peering cautiously over the edge of a ditch. They belonged to a little, bewildered Russian. The Germans had captured him, put him into German uniform and told him to drive an Army waggon. He washed dishes gladly at RHQ for a day or two, then went back to the prisoner-of-war cages.

At this time the Scottish Division was ordered to take over the bridgehead in which the 50th Northumbrian Division was fighting hard across the Albert Canal south of Gheel. To do this a journey of about ninety miles had to be made, and it was on the evening of 12 September that the first of the Scottish Division's infantry, the Cameronians, went into the bridgehead. On 10 September the regiment drove from Oyke to Breendonck, a small town on the main road between Brussels and Antwerp. To the regiment Breendonck is memorable for its brewery, its dance and its concentration camp, or what had been its concentration camp. In the brewery RHQ was quartered. The dance was given that evening by the townspeople—thrilled with new-found liberty—in honour of the regiment. The congestion at Hampden Park when Scotland meets the ancient enemy has never been greater than the crush in the little dance hall. The dancing, in the Belgian style, was vigorous. It was the regiment's first night 'off the leash' since landing in Normandy, and it was the townspeople's first opportunity to celebrate liberation in such fashion, and everybody was flushed, perspiring and happy.

The concentration camp in Breendonck had been established by the Germans; now it contained those of the guard who had not been swift enough to get away and an increasing number of people said to be collaborators, the women with their heads shaved as a mark of their disgrace. Outside the camp hundreds of Belgians shouted, danced, sang and shook their fists at those within.

The division's knowledge of what was happening in the Albert Canal area was scanty, so A Squadron patrols went out from Breendonck on 11 September in search of information. The report sent to divisional headquarters that night contained the following facts: that the bridges over the canal were demolished and no other crossing places had been found; that the 61st Reconnaissance Regiment was south of Herenthals, and the 4th Welch at Larrenburg; and that enemy were seen north of the canal at Schaats, Herenthals, Diestenberg, Vierseldijk and Massenhoven. Positions of bridges standing on Petite Nethe and La Nethe were given. Divisional headquarters were informed that the general impression was that the enemy was not holding the canal in great strength.

At Breendonck A Squadron had the misfortune to lose Lieut Higgs, who was injured in a motor accident.

On 12 September, while A Squadron continued to reconnoitre, the regiment went on to Vorst, a village two miles south of the Albert Canal. Entering the bridgehead that evening, the Cameronians confirmed that the opposition on the perimeter was determined, and the regiment's orders for the following day were to make a detailed reconnaissance of the canal area. Next day, however, the infantry found that they were opposed only by rearguards, while the early-morning reports of B and C Squadron patrols also indicated a withdrawal from the canal line. The chase was on again; A and B Squadrons hurried over the only bridge and headed for the Junction (Meuse-Escaut) Canal, between five and seven miles away.

A Squadron patrols, on the left, were not hindered until they drew near to the bridge north of Gheel and the bridge on the main road to Rethy. Then they met slight resistance on the near bank, and came under heavy fire from the far bank. They reported that both bridges were demolished.

B Squadron, on the right, made for the town of Moll and the Donck bridge two miles beyond, which air reconnaissance had reported to be still standing. The main road between Gheel and Moll was cratered; the squadron went south of it. At two o'clock in the afternoon the leading patrol was halted in the centre of Moll, where two cars were knocked out in an action commemorated by a scar on the face of the town clock. Sgt Maxfield, Sgt Litton, Tpr Marshall, Tpr Sarl and Tpr Ritchie were wounded. The 2nd Gordon Highlanders came up and cleared the town after sharp fighting with the German rearguard. Behind the

Gordon Highlanders were the Argyll and Sutherland Highlanders, mounted on the tanks of the City of London Yeomanry in readiness for a dash to the Donck bridge. At half-past three a loud explosion in the north was heard; at half-past six it was confirmed that the bridge had been blown up.

On the Junction Canal the Germans made a stand, and for a week the 15th Scottish Division—first 44 Brigade and afterwards 227 Brigade—had some of its hardest and most costly fighting to preserve the small bridgehead which the 8th Royal Scots seized across the canal north of Gheel on the night of 13 September. On the same night the 6th King's Own Scottish Borderers also crossed, near the Rethy bridge, but they had to withdraw because the Germans flooded the area by manipulating the lock gates. The regiment stayed south of the canal, quartered among the hospitable people of Meerhout and Moll, and patrolling the factories, straggling suburbs, woods and marshes in the canal area to prevent German infiltration. The difference between doing a little peaceful shopping in Moll, or sipping a light beer in one of its cafes, and watching for a marauding German patrol, or listening for the sudden scream of a shell in a deserted canal factory, was only half an hour's walk along a very ordinary-looking, straight suburban road. On the night of 15 September Lieut Michael Morris, of C Squadron, with two sergeants, led the way for the 2nd Gordon Highlanders, who tried to cross the canal by lock gates two miles west of the Donck bridge in order to draw off some of the great pressure by the Hermann Göring troops on the bridgehead. The Gordon Highlanders were pinned down by machine-gun fire, and the attempt failed.

That day Field Marshal Sir Bernard Montgomery had visited the Scottish Division and presented medal ribbons. 'I hope,' he said, 'that you will tell your folk at home that I came here today and told you that the 15th Scottish Division had done magnificently.' The regiment provided the guard of honour, commanded by Captain L. T. Ford, and was complimented by Major General Barber on its smartness and bearing.

On 17 September C Squadron relieved the Argyll and Sutherland Highlanders in the Donck bridge area. It was eerily quiet there, among back gardens, deserted except for a few forlorn hens, and among the empty, echoing factories with their machinery dusty and idle, and among the woods. Intermittently shells shattered the quietness. From the factory at the Donck bridge the Germans could be seen on the other bank, fewer than fifty yards away. That day eyes looked up to watch the Dakotas and Stirlings and gliders flying to Arnhem, and good wishes went with them through the puffs of anti-aircraft shells ahead. In the afternoon C Squadron headquarters defeated Moll at football. It was an exciting game, and the score was broadcast at intervals to the patrols watching the canal.

By day C Squadron assault troop, supported by machine gunners of the Middlesex Regiment, made a strongpoint in one of the factories. At night the troop withdrew to houses nearer to Moll. On 18 September a strong enemy patrol crossed the canal and captured two assault troop men who were guarding one of the approaches to the factory. The close nature of the country made it impossible to guarantee against surprise, and the Germans on the other side of the canal were able, enterprising soldiers. The possibility of a German crossing which would be more than a patrol led to the placing of the 8th Royal Scots, two companies of the Middlesex Regiment (machine guns and mortars) and artillery under the colonel's command, but no attack came.

The Gheel bridgehead had served its purpose as a diversion from the Second Army's main thrust towards Arnhem, and on 20 September the division was ordered to withdraw from the bridgehead, hand over the rest of the area to the 7th Armoured Division and go into Holland on the following day. On the last day in Belgium Lieut Colonel Grant Peterkin received immediate posting instructions to go to the 43rd Wessex Division as GSO1. He addressed the squadrons and issued the following Special Order of the Day:

Today I have been ordered to relinquish command of the Regiment and return to the Staff.

In this my final order I wish to thank all ranks for their very real and loyal co-operation and help which have always been extended to me, and to wish you good-bye and good luck.

To me fell the honour to reform, train for Active Service and lead into action the 15th (Scottish) Reconnaissance Regiment. We have now reasonable excuse to consider ourselves the best regiment in a very fine Division. Much of this is due to the fact that we have been a happy family in which everyone did his best, and it has been easy through all your efforts to achieve success.

We have had our trials and tribulations, but when the time for judgement came we were able to show to all and sundry how well we could do.

I shall never forget the many very happy days we have spent together, nor shall I ever forget the Regiment. I shall follow your future achievements in war and peace with undiminished interest.

That every one of you will give to my successor the same co-operation and willing assistance I am certain. Continue to work and play with the same cheerfulness and determination, and let everyone ensure that he never sullies the name of this Regiment that I look upon as mine.

It is a sad day for me, but your continued success will help to soften the blow.

Good luck to each one of you, both in the remaining days of the war and in the difficult days of the peace to follow.

B Squadron remained in Moll with 44 Brigade until the 7th Armoured Division had completed its occupation of the area, but at first light on 21 September the rest of the regiment began its drive to Holland. In the centre of Moll, on this cold, misty morning, Lieut Colonel Grant Peterkin took the salute from his regiment for the last time and wished it luck as the long line of vehicles headed for a new country. Everybody was sorry to say 'Goodbye' to that tall figure in the mist—'the old man'.

He had given the regiment its character, its spirit and its methods. His enthusiasm was infectious, and he had the knack of getting the best out of everyone. On the cloth model at Felton he had plumbed the depths of his officers' ignorance, but in such a skilful and delightful way that they had left each exercise brimming with new knowledge and confidence. He may not have known that there was almost violence in the sergeants' mess over the vexed question of whether the porridge should contain sugar or salt, but in those days of training there was very little which escaped his eye or inquisitive cane—certainly not the Nissen hut full of snoring officers 'whose batmen hadn't called them for PT.' At sport the regiment's teams were always spurred to greater efforts by the presence of the colonel, racing up and down the touchline with brandished cane.

Battle increased the regiment's admiration of a leader whose appreciations were accurate and decisions swift, who appeared among the forward troops when things were at their 'stickiest', and who had a racy way of keeping everybody 'in the picture'. Just as his cane had poked into every corner of the regiment in training, so his jeep, with shining Reconnaissance Corps badge, waving aerial and the good-natured Corporal Ridge, bustled into every corner of the regiment in action. It was always a welcome sight.

After Lieut Colonel Grant Peterkin had left, it was learned that he had been awarded the DSO for the way in which he led the regiment in France and Belgium. From GSO1 of the Wessex Division he was posted to command the 1st Gordon Highlanders in the 51st Highland Division, and in that command won an immediate award of a Bar to the DSO in the fighting between the Maas and the Rhine. He was wounded in the assault across the Rhine. Later he was given command of a brigade in the Highland Division.

In the reorganization which resulted from the colonel's posting Major Smith became commanding officer, Major MacDiarmid second-in-command, Lieut Blount captain and adjutant, Capt Liddell second-in-command of C Squadron, Capt Ford officer commanding Headquarter Squadron and Major Gaddum officer commanding A Squadron.

For his courage in leading patrols in the Avelghem area and on the Junction Canal Sgt S. Kirrage, of C Squadron, was awarded the Croix de Guerre 1940 with Palm.

Tony Royle wrote in 1996: in 1944 – I was, as Lieut E.A. Royle MC, the Troop commander of No.9 Troop, C Squadron. The Squadron Commander was Major Harry Mills. Sgt.Hanby and Trooper Neville were members of my Troop.

On 28/29 August, the Division crossed the Seine and formed a bridgehead to allow the 7th and 11th Armoured Divisions to advance to seize Antwerp and they were reported to be in Ghent on 4 September. With such rapid advance, a mass of Germans were trapped to the west and the supply lines were cut from time to time, stopping supplies of fuel and ammo to the Armoured Divisions. The Regiment was ordered to move and stop this cutting off of supplies. I think we arrived at Avelghem in the early hours of 6 September and went on patrol westwards around first light. My lead car, commanded by Sgt Hanby was I think knocked out before mid-day. We came across a lot of Germans. We thought they were surrendering, but suddenly from the right an anti-tank gun, not a panzerfaust, knocked the car out.

We withdrew some 300/400 yards to a crossroads where there was a railway bridge over the road and also a bend in the road, and we set up an ambush. After a while, a bus full of German soldiers, escorted by motorcyclists, drove into the trap and were destroyed. We withdrew a further mile and set up another trap, but no enemy came our way and at dark, we were ordered to come into base. On the 7th, or it may have been the 8th, I returned to the place where Sgt Hanby's car had been knocked out, but the area was not clear and I was unable to extricate the bodies of the crew. I returned a day later with the Padre, Capt. Reverend Bradbrooke, with sheets and ropes. On our arrival, the car was empty, but some Belgians who lived nearby, told us that the rescue services (air raid) had taken them to Deerlijk cemetery. They had been placed in boxes and an 'X' marked the body of the 'chaffeur', i.e. Trooper Neville. They, plus as many as was possible, climbed on my car, and they guided us to the burial grounds. Two shallow graves had been dug and the boxes were there. They asked us to delay our service as others may wish to attend, and some twenty or so, did so, some with flags. The wartime burial service in the field is short, but that service, conducted by our Padre, was the most sincere funeral I have attended.

The next day we were heading north, and the next real rest was at the blown bridge at Moll/Ghent on the canal there. My Troop lost two Bren Carriers on the 6th, and two members went missing but turned up later as POWs. (The village where the ambush took place was later identified as Vichte.)

In 1948 I received a letter from either the Allied War Crimes Commission, Belgium Section, or it was the Belgium War Crimes Commission, asking for details of the bus ambush. I gave them all the information I had; they thanked me and said that it confirmed the information they had been given. They thanked me, and my Troop for helping in the liberation of Belgium. The main purpose of their contact was to seek information as to whether any Belgian civilians assisted me or took part in the ambush. A German officer believed that it was the local

Resistance that had carried out the ambush, so the Germans had shot some local residents out of hand. I informed the commission that no civilians had assisted us; I had chosen the location, positioned my troops and executed the plan. The locals took no part in it. Of course, they could have warned the Germans of our presence, but, as excellent allies, did not do so, and offered the enemy no help whatsoever.

* * * * *

The third member of the Neville and Hanby crew was Trooper Hoolachan, he managed to extricate himself from the car and dodging bullets he used the cover of a ditch and a small railway.

* * * * *

Armand Deknudt:- The first house he reached belonged to Emiel Tack who said 'one soldier escaped, he had black curly hair, a tall handsome lad, but he was badly burnt, he had lost his helmet. He had to cross ditches and the railway whilst the Germans were firing at him.' He finally got to my back garden. At that time there stood a pump and my parents held the boy under the water, but he cried in pain. He went to the rear of our house and then my father took him to the centre of the Belgiek.

At the Belgiek, Hoolachan was looked after by the caring hands of Leentje (Helena), of the café 'The Little Cross' she said 'This Englishman came into our home, I attended him. My mother said that buttermilk was good for burns and we had some fresh from the farm. We got it here from the Coudyzers farm. We rubbed him all over with buttermilk in the kitchen. Gilbert Coudyzer then took the soldier on his bicycle and drove him via a back road to Doctor Isebaert at Vichte.'

* * * * *

Armand Deknudt lived in Deerlijk throughout the war and was fourteen-years old at the time of liberation. In addition to his own experiences he has researched the events of the time relating to the area. His investigations found that a young woman called Christiane Degezelle observed the action from an upstairs window in her house on Hoogstraat. She waved to the crew of an armoured car who returned her greeting; a hundred metres further down the road as the vehicle approached the crossing with Rodenbachstraat, she heard a blast and the vehicle was hit. There had been a fatal error and a round from a British anti-tank weapon had been mistakenly fired at the recce car, killing Troopers Davies and Miggins. Their graves in Ooike churchyard and Sgt Hanby's and Tpr Neville's in Deerlijk are cared for by Armand and the grateful residents of the town.

Resistance to the German occupation had been organised by the 'White Brigade' but Armand recalls that they were prudent not to shoot up the endless columns of retreating troops, as reprisals would have been severe for the local inhabitants. The 'White Brigade' was so called because of the colour of their uniforms, local factories under German control produced the cloth but not all of it reached its intended destination!

Thomas Marshall:- I have a very strong memory of 7 September as I was one of the armoured car drivers. Our target was the crossroads on the edge of the town, as it was the escape route of the retreating Germans. With our customary cautious approach, I parked our car about 100 metres from the crossroads on the left hand side of the road, hugging the brick wall which had some overhanging greenery providing excellent camouflage. A cul de sac on the opposite side of the road which was an escape from enemy guns if we were noticed. Whilst keeping an eye on the crossroads, three or four of our armoured carriers of the Assault Troop came up and parked very closely behind me, which at the time, I thought was the wrong thing to do. We did not wait long before the Germans started to move over the crossroads on their escape route and it wasn't long before they noticed us. We had fired at a party of the enemy until our machine gun jammed. On giving our position away, the Germans started to manhandle a 88mm self propelled gun around the corner, so they could get their sights on us. As soon as I noticed the barrel of the gun poking around the corner, I put my car in gear and got across to the cul de sac as quickly as possible. As I completed the manoeuvre the Germans commenced firing and set ablaze the armoured carriers. I turned my car around in order to see what was going on and to be positioned for a rapid exit if required.

Whilst there a brave civilian was trying to watch the Germans in the courtway and attempted to give us information but he had to vacate his position because he was spotted and rifle fire only narrowly missed him. Our 6-pounder anti-tank gun, which belonged to the Assault Troop, positioned the weapon alongside us which afforded them a clear view of the crossroads. As things started to 'hot up' our 6-pounder fired at an armoured car which had stopped right on the centre of the crossroads. I pulled my car up very slowly, so that I could see what our gun had fired at. To my horror, I could see that it was one of our own cars that had entered from a different direction. It had been hit right in the centre; I saw the Commander get out and run but sadly the two other crew members who were my friends were killed. I had witnessed a very tragic case of mistaken identity, which has stayed with me all my life.

We were still in a very dangerous position, as the Germans were gradually closing up around us as they realised we were blocking their line of retreat. I witnessed another member of our troop becoming a casualty, he had laid down behind a Bren gun but the Germans had fired a shell at him. I do not know whether he was killed or not because it would have been suicidal to try and reach him. Eventually we were ordered to withdraw. Whilst waiting, the Germans were firing their guns across our only escape road every four seconds. So, in between each three shots, there was a time lapse of three or four seconds. I had to work out the best time lapse of those shells. So with a wounded officer and some of our assault troop clinging to the side of my car, I made the escape. We were still not out of danger. I was taking evasive action down the escape road by swerving from one side of the road to the other, four shells narrowly missed us. I could not get down the next road quick enough to get away from the gunfire. We waited a while and then had another try to reach our Troop HQ, which we achieved.

They were located in a café and with a great thirst for a drink, I ordered a beer and was asked to pay for it! I didn't think it a very generous gesture in charging me for a beer when I was trying to liberate their country from the dreaded Nazis.

We were still not finished. With the information supplied by the Recce, the decision was made to send in the infantry. We were informed that our car would conduct the liaising which meant sending progress reports back via our wireless.

It was early evening and we were all waiting on the start line for our artillery to lift their shelling of the town. Then we were given the order to attack. We began to follow the infantry into the town but had to halt because they were receiving fire from the houses. The infantry sergeant approached and asked if we could take the lead and silence the Germans in their concealed positions. So with a few cheers from the 'boys' we pulled to the front and sprayed our guns each side of the road at the houses and the infantry followed up and cleared the remaining enemy out.

The town was taken and I do remember the infantry doing a 'knees up' (dance) and making merry with the public. There is not much more I can remember of that day, except that it was becoming very dark and we took up position near a house. The family of two young girls and their mother came out and gave us the usual cuddle and kisses that made us feel that it was all worthwhile. Whilst we were talking to this family, we heard a loud noise from down the road, we hustled the family away and our gunner went to investigate. It turned out to be a horse wounded in the fighting which was dragging its entrails behind him. Our gunner put the poor animal out of its misery. Of the battle in Deerlyck, there were 300 German prisoners taken but it had been at a cost.

Arthur Watkins:- 'Time spent in reconnaissance is seldom wasted'.
On 13 September 1944, a 'Heavy' Humber Scout Car of No. 6 Troop B Squadron approached the small town of Moll. The crew, Corporal Reg Ray and Troopers Arthur Watkins and George Bunn, had been informed by the Belgian Resistance that the Germans had withdrawn and their orders were to ascertain the true situation. There was no apparent sign of life as the vehicle came to a halt in the town square but as the populace realised it was an allied machine, they began to appear in numbers, climbing up on the car with welcoming flags. Arthur Watkins, the radio operator/gunner, observed a petite elderly lady pushing

her way through the crowd, calling out with a strong welsh accent 'Is anyone there from Cardiff?' Corporal Ray was in fact from the Cardiff area and a lively conversation developed. Suddenly the vehicle came under small arms fire with shots bouncing off the car. The people scattered. Arthur was just attempting to locate where the fire was coming from through the telescope on the gun-sight when he felt a tug on his shoulder and heard the distinctive welsh voice cry, 'They are in the church.' The Welsh lady was standing on the engine hatch leaning into the turret 'spotting' for the crew. Calling for her to get down and take cover, Arthur placed a couple of well-aimed 2-pounder HE shells into the church tower to silence the Germans. (He learned later that ten or twelve were killed).The vehicle then moved forward past the church and awaited the arrival of the 2nd Gordon Highlanders who came up and cleared the town after some sharp fighting with the German rearguard.

During the day, two of the 15th Recce vehicles were put out of action with five members of the crews being wounded. Arthur and George Bunn returned at the first opportunity the next day, concerned as to the well-being of the Welsh lady. It transpired that her maiden name was Evans and that she had married a Belgian miner who had been working in South Wales, the pair of them eventually settling in Moll. Arthur left his address with the lady and eventually a postcard arrived in England depicting the market place pre-war and a note stating 'this is what the church should look like!'

*   *   *   *   *

In September 1995 on one of the reunion visits, Arthur Watkins revisited the exact spot of his wartime encounter. George Bunn was eventually traced and was delighted to meet up with former comrades; he died aged eighty-four in August 2007.

Tom Marshall was a driver of one of the cars knocked out in this action; wounded he took refuge in the cellar of a house. Whilst in Moll a young boy, Eugene Offner, gave Tom a photograph of himself. Fifty years later Tom was invited back to Moll and met again Eugene, now a Doctor. Tom died in 1998 aged eighty-four.

*   *   *   *   *

Ernie Clarke:- From the earliest days the Regiment was always known as 15th (S) Recce Regt, until the arrival of Lieut Colonel K.C.C. Smith. From then on we were to be known as 15th Scottish Reconnaissance Regiment—no short cuts, no brackets. And so it was! We had crossed the Rhine and were well up into Germany way out on our own, when an American unit in a jeep raced up to RHQ and a voice roared out –'Say is this the 15th Recon Outfit?' I will never forget the look on the Colonel's face.

Clive Ridge:- When Lieut Colonel Grant Peterkin left the Regiment to join the 43rd Wessex Division it was a sad day. We thought he was a great leader and all the Regiment thought he was 'the best'. It was a sad day for me. Major Smith our second in command became our CO so I had a new driver! One thing changed; I had to do the map reading.

Our routine was very much the same each day. Late one night Colonel Smith was issuing orders at one of the Squadron HQs for the following day; he had instructed me to find something to eat. It was dark and as I approached the HQ the sentry on guard challenged me from some distance, 'Halt, Who goes there Black'. I thought no, it is after midnight and the password would have changed for that day and I did not know the correct reply! I thought it cannot be 'White' surely, that would be too easy. Thinking quickly I shouted 'Magic', I heard the bolt click on the rifle, 'it's me, it's me, Corporal Ridge,' I bellowed. The officer of the guard came out and gave me a right rollicking!

We took one jeep over to France and that was replaced soon after Lieut Colonel Smith took over. I was in both jeeps from the first day to the last serving as driver/operator 15. Each jeep completed approximately 22,000 miles.

Len Watson:- I had just returned to base after nine days' continuous patrolling, tired and unshaven, when Sgt Major Franks said 'You are wanted on a special guard of honour for Field Marshal Montgomery.' Being six-feet tall I suppose was the reason for being selected, Arthur Watkins and I had previously led many church parades. 'Get a shower and haircut, the crew will blanco your kit.'

Len is extreme right of the second row in the photograph.

Arthur Watkins:- We were in a small town and were talking to a family who implored us to rescue their twenty-year old son from the local prison; he had been arrested for resistance activities. Without any orders we drove to the prison where the jailers would not surrender without a fight so I put a 2-pounder shell through the door. We entered and freed the young man in question. I remember the place was whitewashed throughout and there were instruments of torture and evidence of its use in the place. Len Watson rode on the back of the armoured car and remembers the incident clearly. This was Breendonck where the Germans had turned an old fortress into a torture chamber.

James Ferrier:- We entered a small village and came upon a lorry of German troops; I destroyed the vehicle and shot up the troops and we continued on to the village square which was packed with infantry and an anti-tank gun pointing our way. I had a HE shell in the 37mm and knew it would not penetrate the armour shield of the gun and so placed the shot underneath it. I thought if these are front line troops we are in trouble as they are bound to have personal anti-tank weapons, and so I proceeded to shoot up the square with machine-gun fire whilst young Rex Miller, the driver and one of three brothers from Chile, drove the car out of the centre. When we reported back to the Troop the car commander was sent back sick and Peter Kerridge told me to take command of the car.

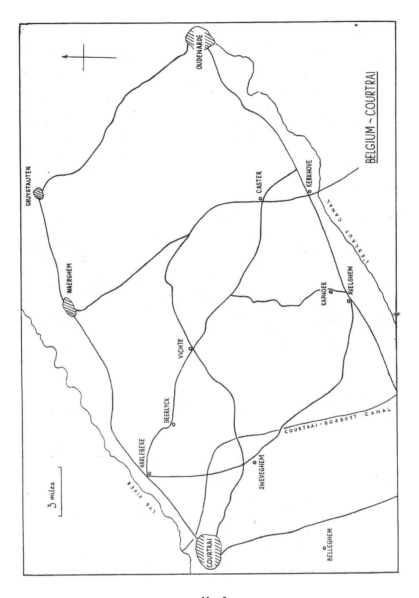

Map 5

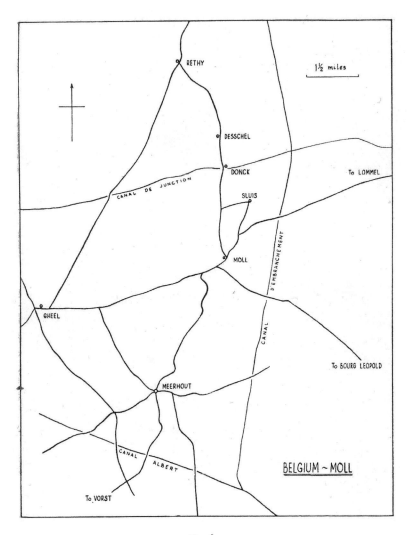

Map 6

The Regiment in convoy through Falaise

FM Montgomery and Lt Gen Barker
Major K.C.C. Smith with cane

'Tiny' Barber (left)
FM Montgomery shakes hand with Major K.C.C. Smith

Major K.C.C. Smith; 'Tiny' Barber; Lt Gen Barker; FM Montgomery

FM Montgomery decorates 'Tiny' Barber - at 6 feet 8 inches the tallest General in the British Army

Field Marshal Montgomery inspects Guard of Honor, 15 September 1944, supplied by the regiment under
Captain L.T. Ford
Len Watson, far right; Bert Bonner 4th from left, front row

Thomas Marshall

Christiane Degezelle

Armand Deknudt

Tony Royle

Thomas Miggins

Arthur Watkins; Welsh lady; George Bunn

Arthur Watkins; Tim Chamberlin and Alan Westby at the same spot fifty years later

Moll Church before 'alterations'

Arthur Watkins and George Bunn, 2001

15th Scottish vehicles in Vichte
7 July 1944

CHAPTER XI

BEST, HELMOND AND BEST AGAIN

Map 7

On 21 September the regiment passed through Lommel, crossed the Escaut Canal, entered Holland two miles farther north and drove on to the Eindhoven area, gazing with awe at the dark splendour of the uniforms of the Dutch police and sharing chocolate and cigarettes with the people who crowded excitedly round the vehicles whenever the column halted. The large town of Eindhoven, dominated by the Phillips radio factory, was part of the area which had been freed only a few days before by the airborne forces and XXX Corps in the dash to Nijmegen. A mile or two to the north of the town the Welsh Division— to be relieved by the Scottish—and the Germans faced one another across the Wilhelmina Canal. C Squadron patrols, sent out to glean information about the district for divisional headquarters, reconnoitred bridging sites south of Oirschot and Best, met Americans of 502nd Parachute Infantry Regiment, who were holding the Zon bridge four miles east of Eindhoven, and found that small groups of enemy were still fighting south of the canal.

When Lieut Gray's patrol reached the canal a deputation under a German officer crossed from the opposite bank with a white flag to discuss surrender terms. The officer seemed to be willing to surrender but his companions persuaded him to decline, and after a very correct military parting the Germans rowed back across the canal. Events were to prove that both surrender and retreat were far from the intentions of the Germans on the other side.

The road from Eindhoven to the canal was wide and straight, and on the far side it continued straight towards Boxtel and s'Hertogenbosch in the north. About a mile beyond the canal were the Best crossroads, and beyond them the road lay between woods. At the crossroads one road went left and west through the small town of Best, across a railway and on towards the city of Tilburg. The road in the opposite direction ran between the canal and the woods, through the straggling hamlet of Vleut and by lonely farms, to St Oedenrode. American paratroops were fighting in groups in the area, but in the main the Germans held the canal line nearly to St Oedenrode, where the Nijmegen corridor stretched to the north. The Scottish Division's intention was to cross the Wilhelmina Canal and strike north towards s'Hertogenbosch to relieve the pressure on the corridor.

On the night of 21 September 46 Brigade crossed the canal south of Best, and by dawn the crossroads had been taken. The regiment waited along the road between Eindhoven and the canal ready to be called across to break out of the bridgehead—A Squadron towards Boxtel, and C Squadron west towards Oirschot. But there was no break-out. A Squadron's patrols found the enemy firmly in position about a mile north of the crossroads, and when a counter-attack, supported by heavy mortaring and airburst shelling, drove the Glasgow Highlanders from their foothold in Best it was obvious that there was no opening to the west for C Squadron. The regiment stayed south of the canal, setting up headquarters in the school at Aacht. Next day it waited again for 'Tally ho', the words which were to unleash it, but again the wait was in vain. While the Lowland Brigade fought its way into the centre of Best, and 46 Brigade was engaged north and east of the crossroads, A Squadron patrols, supporting the infantry, searched both sides of the Boxtel road without finding any gaps in the German defences. These formed a continuous front through a flat country where the woods were thick and the few open spaces were divided into many fields bordered by ditches, high banks and lines of trees. It was a country suited to defence, and the infantry's progress was slow and costly. The regiment did not move its headquarters across the canal until 27 September, and then only to Vleut. By that time Best had been occupied as far as the railway, and the road east to St Oedenrode had been opened. But the Germans remained firmly planted in the woods just north of the road, in spite of the advice to surrender broadcast by Capt Rosdol, the division's intelligence officer, and shrieking rocket attacks by Typhoons, one of which, its tail shot away as it dived, went straight down into the woods. Everyday A Squadron had patrolled forward from the bridgehead along the main road and up forest tracks, plotting the enemy's positions. C Squadron had guarded the bridge built by the Royal Engineers across the canal, and its assault troop had manned observation posts in the Bata shoe factory on the south bank of the canal, opposite Best. Having found the tracks too bad and the enemy too strong in an attempt to advance west, B Squadron moved on 26 September to St Oedenrode and patrolled between the River Dommel and A Squadron's patrols in the woods north of Vleut. On 26 September Tpr T. F. Cross and Tpr I.T.M. Stewart were killed.

The regiment's move to Vleut on 27 September was to take up positions in the woods as infantry. This was done by C Squadron while B Squadron continued to send out its patrols from St Oedenrode and A Squadron, at first, rested south of the canal. RHQ, in houses strung along the road, was within hail of C Squadron headquarters in a farm across a small field, on the very edge of the woods, and two or three hundred yards inside the woods were the slit trenches of the squadron's forward posts. Sgt 'Chunky' Davidson and his signallers at RHQ got out the field telephones and cautiously laid cable through the woodland rides.

The Dutch people were still occupying their houses and farms, but over the area by day there was that stillness which descends when opposing armies are close, each hidden from the other and keeping constant vigil. At night the woods were intermittently alive with the chatter of small arms and the glow of tracer bullets. Night was the time of foot patrols. The lighted signs at RHQ were a source of alarm to its neighbours until Sgt Hine, of the regimental police, was persuaded to mask them.

This is Capt Kemsley's story of his first night at Vleut:

I was turning in on the floor in a little house occupied by an old couple when the woman, a white-haired cripple with her leg in irons, hobbled in to me, weeping. I could not understand her, except that it was obvious that she was upset by the fighting. She made me follow her into the bedroom, where her husband was in bed. I gathered that he had been wounded by a mortar or shell. He was stone deaf and could not hear the firing which was upsetting his wife. She seemed to think that if I got into bed with them they would be safer, but by patting her shoulder and using the few words of German which I remembered from school I managed to convince her that nothing could happen to them. She went to bed and I went back to my blankets. Next morning she took me to a little chapel in the attic. Some days later we left the area, and when we returned the house was empty, with a shell hole in the roof.

The soldier who could be spared could leave the mud and tense quietness of Vleut, drive into Eindhoven in a quarter of an hour, take a hot bath or swim in the modern public baths and go to the pictures. Drivers always pressed hard on the accelerator when they reached the bridge over the canal. German shells often landed there, and Capt George Pearce, the technical adjutant, once had hurriedly to forsake his jeep for the ditch near the bridge. Tpr Templeman had a similar experience while driving his half-track between the Best crossroads and Vleut, and A Squadron suffered casualties from shelling as it went in convoy along this road. The regiment's casualties in this period included Cpl D. L. Atkin, Tpr F. L. Griffiths and Tpr F. Taylor, all of whom were fatally wounded.

For six days C Squadron filled the gap in the woods between the 2nd Gordon Highlanders and the 2nd Argyll and Sutherland Highlanders while on the right A and B Squadrons patrolled the muddy tracks to help the Lowland Brigade, fighting slowly forward to capture the village of Fratershoef, and to help 158 Brigade of the Welsh Division, which was north of the Dommel. One night the divisional staff feared that the enemy was about to attack the road in

C Squadron's area but reconnaissance by Colonel Smith in his jeep revealed that the 'danger spot' was serenely occupied by a searchlight detachment engaged in the old military art of 'brewing up'. The humour of his report was not appreciated by the divisional staff.

It was while the regiment was at Vleut that the LAD, working to the colonel's own specifications made from sheet metal the portable latrine which was the pride of RHQ and a source of wonder to all visitors. It looked like a sentry box and was called the Thunder Box.

On 2 October the 51st Highland Division began to take over the Best-St Oedenrode area so that the 15th Scottish Division could have its first official rest as a division since landing in Normandy one hundred days before. On 4 October the whole regiment was comfortably housed in the schools and halls of Helmond, ten miles east of Eindhoven. What a wonderful time the next fortnight was! Enough sleep; the benediction of hot baths; the gaiety of the dances in B Squadron's cafe; the place by the fire in hospitable Dutch homes; and the chance to do all those odd jobs which had been accumulating. Vehicles were 'spring cleaned'. Weapons were stripped. The crusts of many meals were scraped from pots and pans, and many an obstinate portable cooker was persuaded to work again. Best battledresses were pressed and worn, and, permission having been given for the wearing of collar and tie when walking out, shirts were sent to good Dutch wives to have tails turned into collars.

C Squadron had billets opposite a large monastery, and the 'OC Monks' allowed the vehicles to be harboured in the grounds, behind a wall about twenty feet high and gates that were bolted at seven o'clock each evening. The bearded monks were the soul of kindness, bringing to the squadron frequent gifts of fruit. They were fascinated by the armoured cars, and during morning maintenance the 'OC, Monks' was continually chasing them back to their devotions. It was probably just as well that he did not catch the one who clambered into the turret and started swinging it round like a veteran of the campaign! A combined 'C Squadron-Monks Squadron' photograph was taken, with the cars as part of it.

Resting in Helmond was not without its hazards. On the way through France Major Mills had acquired a caravan—an abandoned German four-wheeled trailer —which lumbered along in the wake of his half-track and incurred the frowns of the Royal Engineers whenever it had to be disconnected and manhandled across any bridge too frail to bear the weight of both vehicles at once. The exit from the caravan was steep and not easy, and one morning in Helmond the major appeared at breakfast behind the blackest of eyes and the reddest of skinned noses. Capt Kemsley, too, suffered slight disfigurement when he stepped absentmindedly from the rear of an ambulance which happened to be moving.

On 6 October the people of Helmond flocked to the castle to see and hear the massed pipes of the 15th Scottish Division playing for the first time on the Continent, and two days later, a Sunday, the regiment marched through the town to church behind the pipers of the 2nd Gordon Highlanders.

The same day the regiment was placed under command of the 11th Armoured Division, and in the evening B Squadron, moving out to the area of Milheeze and Deurne, took up positions in marshy, wooded country on the eastern edge of the Nijmegen salient. These positions, which linked the 11th Armoured Division with the 7th US Armored Division on its right, were held by the squadrons in turn for eight days while the rest of the regiment remained in Helmond and, for the latter part of the time, the 3rd British Division advanced on Venraij from Overloon. In front of the squadron positions was a canal. On the morning of 9 October a foot patrol from B Squadron was ambushed while going towards it, and Lieut E. W. Goodrich, who had lately joined the regiment from the disbanded 59th Reconnaissance Regiment, did not get back. Later it was learned that he had been killed. On 15 October B Squadron patrols confirmed reports that the enemy had abandoned the canal line, and the 11th Armoured Division began building the bridge over which it crossed to join the 3rd Division. After C Squadron had spent a day keeping watch from the canal and B Squadron's I Troop had spent a night guarding the new bridge against attacks by saboteurs that never came, the regiment, complete in Helmond, came under command of the Scottish Division again.

The next orders were to return to the Best–St Oedenrode line as part of 227 Brigade Group, which was to relieve two brigades of the Highland Division and the 2nd Derbyshire Yeomanry. This was part of the redistribution of XII Corps formations for Operation Pheasant, planned to drive the stubborn Germans back from the western edge of the Nijmegen salient and out of s'Hertogenbosch and Tilburg. The 7th Armoured Division and the Welsh Division were to advance on s'Hertogenbosch from the north-east at dawn on October 22nd, and later the Highland Division was to attack from the east and swing south-west to Boxtel and Esch and Vucht. The Scottish Division was to help the Highland Division by clearing the Germans from the Best– St. Oedenrode—Boxtel triangle, and to drive west through Oirschot and Moergestel to capture Tilburg while the 7th Armoured Division made for Loon-op-Zand, to the north-west.

At dusk on 19 October the regiment went back into the gloomy woods of Vleut, more windswept, rainswept and muddy than before but still occupied by the unseen Germans, whose line had been pushed back about a hundred yards. The regiment found new holes in the roofs and walls of its billets, and new signs everywhere—'Stop here,' and 'Under observation— run,' and 'Don't go beyond this point.' It missed the chance encounter with the American paratroops, who had been met here before, ready to barter a fur-lined flying suit for a bottle of whisky and quite modest about their gallant part in the opening of the road to Nijmegen—'Jees, were we glad to see those Churchills arrive?'

The trappings of the regiment's command post— the maps and map boards, talc, chinagraph pencils, lists of codes, field telephones and lines, wireless headsets and leads—were spread out in the same small front room, behind demure lace curtains and under the inevitable crucifix which looked down from the wall. Major Mills, visiting RHQ one afternoon, saw from this room shells bursting all round the farm where his squadron had its headquarters, a field away. Hurrying back, he found everybody safe and Capt Jack Lane not yet sufficiently awake to realise that he had won for himself a small niche in C Squadron's hall of fame by sleeping soundly through a racket which had sent all his companions scurrying for cover. C Squadron had returned to its old positions and a delicious crop of apples and pears, and this time the whole regiment was strung out as infantry in the woods, having taken over from the strength of a brigade. B Squadron, reinforced by C Squadron's assault troop, occupied an unpleasant area called The Box, so close to the Germans that they could be heard coughing and moving in their forward posts. The Box was often under fire, and there Sgt Holland and Tpr Reetham were wounded. One burst of mortar bombs caused seven casualties in B Squadron's assault troop. On 20 October Tpr R. Dodd was killed.

At dawn on 24 October Major Gordon picked up the field telephone in The Box and said 'I hear no coughing this morning'. It was a message which began an advance which liberated a city; three days later, after a dash which B Squadron led, Tilburg was free. The colonel told 227 Brigade Headquarters that he thought the enemy had withdrawn from the regiment's front in the night. He ordered C Squadron to patrol beyond B Squadron's positions, and A Squadron to explore the main road to Boxtel. Mines and booby traps were found, but not Germans. Brigade Headquarters, a little sceptical about the colonel's first message, decided from a study of night patrol reports that the situation had indeed changed, and at ten o'clock in the morning permitted the regiment to forsake its infantry role and become a mechanised reconnaissance regiment again. While A Squadron went up the Boxtel road, and C Squadron continued its patrols along the woodland tracks, B Squadron began the advance through Oirschot and Moergestel to Tilburg.

Lieut Gordon Dalton has described the advance to Boxtel:

My orders were brief—'Get to Boxtel'. My route was simple—straight along the Best-Boxtel road. But after going about a mile and a half we saw two civilians jumping up and down on a fallen tree, waving a white flag, and found before us a road block consisting of more than a hundred stout trees and the usual booby traps. In the centre of the block was a concrete pillbox. On either side were the woods.

Lieut Harry Green arrived with his carriers, and he took to the tracks to the left of the block while I went to the right. One of the carriers struck a mine, and the driver, Tpr Taylor, was killed, and Sgt Heath badly shaken. The Germans, however, had left a perfect detour on each side of the road block. Reaching the main road on the far side of it, we saw Lieut Green's carriers going flat out for Boxtel and gave chase in our cars, whose greater speed soon brought us level. The race was cut short when Lieut Green was ordered to consolidate on the railway crossing while we went into the outskirts of the town. We met no enemy, but came under fire from the Highland Division, which was shelling the town. After we had sent a message back to squadron headquarters and it had been passed on, the shelling stopped.

The bridge into the centre of Boxtel had been blown up, so an assault section crossed the river in an assault boat, pulled across by joyful Dutch people on the far bank. Soon afterwards the message 'all clear' was received. I went back to my car to enjoy my haversack rations, only to find that Dutch children had scoffed the lot. But my driver, L/Cpl Berry, never failed me, and only a few minutes elapsed before he appeared with 'lunch for one, sir'. Meanwhile the rest of the troop was posing for photographs. It was just as well that the colonel did not appear!

While we were waiting for the assault section to return, a member of the Dutch underground movement passed to me a written message from an American airborne officer who was with 120 men behind the German lines. He stated that they had casualties and would need transport. The civilian who brought the message gave me their location and the positions of three anti-tank guns which we should encounter if we went to the rescue. I sent the civilian back with the message 'Keep smiling. Help coming.'

To my regret, we were not allowed to free them. Instead, the matter was left to the Highland Division, as it was on that side of the river.

The assault troop returned, having confirmed that the Germans had evacuated Boxtel on the previous night, and in the dusk we went back to harbour. As we were pulling out amid murmurs of 'Stay and protect us' a frantic Dutchman ran up, spluttering Dutch. Rather than stop to translate his outpourings, we hauled this somewhat elderly gentleman on to my moving vehicle and took him to RHQ, only to discover that he was simply expressing his worry that the Highland Division would shell Boxtel again during the night. Driving him back to Boxtel in a jeep through the darkness, I was so preoccupied with the problem of returning through the division's outposts without being shot that I forgot all about the blown bridge at Boxtel, and pulled up with screeching brakes and one wheel over the river. The local people hauled me back, and the jeep's speed took me back through our lines before they realised what the 'tornado' was.

That day A Squadron headquarters, moving forward because the thick woods made wireless communication difficult, had come to the road block and taken a track different from those used by the leading troops. There was a dull bang as the command half-track hit something. There was another bang when Tpr Ives, the driver, got out to see if a tyre had burst, and a third bang when Tpr Balfour, one of the wireless operators, got out to find out what was happening. Major Gaddum left the vehicle on its other side; there was another bang. The half-track had struck a nest of Schu-mines, some of the first the regiment had come across. This misadventure taught the regiment that the leading troop must mark clearly the route which it takes when a diversion has to be made. Major Gaddum, Tpr Ives and Tpr Balfour were all wounded, and Major Gaddum died as a result of his wounds.

Meanwhile B Squadron, followed by infantry and tanks, was racing towards Tilburg, in spite of road blocks, rearguards and blown bridges. But that is so much B Squadron's story that Lieut P. D. Peterson who was in the van, shall tell it in the next chapter.

On the regiment's arrival in Holland Lieut K A. Pearce joined A Squadron from the 59th Reconnaissance Regiment.

Clive Ridge:- The Colonel could call on a flight of three rocket firing Typhoons, if we were being held up by a Tiger tank or similar serious obstruction. The Colonel would ask the section being held up to put up yellow smoke to identify their position, then the fighters would come in, dive, fire their rockets and clear the problem! I remember clearly one attack; as they dived one behind the other the rear aircraft fired his rockets too soon hitting and destroying the central aircraft. The Typhoons proved invaluable on many occasions smashing the fearsome Tiger tanks most effectively.

Ernie Clarke:- recalls the same incident, on or about 28 September 1944, RHQ was in the woods of Vleut about a quarter of a mile from the front line the middle aircraft hit by rockets from the third went straight down into the trees.

Edwin Reetham:- Whilst recovering from wounds Edwin Reetham a Bren carrier driver with B Squadron received a letter from a boyhood friend, Dick Lyons, explaining that he was flying Typhoons. Edwin replied that they were full of admiration for their exploits and of the inestimable value they placed on the support they received from this low flying aircraft at critical times. The letter was passed around the pilots mess and this gave some comfort to Edwin when he learnt that his friend was killed in action near Venlo, Holland in February of 1945.

* * * * *

John Arnold was found badly wounded on 29 September; he had received shrapnel wounds from an exploding 88mm shell to his head and both arms. He was taken to No 23 CCS NW Europe on the 30th, his mother received notification that he was dangerously ill. The Doctor who examined him arranged for his immediate transfer to St Hugh's College in Oxford which had been converted to a specialist head injuries unit.

During treatment John had a steel plate inserted into his head but the injuries caused total paralysis down the right side of his body and he had lost the power of speech. The brilliant, dedicated staff at St Hugh's helped him to walk again and a marvellous speech therapist enabled John to speak again. John spent two and half years in hospital before being discharged and attended specialist consultations and check-ups for the rest of his life.

Whilst based in Pontefract John had met a local girl called Audrey and in the true spirit of 'love conquering all' they were married on 16 August 1947, they had two sons and enjoyed a full and happy life together.

Alan Westby:- We were billeted in a Dutch farmhouse where the owners had not fled the fighting and were still in residence. We all trooped into the kitchen intent on finding a place on the floor whereon to kip down for the night. The farmer's wife bustled in to ask if one of us would like to sleep in a proper, soft, white bed instead of on the hard floor. Now if I had had a few more years on my back, alarm bells if not bells of anticipation would have rung, but to a nineteen-year old a comfortable night's sleep was all important. I accepted!

The lady opened the double doors of a cupboard in the wall of the kitchen and there on a shelf was a nice, clean, white bed. As bedtime approached I got ready for bed and climbed into the cupboard. I was almost asleep when my hand touched hair, in fact it was a beard! Apparently my benefactor had shoved me in alongside Grandpa! Never one to look a gifthorse in the mouth I turned over and slept the sleep of the just until morning.

Gordon Nursaw:- We were in a house at Best some short distance down the canal was an overhead bridge and beyond this on the left was the Bata Boot Factory. Up until now no looting had taken place as far as I was aware but now many people took boots from the factory, some taking several pairs. The owners complained bitterly and all had to be returned except one pair per person!

The front line was a short distance away, close to which was a huge refrigerated warehouse, blazing fiercely. Some of the lads braved the road to the warehouse and came back with salvaged barrels of butter and sides of bacon; they could easily have been killed, but we did enjoy bacon cooked in butter!

Ernie Clarke:- I always remember Walter Kemsley's concern about the old couple in the house at Vleut. Whilst on holiday in Holland in the 80s, I visited Vleut. It was difficult to identify houses because so many new ones had been built, but I felt I recognised a particular area. There was a man working in a shed, making clogs and I asked him if there was anyone around who could remember the war and an old crippled lady and her deaf husband. He said 'my dad is still alive, and he was here then – I'll call him' and would you believe it – yes, he remembered that old couple, and they had survived for a few more years. I was pleased to able to inform Walter Kemsley of this some years later.

9 Troop C Squadron fraternise with the locals
Two Dutch women wearing Zoot suits borrowed from J. Laurie and Oscar Thomas

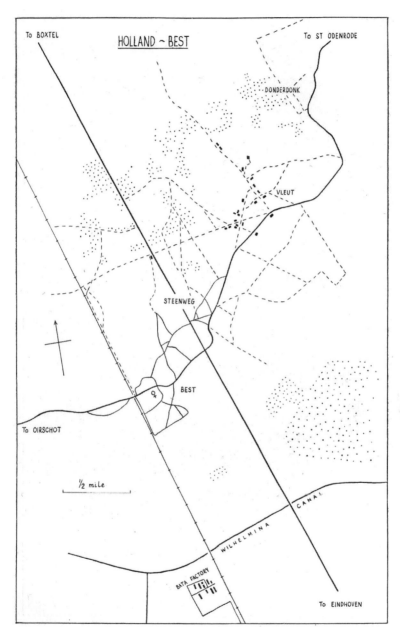

Map 7

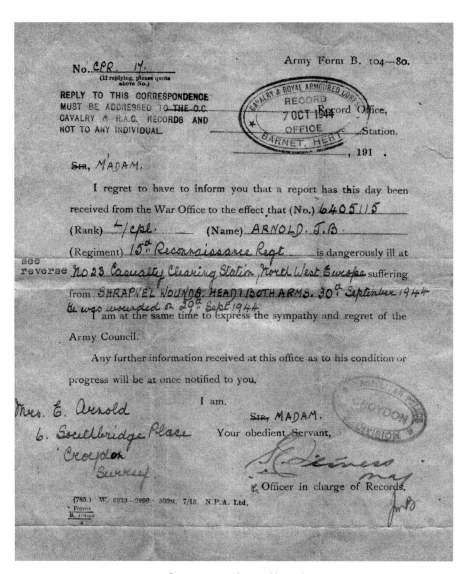

Notification sent to John Arnold's mother

CHAPTER XII

FULL CRY TO TILBURG

Map 8

This is Lieut Peterson's story:

The only B Squadron troop not completely divorced from its vehicles in the woods of Vleut was 5 Troop, so on 24 October it was given the job of heading the advance towards Tilburg in its armoured cars. Orders were received from the colonel, and at two o'clock in the afternoon the troop moved over the Best crossroads, having waited in vain for a wireless report that the leading infantry, the Cameronians, had reached the far side of Best. At the Best railway crossing the reason for their delay was clear; the crossing had been 'lousy' with mines. Our arrival coincided with the removal of what we hoped was the last one, and after a survey on foot the troop crossed safely, led by L/Sgt Grice's car. The Cameronians were left behind.

A few hundreds yards farther on we went round a bend and came upon the first obstacle: large trees lying across the road. It was a harmless obstruction, but one which made it necessary to use cars and tow-chains and machetes to clear a way for the troop. These trees, similar obstacles and mines were the only hindrance on the road to Oirschot. When that town, the halfway mark towards Tilburg, was drawing closer we met a civilian and asked for information. We gathered that about four hundred yards away, round a bend, was a large gun, pointing towards us. The cars were moved a little closer, into covering positions, and a small foot patrol went forward to investigate. A gun there certainly was, but it had long ago fired its last round and it sprawled drunkenly half in a ditch and half out. Probably the civilian had tried to tell us this, and we had not understood.

Just before entering Oirschot we were met by two members of the Dutch Princess Irene Brigade—an odd experience to come across khaki-clad figures on bicycles while leading an advance. It was the first time we had encountered this force, and it was hard to explain on the wireless in code who these friends were. Some people still believe that we met a fighting force of Free Chinese. The Dutch soldiers had crossed the Wilhelmina Canal the previous night and had spent the day exploring, but with nothing 'in the bag'. This meeting gave us added confidence as we probed into

Oirschot. Two patrols made a lightning reconnaissance through the town and met on the far side, beyond the battered church. They reported 'All clear'. The report of the situation wirelessed to Major Gordon, coming up behind us with the remainder of the squadron, was well received; it fairly begged for his order, so often heard—'Push on'. Push on we did. Then with Oirschot well behind us, we ran off our maps, and had to stop. While the troop kept one eye on the ground and the other on the No. 2 Cooker the troop commander returned to Oirschot, where squadron headquarters were surrounded by a milling, cheering, chattering crowd which obscured all but the aerials of the command vehicle. One well remembers the idol of the hour, Major Gordon, a little perplexed (or was it anxiety?), but happy at the turn of events and eager to get on with the job. Capt Boynton, whom everybody knew as Johnny B, was tickled to death by the day's successes and the reception. Even the calm Sgt Sheppard was regarding the situation with obvious enjoyment whenever he could allow his attention to stray from the wireless. Major Gordon made the sacrifice of his own map, and troop commander rejoined troop—giants a little refreshed. The orders were simple and to the point: 'Centre line: Oirschot-Moergestel. Push on, but don't investigate beyond Moergestel.' How annoying to be so restricted! What a cramp on one's style!

The troop was now joined by the carriers of 6 Troop under the command of Sgt 'Brewey' Reeves, and a three-inch mortar and carrier under the command of Cpl Townsend. We pushed on, uneventfully. Surely, we thought, this cannot last; where is the Bosche today? The first sign that he might not be far away was discovered by Sgt Grice when the leading car reached a small wooden bridge beside a watermill. One side of the bridge was badly damaged. It looked as though the enemy had tried to blow up the bridge but had not had time. Or was this a trick to draw us on and prevent heavy support from reaching us? The bridge seemed safe on the near side. What doubts remained were settled when the first car passed safely over. We went on with increased vigilance, and a few minutes later Sgt Grice, going round a left-hand bend, saw Germans moving in a long narrow wood on the left of the road, about 150 yards ahead. Other Germans were moving around a small hut on the far side of the wood. Tpr Simmons pressed the trigger of the Besa. Back over the wireless went the message 'Contact—wait—out'. The fun was on. For once it was very one-sided.

The troop plan to send the carriers round to the left flank and to fire on the wood with the three-inch mortar was never needed. The Germans were completely surprised and in one way or another eliminated. The final 'bag' was eight prisoners and five dead. The first two surrendered quickly, after fire from all the cars along the whole length of the wood. One, quite a boy, was badly wounded, but the other was unhurt and co-operative, an attitude which may have been connected with the pressure of a pistol in his back. He called out to those still in the wood, telling them to surrender. Nothing happened, so the Besas opened fire again. The performance was continued—alternate shouting and shooting—until four more prisoners came out. Then the troop commander and Sgt Baldwin (The Spiv, God bless the Queen) and the cooperative one went into the wood and captured the last two Germans, who, by good providence, gave themselves up instead of firing the loaded machine gun and bazooka which they had. Tpr Simmons, who was never called anything except Simmo, spotted a German cycling furiously away from the wood. The upper part of his body could be seen above the hedge, about 400 yards away. Simmo aimed deliberately and there was a short burst from the Besa. The cyclist shot from his saddle into the bottom of the hedge, dead. Simmo grinned. 'How far do *you* reckon it is?' he said.

We were now under shell and mortar fire which was accurate enough to make it clear that we were being watched, probably from the rising ground beyond the long straight road ahead. We withdrew round the bend and gave a complete report of the situation to squadron headquarters. The light was failing, and as we had gone farther than the infantry could hope to march that evening we were ordered to go back behind the damaged bridge by the mill. The prospect of digging in here for the night was not amusing. We were thankful when the colonel appeared, in good form and with the news that he had insisted on our relief and arranged for infantry to be brought up on the carriers of 2 Troop. What a welcome sight those Jocks were! We abandoned our half-dug slit trenches and went back to Oirschot, a hot meal and sleep. We bedded down in a school. We could have slept on our feet.

Orders for the next day, 25 October, were that Lieut Leppard would lead the advance to Tilburg with 1 and 2 Troops; 3 and 4 Troops, under Lieutenants Jenkins and Gillings, would investigate tracks on the right; 5 and 6 Troops would be in reserve; and Lieut Riesco's troop, lent by C Squadron, would explore the left flank, by the canal. Wednesday's dawn was misty, so misty that Lieut Leppard had to wait for the visibility to improve. After he had left, the command vehicle became an information bureau with liaison officers from the infantry, 6 Guards Armoured Brigade and the Gunners crowding round to listen to the wireless reports of his progress. The going seemed to be good. Headquarters and the reserve troops moved to near the damaged bridge – already repaired by the Royal Engineers so that Churchills could cross. The sun broke through and spirits rose. Lieut Leppard had passed the wood where the one-sided shooting match had taken place on the previous evening, and all was quiet. The troops on the flanks encountered mines, but there were none on the main road. The report of 'Contact' from 1 Troop brought all headquarters to immediate attention.

The troop had gone about two-thirds of the way to Moergestel when an anti-tank gun fired four shots from the left at short range. Visibility was still poor and all the shots missed the leading car, but in reversing it went into a ditch and from that moment was out of action. The crew baled out safely. When Lieut Leppard, leaving the carriers of 2 Troop on the main road as a base, tried to outflank the opposition on the left the soft ground claimed his lumbering Staghound and another car, leaving him only one Humber in action. One well remembers the views of Major Gordon on Staghounds, and his vows about their future.

It was decided at a high level to attack with infantry and the Churchills of 6 Guards Armoured Brigade. Lieut Leppard's depleted force was reinforced by 5 Troop, and the infantry arrived on the tanks, ready for a full-scale sweep from the right flank down on to the anti-tank gun position. But Lieut Leppard had heard sounds of moving tracks, and, although unable to see what had happened in the mist, was convinced that the gun had departed after engaging his troop. We could take a chance on his 'hunch' or allow the delay of an attack which might be against nothing. We decided to take the chance and told the leading Churchills, squadron headquarters and the liaison officer in touch with the Scots Guards. The attack was stopped. Followed by Lieut Leppard in his one car and the carriers of 2 Troop, 5 Troop's cars went down the road towards either an empty gun position or a gun. We passed the ditched car without having even as much as a rifle fired against us, and soon we were in Moergestel, only to find that the bridge over the fast-flowing river had been blown up. Things happened swiftly. The tanks rumbled and jerked their way down the road behind us. Major Gordon, in the highest of spirits and one of his better 'push on' moods, appeared from nowhere, and everyone was thinking 'Now for Tilburg'. It seemed a pretty even bet that the first to cross the river would be the first there. The squadron leader of the Scots Guards threw caution to the winds and ordered a Churchill into the river. It stuck with its rear pointing to the sky. A scissors bridge was called up by wireless, and first across it were 5 and 6 Troops, ordered not to Tilburg but to go through the rest of Moergestel to the right and reconnoitre the bridge at Oisterwijk and if possible, the routes beyond.

The only German seen in Moergestel was a dead one near the junction of the Tilburg and the Oisterwijk roads. He had not been dead long, and was obviously the work of the Resistance. Sgt Grice, in the lead, set a cracking pace. Ahead was a dense wood—not a pleasant prospect. The cars raced through with the drivers pressing hard on the accelerators. There were concrete pillboxes beside the road and we saw figures moving among the trees as we flashed by. But the Germans were surprised; there was no opposition. Breaking out of the wood, we saw the church steeple of Oisterwijk in front, open country on our left, and on our right a long row of houses which gave cover against observation from the right flank. A few hundred yards ahead, where, according to our maps, the river was bridged, large trees were lying across the road, and their leaves and branches blocked our view. Sgt Baldwin and Sgt Grice went forward with their cars and reported that the bridge had fallen into the river. When two carriers went up to try to tow the trees aside a long burst of machine-gun fire from the other side of the river raked the area. A second attempt brought down more intense fire, which included shells. The carriers were withdrawn, and the troop took cover, watching the far side of the river and firing Besas at places which might have been machine-gun nests. The shelling increased. It was obvious that 88 mm guns were being used, and the indications were that the enemy intended to make a stand behind the river.

When we wirelessed back our report, Capt Boynton, who received it, was at first incredulous; he could not believe that we had gone so far in so short a time; he thought that we had given the wrong map reference and must mean a small bridge, passed almost unnoticed, on the outskirts of Moergestel. His delight on being convinced that we were right was good to hear. We were ordered to withdraw out of the shellfire; as we started to go back to the Moergestel side of the wood a shell screamed over the rear of the troop commander's car, landed in the bank about six feet away and covered the vehicle with a shower of earth and stones. On the way back Tpr Simmons was seized violently with diarrhoea, but the wood was no place in which to loiter and even less a place in which to be caught with pants down, so he had to suffer, not in silence, until the cars had settled at the junction of a road and track on the Moergestel side of the wood. He began to scramble from the turret, but a second later fell back into the car, hit in the chest by a sniper's bullet. This chance shot put Simmo out of action until the following March. The troop was the poorer for his absence.

It seemed only a matter of minutes before we saw supporting arms of every kind streaming past us towards Oisterwijk. We received from Major Gordon his famous message, perfectly coded: 'The big Sunray has been here and is highly delighted. I mean the long Sunray, the longest and leanest Sunray of them all. Well done.' Afterwards we heard that, unknown to Major Gordon, the 'long Sunray', Major General Barber, was standing beside the jeep from which the message was transmitted.

While 5 and 6 Troops were in position by the wood other parts of B Squadron and Lieut Riesco's cars were searching for an intact bridge east of Tilburg. At five o'clock Lieut Leppard found one, near Moerenburg, whence it would be possible to attack the main railway bridge over the Wilhelmina Canal. Two more troops were rushed to strengthen the bridgehead. At dusk the enemy realised that the bridge was standing and in British hands, and after using small arms and finding that the bridge was well held the Germans shelled the area heavily. The 9th Cameronians relieved B Squadron at seven o'clock.

On 26 October C Squadron patrolled the Wilhelmina Canal south of Tilburg, meeting 4 Armoured Brigade and reconnoitring the roads, while 46 Brigade dealt with the opposition in the Oisterwijk area, and 44 Brigade prepared to attack Tilburg from the south. The attack opened at half-past eleven on the following morning, and soon after two o'clock the infantry had reached the outskirts of the town. At half-past two the commander of 44 Brigade reported 'sounds of jubilation from the direction of Tilburg'; half an hour later the town was declared liberated. As the infantry advanced cautiously they were seized by jubilant Dutchmen and carried off into the city. That night and the next they were feted as never before.

It was not altogether by chance that the regiment did not move into Tilburg, the city which it had done so much to set free. There were strong rumours that all was not well in the Helmond area, and it was obvious that the division would be unemployed in the west now that Tilburg had fallen. The colonel did not want to leave Oirschot; he thought that the regiment should stay there, concentrating on maintenance. He was over-ruled, however, and on 28 October RHQ, A Echelon and A and B Squadrons were concentrated at Moergestel, and C Squadron at Best.

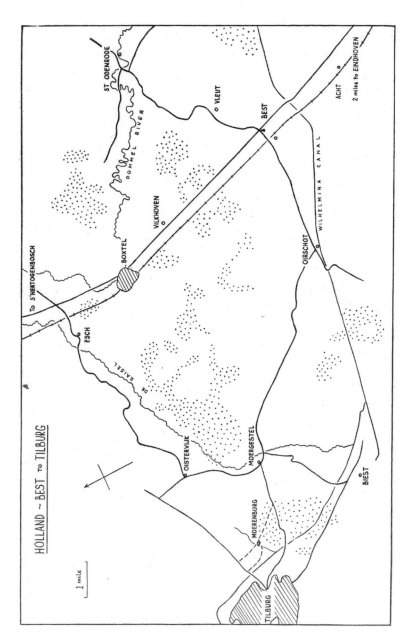

Map 8

B. Squadron reach Oirschot. Lieutenant P.D. Peterson searches prisoners

B. Squadron HQ move into Oirschot

The Scissors Bridge laid at Moergestel by 6 Guards Armoured Brigade

Scissors Bridge Moergestel - fifty years on
Len Watson and Arthur Watkins, September 1995

Liberation of Dirschot. Major Gordon talks to the civilians (Imperial War Museum - B 11272)

Lieut A.E. Gillings Croix de Guerre
Silver Star
Famous sheepskin coat in Bren
carrier

Scissors Bridge, Moergestel - laid by 6 Guards Armoured Brigade
15th Recce were one of the first to cross the bridge

CHAPTER XIII

LIESEL, MEIJEL AND THE PEAT BOGS
Map 9

There was to be no time for the Scottish Division to linger in Tilburg for any ceremony of liberation after the first spontaneous welcome. The Germans had struck suddenly in the bogs south-east of Helmond. Beginning a counter attack across the Deurne Canal between Meijel and Liesel, ten miles from Helmond, on 27 October, a large force of tanks, infantry and artillery had driven back outnumbered units of the 7th US Armored Division and had advanced from Meijel north along the road to Liesel and north-west along the road to Asten. There was anxiety in Helmond. To meet the threat the Scottish Division hurried back from Tilburg on 29 October over the roads it had so recently travelled, through Oirschot and Best. By this time it was reported that the Germans advancing north had enveloped a small American force holding out in Liesel and were within a mile of Deurne, and that the enemy was two miles from Asten on the Asten-Meijel road, to which parts of a British artillery regiment had been rushed. For more than twenty-four hours these British guns had been firing with hardly a pause, breaking up German concentrations and engaging oncoming tanks over open sights. There was no news of the situation between Liesel and Asten. The Scottish Division's infantry battalions went into action as they arrived, and by nightfall on 29 October the division had blocked the routes of the German advances, with 227 Brigade across the Asten-Meijel road south of Heusden, the Lowland Brigade across the Liesel-Asten road west of Liesel, and 46 Brigade astride the Liesel-Deurne road. That night the Americans withdrew through the division's positions. The Germans, in spite of more attacks, could come no farther. Next day the job of pushing them back over the bogs began – a job which was to last more than a fortnight and mean hard fighting in cold, wet, desolate country.

It was country ideal for defence. The peat bogs stretched for miles, flat, lifeless, windswept, rainswept and pockmarked with black pools where shell holes had filled with water. The hulks of destroyed American and German tanks stood out darkly on them. To move across them was to invite the swift attention of the German artillery. The only roads across them were the three forming a triangle between Asten, Liesel and Meijel, and these the Germans mined and shelled. Where the flatness of the bogs was broken, it was by the dense bulk of fir plantations, suited to German infiltration. Somehow— goodness only knows how—the Dutch people had managed to farm some of this bleak land, and the regiment found that one of the few redeeming features of its part in these operation was the chickens and pigs wandering about the deserted, battered farms. Chicken pluckers and pig shavers, professional and amateur, were kept hard at work. Their activities, however, lacked the seal of official approval, and Capt Liddell had an embarrassing five minutes when the divisional commander unexpectedly visited a C Squadron headquarters adorned with five plucked chickens hanging ready for the pot. Fortunately, General Barber had the Nelson touch. After a muttered 'Lot of chickens getting in the road of your carriers,' he drove off in his jeep—without seeing the other two dozen chickens and two pigs ready for cooking at the rear of the house. From its boggy fastness Lieut Kerridge's troop (A Squadron) sent to RHQ by Dingo a pig prepared for the oven adorned with Reconnaissance Corps flashes.

It was in the bogs that the regiment really learned the full value of its carriers, quite apart from the excuse which they provided for dead chickens. On the long runs—the 'swans'—through France and Belgium they had been cursed as a drag and a nuisance; their tracks were so vulnerable to the cobbled streets. In the bog country, where the cars were confined to unpleasant excursions on the shelled, mined roads, the carriers were able to explore the muddy tracks across the peat, and their crews plotted many minefields and pinpointed enemy positions.

After a night in Helmond, where a bomb made a crater twenty feet deep and forty wide in B Squadron lines, but caused only two minor casualties, the regiment was driving south beside the canal before dawn on 30 October. Headquarters were set up in Zomeren. A Squadron, now commanded by Major Ford, patrolled east from Ommel, two miles north of Asten, and the cars reached the Deurne-Liesel road. Two managed to enter Liesel from the north, but both were knocked out by an anti-tank gun in the town. Their crews got away unharmed. B Squadron patrols went south to find out the dispositions and intentions of the 7th US Armored Division on the right, and C Squadron was engaged south and east of Heusden. To protect the right flank of the Glasgow Highlanders a troop of carriers, 10 Troop, commanded by Lieut Michael Morris, kept watch on the edge of a large wood south-west of Liesel. In the afternoon the Germans attacked with infantry and tanks in this area, and tried to outflank the Glasgow Highlanders by infiltrating through the wood. The carrier crews stood firm, although outnumbered and under heavy fire. Cpl A. J. Hartley was killed in a forward post, but Tpr J. Bolton, who was with him, fired his Bren at the advancing German infantry until he had used all his ammunition. Then he used his pistol. When told to withdraw he collected his thirteen empty Bren magazines. He was awarded the Military Medal. So was Tpr William Coburn, who fired a Bren until his magazine was shot away, then, slightly wounded, seized a rifle and continued to engage the enemy. It was not until the Glasgow Highlanders had had time to adjust their positions to meet the threat that Lieut Morris safely withdrew his small force, leaving many German dead. He received the Military Cross.

By the night of 30 October, which R.H.Q. and B Squadron spent at Zomeren, A at Ommel and C at Heusden, what had been a confused situation was clear—thanks partly to the regiment's patrols. Not only was it clear, but under control. The infantry were within a quarter of a mile of Liesel on the north and west, and next day the 7th Seaforth occupied that small, stricken town, and the 6th King's Own Scottish Borderers passed through and cleared Slot.

B Squadron again went to the south of the division's front, protecting the right flank of 227 Brigade and maintaining liaison with the Americans. The dominating position on this flank was a school, from which the boundary between the two divisions could be kept under observation. The B Squadron troop ordered to occupy this position found it strongly held by the enemy. The Americans were not prepared to occupy the school themselves, although it was just inside their area, but they were ready with help for the troop in the shape of two self-propelled guns, which fired at the buildings at a range of 200 yards. The troop mopped up as the Germans fled. Prisoners stated that their party had numbered twenty-two, of whom thirteen were killed and seven captured. They belonged to the 6th Para Lehr Regt Hermann. First B Squadron, then A Squadron, kept the school constantly manned, using it as an observation post and as a base for foot patrols into no man's land—patrols which preceded a successful attack on an important feature by the Argyll and Sutherland Highlanders. The school's value as a look-out was proved when watchers saw a Panther tank on the move and called for artillery fire; after a 'stonk' by medium guns the Panther was not seen moving again. Later the same day the school was bombarded by nebelwerfers—rocket mortars—and self-propelled guns. The division's artillery would not reply, because the German guns were outside the division's boundary, so off went Major MacDiarmid to seek the help of the Americans. Sure, they were willing to help, delighted to help. How many guns did he want? They brought a large concentration of heavy guns into action. They were enough.

Meanwhile the advance down the road from Liesel to Meijel continued slowly with hard fighting, in which the infantry were supported by tanks of 6 Guards Armoured Brigade and patrols from C and B Squadrons. Some of the patrols which the regiment supplied were officer liaison patrols with infantry battalions. These gave the battalion commander an up-to-date summary of the situation on his flanks, as well as affording an extra link with his brigade headquarters and with his forward companies when armoured cars were working with them. One battalion commander issued an urgent set of orders to his companies by this means after his own communications had broken down.

The armoured cars advancing down the Liesel-Meijel road were nearly always under fire, partly from 75 mm guns on the east bank of the Deurne canal.

From Heusden C Squadron patrolled down the Asten-Meijel road, which was mined and cratered, and Sgt P. R. Dobson has written of the 9 Troop patrol on which Lieut Royle and an RE officer measured a large crater under shell fire:

The road to Meijel was suicide. Everybody knew that. It was dead straight for the first mile beyond the infantry positions. Then it bent slightly to the right, and continued straight for another mile, finally disappearing into some trees just outside the village. It ran across open peat bogs and marshes and was banked up several feet above ground level. We could read all that from the map, and when we came into the open to the first stretch it was no better than we expected. We were hoping to meet a crater, and eventually we did, but not until we were within a couple of hundred yards of the village. By then we had already pulled three strings of Teller mines off the road, and we had seen many Germans milling about in a wood a thousand yards behind and to the right of us. But if they had been able to get across the marsh they would not have attempted it; they were far too busy with someone else. In addition to the leading patrol we had Lieut Royle in his heavy car and an RE officer in a Morrisette. It was obvious that we could not pass the crater so we turned the cars while the two officers went up and gathered information about it. Then, after we had done all this and sent the information back, a sniper fired from the left. He was a bad sniper, for he completely missed four of us standing in a bunch, but when his big brothers joined in they showed him a thing or two. They evidently had four 88s in the village, and, although firing indirectly, had the road pinpointed all the way. The Morrisette was at a farmhouse half a mile away, while the second heavy car was at another four hundred yards behind us. As I dived into my car I saw that the RE officer had been hit, but he managed to jump on Lofty Dullaway's car, and I held my door open for Lieut Royle, who was in the ditch. I thought he would get on the other car, so we started off, passing the second heavy, and stopped at the farm, where we put the wounded officer on the Morrisette. We had been followed all the way by shell fire, and while turning the Engineer's car—a tricky operation because of the thickly mined verges—Lofty was hit in the leg. Then we discovered that Lieut Royle had not been on either car. L/Cpl Songhurst started to move up to find him, but was immediately pinpointed, and Bill Thomas had to do a very hasty and tricky bit of backing. Finally we got the three cars together at the farmhouse, and were just arranging for a party to go up to the crater on foot when a familiar voice hailed us from the ditch. It was Lieut Royle, safe, sound and soaking; he had crawled about six hundred yards to us. I never knew why he did not come back on the cars, but I strongly suspect that he stayed to locate the guns that were firing at us. For that action alone he deserved the MC which he was awarded soon after.

On 5 November B Squadron took up positions in the bogs facing the Deurne Canal on the division's left flank, becoming part of the flank protection which 46 Brigade was providing for the attack on Meijel that day. The attack, preceded by a tremendous barrage by British guns, was not successful. The ground was waterlogged and mined, and one after another the Grenadier Guards' tanks advancing with the infantry were bogged or blown up or hit by shells from the 88 mm guns which commanded the open approaches to the town. The division's gunners laid a thick smoke screen to help the crews of twenty-three bogged tanks to reach safety. The attack was called off.

For the next fortnight the regiment had one squadron watching the left flank in the bogs between Liesel and the Deurne Canal; one squadron in reserve at Heusden, and at first keeping a patrol in the school on the southern boundary; and one squadron resting in Helmond, which everybody regarded as home. The squadrons were switched every two days. Two days in the bog were not long enough to be a great strain, and at Heusden there were comfortable billets in the school. C Squadron especially will always remember the kindness of the Head Master's family who lived in the house next to the school. His wife was 'Mutter' to everyone.

On 9 November XII Corps, consisting of the 49th, 51st and 53rd Infantry Divisions, 4 Armoured Brigade and, later, the 7th Armoured Division, relieved the Americans on the right of the Scottish Division in readiness for the winter attack eastward to the banks of the Maas.

On the night of 11 November an infantry patrol reported that there was no sign of the enemy in Meijel, and this news was confirmed by an officer and private of the King's Own Scottish Borderers, who hid in the town all day on 12 November. On 14 November the infantry moved into Meijel, a town of gaping walls and roofs, a town so mined and booby-trapped that it was a danger to the incautious for weeks afterwards.

The regiment's experiences around Liesel and Meijel and Heusden had shown that for reconnaissance in this type of country a geological survey map was required. This type of map had proved invaluable in selecting training areas in the United Kingdom; peat is impassable to all kinds of vehicles. The only solution appeared to be to find such a map. Colonel Smith despatched an officer patrol with strict instructions not to return without one. The patrol consisted of the intelligence officer, Lieut Isaac, and Jean Wahl, the Free French liaison officer who lived and worked with the regiment for most of the campaign. They found a map in Tilburg. The vital information was extracted and reproduced on 1/25,000 maps; it proved an invaluable guide in the advance to the Maas.

The regiment's losses in the fighting to drive the Germans back beyond Meijel had included the deaths of Cpl F. C. L. Eaton, L/Cpl F. Behling, Tpr E. W. Taylor, Tpr H. W. Greig and Tpr G. H. Thompson.

Major C. R. T. Dove joined the regiment from the 161st Reconnaissance Regiment (Green Howards), and took command of Headquarter Squadron.

Wilkie Wilkinson:-   A member of 10 Troop C Squadron.
We were holding our own against a counter attack. We were dropping them like ducks, for an hour and a half we were holding them. Then he turned nasty and let four Mark 4 tanks loose. Two engaged the carriers with AP and HE, they missed us. The other two engaged the positions with HE and shrapnel wounding Sgt Royce and hitting Tpr Gurney in the eye and face, Cpl Hartley getting it in the back and lungs.

Lieut Bryan White:- Cpl Hartley was killed, Tpr Gurney lost an eye, one MC and two MMs were awarded and Sgt Royce who commanded the carrier section and all the men involved that day can be proud of their performance.

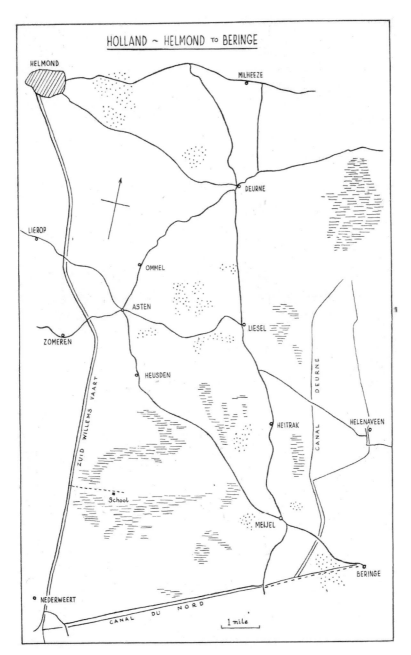

Map 9

Captured anti-tank gun
Oscar Thomas is wearing the German helmet

Officers of B Squadron - Holland 10 November 1944
Standing L to R: Lt D. Peterson 2i/c 7 Troop; Lt R. Fleet o/c 7 Troop; Lt M. Leppard o/c 5 Troop;
Lt J. Davies o/c 8 Troop; Lt G. Paton, Sqd HQ
Seated L to R: Lt K. Jenkins o/c 6 Troop; Capt J. Boynton Sqd 2i/c; Maj A. Gordon Sqd Commder;
Lt A. Gillings 2i/c 6 Troop; Lt W. Falloon 2i/c 5 Troop

CHAPTER XIV

THROUGH MUD TO THE MAAS

Map 10

The 15th Scottish Division's part in the clearing of the Germans from the country between the Deurne Canal and the River Maas was a battle against rearguards, mines, craters, demolitions and, surpassing all else, mud—November mud which clogged and clung or squelched and oozed, and spread so wide and lay so deep that it soon obliterated the poor tracks which were the division's only eastward roads. These were strewn with bogged vehicles, and units found that a sea of mud could split them almost as effectively as a sea of water, in spite of the Royal Engineers' valiant efforts to keep the way open with Corduroy track. For the regiment this advance was chiefly the story of C Squadron and the Weasels. Just as B Squadron had its glorious hour on the roads to Tilburg, so with C Squadron on the quagmire to Sevenum and beyond. The Weasels, light, unarmoured and broad of track, were the only vehicles which could be guaranteed to cross the mud. The colonel had had the foresight to obtain some through VIII Corps; it was not long before they were being sought by every unit in the division, and it was only with difficulty that enough were retained to keep C Squadron supplied.

The division, the right flank of VIII Corps, was given two routes east from the Deurne Canal. One, called Skye, ran from Meijel through Beringe to Sevenum, and was 227 Brigade's; the other, called Ayr, ran from Liesel to Sevenum through Helenaveen, and was 46 Brigade's. In the north the 11th Armoured Division and the 3rd British Division were advancing; in the south XII Corps. The XII Corps attack across the canal on the right had already caused the enemy to start withdrawing from the Scottish Division's front by 20 November, when the division's advance began. The 51st Highland Division had reached the Meijel-Venlo road at Beringe, Panningen and Helden, and farther north A Squadron patrols had crossed the bogs east of Liesel to the Deurne Canal on 19 November and Lieut Dalton had swum across the cold canal without finding any Germans. That evening C Squadron relieved the Royal Scots Fusiliers in part of the line near Meijel and lost two vehicles, but no men, on mines.

The advance of 227 Brigade towards Sevenum on 20 November was reconnoitred by B Squadron, which, having a troop from C Squadron under command, also patrolled ahead of the Lowland Brigade, pushing north to Helenaveen from Beringe. The patrols to the north reached the outskirts of

Helenaveen by noon, and met enemy and mines in the woods south of the village. They handed over to the Royal Scots Fusiliers. The patrols to the east soon discovered the dreadful truth: that the division's way to Sevenum was little more than a track across the peat bog. They sent back a route report, kept the infantry supplied with warnings about mines and craters, and had brushes with the enemy on the route and the right flank.

On one of B Squadron's patrols Tpr K. Gaskill, in the leading car of Lieut Gillings's troop, was firing at six Germans when his face was grazed by a shot which pierced the turret, having been fired at point-blank range. It had come from two more Germans, in a slit trench. Gaskill was only five feet four inches tall, and from his seat in the turret he could not point his gun down enough to engage his attackers, so he stood, with blood streaming down his face, and shot them. He had already hit four of the six other Germans.

That day B Squadron lost Lieut Martin Leppard, wounded while leading his men on the way to Sevenum. About three or four miles from that town they came upon an enemy outpost and engaged it and took two prisoners, although under machine-gun fire from the left flank. Unable to outflank the main German position with his cars because of the peat on either side of the track, Lieut Leppard called up a section of the assault troop and took it forward on foot. Two more outposts were forced to surrender and prisoners were sent back to the cars, but on nearing the main position the section came under accurate machine-gun and rifle fire, and Lieut Leppard was hit in the leg while helping another man who had been wounded. Lieut Leppard crawled forward again, but his small force was not strong enough to overcome the opposition, so he withdrew it to a position from which he was able to give covering fire for an infantry attack. He was awarded the Military Cross.

On 21 November C Squadron took over from B Squadron the task of reconnoitring in front of 227 Brigade on Skye, while in the north, Helenaveen being captured in the morning, A Squadron patrolled Ayr. It was a day of biting wind and driving rain, under which the mud spread and deepened. On both routes the patrols met rearguards, mines and demolitions. At night A Squadron was able to return to Liesel, but, because of the mud on Skye behind it, C Squadron, having reached a demolished bridge at Achterste Steeg, had to spend a cold, damp night in the open, halfway between Sevenum and the regiment's base at Beringe. The first party had just returned from the newly begun short leave in Brussels, and the wonders and luxuries of hotel life there were described that night to a C Squadron group huddled among frogs at the bottom of a dried-up well, into which the rain dripped through an improvised roof. At dawn the squadron, chilled and stiff, was heading for Sevenum again. A scissors bridge was placed across the gap at Achterste Steeg, and by ten o'clock Sevenum had been entered by Lieut Royle's troop, explored and reported clear of Germans but not of demolitions and mines. The church tower had tumbled across the street: that same church tower which the British higher command had spared, wishing to do as little damage as possible, in spite of its use by the enemy as an observation post and the consequent requests by the commander of 227 Brigade that it should be attacked by Typhoons. North of Sevenum were mines and craters, and opposition at the railway station, but C Squadron's patrols pushed on; by four in the afternoon Lieut David Richford had reported that the enemy had gone from Horst, three miles to the north. Two villages were also reported clear. Meanwhile the rest of the squadron's vehicles had been pushed and towed and dragged and driven through the mire from the previous night's harbour to Sevenum, where the squadron spent the night with the Gordons, who had struggled through the mud of Skye on foot. In the north A Squadron had patrolled along the Helmond-Venlo railway from Deurne towards the village of Amerika.

The corps commander sent this message to the divisional commander: 'Gen Barber from Gen O'Connor. Many congratulations on magnificent work carried out by all your troops and particularly your Recce Regt and Engineers in today's appalling weather. Very well done.'

The good-natured face of Cpl Ridge, the colonel's driver and wireless operator, wore a slightly puckered look these days as he contemplated the muddy misadventures which must be endured so that the colonel could visit his forward troops from Beringe— misadventures such as these:

Going to visit C Squadron, we put the jeep into four-wheel drive and low-ratio bottom gear, and started to plough our way through. We passed many bogged vehicles, but we got through to squadron headquarters in Sevenum. We left again about three o'clock, and on the way back we were stonked by mortars; as we were the only car on the road at the time it looked as though someone was out to get us before we got back to RHQ. However, Colonel Smith decided to push on. After going about two miles we came again to the sea of mud; by this time the wheeled track and the tank track were pretty much the same—both pretty deadly. We were almost brought to a stop by the mud, so I suggested we should change to the tank track, which seemed at that point to be better than the one we were on. So we tried the tank track. We had gone about twenty yards when the jeep sank up to its axles. Of course, the colonel was very pleased, but, after all, anybody can be wrong. I dug, but the mud came back as fast as I dug it away. A carrier from an infantry battalion came along, and towed us out. Off we went again, with the jeep doing its best and me praying that it would keep going. It sank again. I got out, shovel in hand, spirits low. Then we saw one of C Squadron's Weasels going merrily along about a hundred yards ahead and the same way as we had been. We shouted and I went after it. I was wearing gum boots and they kept sticking in the mud, and I was not making much headway. But the Weasel stopped to tow Major Gordon's car, which was well bogged, and after he had been rescued we were pulled out. Next day we gave up the jeep for a Weasel. I could not drive it, so Major Gordon drove and I rode in the back with the colonel and the wireless set and batteries. We were doing fine until we hit a terrific bump. The colonel and I were thrown into the air and fell in a heap in the back; the wireless set came off its mounting, and the batteries were all over the floor. After some comments on Major Gordon's driving by Colonel Smith, we continued to Horst, where C Squadron was. On arrival we found we were minus one complete spring, but as usual we eventually got back to RHQ—after a rather bumpy journey.

On 23 November the divisional commander wanted reports on Kastenraij, Tienraij, Brock and the woods south of Brock, all in the sodden country near the Maas, so it was a dawn start for C Squadron's patrols again and another hard day in the driving rain. Soon the wireless at squadron headquarters, manned with unfailing cheerfulness by Sgt Dutch, was telling the same sort of story as it had on the previous two days. 'Hello Able one. Road block consisting of ten felled trees with mined verges at road junction ....' 'Hello Able two. Mines at track junction .... Bridge blown at ....' 'Hello Able three. Track impassable at .... owing to flooding of dyke. Entrance to track at .... cratered and mined.' From Lieut Royle came 'Hello Able one. Contact at figures .... Wait. Out.' Then, a few minutes later, 'Hello Able one. Jerries took refuge in a hen coop. I fired a few rounds of 37 millie but all I can see is a mass of chickens and feathers.' All the tasks were achieved. Kastenraij, which had been an objective of the 3rd British Division, was reported clear soon after noon, and the infantry of that division were able to march in unopposed. They were surprised to find C Squadron already there. Brock and its woods were reported clear about the same time. Sgt Dobson shall tell of the journey towards Tienraij:

The road junction outside Horst, where we intended to turn right to Tienraij, was completely blocked by fallen trees. After a circuit of two or three miles over rough tracks and fields, we again reached the main road, and found a track on the other side leading to our objective. Owing to the possibility of mines, the three commanders, Lieut Royle, Sgt Dullaway and myself, took turns to walk in front of the cars. Reaching a junction where there were several scattered farms, and where we hoped to turn back to the main road, I saw that Lieut Royle, who had been walking in front, was surrounded by excited Dutch people. When I got there a voice yelled 'Hey bud, come here and let me shake your hand.' It was an American airman who had been living among the Germans for three months as a deaf mute. The heroine of the day was a young and beautiful Dutch girl who had rescued him and prevented the Germans from discovering his secret.

The main road was blocked by a blown bridge, so we continued along our track. After we had gone about a mile across open ground a Spandau opened fire from a large wood six hundred yards away on our right. Behind it was Tienraij. The Germans had held their fire until the first car had gone up to Lieut Royle, who had been about four hundred yards ahead, and it seemed that they had been trying to draw us into something heavy. But nothing heavy opened up. We returned the fire, and turned the cars round behind some haystacks. After staying there some time we were ordered to withdraw.

Dusk was approaching, and we had about a mile of open ground to cross before we reached the cover of the farm houses. I went about four hundred yards in my light car while the other two gave cover with their fire. Lieut Royle had ordered us to turn all our firepower on to the wood, and, such an order being a rare one, we took full advantage of it. My gunner, Tpr Jones, did wonders with the Bren, even while we were moving. As soon as we stopped the next car moved; always we had one moving and two firing. As we approached cover I grabbed the spare Bren, anxious to join in. By a miracle I avoided decapitating an inquisitive Dutchman who ran right in front of the gun as I stood on my seat, firing from the hip. My driver, the one and only 'Oscar' Thomas, loath to leave the scene without 'having a go' himself, was finally persuaded to 'snake' round the corner, and we watched the heavies come round in turn, each stopping to send a final shell into the wood.

On the way back we picked up the American and his rescuer. Mr Royle gallantly carried her through the mud to my car amid the cheers of the villagers. After picking up three quite willing prisoners from a nearby farm, we returned to Horst. I had a very interesting conversation with the Dutch girl on the way back, and learned much about the German soldier.

As a result of C Squadron's work in the rain that day much was known about the narrowing strip of flat, hedgeless, brown fields and dark woods left to the Germans on the west bank of the Maas. The squadron's patrols were out again on 24 November, hampered now by flooded and collapsing roads, and 9 Troop, going again towards Tienraij, found that Germans had advanced their standing patrols by about a thousand yards in the night. Capt Lane, who had become the squadron's rear link officer and was soon to join the instructing staff at Sandhurst, was sent to investigate a large dyke, which he waded conscientiously, through thick mud and almost freezing water, to reach the far bank. There he met his driver, L/Cpl Wiseman, pardonably self-satisfied at having crossed dry by a footbridge discovered just round the corner.

On 25 November 227 Brigade resumed the advance to the river, and C Squadron, being still the only one on the Sevenum side of Skye's obstructing mud, again led the way. This time white flags hung from the church and other buildings of Tienraij; the Germans had withdrawn to the outskirts of Swolgen, a mile farther on, where the patrol contained them until the Gordons came up with the tanks of 6 Guards Armoured Brigade. Lieut David Richford, who had succeeded to Lieut Gray's command when Lieut Gray became captain and joined the RHQ staff, took his cars to the outskirts of Broekhuizervorst on the banks of the river. The enemy was strong here. Sgt Millroy's light car, in the lead, came under fire from a house, and a bazooka narrowly missed the rear wheels. Backing, the car went into a ditch. 'Bale out' said Lieut Richford on the wireless. 'Bale out be ....' said the old cavalryman, 'I've got a thousand fags in here and they're not for the bloody Jerries.' So he laid smoke, and under its cover another car dashed up and fixed a tow rope to the one in the ditch while Sgt Millroy himself ran up to the house from which the fire was coming and pitched grenades through a window. Another position he attacked with his Bren, and the patrol supported infantry storming the strongpoint. Sgt Millroy received an immediate award of the Distinguished Conduct Medal.

The buoyant Lieut Johnny Bosch took his carriers along the Tienraij-Venlo railway, and his comments on his difficulties—in the manner of the raconteur born—made it quite clear that had he been in command of a flotilla of motor torpedo boats instead of a troop of carriers far more would have been achieved.

Back to the river the German rearguards were being pressed, fighting their delaying actions with undoubted skill under conditions which favoured them. In the north the infantry of the 11th Armoured Division, floundering across swamp and bog, had found C Squadron already in front of them at Horst. In the south the 49th Division had come to a halt only at the gates of Blerick, the German riverside stronghold opposite Venlo, and, having got thus far, was able to allow the Scottish Division to use the good road through Maasbree to reach Sevenum and Horst from Beringe. So, at last, it was 'Goodbye' to the mud of Skye, and no tears of farewell. The rest of the regiment moved up: RHQ and A Echelon to a farm at Voorste-Steeg, B Squadron to another at Ulfterhoek, between Sevenum and Horst, and A Squadron into Horst. These Dutch farms were invariably one great building, with house and byre and barn all under the same roof. Their floors were always littered with children. Always the crucifix looked down from their walls. In the field opposite the farmhouse which sheltered RHQ there was much digging, and from out of the earth the farm people brought a long red lorry, which had been buried throughout the German occupation.

There was work for both C and A Squadrons on 26 November, when the division continued to close up to the bank of the Maas. Still leading 227 Brigade, C Squadron troops gained their objectives at Wanssum and Blitterswijk by 10.30 and stayed there until the Highland Light Infantry took over the positions at noon. Another troop, with the Glasgow Highlanders, found that there was still strong opposition in the area of Broekhuizervorst. A Squadron led 46 Brigade, whose task was to clear eastward from Horst towards Grubbenvorst and Houthuizen. The woods east of the railway were extensively mined, and the tracks difficult. As the river was approached the opposition stiffened at points where the Germans were still using ferries. Lieut N. R. Kenneford was killed. He was in command of carriers which were sent with Lieut Dalton's cars to seize and hold the village of Grubbenvorst. Lieut Dalton has described what happened:

We decided to enter Grubbenvorst in a pincer movement, the carriers going to the left and the cars to the right. The progress of both troops was slow owing to large craters. Lieut Kenneford said on the wireless that he was on the outskirts of Grubbenvorst and was taking in a foot patrol. Sgt Kirman's car patrol was now with the carriers, but was held up because the railway crossing had been blown up. There were mines on the other side of the crossing. The cars gave covering fire to the foot patrol until it was out of sight.

Lieut Kenneford reported on the wireless that the village was clear, and I told him to take up defensive positions, saying that we were coming in to strengthen him. In the meantime I had met a patrol from another reconnaissance regiment, which stated that it had been in Grubbenvorst and that 'trigger-happy' Germans still held the village. However, the carriers were in, so we started to join them, taking the same route—a muddy track which gave the cars no end of trouble.

We came within sight of the carriers while we were going along a narrow track with a fence on the left and a drop of three or four feet on the right. Sgt Kirman's car, leading, became bogged, and as the stationary troop presented an ideal target I reversed my car—the last one—to ease the congestion, but we only complicated matters by bogging ourselves with a list forty-five degrees. Sgt Craig, however, had squeezed his vehicle between the fence and Sgt Kirman's and was moving into the village. Then, suspicious, he halted.

Pandemonium began. Germans appeared, firing in all directions. Sgt Craig's vehicle caught fire, and as he was withdrawing to extinguish the flames his gunner, Cpl Dawson, was helping Sgt Kirman to hold off a bayonet charge by about a dozen fanatical Germans who had taken us by surprise from the rear. At the same time the carrier sections were engaging snipers in the village. Next we got a packet of 'whining Winnies', and the situation had become so chaotic that I ordered everybody to withdraw as best he could.

When the last car, Sgt Kirman's, was about to withdraw he saw Tpr Prendergast running beside a hedge. Prendergast told him that two carriers were still in the village, their crews pinned by sniper fire. Sgt Kirman blazed away at the snipers while the carriers got out. I jumped on one of them, my bogged vehicle having to be abandoned.

We withdrew behind a wood, where a roll call showed that three were missing— Lieut Kenneford, Sgt Daurnhime and Cpl Trimnell. Soon afterwards Cpl Trimnell appeared with the news that Lieut Kenneford had been killed by a sniper while taping off mines. He knew nothing of the whereabouts of Sgt Daurnhime.

Later in the day I went into Grubbenvorst with a company of infantry, and found Sgt Daurnhime wounded but in good care at a convent.

Lieut Kenneford's death robbed us all of a friend.

Wounded in the arm, and with his eardrum perforated by the explosion of a mine, Sgt Donald Daurnhime had fought on in the village, and his courage and devotion to duty were rewarded with the Military Medal.

By nightfall on 26 November a few ferry sites were all that remained to the Germans west of the Maas on the division's front. They were left to the infantry.

A little to the south the German paratroopers, penned in Blerick with their backs to the river, looked out on the 49th Division from behind minefields, a thick belt of barbed wire and a formidable anti-tank ditch. On 29 November the Scottish Division, relieving the 49th, was given the task of capturing Blerick. The attack—it was called Operation Guildford—was made on 3 December by the Lowland Brigade and directed by its new commander, Brigadier H. C. H. T. Cumming-Bruce, DSO. On the night of 2 December the Glasgow Highlanders made a great to-do north of the town, in the riverside strip of woods and fields where B Squadron had taken up positions on 29 November to protect the left flank. Gramophone records of tanks forming up were played; the defenders of Blerick were deceived. They expected attack from the north. Instead, after four hundred guns had fired into the town for two hours next morning, the mine-clearing flails, the portable bridges, the flame throwers and the mortar projectors of a Churchill tank breaching force swept across the open country from the west. Behind them the magnificent Lowland infantry rode into the assault on Kangaroos (Ram tanks without turrets). By four o'clock in the afternoon Blerick had fallen. C Squadron, manning six lanes, controlled the traffic going into the assault as the same squadron had done in training on the Yorkshire Wolds. The flow of vehicles over the muddy approaches was smooth, and General Barber congratulated the squadron. To the regret of everybody in the regiment, its genial medical officer, Capt Watson, broke his massive jaw when his car went over a mine in this attack. He was succeeded by Capt J. Orr, RAMC, who was to win a similarly high place in the regiment's esteem.

It was at the end of November that Sir Richard O'Connor relinquished command of VIII Corps, and the regiment felt that it was parting from an old friend. But his successor, Lieut General Evelyn Barker, CB, CBE, DSO, MC, who left the 49th Division, was also an old friend. B and C Squadrons had known him as their divisional commander in the old days of the 54th Division, and his camp commandant, Major 'Pippin' Cox, was even better known as the former quartermaster of the old 54th Reconnaissance Battalion.

Details of Sgt Millroy's DCM appeared in the *London Gazette* on 1 March 1945.—

North West Europe. When operating in the area of the River Maas on November 26th, he was the Commander of the leading car in a patrol sent towards the river near Swolgen. On approaching some farm buildings east of Swolgen the car was damaged by fire from machine-guns and bazookas. Although his car was out of action, Sgt Millroy remained in it and engaged the enemy with his Bren gun until all the opposing positions were located. Ascertaining that there were two enemy positions covering the road, Sgt Millroy, with total disregard for his own safety, then dismounted from his car and under a hail of fire rushed one of the enemy positions, destroying it with three grenades. He then returned to his car, took his Bren gun and advanced on foot to engage the second enemy position. This he did with such good effect that an infantry platoon which was following up the patrol was able to get round behind the position and capture those holding it without suffering any casualties.

Trp L Thomas (Oscar)

Lieut David Richford's Humber, C Squadron, 1600 hrs 22 November 1944 - Horst

23 November, Horst

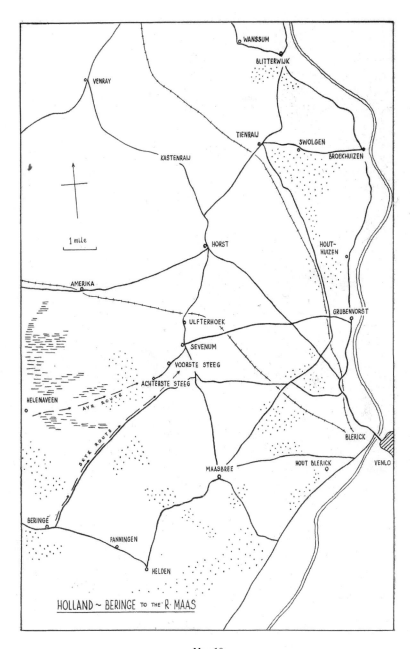

Map 10

CHAPTER XV

ANNA HOEVE AND HOUT BLERICK
Map 11

Go east out of Sevenum, being careful how you drive round the sharp corners when you leave the centre of that small town. Cross the railway line and go on between the straggling farms until you come to the wide main road which runs south to Blerick, parallel with the Maas. Turn right here, and drive a short way towards Blerick. Then turn right again, this time on to a track between fields without fence or hedge. (You may have to do some adroit steering along here: there used to be a soft patch.) Turn left and bump along another track towards Blerick again. Soon you will come to Anna Hoeve. The country is flat, this country beside the Maas, and if it is winter you will find it dreary. Just beyond the long bulk of Anna Hoeve, and on the far side of the Blerick road, the sombre woods seem to be frowning at you. On the farms the few buildings rise, austerely angular, from the winter drabness of the level, hedgeless fields. Such a farm is Anna Hoeve. Until 22 December it was the headquarters of the three reconnaissance squadrons in turn as, week about and under brigade command, they guarded a long stretch of the Maas while the rest of the regiment was out of action.

It was really too long a front to be guarded adequately by one squadron. It stretched from just south of Grubbenvorst to just north of Blerick, and it was a good half-an-hour's walk from the northernmost troop headquarters—a wooden bungalow in a clearing—to the southernmost—a house just off the Blerick road, beyond the broad stream which the Royal Engineers had bridged and the railway bridge which the retreating Germans had reduced to lumps of masonry. And walk it was in the day time, at least along that part of the main road where vehicles could easily be seen by the enemy watching from Venlo. A railway—the one whose bridge had collapsed—runs roughly parallel with the road and the river, between them. To reach the Maas from Anna Hoeve you must cross fields, then the main road, then open scrubby country, then the railway, a strip of meadow, a tongue of wood and another road, which runs beside the river. Down towards Blerick the main road and the railway run side by side. From slit trenches, from the houses at the southern tip of the tongue of wood, from the house perched above the railway cutting, the squadron look-outs spied all day on the Germans across the 150 yards of water, and watched the distant white vertical trails which showed where rockets were being fired at Antwerp. The Germans looked out from similar hiding places on the other side. Sometimes their shells shrieked over, ripping into the woods. Sometimes, on cloudy days, their new jet fighters swooped over, streaking ahead of their sound, too fast for the Bofors gunners who were staying at squadron headquarters. Nights were tense. Look-outs were replaced by listening posts close to the river. Ears were strained for the sound of a German patrol coming across by boat; eyes peered into the darkness until familiar bushes became crouching men. It was not the policy to cross to the German side, but the German patrols crossed frequently at night and slipped easily through the thin screen of outposts. Capt Kemsley, Sgt Sheppard, Cpl Russell and Cpl Stevenson, looking for a fault in the field telephone line down the Blerick road one night, found a cut in the cable that was obviously intentional: the patrol had even crossed the main road and gone into the woods to the west to bazooka vehicles of the Middlesex Regiment parked at a farm not far south of Anna Hoeve. The C Squadron troop nearest Blerick found a German outpost of one man on the west bank of the river. His relief was overdue, and he was a not unwilling prisoner.

In the early part of the time on the Maas it was impossible to drive all the way down the Blerick road because the stream south of Anna Hoeve had not yet been given a bridge to replace the one which the Germans had destroyed. It was at this time that a Dutch man arrived one night at an A Squadron post, saying that his wife was about to give birth to a baby somewhere on the bank of the Maas. So Lieut Ray Parker set out with a small party on the midwifery expedition which he describes:

The Dutchman had arrived at Dalton's troop position just north of mine. Dalton passed him over to me, and it was arranged that an ambulance should come down behind the wood which was my troop location. The ambulance arrived with Sgt James, the squadron signals sergeant, and we set out on foot—Sgt James, Sgt Williams, the Dutchman and myself. We took a stretcher with us.

The Dutchman could not speak a word of English, and I was suspicious. As we went along in single file I had my hand not far from my pistol—if it were a trap, he was certainly going first. We clambered over the tree thrown over the stream, scrambled over the wreck of the railway embankment and went along a very quiet path to a silent battered farmhouse within fifty yards of the Maas. Still suspicious, I left Sgt Williams outside with his Tommy gun while I followed the Dutchman into the house. The only habitable place was the cellar, and there, sure enough, was the woman, lying on filthy bed linen.

Much relieved, I called the whole party in, and the patient, thinking no doubt that I was the doctor, promptly displayed the affected parts. I felt bound to attempt to judge how long we had. There were obvious signs of an approaching birth, but I felt that we had at least an hour, so I decided to carry her back.

It was a frightful job to get her up the stairs. They were too narrow for us to bring her up on the stretcher, and she had to walk with what help we could give. Once on level ground she rode safely on the stretcher, making so much noise that if a German patrol had been about we would have been even more unhappy. However, things went well until we reached the blown railway embankment. It was hard enough to get her over the rubble, but the main difficulty was the stream. We could not carry her across the tree on the stretcher, so there was nothing left but to let her more or less walk over. One of the sergeants crossed first and held the tree steady on that side and the other sergeant held it on the other side while I went over with the woman clinging to me as best she could. And how heavy a pregnant woman is!

Once across the stream it was plain sailing—on to the ambulance and off to hospital. The baby was born about two hours later.

The days and nights on the Maas were a busy time for the regiment's signallers. Field telephone lines had to be laid alongside track and wood and road to connect all the posts with the switchboard manned night and day in the front room of Anna Hoeve, from which other lines went back to brigade headquarters in Sevenum and north to whichever battalion of the 3rd British Division was in Grubbenvorst. At any time of the day, along the Blerick road or on either side of it, you might have come across a small party, perhaps with jeep, perhaps without, but certainly with drums of cable, 'Don Five', borrowed ladder, pliers and spades, working under the direction of one of the three squadron signals sergeants—James, Sheppard and Dutch—or Capt Kemsley, Sgt Davidson or Cpl Stevenson from RHQ. The work was made harder by the fact that the regiment's official equipment, bristling with wireless, contained little for line communication—five field telephones, to be exact. However, past scroungings and current borrowings provided enough equipment to make the improvisation of the rest worth while. (The regiment had a good friend in Jim Shields, the Royal Signals quartermaster.) The lines to some positions, being under observation, could be laid only after dark. Here is the signals officer's account of one these nocturnal expeditions:

In the back room of Anna Hoeve Major Gordon spread his maps among the litter of kit, and thought about the German patrols. He decided to set a trap for them by putting a night post in some buildings near the river, on the far side of the tongue of wood. That meant joining a line to the line which already ran beside the wood to the houses at the southern end, and taking the new line along the path which cut through the wood, then across the road and into the buildings. It was a job for darkness. At dusk off went Lieut Peterson with his men to occupy the post, and off went Cpl Stevenson with me to lay the line. As we crossed the railway one of the Middlesex at the post there warned us: 'Mind our trip wires across the track when you come back.' We thanked him and went on. The path through the wood was not long, but the wood in the dark was not comforting. I went through it without lingering, pistol in one hand, cable in the other, Stevie paying out the line from the edge of the wood behind me. When I returned he was joining the lines, and not to be seen in the darkness. Neither could find the other until one of us hit on the idea of softly whistling morse. Glad to have the job done, we hurried back towards the railway. It was not until I walked clean through it that I remembered the Middlesex trip wire, but whatever flare or infernal machine was attached failed to go off. Next day, back in my billet at RHQ, I received from Templeman a somewhat dramatic welcome: 'Whew! If anything had happened to you out there it would have been on my head. I forgot to tell you that I took the ammo out of your pistol in case the kids here got hold of it.' But I was never much of a shot, anyway.

On 9 December the regiment, except for the squadron at Anna Hoeve, went from the Sevenum area to Lierop, near Zomeren and close enough to Helmond to compensate for the fact that quarters were mainly barns and hay lofts disposed along muddy tracks. The Maas squadron and the rest of the regiment were now in quite different worlds: the one looking out across a deserted river for glimpses of a hidden enemy; the other well out of range of German guns and near a canal which was soon to be crowded with cheerful Dutch skaters. After calling for the despatches at the Lierop tailor's shop in which L/Cpl Holderness had neatly spread his signals office (who will forget the jolly, friendly young people there?), Tpr Merryman or Tpr Yount would set off in the hard-worked signals jeep on a daily round which covered nearly fifty miles, through Asten, Meijel, Panningen (divisional headquarters), Maasbree and Sevenum to Anna Hoeve, and back again. The arrival of the signals jeep bringing the mail was always a great moment of the day at Anna Hoeve.

Field Marshal Montgomery visited the division again on 13 December and presented medal ribbons, twelve to members of the regiment. 'In this fighting no division has done better, and it is a first class show' he said. He gave details of the leave scheme which was soon to be started. In the regiment the colonel drew names from a hat to decide the order in which people should go. Everybody was agog. The names of Capt Liddell and Sgt Gilbert came out first and second.

It was decided to replace the Anna Hoeve squadron with infantry in order to have more men on this long stretch of the Maas, and the regiment was ordered to take over another part of the front—at Hout Blerick, a mile south of Blerick—on 22 December. On the night before the change the A Squadron position at the southern end of the tongue of wood was rushed by a strong German patrol, which clattered off jubilantly down the river road with nine prisoners. The Royal Scots Fusiliers relieved A Squadron on the afternoon of 22 December, and the same day C Squadron went into Hout Blerick, taking over from the King's Own Scottish Borderers.

To reach Hout Blerick from the west you drive straight on from Maasbree instead of turning left, which is the way to Sevenum. The road slopes gently down to the river, and near the river you turn off to the right to go into the village. That December it was advisable to turn right sooner and go the 'back way', along a bumpy track beside a wood, because the country near the river was under German observation. Hout Blerick was badly damaged and almost deserted—eerie as only an empty village in a grey December can be. Squadron headquarters were in the crypt of what remained of the church, and connected with the troop strongpoints by a complicated system of field telephones. The most unpopular position was 150 yards from the river, and could be relieved only at night. It was decided that the squadron at Hout Blerick should be reinforced by members of Headquarter Squadron.

The weather became colder and colder, and the rutted tracks like iron. The vehicles had anti-freeze in their radiators, but the engines had to be run at intervals during the night. In spite of many precautions, some wireless batteries froze and burst. The canals froze. There was alarm lest the Maas itself should freeze. The long nights in the slit trenches were agony, and the rum ration the most precious thing in the world. At Lierop the smooth running of RHQ depended on the Valor oil stoves, for which Sgt Davidson, the intelligence sergeant, was made responsible. A burnt out wick was a major crisis.

Sgt Davidson asked for a new one. All the Scot in the colonel was shocked. 'Heavens man! A wick should last two years. All the rooms in my house are heated by Valor stoves' he chided. To which the harassed sergeant replied, 'I'm sorry sir. In England we use electricity.'

The approach of Christmas brought another crisis: a bomb fell on the Helmond hall which had been booked for A Squadron's Christmas dinner by Lieut Harry Whitham, who combined the manifold duties of PMC, entertainments officer and liaison officer with breezy efficiency. But in Harry Whitham the hour had found the man, and both A and B Squadrons had a gay Christmas Day in the town of their adoption, a day for which thanks were shared by the entertainments officer, the quartermaster, Lieut Hughes, and

Major Kemp. Headquarter Squadron spent the day equally cheerfully in Lierop, where the sergeants ferried early-morning tea in jeeps and the sergeants' mess band entertained after dinner. The only musical instrument in the band was a cornet wielded by Sgt Major Leslie Evans in a manner reminiscent of the buskers outside Blighty's public houses. The piece which proved most popular was 'The Skater's Waltz' possibly because it was the only recognisable one.

C Squadron was still at Hout Blerick. Its festival was postponed, but even at that desolate village there was something of the spirit of the season. On Christmas Eve the Germans decided to forego their routine 4 p.m. shelling, and that night, which was cold, clear and very still, sounds of festivity came from the far bank of the river. On a Christmas morning white with frost the only sound was a church bell across the Maas. The colonel came, and the padre, who conducted short services. At dusk the enemy deemed Christmas over and began shelling again. In the evening a 'flap' was relayed to the squadron from 'higher up': German patrols were expected. A trap was laid; all the way along the front a riotous party was simulated with singing, bagpipes, trumpets and flares, which masked a general stand-to. No patrols came. Relieved by B Squadron on 28 December, C Squadron swept into Helmond two days later for its belated Christmas party, recounted by Capt Liddell:

The entertainments officer had done us proud. The party was in a Helmond cafe which looked more like a church inside, with its gallery and organ. It was so large that the whole squadron was able to sit together while officers and sergeants rushed hither and thither as waiters. Everything went off with a bang, including the electric organ, which was most popular. We started it with the help of the proprietor. Then he disappeared, and we could not get it stopped. Brigadier Cumming-Bruce, who had come along from 44 Brigade, did his best to compete with it for a while, but we had to fetch the proprietor and ask him 'for Pete's sake' to turn it off. Major MacDiarmid, representing the colonel, also spoke a few words in his own inimitable way. Then the squadron got to the serious business of the day.

The Q department had managed to procure real English beer. There was not much, but a 'hell brew' was also ladled out, and soon some wonderful acrobatic feats were being performed. Nobody knows how Sgt M got up to the statue twenty feet above the floor. How he got down again without breaking his neck is an even bigger mystery.

Then we had Trooper F. 'Geordie', loud in his praises of Lieut R. Using the adjective which in the Army meant everything except what it really meant, he declared Lieut R. to be the best officer of all the officers. The other officers were not quite certain how to take this, but that mattered not one whit to Trooper F., who proceeded to take them in turn and deliver a short homily on their characters—in most cases a very accurate sort of thumb-nail sketch.

By this time everything was going with a swing, including some of the chairs, and the proprietor was beginning to look a bit pale. Sgt Major Ward sized up the situation and decided that fresh air would be beneficial to the company, so everybody was turned out to cool down for a couple of hours before the dance, which started at seven o'clock. It was amazing, the difference those two hours made. A sober and respectable, but cheerful, gathering welcomed the Dutch girls, who turned up in large numbers. The organ played again from time to time, and everybody had a grand time. One and all sang loudly the praises of the entertainments officer, and voted this one of the best, if not the best, Christmas in the Army.

The Tam o'Shanters, the division's concert party, played 'Dick Whittington' magnificently in a long run at Zomeren, and a Dutch concert party came from Helmond to Lierop to entertain the regiment. This poem, written by one of the performers, was read with great feeling by its author:

TO OUR LIBERATORS

We sighed and sighed in slavery; we cursed the horrid Huns.
Then after years of pining, hark! The sound of saving guns;
Our trembling hearts cried out for joy in spite of bomb and shell,
For was not Heaven coming after years and years of hell?

We prayed and prayed, and Heaven made our faithful Friends break through.
They forced the enemy's strong defence; they drove him on anew.
And lo! From every window burst our colours glad and free,
Our long forbidden Orange shone: a sun of victory.

A little shy, we try and try to thank you, gallant Men
Who came to bring us liberty and make us live again;
Our Dutch is double Dutch to you, but may you understand
The language of our children's kiss, the shake of grateful hand.

God speed you on your glorious way to Victory and Fame;
For ever in our history be praised your Army's name;
Hurray for glorious England, Wales and Bonnie Scotland too,
For Irishman and for the States; good luck to all of you!

In reply to this tribute the following poem was reproduced in a Helmond newspaper:

TO HELMOND

Our stay with you, so short has been
but you have made us feel
t'was worth our while in freeing you
from the yoke of the NAZIS heel.

From Scotland, England, Ireland and Wales
we came to set you free,
and pressing forward we must go
to hasten VICTORY.

But we shall not forget you
and the kindness you have shown
in this small DUTCH town called HELMOND;
you have made us feel at home.

We hope that when this War is WON
and free men have their say
we can return to visit you
for a peaceful holiday.

But meantime let us forge ahead
until that day is near
when we can meet in quiet content
and raise a hearty cheer.

FROM A SOLDIER.

On New Year's Day the Luftwaffe made its last really great gesture; it was with surprise at first that members of the regiment saw black crosses on the wings above Lierop's roofs. But these fighters were not interested in Lierop. There was more activity in other parts of the division's area, and several of the attacking aircraft were shot down. Major MacDiarmid, on a journey back to RHQ, had to dive for a ditch.

On 7 January all the regiment that was in Lierop was inspected by Maj Gen Barber on a snowy field and marched to church behind a pipe band from the Lowland Brigade. The squadron watch on the Maas, continued in the snow, and white overalls were issued.

There was one never-to-be-forgotten exchange when one of the squadron patrols returned on a freezing night:

Shivering sentry in slit trench (whispering): 'Who's that?'

Patrol leader (whispering): 'Who's that who said "Who's that?" '?'

Shivering sentry: 'Who's-that-who-said-who's that-when-I-said-who's-that?'

On 8 January the regiment was ordered to provide a squadron as the division's mobile reserve, under command of a brigade group at Roggel, six miles south of Meijel, and the new system was that the squadrons spent a week in each position: Hout Blerick, Lierop, Roggel. RHQ and A Echelon moved south over the slippery roads to a camp of huts—wooden, dishevelled and draughty—at De Heibloem. On 20 January the division was relieved by the 6th Airborne Division, fresh from the Ardennes, and 1 Commando Brigade. Two days later the regiment, except for A Squadron (not yet relieved at Hout Blerick), drove to Boischot in Belgium. Never again was Helmond to be near. That was sad. But there was no grief in parting from the cold slit trenches by the Maas.

On 29 November, 1945, the 'Ost Brabant', the daily newspaper of Helmond, stated: 'All British elite—troops have been stationed at Helmond between November and December, 1944, including the 15th Scottish Recce Regt (whom the Helmond people called their 'own army')'.

On the Maas front Tpr S. D. Robertshaw was fatally wounded.

In Holland the regiment had been joined by three officers from the 59th Reconnaissance Regiment—Capt D. E. Jackson (to B Squadron), Capt G. B. Salmon (to C Squadron) and Lieut G. M. Paton (to B Squadron). Lieut P. G. Vroome also was posted to the regiment, and he went to C Squadron.

George Blount:- The 'Wee Mac' recalls the Winter of 44-45 when the regiment was dug in on the banks of the Maas. A nightly rum ration was the entitlement but many of the A Squadron 'Jocks' did not avail themselves of the warming fluid. The outcome was that George accumulated a surplus of fourteen gallons! This was passed onto the RSM to provide a rum punch for Christmas and the New Year (English and Scots respectively). The RSM's idea of a punch was 14 gallons of rum, one cupful of water and a solitary orange; served in brimming mugs it resulted in many prostrate troops and a surplus of hangovers!

Medical Section with White half-track
Back row (L to R): Dvr Wright (RAOC); Tpr Colquitt (RHQ); Dvr McCullen (RASC)
Middle row (L to R): Tpr Etheridge (A Sqdn); L/C Woodcock (A Sqdn); L/C Anderson (C Sqdn);
L/C Knight (B Sqdn); Tpr Donovan (B Sqdn); Cpl Matthews (RHQ)
Front row (L to R): Tpr Murdoch (D/O RHQ); Tpr Andrews (C Sqdn); Sgt Ponting (RHQ);
Capt Watson (MO RHQ)

Back row: Len Watson; unknown; 'Crasher' Clarke, Feally
Front row: Lt Gillings; Lt Leppard; Lt Falloon; Walters

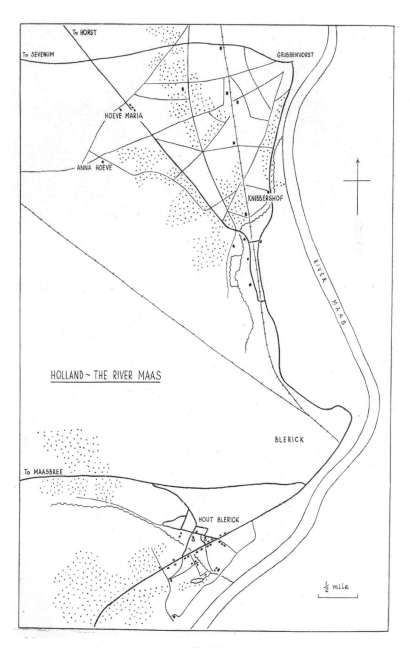

Map 11

Awards to Division - 13 December 1944
15th (S) Recce officers in black berets
Front row, left: Major P.T.I. MacDiarmid
Second row, 2nd from left: Capt K.W. Gray, Lt P.C. Kerridge; Lt M. Morris; Capt G.R. Blount

Kingsley Gray receives the Regiment's first Military Cross from FM Montgomery - 13 December 1944

21 ARMY GROUP

PERSONAL CHRISTMAS MESSAGE
FROM THE C-IN-C

(To be read out to all troops)

1. The forces of the British Empire in western Europe spend Christmas 1944 in the field. But what a change has come over the scene since last Christmas.

The supreme Battle of Normandy carried with it the liberation of France and Belgium.

Last Christmas we were in England, expectant and full of hope; this Christmas we are fighting in Germany.

The conquest of Germany remains.

2. It would have needed a brave man to say on D day, 6 June, that in three months we would be in Brussels and Antwerp: having liberated nearly the whole of France and Belgium; and in six months we would be fighting in Germany: having driven the enemy back across his own frontiers.

But this is what has happened.

And we must not fail to give the praise and honour where it is due:

" This was the Lord's doing, and it is marvellous in our eyes."

3. At Christmas time, whether in our homes or fighting in the field, we like to sing the carols we learnt as children; and in truth, this is indeed a link between us and our families and friends in the home country: since they are singing the same verses. The old words express exactly what we all feel today:

" Glory to God in the highest, and on earth peace, good will toward men."

That is what we are fighting for, that is what we desire: on earth peace, good will toward men.

4. And so today we sing the Christmas hymns, full of hope, and steadfast in our belief that soon we shall achieve our hearts' desire.

Therefore, with faith in God, and with enthusiasm for our cause and for the day of battle, let us continue the contest with stout hearts and with determination to conquer.

5. And at this time I send to each one of you my best wishes and my Christmas greetings.

Wherever you may be, fighting in the front line, or working on the lines of communication or in the ports, I wish all of you good luck and a happy 1945. We are all one great team; together, you and I, we have achieved much: and together, we will see the thing through to the end.

6. Good luck to you all.

B. L. Montgomery
Field-Marshal
C-in-C 21 Army Group.

Belgium.
Xmas, 1944

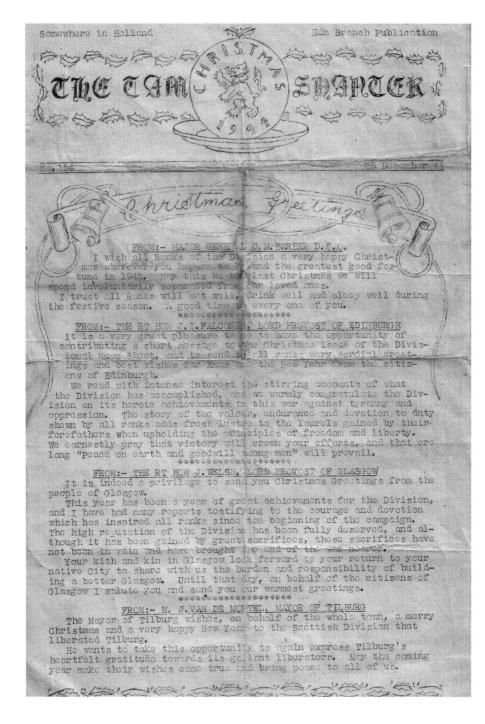

Somewhere in Holland   Edn Branch Publication

THE TAM O'SHANTER

CHRISTMAS 1944

No. 154   25 December 44

Christmas Greetings

FROM:- MAJOR GENERAL C. M. BARBER D.S.O.
I wish all Ranks of the Division a very happy Christmas wherever you happen to be and the greatest good fortune in 1945. May this be the last Christmas we will spend involuntarily separated from our loved ones.
I trust all Ranks will eat well, drink well and sleep well during the festive season. A good time to every one of you.

FROM:- THE RT HON J. I. FALCONER, LORD PROVOST OF EDINBURGH
It is a very great pleasure to me to have the opportunity of contributing a short message to the Christmas issue of the Divisional News Sheet, and to send to all ranks very cordial greetings and best wishes for Xmas and the New Year from the citizens of Edinburgh.
We read with intense interest the stirring accounts of what the Division has accomplished, and we warmly congratulate the Division on its heroic achievements in this war against tyranny and oppression. The story of the valour, endurance and devotion to duty shown by all ranks adds fresh lustre to the laurels gained by their forefathers when upholding the principles of freedom and liberty. We earnestly pray that victory will crown your efforts, and that ere long "Peace on earth and goodwill among men" will prevail.

FROM:- THE RT HON J. WELSH, LORD PROVOST OF GLASGOW
It is indeed a privilege to send you Christmas Greetings from the people of Glasgow.
This year has been a year of great achievements for the Division, and I have had many reports testifying to the courage and devotion which has inspired all ranks since the beginning of the campaign. The high reputation of the Division has been fully deserved, and although it has been gained by great sacrifices, these sacrifices have not been in vain and have brought the end of the war nearer.
Your kith and kin in Glasgow look forward to your return to your native City to share with us the burden and responsibility of building a better Glasgow. Until that day, on behalf of the citizens of Glasgow I salute you and send you our warmest greetings.

FROM:- M. J. VAN DE MORTEL, MAYOR OF TILBURG
The Mayor of Tilburg wishes, on behalf of the whole town, a merry Christmas and a very happy New Year to the Scottish Division that liberated Tilburg.
He wants to take this opportunity to again express Tilburg's heartfelt gratitude towards its gallant liberators. May the coming year make their wishes come true and bring peace to all of us.

No. 154   THE TAM O'SHANTER   25 December 44

EUROPEAN FRONTS

Western Front

News of the Ardennes battle grows increasingly better. The position now is that we have brought the Germans to a halt, at least for the present, and pressure is being brought to bear on the enemy from both flanks.

On the north, Monschau is firm, and the Allied line from Elsenborn, through Malmedy, to Stavelot which, in spite of reports to the contrary, is still in our hands, has withstood strong attacks, and has even been the scene of a slight withdrawal on the part of the enemy.

Further south, St Vith is in German hands, but our hold on Vielsalm, to the west, is containing the enemy in this region.

It is the push between St Vith and Bastogne that has gained most ground, but here, too, it seems that the spearhead has been blunted. The towns of Marche and Rochefort, which stand about 20 mls from the Meuse, are in American hands, and it is probable that part of St Hubert is still held. Around Bastogne itself, to which the Americans are clinging doggedly there is evidence that the German ring has been loosened. At the other end of the line, Echternach stands firm.

Yesterday, the weather was again in our favour. The Americans sent over the largest force ever despatched on a single mission. In a stream 400 mls long, over 2,000 bombers and 900 fighters swept over to bomb communication centres and airfields behind the German lines. Details of results are not yet available.

Italian Front

In Italy, 8th Army troops continue to improve their positions along the river Senio, and are tightening their squeeze on the German positions on the eastern bank.

Russian Front

By advancing 25 mls in 3 days, the Red Army has broken through the strong defensive zone to the south-west of Budapest. The main German retreat line from the capital to the west has been cut, and the city is three-quarters surrounded.

GREETINGS

FROM:-
GARNET WILSON,
LORD PROVOST OF DUNDEE
****

I send Christmas greetings from the citizens of Dundee to all ranks of the Division.

Our thoughts are with you, as we see in the glow of the street-lamps now lit again messages of hope for you and for ourselves.

The days of warfare are numbered. May happy days lie ahead of you all.

CHAPTER XVI

THROUGH FLOOD INTO GERMANY
Maps 12 and 13

On the afternoon of 9 February, driving east along a road wet with thaw, the regiment passed one of those headless, armless busts of ample curves which dressmakers use. Propped against it beside the road was a board on which somebody had scrawled 'Nix good for Tommy'. It was an introduction to Germany. Several miles behind were the Dutch border and Nijmegen. Ahead were the Siegfried Line village of Nutterden and the town of Cleve, or the rubble, craters and tilting walls which had been a town before the Lancasters flew over two nights ago.

The First Canadian Army's great winter battle, the clearing of the country between Maas and Rhine was nearly two days old. C Squadron, the traffic policemen of the Wolds and the attack on Blerick, had been on point duty again in the Siegfried defences while the Scottish Division's infantry broke through them to the Materborn heights above Cleve, overcoming an enemy stunned by the thunder of a thousand guns. Hopes were high. General Crerar, commander of a Canadian army enlarged by five divisions and other formations from General Dempsey's Second Army, had announced, 'The operations which we are about to undertake are of the greatest possible importance. Indeed, the result of them can lead to speedy and complete Allied victory.' The regiment was going into a battle of movement for the first time since the November advance to the Maas.

Its part in this Operation Veritable followed days of preparation and secret planning in a cold Tilburg monastery, a nightmare of a drive through the darkness to Nijmegen, and a day of lying low there, with signs masked so that there should be nothing to tell the Germans that the Canadian Army was being reinforced. The move to Boischot on 22 January had been something of a mistake; it had happened before the arrival of the change of plan which was to send the regiment to Tilburg. But it was a mistake which nobody regretted, for Belgium went to the head like wine. Many had snatched a few hours of gaiety in Brussels by the time that the long line of grey vehicles went north again, over ice and through fog, to the Trappist monastery where the bearded monks wore white robes or brown, were helpful in silence and brewed Trappisten Bier. A Squadron was not in the monastery, but in houses on the southern edge of Tilburg, and a V1 exploded there without causing loss of life to the squadron. Five officers posted from the 38th Reconnaissance Regt had arrived just in time for the journey to Tilburg. They were Lieutenants P.C.H. Ambler, M. A. Bays, E. H. Jellinek, M. B. McFall and G. S. Browne.

On 7 February the regiment settled sleepily in Nijmegen schools and houses after driving secretly through the night. It was a slow, lightless drive with straining eyes over a road which wound above low-lying fields, threatening the driver who dozed with a plunge to disaster down the steep embankments. When the column reached the floating bridge which shivered on the tide of the Maas and seemed to disappear beneath the front wheels, then courage failed, and lights flicked on, and for a few minutes there was all Blackpool front on the move. Captain Fordyce, who had recovered from his Normandy wound, finished this drive, went off immediately to collect NAAFI rations, was in a collision and had to go to hospital again.

The Veritable attack, conducted by XXX Corps, began on the morning of 8 February, with the Scottish Division in the centre, lunging at Cleve. On its left, in the flooded country beside the Rhine, were the Canadians; on its right were the Welsh Division, beating through the Reichswald, and the Highland Division, on the plain between forest and the Maas. After the fall of Cleve the Wessex Division—it was planned—was to pass through and strike south at Goch. The Guards Armoured Division was to break out, dominate the high ground north of Sonsbeck and seize the main road bridge over the Rhine at Wesel. In addition to C Squadron's point duty in the Siegfried Line, the regiment was given these tasks in the planning: to reconnoitre the advance of columns on Calcar and Udem from Cleve; and to find roads between Cleve and the Reichswald over which the 2nd Household Cavalry could dash towards Goch.

General Crerar had laid down: 'Whatever the difficulties of ground and weather, the forward thrust through the enemy and his defences will be pressed without respite. He must be given no time or opportunity to collect his thoughts or resources.' And so it was as the regiment drove towards Nutterden in the gathering dusk on 9 February, with the Siegfried defences prised open, the enemy still reeling from the first shock of attack, and the infantry of 44 Brigade on the Materborn heights above Cleve. But there was to be confusion and delay as the Wessex Division (released before Cleve was cleared), the Scottish Division and the Germans jostled each other in the ruined town. The enemy was to rally. There were to be days of hard fighting against foe and flood before the fall of Goch, Calcar and Udem. The Rhine bridge at Wesel was never to be seized intact.

On the opening day of the attack 46 Brigade had taken Frasselt, and 227 Brigade—in spite of the presence of mines and the absence of tanks, bogged before reaching the start line—had got to Kranenburg on the main road to Cleve. By next morning the Lowland Brigade, delayed by the congestion on the only road, had managed to get only the 6th King's Own Scottish Borderers into position for the assault on the main defences, but the Borderers almost completed that phase on their own. They crossed the anti-tank ditch and went on in Kangaroos to capture Wolfsberg, a mile beyond it, by 9.30 a.m. Ten German officers, 230 men and a battery of medium guns fell into their hands. By ten o'clock 227 Brigade infantry were in the fortified village of Nutterden.

While the infantry advanced through the mud and fortifications of the Siegfried Line under the eyes of C Squadron, the rest of the regiment was waiting tensely in Nijmegen. In the school which was headquarters the planning maps showed arrows pointing boldly towards the Rhine; the colonel, anxious to be going, talked of 'cracking the whip'. On the morning of 9 February came the warning to be ready soon to probe towards Udem and Calcar. B Squadron was given the Udem route, and A Squadron Calcar. The Cleve road, it was stated, would be cleared for the regiment, but the colonel, knowing the vast amount of traffic which had to use it, was doubtful about this, and sent an officer patrol from B Squadron to investigate another way. This was under two and a half feet of water. When the regiment started out from Nijmegen in the afternoon it was on the main road, a road by no means clear, and not until the light was fading did B Squadron's leading cars reach the crossroads in Nutterden. In an attempt to get round Cleve the squadron went to the right, following a poor road which wound its way up to the high wooded ground above the town. The orders to push on in the little daylight which remained were urgent, but the patrols were hindered by tanks and Buffaloes returning from placing the infantry on the high ground, and little progress had been made by six o'clock. Further orders were sought from divisional headquarters, because reconnaissance in vehicles by night had always proved hopeless. This time, however, the regiment was told to do everything it could to get on and to try to seize the railway embankment between Cleve and the forest. The task we given to B Squadron, and searchlights were sent forward to light the way as best they could. What happened that night, while B Squadron headquarters listened anxiously to its wireless on the hill above Nutterden, and RHQ listened in a cellar in the village, is a story for Lieut Gillings to tell:

We had been called in from patrol at half-past nine that night, and I was visiting my night alarm posts when the squadron leader sent for me. 'I want you to take a patrol through Cleve,' Major Gordon said 'You will get as far out towards Goch as communications will allow. I have arranged for the searchlights to move as far forward as they dare, and they will a least help you into Cleve.' So you have arranged for b—searchlights, I thought. The thought of going on a patrol at night with cars made me feel awful.

I returned to the troop and called them together 'I want six volunteers for a risky job,' I said, and told them what it was. Tpr Slaughter (Tod to everyone from colonel downwards) was the first—he always was. Tpr Gilbertson. Tpr Ward. Sgt Short said he would be my driver. We emptied our pockets of everything but cigarettes. The plan was to move forward in bounds of two or three hundred yards until we reached the line of our infantry, and then see what support we could get from the searchlights once we reached the high ground overlooking Cleve. I was told that Capt Boynton would be a wireless step-up if communications became difficult.

Tod was doing an excellent job in the leading car, stopping every so often, dismounting when in doubt. He would report 'O.K.' on the wireless, and away we would go again.

We were nearing the high ground now, and the two cars were close to one another. If only, I thought, we can reach that high ground all right we'll have every chance of success. Just short of the crest we stopped; Tod was reporting 'shapes' moving down the road towards us. They were nearer now and recognizable as men in single file. They must be our own infantry, I thought, because there was nobody between them and squadron headquarters, a mile or so down the road. We went to the top of the hill and halted beside the file. They walked past without looking up at the cars; they were so close that I could have touched them. Gilbertson was counting them . . . nineteen, twenty, twenty-one . . . I wanted the comfort of knowing they were our infantry. But were they? .... twenty-two, twenty-three, twenty-four. I had to speak to them. Surely they had seen the cars. 'Hullo Jock,' I shouted. There was no reply.

Tod was out of his car and walking over to them. He said something to one of them, and in a flash he was beside my car. 'Blimey, they're bloody Jerries,' he said. 'Turn your car round, Tod,' I told him, and shouted 'Is there an escort there?', still not believing that the enemy could be so near to our lines. Again no reply. I jumped down to back my car round. Gilbertson was caressing a couple of grenades longingly. I knew now that there was no escort, and decided to usher them quietly back to our lines. A voice shouted from across the road, 'Hey, Jock.' 'What do you want ?' I said. The answer came instantly—a burst of Schmeiser.

Jesse Owens' record was broken, and I was back in the turret in a few seconds. Sgt Short had the car turned around beautifully and was moving down the road to catch up Tod and the Jerries almost as soon as I was on it. Gilbertson was blazing away at the German who had fired at me, and Tod was letting his twin K guns go for all he was worth. The Germans had dived for the ditch. Not an hour ago we had been scared of the dark; now we were grateful for it. A mile back we met Capt Boynton, and I told him what had happened. He decided it would be foolish to take the same route, so we set off to find another way through.

This time we went along a track which, according to the map, blossomed out into the main road somewhere in Cleve. We passed the two searchlight crews sitting in front of the forward infantry, but looking quite happy. We had gone about five hundred yards when a man ran up and gasped, 'My platoon of machine guns has been over-run. Can you get help?' After sorting out his rather incoherent story, Captain Boynton said we would have a look, with the idea of sneaking into Cleve through these positions. When we reached the top of the hill we saw several houses alight, ammunition exploding and small battles going on everywhere. We were silhouetted against the fires, and we received bursts of Spandau and grenades. It did not take us long to realise that we would not get through that way, and we had begun to look at our maps for another when a wireless message called us back to squadron headquarters for fresh orders. On the way back we heard planes, and if it is possible for planes to sound German these did. Two planes swooped and dropped two bombs near the searchlights, but the steady beam continued. We sighed with relief. The planes came back and tried to machine gun the lights. Still the same steady beam. Eventually the aircraft went. How we admired those searchlight crews!

Major Gordon told us that we were to lead an armoured column along our original route, and when I explained to the commander of this column what had happened there he said, 'Will you go forward again? If you find anything in the same position I will bring my tanks up and clear it.' That was fair enough! Sgt Grice, Tpr Fisher and Tpr Bates came this time in a third car, and I had Tpr Wise as my driver. This was a great show of courage on his part, because he had been suffering from an attack of nerves for some time. He told me afterwards that he came because he thought he would regain his nerve. He did.

We set off again, with Capt Boynton as liaison officer with the tanks. Tod again did his job admirably. He spotted the roadblock which had been erected for our benefit and gave the Germans several bursts before they saw him. His steady voice came back over the wireless—'Contact'. Two Spandaus were now firing back fairly accurately, but we were slowly reversing towards the tanks. The commander of the column immediately sent off six Shermans and a platoon of the 43rd Division infantry, and the position was cleared in an hour while we watched.

It was decided that as the six tanks were in front we should follow them through Cleve, and take over the lead again on the other side of the town. Amazingly, the men in the tanks read their maps through streets which had become craters and heaps of rubble. The cars followed. Commanders were out of tanks and cars, guiding the drivers round craters where there were only inches to spare. Occasional firing down streets and into the few remaining houses was the only reminder that this was more than a severe test of night driving. In the centre of the town Sgt Grice's car was swallowed by an enormous crater; it looked as if a crane would be needed to get it out. 'Are you all O.K.?' I shouted. He answered, 'Yes, we'll be all right here.' I hated leaving them, but we simply had to get on.

On the far side of Cleve the commander of the column called a halt until daylight. After what seemed an eternity dawn broke, and we went forward, past the leading tanks. Firing began in a copse on the left when we had gone three hundred yards, but the infantry were soon in action, and we continued down a straight road bordered by trees. There were fewer craters, and in daylight they were easier to avoid.

Ahead something flashed and banged. Up went my leading car. I thought I saw two bodies bale out, and breathed a sigh of relief. But what bad luck that Tod's car, the smallest of all the vehicles there, should be the one hit! We were about fifteen yards from Tod, so out baled Gillings and crew—quicker than that! I started to go forward to the knocked-out car, and met Ward, the driver, coming back, quite unshaken. 'Where's Tod?' I asked. 'I think he baled out all right' he said. We waited a little while for him to appear. Then Wise and I had a look at the car. Tod was inside; he must have died instantly. He was a fearless man.

The tanks were trying to get what cover they could. A Sherman came up to us and put a shot straight down the road. The reply came instantly, and up went the Sherman, followed immediately by a Honey. Another Sherman crept up. Apparently the crew could see the enemy; we could not. The Sherman's first shot knocked out the German gun. There were cheers, followed by swearing when a shell from another German weapon hit a Kangaroo. The Sherman fired again, and the enemy became a ball of flame. We found afterwards that the Germans had a self-propelled 88 mm gun and a Tiger tank.

I do not know why, but we did not go farther that day. Capt Boynton placed our cars on the outer edge of the reserve tanks, and one man in each crew kept watch while the tanks and infantry tried to get round another way. The road came under heavy mortar fire. Capt Boynton's car had broken down when we first entered Cleve, but the driver, Tpr Cheeld, repaired it and caught us up. The wireless operator, Tpr Edwards, was able to send back almost a running commentary on the battle of the tanks, being between the Shermans and the Germans, with what he called 'a grandstand view'.

That night we were called back to the squadron, and on the way we came upon the car that had fallen into the crater. The previous night, in the centre of a town still occupied more by the enemy than by us, Sgt Grice and his crew had taken more than thirty prisoners. Fisher sat by the road with his Bren, and Bates found a cellar and put the Germans into it as they were collected. One officer tried to drive by in a car, but a shot from Sgt Grice's pistol changed his mind. We buried Tod in the local cemetery.

Capt Boynton received the Military Cross. The Military Medal was awarded to Tpr Ward and Sgt Grice, who, like Lieut Gillings, was already holder of the Croix de Guerre.

While B Squadron's patrol was in Cleve on the night of 9 February several reconnaissance parties from the Wessex Division called at the regiment's command post in the cellar of a house next to one of the concrete forts in Nutterden. The visitors thought that Cleve was already in British hands and that they could motor through the town, signposting the way for their division's advance on Goch. RHQ persuaded them that this would not be advisable. Early on the 10th the regiment reported to headquarters of the Scottish Division that there appeared to be only a few disorganised enemy in Cleve, but added that no definite conclusion should be drawn until daybreak. That night a large gun lobbed shells into Nutterden from across the Rhine.

Daylight brought from B Squadron reports of confused fighting in the centre of Cleve, where there were now parts of both Scottish and Wessex Divisions as well as the German defenders. A Squadron's orders to pass through the town and reconnoitre towards Calcar were cancelled when it was realised that the place was not yet sufficiently clear. Daylight also revealed enemy groups on the high ground, and B Squadron headquarters were involved in a skirmish when they tried to go into Cleve that way. Indeed, the infantry were engaged for some hours in the wood beside which the searchlight crews had stayed without apparent concern during the night. On 11 February the Scottish Division's infantry systematically cleared the northern part of the town, crossing the canal, while the Wessex cleared the southern part. At five o'clock in the afternoon divisional headquarters ordered the regiment to get information about the road to Calcar, and A Squadron, which had stood down after patrolling in Cleve, was on the road again within a quarter of an hour. Its patrols met the enemy soon after passing through the infantry's forward posts, and darkness made further reconnaissance impossible.

Late that night the small, smoky front room of the house at Nutterden was crowded. The remains of supper were pushed aside, the maps were spread out, and in a silence that was tense the colonel gave out the orders for the dash to Calcar which was to begin at dawn. The 7th Seaforth were to go in Kangaroos, with supporting arms. The regiment without B Squadron was to lead. 'We shall seize and hold Calcar,' the colonel said. 'We shall probably be surrounded and cut off for several days . . .' The regimental orderly room staff discoursed on wills, then packed away the files and typewriters, primed grenades, cleaned Brens and rifles and made the PIAT ready.

But the event was something of an anti-climax, although not for those face to face with the fierce opposition which sealed the Calcar road against any such swift, spectacular advance. That day the regiment's headquarters went only as far as the shoe factory beside the main road on the western edge of

Cleve, a mile or two from Nutterden. And in the shoe factory they stayed for several days. A Squadron crossed the improvised Class 12 bridge over the canal in Cleve early in the morning, and found the enemy on the south-eastern outskirts of the town. The Kangaroos could not go over the canal until a stouter bridge had been completed, and it was not until about 12.30 that the vanguard started down the Calcar road. The infantry and tanks fought their way forward, and whenever there was a pause in the fighting A Squadron's patrols went ahead again. But it was slow progress. The Germans had sited their defensive positions well, and their artillery, which had been considerably reinforced, kept the few roads under accurate fire. Large railway guns were sending shells with a nasty gurgle from across the Rhine. Deep ditches prevented the Kangaroos from deploying, and some were hit. By dusk the column had advanced two miles, and the infantry concentrated for the night around the village of Qualburg while A Squadron came back to the rest of the regiment in Cleve. On the left flank the Canadians had made good progress across the floods in their Buffaloes to occupy Greithausen and Wardhausan.

Next day C Squadron took over from A Squadron the task of reconnaissance, and the patrols which passed through the Seaforth in Qualburg at dawn found that the Germans had pulled back during the night. Hasselt, a mile beyond Qualburg, was reached by eleven o'clock, after mines on the main road had been by-passed. A carrier troop was left in the village to await the infantry, and the armoured cars went on. But this swift start was a deceptive introduction to the enemy's intentions for the day. The Germans waited in strength half a mile beyond Hasselt, and C Squadron's patrols came under such heavy fire from guns and mortars that they had to withdraw. The patrols which explored to the right and to the left of the main road also met determined opposition.

That night, the night of 13 February, the Germans blew up a dyke in the Alter Rhine, and the floods spread and deepened with this new onrush of water. C Squadron tried to find a way round them while the infantry of 46 Brigade carried out limited operations against the strong German positions on the main road beyond Hasselt. No way was to be found. The water had reached the tops of the hedges. Lieut Bosch was told by wireless to find out whether the railway on the embankment could be used instead of the road. He asked for rubber reconnaissance boats. This is his account of what happened:

Half an hour later the boats had not arrived, so I asked what had happened to them. The answer was that it was thought that I had been joking. Soon afterwards the boats came, and we set off on our patrol. Our plan was to paddle along the line and test the depth of the water with the paddles, prodding to see whether there were any shell holes. None of us was very skilled at using boats, and at first we made no headway, but went round and round. This was great entertainment for those who were watching. Next we grounded on the signal wire, then had a narrow escape from puncturing our craft on a holly bush beside the line. When we had gone 150 yards we were sure that the route was no good for wheeled traffic, so we decided to put back. But we could not paddle against the flow of water, and we had to get out and wade, often waist-deep, towing our boats.

While 46 Brigade and the Canadians were engaged in hard fighting on the Calcar road, the main Corps thrust was switched south to the dry ground and Goch, the Scottish and the Wessex Divisions advancing from the north and the Welsh and the Highland from the west. It was tank and infantry and artillery work, and for some days there was little for the regiment to do. The floods had swept across the main road between Nijmegen and Nutterden, divorcing A Echelon, Major Kemp's boys, from the rest of the regiment. On 16 February the three-tonners splashed through from Nijmegen, but the smaller vehicles had to wait. The floods had endangered the whole system of supply; on the first night one of the main artillery dumps was submerged. But the RASC drivers were heroes equal to the crisis. For two days they drove, red-eyed for want of sleep, over treacherous roads, pausing to eat only when their lorries were being loaded or unloaded. In the fierce struggle ammunition was never wanting.

On 19 and 20 February A Squadron patrols reported on the fighting in and around Goch, where the Lowland Brigade and the Highland Division were in action. Lieut Ansley met an old friend, Lieut Col Grant Peterkin, now commanding the Gordons in the Highland Division, and from him gained information about the progress in the south. On 19 February the regiment's headquarters were shifted from the shoe factory to some of the fine hospital buildings at Bedburg, just outside Cleve on the road to Goch.

On 21 February, with the Highland Division withdrawn to refit and the Welsh re-forming north of Goch, the Scottish Division was engaged south and east of the town against an enemy who would yield nothing without a bitter fight and who had brought into action his largest concentration of guns since Normandy. B Squadron was sent to the division's left flank—the woods around Schloss Calbeck between Goch and Buchholt, to the east. It was the beginning of two days' ordeal by shell and mortar and mine for B Squadron, and particularly for its assault troop and C Squadron's assault troop, with which it was reinforced. Later it was also reinforced by the assault troop from A Squadron. Those days have been described by Capt Boynton:

At first car patrols under Lieut Gillings were sent to make contact with the infantry, and they found the going very difficult, their only way being over poor tracks. The patrols carried out their tasks, but not before the Staghound had ditched itself on a track leading to the schloss, which was the headquarters of one of the infantry battalions. The squadron established its base on the reverse slope of a hill near the headquarters of another battalion, and it was here, when the day's work was thought to be done, that the brigadier pointed to the end of a long, thin strip of wood and said, 'Get your squadron in there.' The squadron commander's jaw dropped slightly—the position was about a thousand yards ahead of the dug-in infantry.

A patrol under Lieut Browne—in his first action with the regiment—set out to find a way through the wood to the place indicated by the brigadier. Several men were blown up and severely wounded by schu-mines. It was hard, with the maps available, to follow the tortuous tracks through the wood. The patrol could not reach its objective.

At the same time Lieut Arthur Buck took a carrier patrol through the Argyll and Sutherland Highlanders in an attempt to get to the tip of the wood from the outside. Approaching the village of Buchholt, he met the forward infantry and was told that his route was under observation and fire from the Udem defences. The troop went on down a forward slope, and, coming under machine-gun fire from a group of buildings, attacked the position and took thirty prisoners, in spite of the fact that the Germans had a tank. Its crew surrendered. Lieut Buck was awarded the Military Cross.

It was impossible, under heavy artillery and mortar fire, to reach the end of the wood this way, and when darkness fell the assault troop and C Squadron's assault troop were standing by, ready to occupy the position but unable to do so because nobody had yet been able to get to it. In the darkness a small but determined foot patrol under Lieut Shirley was successful, and he reported that the end of the wood was free of enemy. So, about eleven o'clock, the assault troops were driven to the schloss, which was being intermittently but accurately shelled. By a miracle no shells dropped while they were disembarking there, and after what seemed ages they set off on foot.

Lieut Shirley's and Lieut Browne's troops dug themselves in, and seemed quite happy when visited in the night. In the morning, however, a patrol under Lieut Shirley stumbled on more mines and came under Spandau fire. About the same time a German tank or self-propelled gun appeared with supporting infantry and shelled the position, where there were no anti-tank weapons. Two members of the patrol were killed in full view of the troops. As the position could easily have been surrounded, it was evacuated and fresh positions were taken up in line with the infantry, where Capt Jackson took command. These were held under heavy shelling until the infantry relieved us on the afternoon of the following day. During the shelling two slit trenches collapsed through pressure, and there were several casualties from shellshock. One man, unable to stand the strain, jumped out of his trench, shouting and singing, and was killed by the next stonk. Excellent patrolling was done from the new positions and Germans were reported in the tip of the wood.

Throughout the two days the tension was unbroken There were constant difficulties in supplying the posts through the mined and shelled woods, and casualties were quite heavy, considering the number of troops used. When being relieved six people did not manage to get away between the stonks, and they were wounded. Lieut Gillings, taking the relief platoon to the positions, was so anxious to get away that he relieved by error half the adjoining infantry platoon. An irate platoon sergeant duly got his men back into their trenches. Lieut Falloon was wounded in the eye near squadron headquarters, and Lieut Jellinek in the hand at the schloss.

The colonel visited the position in the wood with Capt Liddell, who had been commanding C Squadron from the beginning of Veritable because Major Mills was in England. Their visit to the shelled slit trenches was the occasion of the classic remark of C Squadron's one and only 'Bomber' Day, who had served the squadron with varying fortune from the days when he made his truck run on string and wire in the old 54th Division.

'How are you getting on?' the Colonel asked. 'All right, sir. It's nice to see some—' said 'Bomber' Day. Capt Liddell has described this visit:

The journey down from Goch was comparatively peaceful until I reached the schloss, which was being used as temporary headquarters by infantry, artillery observers, engineers, signallers and everybody else who could squeeze himself under its last remaining roof (the ground floor one). Our old friend Doc Pooley was running a casualty collecting and clearing station, and he was a very busy man. I stopped just short of the schloss courtyard, wondering how long it would take me to pluck up courage to dash across the intervening thirty yards and squeeze myself under that solid-looking roof, for the courtyard itself was a most unhealthy place. Several carriers were burning in the middle of it, and every few seconds another load of shells would crash down. I had just decided to make a dash for it when the colonel arrived in his jeep, so we nipped across together. We soon found Jellinek, who was acting as post-box between the assault troops and his squadron headquarters. I was glad to see him, because, although I knew where the assault troops were supposed to be, I had only a vague idea where that was on the ground, and I was not keen on wandering more than necessary among the large lumps dropping on the wood. The colonel and I set off at quite a sharp infantry pace in the direction indicated by Jellinek, and it did not take us long to find the assault troops. It was obvious from the many shell holes and shattered trees about their well-dug position that they were having a very nasty time. But they were amazingly cheerful, and obviously very pleased at having a visit from the colonel. Our journey back to the schloss was, I am glad to say, fairly uneventful, even though my feet tended to stray to within striking distance of the ditches while my thoughts strayed to the basement at Goch where, for all I knew, old Nash might even be beating up a tin of M and V.

The RAF by mistake dropped bombs at night on C Squadron's harbour in the Goch area. This, in effect, was a more friendly gesture than it seemed, for it solved the squadron's greatest transport problem. By good luck nobody was hurt, although several bombs fell near the billets and one on one of the three Carden Lloyd carriers used for towing anti-tank guns. Exploding ammunition set fire to the other two. Joy was unconcealed. Nobody had liked the Carden Lloyds: they had littered the regiment's wake in distress on every long move, and had been the bane of the LAD. Special provision had to be made for them in all the orders for the regiment's convoy drives.

On 23 February the Lowland Brigade was in heavy fighting two miles north of Weeze, and C Squadron carrier patrols spent the day protecting the brigade's left flank under heavy shell and mortar fire, sustaining four casualties and losing five vehicles. In the evening the patrols were relieved by infantry from 46 Brigade. It was the regiment's last action in Veritable. That night orders were received for the relief of the Scottish Division, which was to refit and train for the crossing of the Rhine. The Welsh were to continue the attack on Weeze, and the 3rd British Division was to take over the division's area to the east.

Harbour parties set out for Louvain in Belgium on 24 February, and soon after they had gone the orders were changed and Tilburg was substituted. The regiment drove there next day and settled in comfortable civilian billets among people who had a special regard for the Scottish Division, liberators of the city.

The regiment's casualties in the Goch area had included Cpl C. W. J. Haynes, Tpr R. Bodsworth, Tpr J. D. Meadows and Tpr G. T. Border, who were killed, and Cpl E. A. Hunt, who was missing and later reported killed.

In savage fighting the Canadian Army forced the Germans back beyond Calcar to the Hochwald and on through the forest to the Rhine, whose banks were reached on 9 March. The Ninth US Army's offensive from the Roer, begun on 23 February, had linked with the Canadian offensive at Geldern on

3 March, and by 10 March the Allied Armies were facing the enemy across the Rhine.

Lieut Gen B. G. Horrocks, the commander of XXX Corps, had summed up the results of the first part of Veritable in a message to his corps on 23 February:

'You have taken approximately 12,000 PW and killed large numbers of Germans. You have broken through the Siegfried Line and drawn on to yourselves the bulk of the German reserves in the West. A strong U.S. offensive was launched over the Roer at 03.30 hrs this morning against positions which, thanks to your efforts, are lightly held by Germans. Our offensive has made the situation most favourable for our allies and greatly increased their prospects of success.'

Both General Crerar and General Horrocks praised the Scottish Division's part. The corps commander wrote:

'Your division played the primary role in the initial break-in and, in spite of the most appalling going, it fought its way forward, breached the Siegfried Line and captured the all-important ground on the Materborn feature. You then had some very bitter but successful fighting in the wooded country east of Cleve. You have accomplished everything that you have been asked, in spite of the number of additional German reserves which have been thrown in on your front. It has been a fine performance—Well done, the 15th Scottish Division.'

General Barber told his men, 'No one could have a prouder command, and I salute you all on your great deeds.'

Capt W. J. Jennings joined the regiment. He had been signals officer of the 61st Reconnaissance Regiment, which was in the 50th Northumbrian Division and was disbanded with that great division. He worked with Capt Kemsley an old friend, at RHQ and became signals officer when Capt Kemsley was posted to B Squadron in the following April.

Bernie Higham:- On 18 February whilst the battle of Goch was taking place, Lofty Higgs and I were helping walking wounded back to a medical unit which was based in a nearby schloss. We stopped for a cigarette amongst the lines of stretchers covered by blankets, I sat down next to a man who was clearly in great pain. I lit a cigarette and held it to his mouth which appeared to ease his suffering, I said to him, 'the war is over for you Jock, you will soon be home.' His reply was an agonising cry. I was in the process of giving more cigarettes to the wounded when two orderlies removed the blanket off the first casualty I had spoken to and revealed a German uniform. I realised then that humanity is only the thickness of a blanket!

Alan Westby:-   The Demise of the Carden Lloyd
Somebody had to be blamed! It couldn't have been the Germans for they
hadn't many aircraft left. The RAF just wouldn't do such a thing , it must be the
Americans. Yes! The Yanks were to blame.

It later transpired that we were in a far more forward position than that of
which the RAF had been advised or it was down to poor navigation. Either
way the Yanks were off the hook and it was the RAF who were responsible!
We harboured for the night on the road between Cleve and Goch, just over
the border into Germany. The carriers and the 6-pounder anti-tank guns were
parked at 90 degrees to the road. A carrier then a gun parked alternately in a
line. The lads had slept in holes in the ground, under their vehicles and even in
makeshift tents up to now but here there was a little more shelter for we were
billeted in a ruined hotel over the road from the vehicles and guns.

A soldier's bed is an important piece of equipment and great care is taken in its
construction. Each man has a minimum of two blankets which are made into
a flat tube with as much thickness of material underneath as there is on the
top, the bottom is folded underneath for no one likes cold feet. The organised
soldier crawls in at the top making sure that his head is near the wall for added
protection, having divested himself of his boots and outer clothing. We were
snug as the proverbial bug until a huge explosion awoke everyone. Dressed
and outside, we saw the first carrier on fire caused by a direct hit from a bomb,
the exploding ammunition soon set fire to the other two vehicles. A cry went
up, 'Save the Guns', so two of us dragged a gun from between the two carriers
and ran down the road with it. I expected to feel a thump in my back as I had
been warned that when you were hit by hot flying metal that is what it felt like.
One gun saved we returned for the other but that had already been rescued.
Inspecting the remains of my Carden Lloyd carrier from a safe distance it was
apparent that nothing could be salvaged. The only personal property I possessed
had gone up in flames, namely a Methodist hymn book and a pair of civilian
shoes!

Len Watson:-   Jack 'Tod' Slaughter was a fine athlete and had won the high
jump at the Regimental Games. He always smoked a curly pipe and wore his
beret with the rim straight across his forehead, not at the more customary jaunty
angle. Jack was a Gunner/Wireless operator in a Daimler Dingo car which was
equipped with twin K guns and these were pretty devastating with fairly rapid
fire. He was a formidable soldier and carried out numerous patrols. He was
involved in the famous 'Moonlight' patrols; I think it was Monty's idea to create
artificial moonlight by a battery of searchlights. Jack took part in this endeavour
to capture some high ground.

Both Arthur Watkins and myself were friendly with Jack and when we were able,
in off duty periods, went out together. He was extremely brave and our officer
'Gilly' can confirm that when patrols were required, Jack would be the first to

volunteer. In my opinion he deserved a medal for his brave leadership on the vast amount of patrols he participated in. Sadly Jack was killed instantly in his Dingo, his driver was fortunate to bale out. We buried Jack in a local village cemetery near Cleve and later his body was re-interred in the Reichswald Forest.

I wrote to his family regarding Jack's death on 10 February 1945, aged just twenty-one and still have the reply his Mother sent to me from their Bristol home. They continued to send Tod's tobacco to Arthur Watkins.

I will never forget Gilly's face when he returned from an 'O' meeting and informed us that a patrol was required to enter the Reichswald Forest, it was obviously going to be a dangerous operation. I cannot remember what the objective was or if there was one other than establishing a presence in the dense woodland. I do not think that Major Gordon would have sanctioned such a patrol, although we had an assault troop that was more experienced in foot patrols. A group of mainly Bren carrier crews was formed, we were dressed in tank suits and although armed we did not have a shovel to 'dig in' if necessary. I recollect passing through a line of infantry in trenches, this we had frequently done in our vehicles but not on foot. We advanced a few hundred yards when Lieut Browne who had just joined the Regiment instructed Cpl Haynes to take a patrol, and me to take the other one; I suppose he had heard that I had led previous patrols. I always carried an American semi-automatic Carbine that I had picked up near the Arnhem drop and had served me well since. I just bent down to tie my bootlace when Cpl Haynes' patrol set off; they were soon in trouble from gun fire and mines.

I remember dropping back to a cutting in the wood drive, and observing the position; Lieut. Browne and some of the others were moving back through the woods. I always carried a Mills grenade and a phosphorous grenade and considered throwing it to cover my withdrawal but then thought it would set the undergrowth on fire and possibly the trees and make the situation worse.

Whilst I was in the cutting observing, a large calibre artillery piece commenced firing; the sound was quite different to any discharge I had previously heard, quite devastating. I made a dash for the infantry trench, I think they were Cameronians of our Division. I jumped into a slit trench in order to get below ground level. The shelling was incredible, it was impossible to survive in the open. I remember seeing Schloss Calbeck some distance away and considered making a dash for it but could not make the entrance out; anyway the roof was now ablaze. To stay above ground was lethal; some shells landed with a thud near our position but mercifully did not explode. During a lull in the shelling Major Gordon and Lieut Gillings paid us a visit as there was very little food; we were young and could manage on rations from one of the wooden packs so food was not a desperate concern.

I shared the digging with the infantry to extend the slit trench under a wall; we prayed that a shell would not land in our hole. It was two days of stress and anxiety! It was the only occasion when I witnessed a soldier go 'bomb happy' he jumped out of the trench and started to sing; he was quickly hauled back to safety!

I noticed that the trees around us were absolutely decimated, the tops completely blown away; some years later I read that timber from the Forest was useless because it contained so many shell splinters.

Sadly we lost five good comrades on this Reichswald patrol: Cpl Haynes whose favourite song in the Pontefract pubs was 'Whispering Grass', Cpl Hunt, Tpr Border, Tpr Bodsworth and Tpr Meadows; they were all experienced on Carrier cars and were all proud of their achievements on many patrols since our Normandy days.

I believe that I witnessed one of the largest artillery barrages of the war prior to our crossing of the Rhine and was on the receiving end during forty-eight hours in the Reichswald, it was not a pleasant experience and those of us that survived it were extremely lucky!

I revisited the area fifty years later on one of our regimental re-unions, this time accompanied by my wife and two sisters. As I walked around Schloss Calbeck I still found it difficult to identify the entrance. Although a new roof had been installed, virtually every brick showed damage from shell splinters.

Arthur Watkins:- In the outskirts of Cleve some Gordon Highlanders showed me a bank and pointed out that the safe could be clearly seen at the back of the building if three sets of double doors were propped open. I lined the safe up and fired a 2-pounder AP round, the safe door burst open and wads of money cascaded into the air. Upon inspection the money appeared counterfeit and I put a few notes behind the radio; it was much later that we discovered that the cash was of real value!

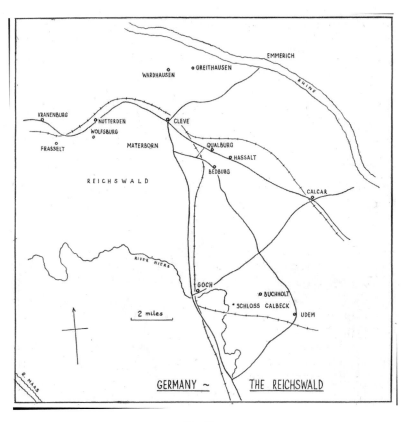

Map 12

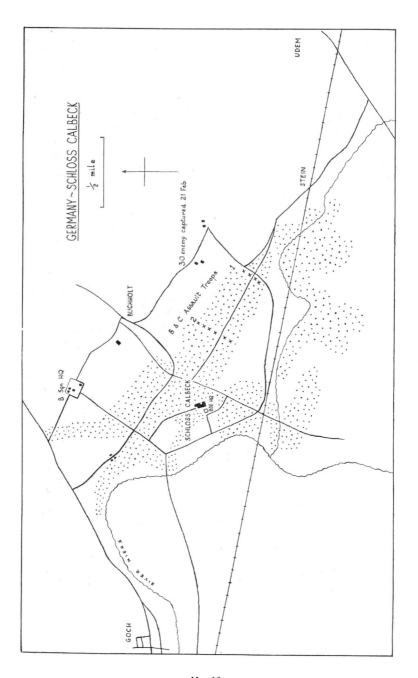

Map 13

A halt on the road to Cleve

The Reichswald Floods . . . on the road to Cleve

Alan Westby - Carden Lloyd Carrier

Only surviving photograph of Arthur Watkins, Len Watson and 'Tod' Jack Slaughter.

'Tod' Slaughter led many patrols in his small Daimler car. He was quite fearless and was killed on 10 February 1945, near Cleve.

Even the Colonel called him 'Tod'. He was the epitome of the experienced British fighting soldier at this stage of the war, never recognised with promotion or awards, but completely on top of his job, brave and resourceful.

British Infantry pressed forward in the wake of armour which has churned this road leading into the Reichswald to a quagmire. Household goods, overturned vehicles and other destruction lined the road which came under heavy artillery fire before the men advanced. Top left is an overturned armoured car with a soldier in tank suit pondering its recovery.

Men of a Scottish Regiment warily advancing through the Reichswald forest. The trees were lobbed and splintered by the terrific barrage which proceeded Monty's new drive. The forest is pitted with Nazi defence posts. Most of the damage was in fact caused by German artillery.

Len Watson and his sisters Trix and Una - Schloss Calbeck, Reichswald Forest, September 1995

CHAPTER XVII

ACROSS THE RHINE
Map 14

The regiment stayed in Tilburg long enough to be inspected by General Barber on the football ground, then moved south on 5 March to share the barracks of Bourg Leopold—a rather dreary Belgian Aldershot—with reinforcement holding units and supply base units. The worst thing about Bourg Leopold was that the RAF had bombed it when it had been occupied by the German Army. The best was that it was only eight miles from Moll, where the regiment already had friends, and not too far from Brussels, where everyone went joyfully in turn for another forty-eight hours' leave. The Scottish Division was planning and practising in Belgium for its part in the crossing of the Rhine as one of the assaulting formations—the beginning of what Field Marshal Montgomery was to describe as 'the last round' in his eve-of-battle message calling for 'the knock-out blow'. As the regiment's part in the assault was to be small, it was not required for the division's dress rehearsal on the Maas, but, for quite another reason, there was much to do in the sixteen days at Bourg Leopold.

The night the regiment arrived there it received a message confirming the rumour that it was to change immediately from Humber armoured cars to Daimlers. This was much the same as moving to a new home, for in the field the armoured car was home to a large part of the regiment, as well as being its eyes and ears and readiest weapon. As each house in a row gains its own character from the way in which it is furnished and lived in, so with the armoured cars—one identical with another to the casual glance as they drove by, but each showing to closer inspection an individuality derived from the belongings of its crew and the way in which they were stowed. The change from one sort of car to the other meant that a tremendous amount of hard work had to be done quickly, for the Daimler, different in mechanism with its fluid flywheel and ability to go backward as fast as forward, required a different technique in both driving and maintenance; and gunners and commanders had to master a new weapon, the 2-pounder, and to accustom themselves to a new turret lay-out. Then there was the question of where to fix the inevitable ammunition boxes crammed with kit. From 7-10 March the tall Humbers were unloaded and handed in to the Second Army Vehicle Park, and the squat Daimlers were collected. The old Humbers had their limitations, but they had worn well under hard use and had been loyal servants. It was to old friends that the regiment said 'Goodbye'.

But there was no time to spend in sentimentality over the old love when the new required understanding and shaping to the regiment's ways. The understanding was acquired in cadres in which the crews trained—first with the old SODs (sawn-off-Daimlers, or, more explicitly, Daimlers whose turrets had been removed)—under the instruction of men lent by the Derbyshire Yeomanry, the Inns of Court and the 11th Hussars, regiments already equipped with the Daimler. The shaping—alterations to adapt the vehicles to the regiment's own ideas and methods—meant many hours of hard work for the LAD under Lieut J. W. Leeming, REME, for the MT staff under the technical adjutant, Capt Pearce, and for Cpl Aveyard and L/Cpl Howie, the instrument mechanics who ran the Royal Corps of Signals workshop in a 3-ton lorry which always accompanied the regiment.

It was apparent that the higher authority which had ordered the change from one type of vehicle to the other had not appreciated the tremendous amount of work involved in carrying it out efficiently. Apart from the handing in of the old Humbers and the drawing of the Daimlers, no arrangements had been made to help the regiment, and the new vehicles were even unserviced, and many of them without oil, when they were collected. Had they not been inspected with the greatest care before being put on the road, many would have been ruined. Higher authority had stated that there were no old Daimlers available for the training of the drivers. Yet in the vehicle reserve depot stood the old Daimlers without turrets—just what were wanted. After gentle persuasion by the colonel they were issued. It was only because the colonel made his own arrangements with the commanding officers of the Derbyshire Yeomanry, the Inns of Court and the 11th Hussars that instructors in Daimler driving and maintenance and 2-pounder gunnery were obtained.

There was one other change at Bourg Leopold—one which caused no regret whatever. On 10 March the anti-tank battery's remaining Carden Lloyd towers were driven and dragged to a vehicle park at Antwerp, where, to the accompaniment of falling V1s and V2s, new carriers were collected to tow the 6-pounders. It was a glad day for the recovery section of the LAD.

At 11p.m. on 21 March the regiment began its drive through Venlo—the town it had watched so long from the other side of the Maas in winter—to Winnekendonck in Germany, where it was quartered in farms to await the crossing of the Rhine. This area near the river was already an amazing sight; almost every hedge and wood sheltered the bridges, rafts and boats with which 60,000 Royal Engineers and men of the Royal Navy were to carry an army across five hundred yards of water. Each of the regiment's squadrons was to supply six half-tracks to tow storm boats and bridging materials to the banks of the Rhine on the eve of the attack. Six carriers were provided to transport Military Government detachments over the river, and two carriers to be a wireless link across it for the RASC. There was no part in the fighting for the regiment until the bridgeheads had been made. Then C Squadron patrols were to land, reconnoitre and link with the 6th Airborne Division, if it had not been already reached by the Scottish Division's advancing infantry.

On the night of 23 March more than 1,300 guns began to fire at the Germans on the east bank, and on the XXX Corps front the Highland Division started crossing opposite Rees. Commanding the 1st Gordons, Lieut Col Grant Peterkin received a wound which kept him in hospital for five days. On the XII Corps front 1 Commando Brigade crossed to Wesel just before midnight, and at two o'clock in the morning the infantry of the Scottish Division, some piped ashore, opened their assault between Rees and Wesel. Twenty minutes later two battalions were complete on the east bank; by dawn there were two brigades, the Lowland and 227. The building of the bridges began. The crossing had gone so much according to plan that to those who did not have to jump from their boats on to a dark and unknown shore it may have seemed much easier than it was. But there was grim fighting at close quarters to force the German paratroops back from their strongpoints, and after the battle the corps commander, Lieut Gen N. M. Ritchie, was to write, 'No one pretends that this was an easy job. It was a mighty difficult one. That the operation was so successful was due entirely to the fighting qualities of the Division.'

At ten o'clock on the morning of 24 March the barking of the artillery on the corps front stopped suddenly, and serenely over the Rhine flew the air armada of the First Airborne Army—more than 1,700 planes and 1,300 gliders. The parachutes opened like hundreds of flowers, and the gliders disappeared behind the woods. Some crashed, some came down in flames. But the objectives, including the crossings of the Issel about seven miles east of the Rhine, were seized. The Scottish Division's infantry reached the most westerly of the Airborne Army's positions in the afternoon. When C Squadron made its way through the bridgehead it found everywhere evidence of the accuracy and deadliness of the airborne attack. Some of the landings had been in the middle of the enemy gun lines, and the guns now stood, intact but silent, beside their dead crews. So great had been the effect on the German artillery that when the squadron crossed the Rhine under a cloudless sky not a single shell interrupted the busy ferries, although there was fierce fighting only three miles ahead.

The Lowland Brigade called for a carrier patrol on 24 March, so 4 Troop was ferried over the river, leaving the rest of the squadron to follow early next day after many hours in the marshalling area. This troop was now commanded by Lieut A. McFall, who called it a 'wonderful bunch'. (But what troop leader did not have a 'wonderful bunch'?) It was the troop of Sgt Royce and Sgt Hubbard, of Cpl Birch (always in gym shoes) and Cpl Harris, of those holders of the Military Medal, Bolton and Coburn, of Bennett, Ireland and Wilkinson, and of course, of Ellis, who always managed to find and wear 'spiv' clothes. Lieut McFall has written of their adventures over the Rhine:

Unable to find the allocated Buffaloes, we got hold of the first we could, and had an ideal crossing, except that Sgt Royce's Buffalo made off on its own and disgorged him on a different beach—not to be seen again for two days. After meeting the King's Own Scottish Borderers, the other carriers went forward to the woods, where we found the headquarters of 3 Parachute Brigade in a large building, surrounded by dead Germans. There was not much we could do, so we went to the Lowland Brigade.

During the night brigade ordered us to patrol through the wood to the autobahn north of Hamminkeln, and we arrived to find our forward troops under fire from self-propelled guns, and several Shermans burning. Breaking from the woods, we saw two white lorries about four hundred yards away. We thought they were ambulances, and Wilkinson was disappointed at not being able to fire the Browning which the carrier sported in addition to a Besa, three clocks, Staghound seats and the cleanest engine forward of the mobile bath unit. We would have been wise if we had fired, because about forty infantry piled out of these lorries when the range had increased and we could not be sure of bagging any. However, they ran pretty fast.

We went on to a farm, where 1 Troop passed through, just in time to leave us with two self-propelled guns, which found us more interesting than we liked. Three DD tanks joined us. One brewed up immediately, Wilkinson's carrier was damaged and a shell came a little too near the back of Bolton's neck. Our efforts at directing the artillery were not very good and did not perturb the SPs in the slightest, but a desperate order for ten rounds gunfire brought over an unexpected wealth of HE which missed the target but played havoc with a company position hitherto unknown. By about four in the afternoon we were able to return to harbour and were glad to find Sgt Royce intact with the rest of the squadron. Cpl Harris and Wilkinson went back for a new radiator, Bolton was patched up, and, apart from the dead cows and the nearness of brigade, all was well with 4 Troop.

Next day we spent in observation in a windmill at Hamminkeln. It was a fairly quiet day except for a thunderstorm in the afternoon. The troop position was in a brewery, which suited all but the troop commander. From then on the troop filled gaps in a wet, cold and very spasmodic line, and after five days and nights without much sleep a rest was welcome.

The rest of the regiment crossed the Rhine by a pontoon bridge on the morning of 26 March. While C Squadron, already working with the Lowland Brigade, continued patrolling on that brigade's front, B Squadron protected the left flank of 227 Brigade, and A Squadron filled a widening gap between the Lowland Brigade and 46 Brigade. Tpr W. L. James and Tpr R. M. Miller, of

A Squadron, were killed. The King's Own Scottish Borderers and the Royal Scots Fusiliers forced a crossing of the Issel—vital to the break-out of the armour—against fanatical resistance, and from there the Lowlanders struck north-east towards Bocholt. The Welsh Division passed through.

On 27 March heavy fighting was reported on all sections of the bridgehead, particularly in the area of Haldern, on the boundary between XII Corps and XXX Corps. On 28 March the regiment was ordered to take full responsibility for protecting the left flank in order to relieve 227 Brigade for an attack on Haldern the next day, but early on the 29th B Squadron's patrols, going forward north of Mehr to give covering fire across the marshland, noticed British troops approaching the brigade's objective from the west. The information was hurriedly sent to divisional headquarters, and 227 Brigade was halted. It was discovered that patrols from the 3rd British Division (XXX Corps) had reported that morning that the enemy had withdrawn from Haldern, and a battalion had been sent to occupy the town. At divisional headquarters similar reports were being received from all brigades: 'The enemy has withdrawn from our front during the night.' The chase was on.

It was a chase which the regiment was itching to join, but the Scottish Division was given a hard earned rest beside the Rhine.

'A great achievement,' wrote General Dempsey to General Barber. 'I send you and the Division my very sincere congratulations. I am sure you are all very proud of what you have done.'

Len Watson:- Crossing the Rhine at Xanten we entered the first German house, inside it was adorned with swastikas and other Nazi material, so we did a bit of damage to the place! As we finished eating off the fine crockery each piece was thrown out of the windows; following this we settled down, no more frustration. 'Mad' McManus emerged from the house immaculately attired in full evening dress complete with silk top hat. 'Mad' Mac was a terrific guy, always shooting at something!

James Ferrier:- On 27 March 1945 3 Troop A Squadron was leading to contact Airborne/SAS. I was not lead car and therefore was standing on my seat looking out of the turret. Tiger tanks had been reported, seen by Charles Millway, in the lead car, but before any action could be taken the first shot hit my car killing my gunner Les James (returned to the Regiment after recovering from wounds received in Normandy) and driver, Rex Miller. Whereas the gunner and driver were killed at once by chest wounds I was hit in the legs and was burnt when the petrol tank exploded.

Harry Green:- I had two Chilean brothers in my troop—they wore BLAV as shoulder flashes (British Latin American Volunteers) their father having been a Scottish insurance man, and I took as much care as I reasonably could not to involve them in the same action together. They were rather special boys and somewhat more refined than most of the men in the Squadron.

In the absence of Peter Ford, Chris Davies sent me on a job at the Rhine crossing. I took carriers and a light armoured car. I asked Chris not to use my troop in my absence, he said he couldn't promise this but would do his best. On my return to the squadron I was met by a very subdued and disconsolate pair of sergeants – Gillespie and Craig – who told me my troop had been used and that the 'Heavy' driven by Rex Miller had been lost. I got hold of his brother and as soon as possible went out and found the car. I stopped the vehicle (brother Miller's light) we were travelling in, some twenty yards short of the burnt out heavy and went to investigate, leaving Miller in his light.

I found two bodies in the ditch – one was the gunner (Leslie James) and the other a legless, armless, headless trunk. It had obviously been burned in the car. The head set was charred into his flesh and it was impossible to identify him. I then clambered into the turret, which was blackened and burned out. I wriggled down under the gun and then saw the exit hole of the 88mm, the path of the solid shot had hit the driver at the very base of his spine and passed out between his feet. I could distinguish the ashes of his legs and also half a burned out skull. I climbed back to the top of the turret and called Miller to come up. He was turning the very badly charred trunk in his hands and looked up at me and said 'I can't tell whether this is my brother or not Sir'. These were exactly his words which I'll never forget. I for my part was thinking, you poor blighter, that is your brother! I then told him to get into the turret of the car so that he could see what I had seen!

James Ferrier was the commander of the heavy that had been lost, he was not the lead vehicle and was standing on his seat looking out of the turret when they were hit; he was seriously wounded and spent nine months in hospital recovering. Leslie James had only recently returned to the Regiment after recovering from wounds received in Normandy. Corporal Ferrier had joined at Felton with Trooper Pollicott who was his usual gunner, 'Polly' had a lucky escape as he was on leave at the time of this action.

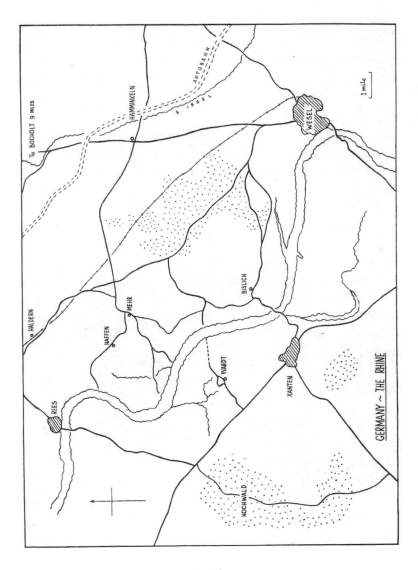

Map 14

CHAPTER XVIII

THE CHASE—TO THE LEINE
Maps 15 and 16

In the low land beside the Rhine the regiment waited while the spring flowers opened and the battle which had become a chase swept farther and farther into the heart of Germany, away from this battlefield littered with broken-backed gliders, burnt-out planes and the weapons and vehicles which the Germans had abandoned under assault from across the water and out of the air. The tanks were in full clatter, with the infantry astride them. Towns east of the Rhine which had been the prerogative of RAF communiques were at last on the Army's maps. On the left XXX Corps was striking north for Enschede and Bremen. In the centre XII Corps headed for Rheine. On the right the maps of VIII Corps were set for Osnabruck, Celle and Uelzen, and 6 Airborne Division was tearing through town and village on the tanks of the 6th Guards Armoured Brigade while the 11th Armoured Division advanced swiftly on its left. For the time being there was nothing for the Scottish Division to do; its part had been to open the flood gates for pursuit. So the regiment waited, and wondered if it would ever join the chase, and passed the time by riding the horses which C Squadron had rounded up and by exploring the litter of the battlefield. Exploring was not without its dangers. The RSM found a panzerfaust— German bazooka— and banged it on the ground to break it, unaware that it contained a propellant charge. By good luck the explosion between his long legs did no more than remove most of his trousers.

On the evening of 2 April the headquarters—in a small farmhouse and tents beside one of the main roads from the Rhine—received the first of the swiftly-changing series of orders which was eventually to place the regiment at the head of the 6th Airborne Division in its dash from the Weser to the Leine. But there was no hint of that then. The regiment was simply warned to be ready to move on the following day, because the Scottish Division had been given to VIII Corps to deal with resistance on the Dortmund-Ems canal while the advance continued. The regiment did move next day, but thirty-five miles north-east to Winterswijk in Holland, although the main part of the division went to the area of Altenburg, near the Dortmund-Ems canal. The command post was set up in the evening in the school at Winterswijk, and what a change it was to receive a glad welcome from the Dutch schoolmaster and his charming daughters after the mute protest of the deserted, untidy houses occupied near the Rhine! This visit to Holland was brief. The situation on the VIII Corps front had changed, and during the night—a night of little rest for the colonel, called repeatedly to the wireless—the regiment was placed under the command of the Airborne Division, which had already by-passed Osnabruck. So, in the chill that precedes the dawn, the long line of vehicles coughed to life and clattered away from Winterswijk in pursuit of the maroon-bereted pursuers.

Nobody knew quite where they would be—they went so fast, these airborne men now tankborne—but there were at least a hundred miles to go, through Bocholt, Borken, Osterwijk and Altenburg and beyond This was the longest and swiftest 'swan' since France, but how different from France! No cheering crowds in the towns, no flowers, no kisses, no wine, no calvados. In the small, neat, high-roofed towns and villages, little marked by war's swift passage, the German people stayed behind their curtains, and showed only the drooping white emblems of surrender. The German civilians who were seen were the very old and the very young, women and the men who had come back from war lacking a limb. They watched without visible emotion. But there were cheers. They came from the small groups of those who had been slave workers and were now trekking west with their bundles, their barrows, their carts and their commandeered German cars, for which they were always trying to wheedle petrol. Frenchmen, Dutchmen, Belgians, men of many nations, delighting in freedom.

Reaching Altenburg in the middle of the day, the regiment occupied what appeared to be an outsize in quartermasters' stores and awaited further orders. In the late afternoon and evening it was on the move again, going through Greven, skirting the battle on the Dortmund-Ems canal, driving beside a line of hills to Lengerich. The night's harbour was Mundrop, five miles south-east of Osnabruck. The 6th Airborne Division was still somewhere ahead, wherever the route labelled 'Pegasus Up' ended. The colonel had gone on in his jeep to find out where that was and get his orders for the following day. The signals officer, the medical officer and Merryman had gone on in another jeep to make arrangements about communications and casualties. For these two jeep parties there were still many miles to go in dusk and darkness—lonely miles up hill and down hill, by wood and farm, with 'Pegasus Up' and the white flags drooping in the villages as the only signs that an invading army had already passed that way. The maroon berets, it seemed, had always dashed on from where they were expected to be. The signals officer ran out of maps and had to place his faith entirely in the sign of the winged horse. Cpl Ridge, the colonel's driver, has told the story of his journey:

The Airborne Division was to have harboured for the night at Bad Essen, but we found the place deserted, so we pushed on. About forty Germans came out of a wood and wanted to surrender to us. Having no time to deal with them, the colonel pointed in the direction from which we had come, and they formed up and marched that way. It was eleven o'clock when we reached the Airborne—at Oldendorf. The colonel went to G Ops, and after midnight we went on to a brigade headquarters for information, and were almost involved in a battle. Returning to divisional headquarters, we found the signals officer and the medical officer there with the other jeep, and at one in the morning we set off for RHQ, with the other jeep following. We put the headlights on. Airborne guards told us to switch them off, as a jeep had been hit by a self-propelled gun earlier in the evening. But the colonel decided to make a dash with the lights on and hope for the best, so we went down the road flat out, with my fingers crossed. I was reading the map by the light of a torch. We came to a canal where a farm was burning on the other side of a wrecked bridge. This was wrong. We went back to the nearest village and tried again. Soon we were at the damaged bridge and blazing buildings again. The colonel said my map reading was ... We tore down another road, the other jeep following and using our tail light as a guide. By now it was half-past two, and the colonel wanted an order group at three. I tried to call RHQ on the wireless, but my batteries were flat. We pushed on through the night, the colonel speechless. We reached RHQ soon after three, but there was no jeep behind.

In the darkness Merryman had noticed a sharp bend too late, and the other jeep had plunged off the road and down a steep bank into a field. There it stuck until an Airborne jeep on patrol roared out of the blackness, and with tow chains rescued the miserable, chilled, drowsy party which had been sharing the night with the howling of a dog at a distant farm. The signals officer, the medical officer and Merryman arrived at Mundrop just in time to join the column on its drive along the route on which they had spent the night.

By the time the regiment had covered the twenty miles through Bissendorf and Rabber to Oldendorf, the Airborne had a bridgehead over the Ems-Weser canal five miles north of Oldendorf, and was about to wheel east for the Weser, thirty miles ahead. The colonel sent A Squadron forward to work with the tanks of the Grenadier Guards. The opposition was light, and progress was good, but the squadron's day was clouded by the death of Sgt Nobby Whiting, who had won the DCM in France and was admired throughout the regiment for his enthusiasm on the soccer field with the regimental side and on the battlefield with his armoured car patrol. Tpr M. A. West was killed at the same time. It was soon realised that working with the Airborne was quite a new experience. Riding their tanks, leaping off them to brush aside resistance with attacks that had reached the perfection of drills, the maroon berets advanced faster than anybody for whom the regiment had reconnoitred before. The colonel has analysed their methods and the ways in which the regiment co-operated with them in the advance to the Leine:

The Airborne Division's normal method of advance was on one centre-line, the leading brigade clearing to about five hundred yards on either side; the second brigade dealing with any large concentrations on either flank; the third brigade probably resting until it could go right through and take up the advance next day. What was required of us was to have a small patrol in front of the leading brigade to give early warning of opposition. On meeting resistance we tried to get all the information we could, and when the 6th Airborne troops arrived they immediately deployed and attacked. We were requested not to get too heavily involved on the centre-line in order not to restrict their supporting fire.

The speed with which the Airborne worked on these small operations had to be seen to be believed. They had the drill absolutely cut and dried. There was no hanging about—the commander merely wanted to know what we had found and immediately deployed the infantry on either side of the road. The tanks followed up, and between them they could clear a fairly large village in about twenty minutes.

The Airborne Division fully appreciated the tremendous advantage which speed gave it, but this form of advance was a nerve-racking business for the leading patrol if there were any enemy in the area, for the panzerfaust can make a mess of an armoured car or scout car. During the whole of the regiment's advance from the Weser to the Elbe, first with the Airborne and then with its own division, the leading vehicles had to expect a panzerfaust when passing through the many woods, rounding any bend or entering any village. As a rule, panzerfaust teams were mounted on bicycles. Because their job was to cause the maximum delay, they normally fired at the first patrol.

On the flanks our task was to sweep through the country, dealing with minor pockets and informing the Airborne Division's headquarters of any major concentrations or any other threat from the flanks. Our assault troops and carriers were invaluable in overcoming the minor opposition, even to the extent of clearing a village. When the resistance on the flank was too strong for us, a brigade was immediately deployed. We were asked to clear up to a start line, and the brigade pushed on, clearing the opposition, with a small patrol of ours in front.

On the evening of 5 April the regiment's headquarters were moved across the Ems-Weser canal to Destel, two miles to its north. The pace of the advance was still a little bewildering. Even such a sedate body as corps headquarters was scampering forward like a two-year-old at Newmarket, and when Lieut Riesco, now assistant intelligence officer, went back thirty miles on an urgent mission to corps for the colonel he found that he was fifty miles behind the head-quarters' new location. The Airborne stormed the Weser at Petershagen on 6 April. Resistance round the bridgehead stiffened with the arrival of German reinforcements and the Luftwaffe, but on the following day the regiment crossed the river and its real gallop began. It was the crack of the whip of the colonel's dreams, although the crossing itself contained no hint of that. Much confusion was caused by the omission of a canal from the map, and twice in ten minutes—the second time somewhat furtively—RHQ drove by the colonel at the same spot. In his expression the second time pain mingled with surprise.

Orders for the advance from the Weser had been given out the previous day at Wegholm, eight miles from the river, where the regiment had concentrated before the crossing. C Squadron was to be on the right, protecting the flank and maintaining touch with XII Corps of the American Ninth Army, which was keeping pace with the Airborne Division. B Squadron had to reconnoitre the way for 5 Parachute Brigade south of the large Steinhuder Meer, and had the special task of dashing for the Leine, thirty miles ahead, and seizing the bridges at Bordenau and Neustadt. The car patrols which led the squadron were commanded by Lieutenants Gillings, Peterson and Falloon, and Lieut Gillings has described the day:

After crossing the river at the inevitable first light, we made our way to the Airborne forward positions and did quite a tour of the bridgehead, crossing railways and canals that were not on the map and going up roads that ended in duck ponds. We had a small battle with Germans who had shot up part of the Airborne B Echelon, which had somehow got to the front. Finally, we got away on our job about eight o'clock.

The airborne colonel said to me, 'Sonny, I want you to go like hell for the bridge, and don't stop for any one. I'll be right behind you.' I had a Humber scout car—with twin K guns—and two Daimler armoured cars, with five carriers following.

Our start seemed ridiculously slow, but I had learned that if your leading car commander knew his job his speed was your speed. We did the first two miles in twenty minutes before we made our first contact—in the village of Rosenhagen. The rush of civilians for cover told us that the place was held by the enemy, and when three German soldiers ran out of a house we knew that they were not prepared for us. The leading car shot past them, wounding all three, and was engaging another six almost immediately. Soon all three cars were in the village, and we were having the time of our lives. Having pinned the enemy to the houses, we used our 2-pounders, and the Besas started the usual fires. Three hundred yards behind us the carriers were engaging two Spandau positions with such good results that they never troubled us at all. But I had forgotten bazookas. We had six slung at us, and two of my cars were damaged. Luckily, only the wheels were hit, so we were able to sit tight and continue burning the village.

Within twenty minutes the Airborne and tanks arrived. If you have ever worked with them, you know that they just rushed right up to the scene of firing, dismounted from the tanks and were in action almost immediately—such beautiful drills. What confidence it gave us to see them in action! The colonel was true to his word. He arrived at the head of the tanks, riding on the bonnet of a jeep, and all he asked was that I get my cars off the road and take the lead again as soon as he had cleared the opposition.

The battle lasted about an hour, and at 9.30 we were ready to go on, having reorganized. My troop was now three Daimler armoured cars. Bill Falloon, a patrol leader and I decided that: (1) never would we stop in close country or in a village; (2) we would decide, if possible, whether or not a village was held before we entered it, and act accordingly. If it were held, we would rush through, and stop only when we were well clear of it, and even then the carrier crews would dismount and circle us to make us bazooka-proof.

We went on at a good speed, sometimes doing thirty or forty miles an hour through a village, always with the three cars as close together as possible. Going through Hagenburg, we came upon a roadblock manned by about twenty Germans, and at the other end of the village the carriers engaged about thirty who had had to let us pass. We stayed in the village—quite comfortable—until the Airborne arrived thirty-five minutes later. The cars went backward and forward all the time, firing at anything that moved. We found that one house set on fire would keep the civilians indoors.

The Airborne troops on the tanks which trundled behind B Squadron's swift cars found their way marked, like a grim paper chase, by the destruction left by the two-pounders, Besas and K guns. Twelve Germans were found dead in a barn which the patrol had riddled in passing because it looked like a German position. Ten more lay dead behind a hedge. The K guns savaged a lorry whose driver was hit by a bullet from the pistol of the leading driver of the patrol. Four German soldiers in a civilian car were wounded when a big Daimler rammed it. German aircraft in a hangar were peppered by the Besas and 2-pounders. About 300 prisoners were taken.

The cars by-passed the airfield at Wunstorf, where anti-aircraft guns opened fire on them. The Airborne men on their tanks cut across to the road beside the Leine, and the leading cars and tanks crossed the Bordenau bridge in a bunch while the enemy scrambled into lorries at the far end of the village. The British paratroops quickly formed a bridgehead, and removed the demolition charges from the bridge.

Without delay B Squadron sent a patrol north to try to take Neustadt bridge from the east, but it met stiff resistance and came under shellfire. Another, going along the west bank, was fired on about a mile from the bridge. A foot patrol went forward and reported that there was no indication that the bridge was destroyed but the area was held by the enemy. That night the paratroopers reached Neustadt bridge after an infantry charge in open order across Wunstorf airfield, but the bridge was blown up in their faces when they tried to rush it. The explosion caused casualties.

On B Squadron's left flank that day Lieut Peterson's four cars of 5 Troop, without support, had cleared twenty miles. Then Cpl Ritson's car was hit by a bazooka, which killed Tpr R. T. Bates, the gunner, and wounded Tpr Hart. Climbing on to the turret to get them out, Lieut Peterson was wounded by a sniper.

On the right flank C Squadron had soon met opposition—in the village of Raderhorst, two miles south of Rosenhagen. Cpl A. Little has described what happened here:

After crossing the Weser our patrol of three cars had left the bridgehead at Bierde, which had been attacked by enemy tanks and infantry in the night. We went on for about three miles, Cpl Lavery's car and mine 'leapfrogging', with Licut Morris's Daimler in support. At the approaches to Raderhorst we came up against an anti-tank gun, and almost immediately bazookas were fired behind us. One hit the Daimler as it drew alongside me, and at first I thought our car had been hit, because both Bradshaw, my gunner, and I were wounded. We hurried back down the road with Cpl Lavery's Dingo while more bazookas burst around us, some only a yard away. All three people in Lieut Morris's car were wounded. Tpr Crouch, the driver, could not avoid capture, and the determined efforts of Lieut Morris and L/Cpl Maxwell to get away were also unsuccessful. A few days later an enemy hospital was over-run, and they were found there and sent to England. We were all very sorry to learn some months later that Maxwell died of his wounds.

C Squadron pushed on through a hard day, having to clear each village, having to contend with tracks which were, at best, bad and at worst only on the map, and having no infantry or tank support until 3 Parachute Brigade joined the squadron late in the afternoon.

A Squadron, which had begun the day in reserve, was soon ordered to go north along the east bank of the Weser to Windheim, which B Squadron's early patrols had reported held by the enemy behind mined approaches. North of this village the 11th Armoured Division was having to fight hard to expand its bridgehead between Nienburg and Stolzenau, and at its request A Squadron cleared Windheim and three more villages, reporting on two important bridges. On this northward advance Lieut Harry Green's troop, attacking a village after one of its cars had been knocked out by a bazooka, was hampered by a Spandau on the flank, but Lieut Green eliminated this position with a grenade, and the village fell. Twelve Germans were killed and twenty captured. This was one of the exploits for which Harry Green was later awarded the Military Cross.

Receiving information of A Squadron's progress, parts of the 11th Armoured Division crossed the Weser to the Airborne bridgehead and went on through the squadron, which then swung east and drove the enemy from Munchehagen, where the armoured division had become involved in heavy fighting.

When a tired regiment went to its blankets on the night of 7 April RHQ was in a hurriedly abandoned SS camp north of Lahde, and the squadrons were scattered miles away—B at Bordenau, A at Munchehagen and C at Wiedensahl. That day the regiment had helped to shatter the Weser line and to lessen German hopes of a stand on the Leine. Success had not, however, been without its price.

Arthur Watkins:- The airfield at Wunstorf was brilliantly camouflaged, close inspection revealing many fighter aircraft dispersed across a wide area. The speed of our advance had obviously forestalled any evacuation plan. I fired 2-pounder HE shells at the nose wheels of the aircraft to effectively disable them. I met the Luftwaffe CO of the base and relieved him of his Belgian Browning pistol and belt; unfortunately this went 'missing' later.

We intercepted a train with many troops returning for leave; they were most upset to go straight into the 'bag' when they were so close to home. One of our troop noted for his shoot-first attitude enthusiastically reported shooting a General. We accompanied him back to the scene to discover one dead Station Master; an excess of gold braid was his downfall!

*   *   *   *   *

A similar event with less severe consequences was recalled by Barry Gibson, a dashing Lieutenant in the 11th Hussars, the day after the war had ended, he was charged with manning a roadblock on the Hamburg to Lubeck autobahn with the objective of apprehending a German General. A great mass of humanity was on the move but eventually the target was captured and sent under escort back to HQ. Barry was surprised and more than a little disappointed when he was admonished on the radio for sending in a high-ranking member of the German Fire Service!

15th Recce troops on captured airfield believed to be 'Wunstorf'
Three Fw 190s appear undamaged

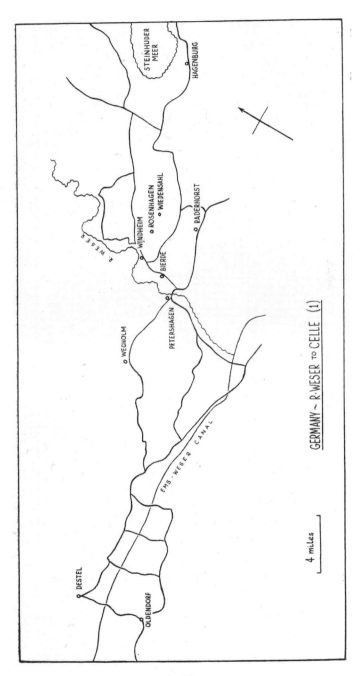

Map 15

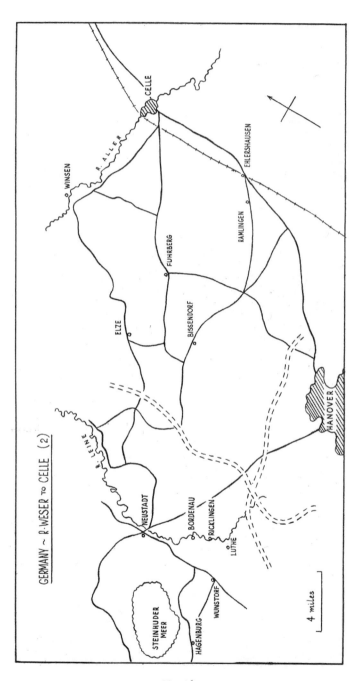

Map 16

CHAPTER XIX

THE BATTLE OF RICKLINGEN BRIDGE
Map 17

Next day, 8 April, the Battle of Ricklingen Bridge was fought. Ricklingen stands on the east bank of the Leine, five or six miles south of Bordenau and not far north of the autobahn to Hanover. It was still in German hands, and there were Germans west of the river. It was reported that they had tanks in Luthe. The capture of the bridge at Ricklingen intact was important, for the Americans needed it, their advance on the right of the Airborne being impeded by the destruction of the autobahn bridge over the Leine. B Squadron sent a mixed force under the command of Lieut Arthur Buck south from Bordenau along the east bank of the river. Three Parachute Brigade, with C Squadron, was to advance on Ricklingen from the west. This is Lieut Buck's account of the Battle of Ricklingen Bridge:

B Squadron had orders to reconnoitre the approaches to the bridge at Ricklingen, to seize it if it was still intact and to hold it until relieved by the 6th Airborne. It was thought that the bridge would have to be held for not more than an hour and a half. The task was allotted to me, and I was given command of the remnants of two carrier troops, the assault troop, the mortars and a 6-pounder. We were quite well equipped with automatic weapons, having Bren guns, Browning machine guns and Sten guns.

It was considered wiser not to go along the west, or 'home', bank of the river for three reasons. The first was that the distance was about double that along the east bank. The second was that to reach Ricklingen by way of the west bank it was necessary to pass through the village of Luthe, in which the Airborne troops were fighting against stiff opposition, including, we understood, four Tiger tanks. (It was deemed more prudent to face the unknown than to face four suspected Tigers.) The third reason was that the element of surprise in attacking from the rear would be much greater than in attacking from the front, where we were expected.

About nine o'clock in the morning we were on our way. Our route lay through close and wooded country, and we were not surprised that the Airborne in the Bordenau bridgehead had suffered casualties from snipers who had worked their way forward through the woods. We moved as quickly as the ground permitted over a rough track, stopping only to investigate likely ambush points. By about 9.20 we were within about half a mile of Ricklingen. Through my binoculars I saw two enemy cyclists pedalling from the west side of the river as fast as they could over the bridge and into the village.

By now the bridge was revealed—a large metal suspension bridge, intact. I felt sure that we had been seen and that the two cyclists were going to warn a demolition party, so I decided to take a chance and make a dash through the village to the bridge. We tore into the village to see several of the enemy running hard for the bridge. A few bursts from our Brownings soon cooled their ardour, and we quickly rounded them up.

The bridge was neatly prepared for demolition, dozens of boxes of explosive being stacked on the pavements and secured under the bridge supports. All were connected by fuse wires. We dismounted and immediately cut all the wires we could see, but in order to make sure that the bridge was safe I got hold of the officer in charge of the enemy sappers and persuaded him to give me enough information to allow us to make all the charges safe. Then I instructed some of our prisoners to climb over the parapet and under the bridge to release the charges so that they would fall into the river. Other prisoners were put to work dumping into the river the explosive which was stacked on the pavements. Meanwhile we took up positions of all-round protection.

The bridge having been made safe, we placed the prisoners in a cellar, and took up prepared positions astride the bridge. The 6-pounder I had sited on the east side of the river, covering the road running into Ricklingen from Luthe on the west bank, where we suspected the four Tigers to be. It was not possible to get all the vehicles off the road, and some had to be parked at intervals along the village street. Half my force I placed in slit trenches on the east side of the bridge, and half on the west. I remained in Ricklingen.

Time dragged on. We saw some enemy 40 mm guns firing tracer in the direction of Luthe, so I made a wireless request to squadron headquarters for our gunners to have a crack at their enemy counterparts.

Just then shells began to fall around us, and we took cover. I made my way along the road in the direction from which the shells came—to see if I could spot any guns. There were no signs of German troops or guns, but one or two civilians were moving about. I had a feeling that there was something up the road, over the crest about six hundred yards away. But my force was too small to reconnoitre any farther, and our task was to sit tight on the bridge until the Airborne relieved us. We had fondly hoped that we would have to hold the bridge for only an hour and a half at the most, but it was now about one in the afternoon, and we had already been in position for three and a half hours. Things did not always work out according to plan, however, and we were more concerned about the Airborne boys, who seemed to be having quite a party in Luthe. The enemy shelling began again, so I asked for artillery fire to be put on the area where I thought the German guns might be. Our shells screamed over, and we got respite from the enemy shelling.

Another hour passed. Sgt Mathews and I looked around the village. I asked some children if they had seen any of their soldiers and tanks. Apparently they had seen one big tank and a few 'little tanks with no tops' but with big guns, which I assumed were self-propelled guns. These had gone along the road—the road from which the firing came—before we arrived in the village. Mathews and I felt a little uncomfortable, as we had found track marks on the road. From their width, the distance between them and the depth of the imprint we could only draw one conclusion—TIGER. I made the village policeman put everyone in the village into cellars, as I expected trouble.

Sure enough, it came!

About two o'clock I was sending a wireless report to squadron headquarters from my carrier, which was about twenty yards along from the crossroads in the village, when I heard the clanking of tank tracks. Sgt Mathews ran up, and, pointing behind me, said: 'Don't look now, but I think that's a tank.' I looked round quickly. About forty yards away, just coming round the corner, was a terrible looking monster with Tiger written all over it. The 88 was pointing right at us, and the muzzle-brake looked the size of a railway engine. The back of my throat felt parched.

My PIAT firer got two or three shots off, but was over-keen and missed the vulnerable parts. The tank blazed away, and we did not see the poor lad again.

I ran along to the next wireless carrier, out of the line of fire, and made a desperate request for tanks to be sent up to support us. I felt sure we would stand a good chance of bagging this Tiger if a couple of Churchills could be sent up. 'No tanks are available' came the reply. We were on our own; the PIAT was out of action; and the 6-pounder was covering a different road.

The Tiger fired its 88 at point blank range into the carrier from which I had come, and the old carrier met its end in a shower of sparks, flames and a cloud of white smoke. The tank slewed round, and I was again in the line of fire. I ran to the next wireless carrier and asked for our artillery to lay a concentration on Ricklingen. We were prepared to risk being hit ourselves just to have the enemy hit too, so that the bridge we had held on to so long might be saved. For various reasons the concentration could not be given, and in a way we were relieved.

By now the Tiger was shooting up our vehicles one by one, and in its wake came two self-propelled guns—the ones which had already shelled us from a distance—and three or four armoured half-tracks.

I went to one of my half-tracks behind some houses to wireless a report to squadron headquarters. All the time my chaps were valiantly firing off everything they had—Brens, Stens, rifles, anything to keep the enemy at bay. I was proud to be in command of such grand men. The fire held off the enemy half-tracks and the self-propelled guns, and made the Tiger keep its lids closed. As I spoke on the wireless at the rear of the half-track there was a blinding flash and a noise of tearing metal. The engine had received a direct hit. We hurriedly abandoned the vehicle, and the flames took possession.

The Tiger had reached the bridge, and tried to make it unusable by firing its 88 at the parapet. This proved ineffective. The tank withdrew into the village, followed by a renewed outburst of small arms fire from my party on the west side.

We got on to the road by which we had arrived—the road where the 6-pounder was sited. The Tiger saw us and gave chase. It seemed a good idea to try to manhandle the 6-pounder round and deal smartly with the Tiger at almost point blank range. We heaved at the gun, one of the gunners nursing an AP shot. But the Tiger opened fire, and we had to abandon the gun, as we could not turn it in time. The Tiger trundled up and ran over the gun, leaving it useless.

There was still no sign of relief, and our ammunition was desperately low. I decided to pull back my party. We fell back some two hundred yards, the Tiger following. The tenacity and strength of the enemy suggested that this might be the leading patrol of a counter-attack on our main column, and I felt that I must get the information to squadron headquarters. I had no vehicles or wireless left, so we had to form up in sections and return on foot. I could not get in touch with my party on the other side of the bridge, but I expected the Airborne to join it at any time and felt that it could stay and welcome the Airborne.

We set off at the double, and by taking to the woods shook off our pursuers. When we reached Bordenau, I reported the situation to squadron headquarters. The squadron stood to and waited.

The party I had left by the bridge sat tight until the Parachute Brigade, having cleared Luthe and doubled for two miles behind its brigadier, arrived and drove the enemy from Ricklingen. The sight of the Airborne men brought a cheer from the harrassed little force. The bridge was saved, and the Americans began to swarm across.

In the defence of the bridge one man was killed and one was missing; six carriers were destroyed and two were disabled; two half-tracks were destroyed and two were disabled; and the 6-pounder was destroyed.

At Bordenau the expected attack did not materialize, and darkness brought welcome relief to all.

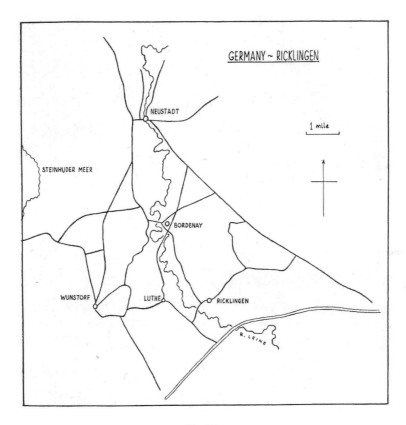

Map 17

CHAPTER XX

THE CHASE—TO THE ELBE
(Including the fight of C Squadron against the Clausewitz Division at Nettlekamp)

Maps 16, 18 and 19

The 6th Airborne Division's headlong advance from the Rhine was halted—by order—across the Leine. When that river was crossed the division had been constantly in action for a fortnight since landing by parachute and glider among the German guns, and now the advance was to be taken over by the Scottish Division, rested after its crossing of the Rhine. The passing of one division through the other inevitably meant a loss of momentum in the pursuit; the result of the delay was met farther east—in the demolitions and strengthened resistance beyond Celle. It was on 11 April that the Scottish Division took up the chase. On 8 and 9 April the regiment had patrolled from the Leine bridgehead, A Squadron reaching points five miles from the river on the second day, and on the 10th the Airborne Division had extended its hold east of the river to include the high ground in the area of Bissendorf and Elze, north of Hanover. It was the last time the regiment reconnoitred the way for the maroon berets. Its orders were to go beyond the high ground and explore towards the town of Celle, which stands on the river Aller behind a screen of forests.

A and C Squadrons set off in the thick mists of morning. On the left A Squadron reported village after village clear, and reached the large village of Fuhrberg, about ten miles east of Celle in the Forest of Fuhrberg, without being opposed, although six German officers and about ninety other ranks were taken prisoner. The squadron established headquarters in Fuhrberg, and the patrols went on towards Celle for another three miles or so. Then they had to stop because a bridge had been destroyed. The woods were so thick on both sides of the road that it was impossible to by-pass the obstacle or the bazooka teams on bicycles which appeared.

On the right flank C Squadron at first had more trouble with the going than with the enemy, finding that many of the poor tracks petered out in fields and woods. The squadron kept in touch with the Americans, now clearing a Hanover whose rafters had been laid bare by bombers as an anatomist lays bare the ribs. As the patrols drew level with the city resistance grew stronger. Lieut McFall, commanding combined 1 and 3 Troops since the wounding of Michael Morris, has described a typical patrol on this day:

Cpl Lavery and Fowler—as usual—were leading. They must have had the best eyes in the British Army, for I do not remember them being surprised on any occasion, even when the bazooka boys came out with a vengeance. Sgt Jacques came next in the order of march, and Sgt Dullaway was in the rear. The cut of the cards had given us the job of coming up from south-east of Celle to seize the bridges east of the town, but that never happened because we came upon the town's ring defences. We did, however, free some men of the 6th Airborne who had been captured just west of the Weser. On the northern outskirts of Hanover we took a large German tank intact, the crew having left it, and the Americans set fire to it. About a mile farther on we bumped ack-ack 88s which were firing at David Richford's patrol on our left. There was also a roadblock, and we laid on an attack while an American photographer, whom we had picked up, took photographs of us in action. We put the 2-inch mortars on an embankment to give covering fire; Cpl Lavery, in the Dingo, was firing from the right of the road; Sgt Dullaway was firing past him; the carrier crews were dismounted and ready to go round the flank. But the squadron leader called the attack off. From about this time we had a section of the assault troop to help us in wooded country, and 'Bomber' Day and Higgs did some wonderful shooting on the principle of one shot, one man.

Next day, 11 April, the regiment again went into the forests around Celle, but this time with the infantry of the Scottish Division hurrying behind to join in the advance. On the road from Fuhrberg A Squadron met demolitions and enemy at the same place as on the previous evening. This was work for the infantry and sappers, and at one o'clock 227 Brigade took over.

On the right B Squadron advanced swiftly through the woods to Ramlingen, but the enemy held the important road junction and railway crossing on the main Celle-Hanover road at Ehlershausen. Lieut Jellinek had a car patrol here. Only a civilian was to be seen—until a man jumped out of a ditch with a bazooka which hit Lieut Jellinek's car at two yards' range, wounding him and the driver. The German was killed, either by his own panzerfaust or by a grenade thrown from the turret of the car. The scout car was hit almost simultaneously, and Cpl H. Rogal and Tpr L. A. Ward, MM, were killed. Lieut Jock Browne was behind with the carriers of 4 Troop, which fired forward and themselves came under fire. During these exchanges Tpr J. Moffat, Lieut Jellinek's gunner and wireless operator, scrambled into the driver's seat, turned the damaged Daimler round in the narrow road and drove it back through the carriers. The Germans were SS troops with guns. After going north and south without finding a way round them, B Squadron kept them under observation until relieved by 46 Brigade late in the afternoon.

C Squadron was again on the extreme right, keeping touch with the Americans and dealing with pockets of resistance. Suspicious of the civilians' behaviour when it approached one village, Lieut McFall's patrol pulled back, looped to the left and approached the place again through pine and birch woods from the north-east. The woods opened into boggy land, and beyond it, two hundred yards away, about forty Germans were marching along the road with bazookas on their shoulders and among them a horse drawing an 88 mm gun. Unseen, unheard, the cars lined the edge of the wood, and at the word 'Go' spattered the Germans with fire from all their guns. Then the patrol melted away into the woods again.

Early on 12 April the 10th Highland Light Infantry, of 227 Brigade, entered Celle and crossed the Aller, the last important river barrier before the Elbe, sixty miles ahead. West of the Aller bands of Germans were withdrawing northward towards Winsen through the forest, and A Squadron sent patrols that way. This is Lieut Gordon Dalton's account of what happened when a patrol consisting of his Daimler and Cpl Coleman's light car went to see if there were Germans at crossroads which the 11th Armoured Division had reported strongly held on the previous day:

Our route was very tricky—thickly wooded on both sides all the way. When we sighted the crossroads we saw movement, which showed that they were still held, and as we nosed our way forward we spotted a cart across the road. By then we were only about ninety yards from the crossroads. More Germans appeared and had a look at us, but not a shot was fired.

As so many Germans had already given in to us on our way from the Rhine, I assumed that this was another surrender, and, standing in the turret, shouted 'Surrender' in German, Dutch and English. But when the other car went forward to drag the cart aside the calm exploded as if a match had been put to petrol. Three bazookas were fired at the light car. They missed. Tpr Judd, the driver, reversed quickly out of sight, and I never saw the vehicle again. We were determined not to withdraw until we had destroyed as much as possible, and Tpr Black, my gunner, set fire to buildings and polished off a few Germans.

The situation was, however, becoming too hot for us, so I decided to get out of it. It was not easy to turn the car round in the narrow road, but L/Cpl Berry did it quickly and skilfully while Black and I kept firing. Suddenly something happened. I thought it was a premature explosion in the breach of the 2-pounder, but, coming to from a daze, found the vehicle listing in a ditch. We had been hit. Automatically I baled out and joined Black in the ditch. I peered through the driver's vision slit, and saw Berry still at the wheel, seemingly dead. Small arms fire prevented us from getting him out. As we crawled away I turned to have a last look at the vehicle and saw Berry struggling to get out, so we immediately returned to help him. He was badly wounded, and his courage was beyond praise. We tore up the legs of my trousers to bandage his wounds, and carried him along the ditch under fire. After crawling about two hundred yards we were all exhausted. Berry's condition grew worse, so Black went off to fetch a vehicle to take him to a first-aid post. Hours seemed to go by before a truck from the gunners arrived. Berry and I were both evacuated to a field hospital, where he was detained because his condition was so grave. I was eventually flown to a general hospital in Belgium, and I regret to say that this was the end of my connection with the regiment and a troop which it had been an honour to lead.

The southern approaches to Celle were so obstructed by demolitions that 46 Brigade and B and C Squadrons were switched north to 227 Brigade's route, and the regiment queued with most of the divisional transport along the Fuhrberg-Celle road, waiting for the bridges at Altencelle to be completed. Other units, seeing the regiment for the first time since it left them near the Rhine, were surprised at its new look. So rapid had been the advance that it had been impossible to replace stricken vehicles except with whatever could be commandeered, and in the line of march sleek limousines, a German ambulance, speckled German half-tracks and even a fire engine went exotically nose-to-tail with the drab, angular armoured cars and bumping carriers. RHQ joyfully acquired a smart car to carry some of the conglomeration of kit from the command vehicle, which was burdened on the move with the personal belongings of several men in addition to its many maps, codes, telephones and forests of aerials and the two wireless sets over which Cpl Pat Stafford and Berny Booty had sweated for long hours in France and shivered for long hours in Holland. Unfortunately, in the new car the looks of a thoroughbred were accompanied by the temperament of a mule, and all the kit had to be bundled hastily back into the command vehicle at a moment when the colonel was directing battle operations from it. It was not one of RHQ's happiest moments!

After struggling along sandy tracks east of the Aller, B and C Squadrons halted for the night at Altenhagen and RHQ at Bostel. A Squadron remained in the graceful town of Celle—where a small and gruesome concentration camp was discovered—a subsidiary of Belsen. The horrible camp of Belsen was only a few miles away, and on the morning of that day a German delegation had arrived at the headquarters of the 11th Armoured Division to negotiate the surrender of a large area around it, because typhus had broken out.

Next day, 13 April, the regiment began the advance from Celle to Uelzen, spread over a wide front ahead of the infantry of the Division and the tanks of 6 Guards Armoured Brigade. The chinagraph pencils had marked the three routes across maps blotched with the green of woods and veined with the blue of streams, and but thinly spotted with the black of villages and farms. B Squadron had the main road in the centre — the road which runs roughly parallel with the railway through Eschede and Weyhausen. On the left A Squadron had its maps set for Scheuen, Rebberiah, Unterluss and Bahnsen, while on the right C Squadron's line of advance was Ohe, Marwede, Bokel and Nettelkamp.

A Squadron encountered only minor opposition until it reached Unterluss, a German artillery training area, where it came upon considerable resistance, an enclosure of girls and an ordnance dump. The infantry cleared Unterluss, a halt was called for the day and Lieut Green became mayor and military commander of Unterluss and spent his time trying to prevent a fight between displaced persons and the German inhabitants.

Demolitions compelled B Squadron to forsake the main road frequently and take to the bad tracks through the woods. Four large craters had to be bridged in fifteen miles, and after the leading patrol had passed through Eschede a bridge was blown up only a few yards ahead of it. Beyond Eschede B Squadron made two notable discoveries: Lieut 'Bumble' Davis found the old Field Marshal van Mackensen in a mansion, and cellars stocked with enough wine to supply the whole division. RHQ had to bump along the railway to reach Eschede. C Squadron advanced over difficult sandy tracks and dealt with pockets of enemy, including a mounted rearguard.

During the night 227 Brigade outflanked the enemy's positions on the main road by a forced march—or drive—through the woods on the left, and only just failed to take Uelzen by surprise at dawn. When day broke Germans with 20 mm cannon in fields on one side of the road leading to the town woke up, rubbed their eyes and stared in amazement at the brigade's column stretched along the road. Then they ran to their guns. In the woods on the other side German machine gunners did the same. Major Dove, the regiment's liaison officer with the column, was brewing his morning tea. His mug jumped on the bonnet of his jeep and came down with a hole through it. The fire from both sides of the road was heavy. Like others, Major Dove and Cpl Macdonald, his driver, took to the ditch, and Macdonald was wounded. Word came along the ditch that the Germans were advancing along it. Major Dove dashed for the cover of a wood, and to his dismay found himself face to face with many armed Germans. Awed by this one-man charge, they surrendered.

That day A Squadron went on ten miles to Bahnsen, and C Squadron, overcoming sporadic resistance, which included Hitler Youth with bazookas, reached Bokel by four in the afternoon. Lieut McFall has described what happened there:

Not liking the look of the main road, we decided to loop along some high ground and come back down the centre line. We broke from the woods, and there in the valley was a company marching east with a waggon of bazookas. Sgt Jacques and Sgt Dullaway went forward to block the road while the dingo and I covered from the crest. The heavy cars dropped out of sight. We thought they were in trouble when we saw the Germans run forward, so we opened fire. Sgt Coe did some wonderful 3-inch mortar shooting, and it was a pity to have to curtail it when we heard irate messages from the other cars that we were shooting rather too close to them. We took one hundred and seventy prisoners. Later we bumped off a staff car, which Cpl Lavery shot clean off the road, killing both occupants.

By dusk C Squadron had reached Wrestedt, fewer than five miles south of Uelzen. On receiving orders to concentrate for the night the squadron withdrew two miles to Nettelkamp. The Glasgow Highlanders were at Stadensen, a mile behind. At Uelzen the infantry had met a determined garrison, and RHQ and B Squadron harboured for the night at Suderburg. At dawn on 15 April the wireless calls to C Squadron were unanswered. On the telephone from 46 Brigade came a report that the squadron had been heavily counter-attacked in the night and apparently over-run.

A patrol was hurriedly despatched from Suderburg under the command of Capt Boynton. It found a squadron, tired, scattered and depleted, which had withdrawn from Nettelkamp after fighting all night against greater numbers and heavier weapons. Lieut David Richford, who had been with C Squadron ever since the old days at Orford, had been killed. So had Sgt E. Fielding, Tpr R. R. Johnson, Tpr L. S. Jackson and Tpr E. T. Cudmore. Tpr F. Strand and Tpr R. G. Gurney were fatally wounded. Fourteen had been wounded. Thirty-nine were missing. Eight carriers, four armoured cars and a half-track had been lost. Gradually the story of the night in Nettelkamp was pieced together.

The attack had been delivered suddenly about midnight by the Panzer Division Clausewitz, a force formed specially to thrust deep into the advancing armies' lines of communication. It was thwarted in this purpose by the resistance of the Glasgow Highlanders at Stadensen, and by the resistance at Nettelkamp of the clerks, cooks, mechanics and 'odd bodies' of C Squadron headquarters, who fought on under the leadership of Capt Liddell and Sgt

Major Ward for hours after the troop positions had been over-run. The surprise which the attackers achieved was made possible by the co-operation of the Nettelkamp people. They had used their white flags of surrender for signalling, and had sent messengers to the Clausewitz force. When the men in the troop positions rushed from their billets to their defence posts in response to the sentries' urgent alarms, Spandaus opened fire on all the exits and guns began shelling and setting fire to those buildings which the squadron occupied. The German infantry had led the attack, softly, in rubber boots. Half-tracks with 20 mm cannon followed them down the main street while self-propelled guns circled the village. The attackers seemed to be drunk or drugged. They howled. They screamed. They took crazy risks.

This is what happened to Lieut McFall's troop:

Things must have moved a bit too fast for the sentries, and we were roused to find our front door—the planned way to our defensive positions—barred by a troop carrier full of Germans. The first of us to the door met a stream of fire, and a sergeant was killed. Thinking that the only thing we had in our favour was that we were an unknown quantity, I decided to get out and have a look round. We got the dead sergeant in, and I set off. I was stuck after going ten yards, and could not rejoin the troop. Some of the troop got away. Some went to ground, as I did. Sgt Jacques was taken prisoner, but freed himself from two armed guards with a block of wood. Only one dead man was left in the house when it burnt down.

This is a sentry's account of what happened to Lieut Richford's troop:

We saw vehicles approaching, and reached the front of the house just as the first one passed—it was a tank, and not one of ours. There were shouts, and a Bren started singing. We dashed in to report. We woke the men. 'Right,' said Lieut Richford, 'cover the road. Don't show yourselves. Keep clear of the windows. Couple of you stand by your guns in the cars. Good luck.' My gunner and I ran out to my car and got ready to fire. We heard the crack of 20 millimetre and the heavy explosion of the 88s. The roof of our house was shattered. A German was shouting guttural commands. Somebody yelled 'Throw out the Tommies.' My gunner said, 'I can't see a thing.' A grenade exploded under our door, and shrapnel shot round the inside of the car like angry hornets. My gunner moaned and slid out, mortally wounded, but I was not even scratched. We lay under the car, and I pressed myself into the ground with my heart beating like a sledgehammer while grenades fell all round. The houses across the road were on fire, making the sky a dull red which new explosions splashed with yellow.

There was a silence broken only by distant rifle fire and by German voices across the road. The remnants of the troop, led by Lieut Richford, crawled up to me. 'Two of the boys have volunteered to stay in the cellar with the wounded. We'll try to make H.Q. and make a stand there.' We crawled across the back gardens towards the open fields. 'Quick, run to hedge and take cover.' Ten yards, another ten to go. A shot whistled over us. We were flat again.

English, spoken with a French accent, floated from the hedge: 'That you Tommee. Hush. We help you get away. We French workers. Come quick . . .' Bill and I went. They were French right enough, but French SS and grinning like devils. We were disarmed. Lieut Richford and somebody else loomed up, and a warning was hissed—'Jerries'. 'Break for it,' he yelled, and fired his pistol. I landed in a bramble. A Schmeisser rattled, and the burst killed our troop leader.

The hedge in which Bill and I were lying ringed a cemetery. We crawled between the graves like men possessed. We tried the church door, but it would not budge. A section of Germans filed by, arguing noisily. We crawled to the far hedge, and were spotted by Germans in half-tracks as we made for the open fields. We lay near one another while they dismounted and searched. They found Bill. One of them stood with his boots inches from my face while they questioned Bill in broken English. After they had taken him away, I walked off, and more shots missed me. I ran into the woods and walked all night, so hopelessly lost that I spun a coin to decide which way to go. In the morning I found that I was in the German lines, where I was captured by a bazooka team. Later I joined Bill and other members of the squadron who had been captured. We were released by the 11th Armoured Division after being prisoners for eight days.

In accordance with the squadron's plan of defence, the assault troop, now commanded by Lieut Peter Vroome, tried to join squadron headquarters, but was surrounded. That left squadron headquarters, and those who had managed to rally there. The howling Germans attacked with guns and machine guns. They tried to rush the defences with half-tracks. They tried to infiltrate on foot. Capt Liddell, slightly wounded, organised his small force to drive them back every time. Sgt Major Albert Ward was wherever the fighting was fiercest, using Bren and rifle and PIAT and the grenade with which he destroyed a

Spandau position. Sgt Harry Gartland, the mechanist sergeant, commanding the left of the defence, leapt from his slit trench and advanced on the attackers, firing his Bren from the hip. Cpl James McDonald, the ammunition corporal, ran forward with a PIAT and knocked out the first of three half-tracks which were bearing down on the headquarters with their quadruple 20 mm cannon firing and infantry ready to leap from them on to the defenders. After the first had been hit, the other two withdrew. Cpl McDonald was wounded in the arm, but he fought on. At dawn Capt Liddell knew that the other troops must have been over-run and that there was therefore no point in staying longer, so he withdrew his weary force in the remaining vehicles under fire from Spandaus which lined both sides of the road out of the village. The squadron leader and the sergeant major were the last to leave.

After keeping watch on Nettelkamp, B Squadron's patrol went into the village with infantry and carriers later in the day. Six German half-tracks had been abandoned, and sixty German infantry surrendered without firing a shot.

The Military Medal was awarded to Sgt Major Ward, Sgt Gartland and Cpl McDonald for their valour at Nettelkamp, and Capt Liddell's conduct of the defence was one of the reasons why he was later awarded the Military Cross.

While the infantry gradually reduced the stubborn garrison of Uelzen—a task which took until 18 April—A and B Squadrons patrolled the country north and south, and C Squadron licked its wounds at Suderburg. The losses of Nettelkamp made the regiment even more dependent on its commandeered vehicles; with these and the patched survivors of that night it had, indeed, enough of the motley in its looks to justify the 'Fred Karno's Own' chalked on the turret of Sgt Dullaway's scorched car. A Echelon sent one of its prizes, a large German lorry, to collect petrol by a route which passed through the 11th Armoured Division, and a patrol of the 1st Royal Dragoons, seeing a German lorry approaching, fired and joyfully reported that what must have been a valuable load had gone up in black smoke. It was a valuable load—the regiment's sports kit. The lorry driver, who was unhurt, was a man from one of the reconnaissance squadrons who had been sent to A Echelon for a rest and told 'It's quite safe there'.

On 17 April the regiment met the 2nd Special Air Service Regiment—the independent command of Lieut Col B. M. Franks, DSO, MC—and the two units, having much the same job to do, decided to do it together. The co-operation begun then lasted until the end of the war in Germany, the SAS patrols in open jeeps sharing the hazards of the regiment's armoured car and carrier troops and winning their unstinted admiration. On its advance from the Uelzen area to the Elbe the regiment also had the support of a platoon of 4.2-inch mortars from the Middlesex Regiment, weapons which could soon persuade the Germans that it was high time to leave a village. A Squadron's patrols on 18 April found that the Germans driven from Uelzen were retreating in disorder, and that night the regiment and the SAS stayed in Bevensen, very much out on their own and undamaged by the aircraft which attacked the column as it entered the village. Next day B Squadron and C Squadron led the way to the Elbe, eighteen miles ahead.

C Squadron, on the left, found a large camp of American and British prisoners of war at Bavendorf, and the 11th Armoured Division became responsible for them. By noon the squadron had reached Neetze, from which it patrolled over the flat country towards the river. The resistance around the riverside town of Bleckede showed that it was to be held as one of the Germans' last crossing places. RHQ, following C Squadron, had one of its major thrills at Bavendorf, where Hitler Jugend, wearing Volksturm armbands, began a stalk with a bazooka. They were seen and fired on. One was captured. He said they were a small reconnaissance party sent to discover British positions and 'brew up' headquarters. RHQ remained extremely alert, but nobody else appeared.

B Squadron, on the right, met opposition on all the roads to the Forest of Gohrde, which was being used as a collecting place for the retreating Germans before they crossed the river. The Military Medal was won that day by Sgt Ronald Trim, commanding a troop which killed twenty Germans and took sixty prisoners in an advance of fifteen miles to the outer defences of Bleckede. He led a successful attack on a road block in Dahlenburg, knocked out a German half-track with fire from his car, and, taking a foot patrol through a wood, destroyed a machine-gun nest and seized a trace of the German positions, which proved valuable to the infantry on the following day.

In Neetze C Squadron had found an international circus. Only the lions and bears were missing. Some said that they had been killed by panzers; others that they had been killed in a Typhoon attack. A performance—the first of many given to British soldiers—was arranged, and the animals expressed their joy at their release from many days' confinement with a display of exuberance which was almost uncontrollable. As soon as they were loosed they careered round the ring, kicking out with zest. Everybody enjoyed it.

On 20 April B Squadron reconnoitred 46 Brigade's advance on Bleckede. The regiment settled in the high-roofed villages of Neetze and Thomasburg to await the assault on the Elbe and reorganize after sixteen days of many patrols, many actions, many hazards, hurried meals and little sleep—sixteen days during which it had led the advance of two divisions for more than 140 miles.

Ken Sadler:- Took part in the action at Nettlekamp. He worked in Germany after the war and was a fluent German speaker. He had made contact with a Colonel Klaus Voss who was a former member of Panzer Division Clausewitz and the author of *Last Divisions 1945*. Ken Sadler and I attended a Panzer Brigade 304 reunion at Heidenheim, Bavaria in 2003. The German veterans, some of whom had served on the eastern front, were less than happy that the excellent Leopard 2 tanks then in service, were to be sold at a knock down price to the Polish Army! Colonel Voss attended a regimental lunch in London in May 2006.

*   *   *   *   *

Requests to the regimental association for additional information produced the following details of individual experiences. Perhaps because the action took place so close to war's end it was fresher in the memory and so more participants responded. This was not a typical action in which the regiment was involved and Victor Sadgrove stressed that it was merely a 'skirmish', a symbolic last gasp of a defeated foe. For the members of C Squadron who were there it was a painful reminder that the Wehrmacht still possessed bite and they mourn their comrades lost so close to the final victory.

Victor Sadgrove:-

Extract from *Path of the Lion* by Charles Lawton.

During the whole of the 14th, the Highland Light Infantry remained outside Uelzen, the enemy making very determined efforts to eliminate them. Soon after dawn they began infiltrating on the right flank, supported by a self-propelled four-barrelled 20mm gun which was shortly joined by three more on the left; rear Battalion Headquarters was cut off and the situation was serious until a squadron of tanks arrived to protect the rear. The Argylls, at the same time, cleared the woods on the right flank. Over 200 prisoners had been taken in twenty-four hours.

In the meantime, 46 Brigade had had the task of clearing the whole of the Corps front; it had split up into three battalion groups, the Glasgow Highlanders on the right, and the Seaforth Highlanders on the left, with the Cameronians in reserve on the right flank; their main problem was to get all their transport forward without using the main Division axis, which was forbidden them. The whole of the area was thickly wooded and the Corps flanks were anything but clear, with odd German battle groups still wandering at large. On the night of 14 April the Glasgow Highlanders were established in Stadensen. A surprise attack during the night by infantry in half-tracks, supported by self-propelled guns, succeeded in over–running a Reconnaissance Squadron at Nettelkamp and then entered the Glasgow Highlanders' positions; most of the buildings were fired by the self–propelled guns, one even attacking Battalion Headquarters and blowing up the signal office. Fighting continued until dawn when the enemy withdrew, leaving behind him twelve self-propelled guns and ten half tracks burnt out; the Glasgow Highlanders' casualties were five killed and forty-seven wounded. This fierce attack was made by a new formation, Panzer Division Clausewitz, which seemed to have been formed from odd units left over from other divisions.

F.M. the Viscount Montgomery in his memoirs states that:

With the Rhine behind us we drove fast for the Baltic. My object was to get there in time to be able to offer a firm front to the Russian endeavour to get up to Denmark and thus control the entrance to the Baltic. In order to speed up the rate of advance, divisions operated in great depth on narrow thrust lines; enemy areas of resistance were by-passed by armoured spearheads and were later attacked from the flank or rear by other troops coming on behind.

As we moved eastwards, the Prime Minister and Eisenhower both became anxious lest I might not be able to 'head off' the Russians from getting into Schleswig–Holstein and then occupying Denmark. . . We reached the Baltic at Wismar on the 2nd May and thus sealed off the Danish peninsular with at least six hours to spare before the Russians arrived.

Their (Germans) present defeat; in March/April 1945 was not comparable to that experienced in Normandy. They had lost so heavily in personnel and territory that they could not again form and equip new divisions. Hitler's Germany now faced disaster.

*   *   *   *   *

The action at Nettlekamp was brutal for those involved but was only viewed as a skirmish in the 'big picture' with unconditional surrender only days away for the Nazi military machine. The day after the night fight at Nettlekamp the 15th(S) Division with its Reconnaissance Regiment chased the Germans, who were retreating back to the Elbe as beaten foes

Lieut M. McFall:- (known in the Regiment as 'Alfie') We had had an arduous day and had advanced quite a few miles, suprised a marching column which was taken prisoner and, at last light, found ourselves in an area free of enemy and well to the right of the organised resistance towards Uelzen. Sgt Telleck, troop sergeant, fixed quarters for the troop, both cars and carriers, performed his usual duties in fixing guard duty, re-arming and refuelling, and I went round the corner on foot to get our orders from Bill Liddell for the next day. As I recall, we were to stand down and go into reserve and, much relieved and very weary, I walked back to the troop. On the way, there was one excitement. The noise of 'tracks', supposedly a tank, came rattling towards the village. I think I got into a hedge and got out my revolver only to see a gaunt and ragged farmer come clattering in from his day in the fields on an aged caterpillar tractor. Yet another confirmation of our distance from the war!

I had a li-lo which I blew up nightly in my sleeping bag, the post had brought the latest Dornford Yates (*Red in the Morning*) hot from Harrods via my Mother.

I put on pyjamas and was soon blissfully asleep. My bed on the floor was just inside the door of the cottage Sgt Telleck had chosen for us. Sited on the junction of three lanes it made a good tactical position. I found my Daimler backed in under a sort of open shed with a tin roof, beside one of our other 'heavies', guns pointing belligerently down the road. I don't give our sentries high marks for failing to alert us sooner, when an enemy SP gun trundled up to park before our door. A sergeant (newly arrived from RHQ as a reinforcement that evening and hardly known to me), and I were the first two out to see what the dickens was going on. Shots from somewhere in the darkness killed him in moments and we got his body back into the house without attracting further fire.

Our position, until we'd found out more of events outside, was a useless one. Our only advantage being that our presence – some dozen of us, was unknown to the enemy as many yards away. I decided to tell the chaps to lie low and went out in order to make my way round the corner to Squadron HQ and get ideas and orders. As things were, we were in no position to launch an attack against unknown odds and unknown numbers.

My first stop was to be my armoured car to collect smoke grenades with which I hoped to make cover for our leaving the cottage. To get there I went quietly down the few feet of path, through the little garden gate and out into the road. A woman was running up and down the other side of the road, screaming to her compatriots about our locations. Not looking where I was going I walked into the back of the SP gun, fortunately not drawing the attention of its crew, and felt the chicken wire which had been welded onto its plating for ease of attaching camouflage. I backed off and found my way to the shed on the corner where my two cars stood. Somebody with a Schmeiser must have seen me and I got a burst or two, fortunately a little high, which pock-marked the bricks above my head.

Daimlers have a door in the hull for access on occasions such as these but, since such occasions seldom arise, I certainly wasn't carrying a key and wasn't even sure where the wretched thing might be. The chap with the Schmeiser stopped me from climbing up onto the turret from outside. Being at the junction, the garden of the cottage ended in a point and I soon found myself lying just inside the fence, attending what I assumed was a German 'O' Group. Certainly a Hauptmann Peters was called for loudly and I made a mental note of his name. There were several fires burning by now and I could see and be seen quite clearly. 'Feign death,' I told myself as a large fellow in a smart greatcoat, came over to inspect me. It crossed my mind that feigning death was not the sporting thing to do but, as he got nearer, I decided to shoot him in the throat should he bend down to inspect me. Fortunately he was called away by name and I took the opportunity to fling a grenade, (which I always carried in the pocket of my blouse), after him and to leg it back toward the cottage door.

Of course, in full view now, there was no chance of going in. To do so would have exposed everybody inside to immediate attention. So I ran past, turned left into the black darkness and took a clothes line straight across both open eyes. It took a few minutes to get my sight back and then I pushed on, hoping to reach Squadron HQ by a back route. I was now in a small farmyard and ahead was the vague shape of a small farmhouse. I eased open its door and found that it led straight into the kitchen where a single candle was burning and an old woman with her crippled son were watching my arrival with anxiety. I made soothing gestures and pointed to their curtained window, which I hoped might bear onto the second lane. Carefully I took up a position there, eased back the curtain, and had a look. Part of the column was forming up to move on. The whole thing looked like a film set with smart, helmeted troops sitting neatly in their half-tracks. I counted thirty-five vehicles, marking as one does sacks of corn arriving in a barn. One, two, three, four downstrokes and one makes five. My tally was on a twenty packet of Players. The good woman kindly gave me a sandwich of black bread and sausage while I was at her window and then urged me to follow her out into the yard at the back. Only then did I realise that I was putting her and her son in danger. One can be immensely self–centred when the going is hot. Obviously she wanted me out of sight but also out of harm's way. She led me into the cowshed, bringing the candle with her, and showed me a small stall between the larger ones for cows. I guessed from a distance by the scent that it was the communal lavatory! There I was put to sit until called for and she retired with the candle to leave me with my thoughts.

My thoughts then, and now, were of small consolation. I had left my troop, admittedly safe and under cover as far as I knew. I had collected the name of one of the officers involved and I had counted thirty-five wagons full of most impressive soldiers. I had no one to pass my information to and, if I moved and was seen might well get this nice old lady and her son shot as traitors - which undoubtedly they were. It was dawn when they brought the schoolmaster to see me. Unable to speak each other's language we conversed in signs. I gathered there were a number of our chaps in hiding and I used the second part of the Player's to write a message saying 'Meet me at dusk in the middle of the village and we will get back to our lines together'.

Very soon after that I was summoned back to my window of the night before to find Michael Riesco, our Intelligence Officer standing in the road outside. I quickly burbled out my news of Hauptmann Peters and the tally of the half-tracks and he bundled me back to RHQ in his jeep. On the way I was shocked to see the mess that our visitors of the night before had made of a squadron of 6 Guards' Tanks and the Glasgow Highlanders who had spent the night in what proved to be our rear.

Cpl Ken Sadler:- During 14 April I recollect driving for what seemed to be hours along dusty forest tracks. Late afternoon we arrived in Nettelkamp where the squadron was dispersed throughout the village. I was with the Mortar Troop attached to squadron HQ which apart from the operational headquarters under the command of Captain Liddell included the Squadron Sergeant Major (SSM), wireless operators, an ammunition and a fuel truck, a section of the Mortar Troop, cooks and clerks. We also had three or four British ex POWs whom we had picked up during the course of the day. During the early evening Captain Liddell held an 'O' Group mainly covering the orders for the following day which was attended by Lieut McFall, the SSM and Troop Sergeants. I heard that Lieut McFall's Troop was to be in reserve. After the vehicles had been fuelled up etc and sentries had been detailed, the rest of us brewed up and went to bed. We were pointed in the direction of a long hall attached I believe to a Gasthaus or similar, to sleep. It was dark by this time.

I was awoken some time later in the dark by someone shaking my shoulder and shouting 'Stand to'. Half asleep I saw it was quite bright: the house next door was on fire. There was also the sound of heavy firing from further down the village. I could clearly hear the distinctive different sounds of a Bren and of a German Spandau (MG42). I remember wondering why I did not hear the long bursts of the Besas (MMG) in the Daimlers firing.

Only later did I learn that the forward troops had been surprised in the houses where they were sleeping and couldn't get into their Daimlers, quite apart from the fact that sitting in the dark in the turret of a Daimler with just a periscope to look through was not ideal, if there were German infantry, whom you couldn't see, crawling around and behind you with Panzerfausts. No one had reckoned with a determined German attack so shortly before the war was virtually over.

I quickly climbed into my tank suit for warmth, grabbed a Bren gun and went outside where I met the sergeant major who told me to take up a position under a 3-ton truck. It was now as bright as day from the fire and lying there in a yellow suit behind the wheel of a 3-tonner did not seem the ideal place to be. I believe the Assault Troop was in a house opposite us somewhere but I had no precise idea where our other troops were. Suddenly we came under machine-gun fire but I couldn't see at first where it was coming from. A little later I saw a muzzle flash and fired a burst from my Bren. At least that was my intention! The Bren fired one round and stopped. I carried out the immediate stoppage action and realised that the weapon was full of sand. During the drive through the dusty tracks the ejection opening cover of the gun must have worked open and the working parts were full of sand. I had no alternative but to strip down the gun, try and clean it a bit and re-assemble. All this in a yellow tank suit in my illuminated position. Trooper Maclean of the Mortar Troop was close by, saw my predicament and gave me covering fire by shooting at the same target. After I had stripped and got the Bren re-assembled I fired a short burst to check. The SSM immediately slid up to me and wanted to know what I was firing at! He said one of our troops might be in the house opposite, or perhaps outside. The whole situation was totally confused as both German troops and our own were mixed up together in different places. The situation was further complicated by the fact that for some reason wireless silence had been ordered until the following day, and there was no radio contact with other troops in the area.

Soon after this Captain Liddell, the Officer Commanding, told me to take up position on the side of a house facing down the road. The ground beneath me was cobbled there was no cover and no possibility of digging in for protection. There was, however, a single house brick so I attempted to minimise my bulk behind it! Things seemed to be comparatively quiet where I was, although there was firing going on all around and I could hear the sound of half-tracks rumbling along the road which I recognised as enemy vehicles. One came along the road at the front of the house and I think it was the SSM who knocked it out with a PIAT. Somewhere in front and off to the side of me, although I could not see him, I could hear a wounded German soldier calling for assistance. He kept calling out what sounded like SAMM—MEE (I found out much later that he was calling out Sani - short for Sanitäter – stretcher bearer). I asked Captain Liddell if I should go out and bring him in but was told it was too risky and should stay where I was. Some time later there was the sound of some scuffling near where he must have been, and hoping it was indeed one of his Sanitäters patching him up, I refrained from firing. There was no one in that position the following day so he must have been collected or crawled away.

There then seemed to be a period of inactivity. About what seemed to be about an hour later I was still keeping watch down the road, I saw a head loom up out of the ditch about ten yards in front of me. I aimed at it and had already taken the first pressure on the trigger when a voice shouted out 'Corporal Vince' (the name of a corporal who apparently the OC had sent out to try and secure assistance as we were either under wireless silence or had lost contact). No man can ever have been closer to death as was Cpl Vince in that split second.

Soon after German infantry must have crawled up near our position and threw hand grenades at us. It took me a few seconds to realise what they were, just a sudden flash and a bang. I fired back at where they seemed to be coming from but could not see if I had hit anyone although it sounded like someone was beating a hasty retreat. Trooper Strand who was somewhere in my vicinity, although I couldn't see him, was hit and was carried down into the cellar of the house which was being used for the wounded. Sadly he died some time later.

Captain Liddell came round again and said that there were no further sounds of firing from other parts of the village and as our Scout Troops seem to have been overrun, we will temporarily evacuate Nettelkamp. 'We will take three half-tracks and get as many of our people out as possible. Wait for the signal.' I heard the signs of activity and two half-tracks start up and drive away, then silence. After waiting for a while I went to see what was happening; as I came round to the front of the house the third half-track was moving away. I shouted and managed to scramble into the overfull transport. Our other vehicles and kit were left behind at this stage. We drove fast down the road to the front of the house for some distance and then there were a few infantry or perhaps artillery soldiers who came running towards us. They obviously realised we were evacuating Nettelkamp and didn't want to be left behind either. They clung somewhere on the outside of the vehicle and we continued our journey back to British positions.

Some time the following morning a counter-attack was being launched by the Brigade, a number of Churchills supported by infantry were moving along the road back towards Nettelkamp. As I wanted to retrieve my Bren carrier (I had something in it which was important to me – but no idea now what it was). I jumped on the back of a Churchill with some infantry and trundled towards our objective. We could see the spire of the church over on our forward right and someone said it was being used as an OP. The tank commander ordered all the infantry off his tank to allow them room to traverse. The third round they fired went through the steeple. The dismounted infantry I had attached myself to carried on marching along a stretch of embankment-type road. We heard the sound of incoming mortar fire and threw ourselves into the roadside ditches. The fire was accurate, the leader of the platoon who was just ahead of me was hit as were several others. Eventually we reached Nettelkamp, the infantry continued with their advance and I detached myself and made my way into the building where we had originally been billeted. Outside the building was the German half-track, which had been hit with the PIAT, the driver was still inside with the top of his head blown off. Some German prisoners were being led away past the courtyard of the building opposite where Squadron HQ had been. There was a dead German soldier lying in the courtyard; one of the prisoners made signs to his escort and was allowed to remove the dead man's paybook and half of his identity disc. I had no idea whether there were any Germans in the building so I poked a rifle round the door with my finger on the trigger. At the far end of the hall I could see one of our own officers and three soldiers with their hands up in the air. They were taking no chances either on getting shot by friend or foe. After giving a report, I resumed the search for my carrier. There seemed very little firing taking place now and it appeared that the desultory mortar fire was the last effort before the Germans withdrew.

I found my Bren carrier unscathed, jumped in and drove off. I did not want to hamper the reinforcing troops coming up so I made a detour back towards my starting off point. I was concerned that they might mistake me for approaching enemy, there were a lot of very trigger happy people around that day. My detour did not go quite as I had planned, somewhere I went adrift and I was driving loosely around the countryside alone between the Germans and our own troops and no longer had any idea where I was or what I might bump into. I came across a hurriedly abandoned German jeep complete with kit and I noticed an ornate dagger issued to senior officers; this was not the place to loiter, so I pressed on hoping to contact British troops. After a lot of uncertain meandering I finally came across a British Churchill tank at a track junction brewing up tea. I scrounged myself a cup and asked them if they could tell me where 15th Recce were. They got on the radio and after a few minutes they were able to give me location instructions and I was able to rejoin the squadron with my Bren carrier. No one seemed to have missed me; they thought I had been sleeping somewhere, only later did someone ask, 'How did this carrier get here?'

Later that day the remains of the Squadron returned to Nettelkamp. The Germans seemed to have carried out a fighting withdrawal. We were to re-occupy our positions and recover vehicles and equipment. About a dozen of our men had been captured. From later reports they were marched from place to place for about five days because the Germans didn't know what to do with them so near the end of the war. They were all treated reasonably well under the circumstances and were all subsequently liberated.

It is of particular interest that the hastily formed Panzer Division Clausewitz did not set out to attack us as such in April 1945. They were to relieve the pressure on Uelzen and their immediate objective was Holdenstedt via Stadensen with the aim of cutting through the American supply routes and making contact with the German Eleven Army in the Harz. They were as surprised to find us there as we were to be attacked by them at night. Indeed, once they had fought their way through Nettelkamp and regrouped, they immediately continued towards Standensen without any attempt at 'mopping up'. This accounts for the number of Recce 'stragglers' still scattered around the village.

Graham Nicklin:- 9 Troop Carriers, C Squadron 14 April 1945
We were all fast asleep in a very nice detached house, when at about midnight the windows came crashing through, shattered by machine-gun fire. My first job was to grab my mate Gordon Nursaw, to get him from the vertical to the horizontal as he stood in the line of fire. Then we all rushed downstairs where I found myself by the front door with Sgt Fielding. There was a frantic knocking on the door, Sgt Fielding opened it and there stood a German lady, who let out a very loud scream and ran back down the path. My head was pressed closely against Sgt Fielding's as we both tried to look through a narrow gap in the door. Suddenly the Sgt made a strange gurgling sound in his throat and shot backwards into the hallway: the poor lad was dead before he hit the floor; the bullet hit him in the mouth.

Then Sgt Kirrage started to get us organised; he sent Sgt Green and two more lads from another troop and an American soldier whom we had picked up earlier in the day and myself back upstairs. I said to the Yank, who had come out of a prison camp somewhere 'we are going the wrong way for you mate.' He replied, 'never mind I'll stick with you.' He was wounded in the hand later in the evening.

Upstairs Sgt Green and I fired a couple of shots out of the bedroom window when he said 'hold it we cannot see who we are firing at.' He was correct; in the dark it was difficult to distinguish friend from foe. Suddenly a burst of machine-gun fire came through the window, so we retreated to the landing, where we stayed for quite a while. I was on the edge of the landing, right at the top of the stairs, when I heard footsteps slowly ascending, I could hear the sound of plaster detached from the ceiling being crunched underfoot by a lone individual. I had a Luger pistol in my right hand pointing at the stairs, then I got a flap on, I did not know whether the safety catch was on or off. Confused, I thought that it might not be a German and was perhaps one of our lads from downstairs, talk about being in a tizzy! Later I discovered that our lads were no longer downstairs, they had forgotten that we were up there. The German reached what I estimated to be about three steps from the top and then gave a very long burst with a burp gun, the flashes lighting up the landing. I think this frightened the guy as he ran like hell down the stairs, little did he realise that he had frightened the living daylights out of me! He must have discussed the situation with his mates because a few minutes later a couple of incendiary shells pierced the roof and started a fire. It was a smouldering fire and the whole place was filled with thick black smoke; we stuck it for about half an hour then we all started choking and decided to get out. The smoke was so thick we all fell over poor Sgt Fielding on the way out.

We went to the back door and saw German troops a few yards away and just then a civilian, an old man, came out of a room with his arms full of blankets. So the five of us grabbed a blanket off him, covered ourselves up and walked down the garden path with the old guy in front. As we approached the bottom of the garden we pushed the old fellow into an air-raid shelter and gave him his blankets back, to which he said 'Danke'. We then went through a gate into a farmyard with a large open-sided barn with a drive through the middle, as we approached one end; two Germans appeared at the other and let fly at us with their machine guns. They must have been lousy shots, a group of five and they missed us all! Sgt Green, the Yank and the other two lads dived to the right over a barbed-wire fence, one of them suffering severe facial cuts. I was too far away to jump so I dived behind a chicken hut. It was pitch black and I couldn't see a thing. I felt isolated; however after waiting a few minutes I dived over the fence, slashing my arm from wrist to elbow. I was wandering around in the complete darkness when a hand grabbed my ankle in a vice-like grip and I fell into a pile of horse manure. The hand belonged to Sgt Green who had kept me under observation all the time.

The five of us then went around the end of the barn past a Bren carrier which was parked up to the straw. As we turned the corner we saw a posse of Germans in the process of setting up a mortar between the farmhouse and some outbuildings. We beat a hasty retreat, climbed onto the carrier and into the barn where we lay on top of the straw. We were all desperate for a cigarette which was of course totally out of the question.

After a while we dozed off but suddenly we heard German voices; cautiously peering out we saw two soldiers examining the carrier. The Yank was snoring loudly and it was obvious that they would fire up through the straw if we were heard so I gently rolled him over and thankfully he became silent.

The next thing I recall is our own 25-pounders shelling Nettlekamp and the two Jerries scarpered like scalded cats (I couldn't blame them). After a while I discerned a figure near the corner of the barn. Curious to learn his identity I crawled over and asked who he was. Recognising my voice that smashing lad Teddy Cudmore of 10 Troop answered. I asked him to join our group but he declined preferring his own position. Shortly afterwards a shell hit the barn, we didn't hear it coming and all of us faded out for a while; when we came to all five of us were wounded one way or another but tragically Teddy Cudmore was killed.

After a few more near misses I decided to vacate the barn and said 'Right lads I'm off to find some more cover, if you hear a shot stop where you are, if not I suggest you follow me down.' Self preservation had become the key factor so I hopped across the farmyard on my left foot as I had sustained shrapnel wounds to my right foot, head, back and arms. I opened a door and found myself in a big farmhouse kitchen; seated at a large table were about twenty-five Jerries. I stood there on one leg looking at them and for a moment I felt really sorry for them, they looked so sad and dejected. One young lad who had a cut on his eyelid said something and his mates moved along the bench on which they were seated to make room for me. This guy then gave me a Player's cigarette which was most welcome. Cutting through my boot lace he removed my boot and sock, he pointed to my field dressing which he then used to bandage my foot.

I was then led to a massive cellar where I sat on some straw; as my eyes became accustomed to the gloom I noticed there were about a dozen women and children across the other side. A few minutes later I was joined by Sgt Green and the other lads. Sgt Green had suffered a serious chest wound so I wrapped my remaining field dressing around him. About an hour later a diminutive German soldier with a Red Cross bag entered the cellar and inquired if we were O.K. I asked if he had a spare bandage for Sgt Green, he opened his bag to reveal that it was completely empty; shrugging his shoulders in sympathy he departed. Mortars near the window kept banging away. A little later a very tall, immaculately dressed German officer came down to look at us; he studied us carefully with his hands on his hips. He then shocked us all by drawing and cocking his Luger, pointing it at the Yank. I really thought the bugger was going to shoot us! Just then the little guy with the Red Cross bag reappeared; he spoke to the officer who gave him a dirty look but replaced the pistol in his holster. The only words I caught was 'Alles Kaputt', I could have kissed the little guy! After that we were released by the Cameronians.

I was the last to be picked up and while I was in the kitchen waiting for a jeep an old lady fried an egg and brought it to me on a plate, apologising for the absence of bread. All the Germans were very kind to me that night (with the exception of the officer).

I travelled by a bumpy jeep to Cologne and then by Dakota to Louvain where I was operated on. Another flight by Dakota brought me back to Swindon, followed by a train journey to hospital in Cardiff where I remained for four months. I was then moved to a recuperation hospital only ten miles from my home; unfortunately my foot would not heal. I endured another operation and an additional four months in hospital. I returned to the Army and was demobolised in 1948. I could not have served with a better group of Officers, NCOs and mates than those who were in 15th Recce.

Bernie Higham:- I arrived at Nettelkamp early evening 14 April. The armoured cars returned from patrol informing us that there were no enemy forces to the front for five miles. I found a bed on the ground floor of a house, undressed to my shirt and underwear, and fell asleep. I was woken by the noise of an SP gun firing outside the window; the only light was from the flash of the discharge. I found my trousers and boots but I was unable to locate my rifle and jacket. The Germans outside were very noisy, I went upstairs to the loft where two comrades were taking cover, we waited for daylight. We came down the stairs but two Germans saw us and took us prisoners. We marched towards the Elbe and stopped at a small town where we were interrogated by an officer who spoke perfect English; I gave him my name, rank and number. We continued our march guarded by two Germans, one old, the other young. We were without food and water for four days, I attempted to eat a raw potato I found in a field but it was inedible. Our guards suffered the same as us except that one had a brown loaf tied to his belt with string. On the fifth day we entered a French POW camp; we were in a hut when one of the prisoners called out 'your comrades they come,' and the two guards ran away. We saw a tank with a white star and knew we were free. I then enjoyed one of the best meals of my life, the Frenchman gave us freshly baked brown bread and butter, blackcurrant jam and fresh milk. I returned to Celle where I was deloused and given a change of clothes, I was walking in the town when I saw a 3-tonner displaying '41' our insignia; the driver gave me a lift back and I rejoined C Squadron.

I learnt later that if I had chosen to stay with the other POWs I would have received six weeks' leave and would have been In England when the European war ended! As it was we continued chasing the enemy to Kiel; shortly afterwards hundreds of Germans were pouring through us in order to escape the Russians who were out for revenge. With hindsight I realise that if I had not seen the recce lorry in Celle I would have spent the rest of my service in Blighty with my family. I was eventually demobbed in February 1947.

Ben Howe:- I served in the Assault Troop, 2 Section of C Squadron and was captured at Nettelkamp, I was a POW for four days, only on the last day did I receive some watery potato soup to eat. I was taken to a POW camp to register my name, rank and number with the Red Cross.

A German officer asked me what part of London did I come from and I replied South London. He sat down took off his cap and said what do they call you? I answered 'Ben' and he said his name was Heinz. He was only about my age and he said to me 'the war is over for you, and it will not be long before it is over for me.' We continued to talk, he wanted to know if I knew the Kennington

Oval. 'Of course', I said 'who doesn't'? It transpired that when he was nine and ten years old he had stayed with his grandparents who lived in Brixton, they had performing dogs which he helped care for. He said he would write home to his father to tell him about the cricket at the Oval. When he returned to Germany his father was keen to hear about cricket as he couldn't understand it. We then went on to talk about the Brixton road and the Empress Theatre where his grandparents' performing dogs had appeared. When he was ten years old his father had entered him into military school; he had last visited Brixton in 1939.

Over the days we would continue our chats about Brixton, the market and going to Saturday morning pictures, whilst all the time other POWs would shout out 'don't fraternise with the enemy.' When finally we were all marched out of there I thought how strange it was that one day we are trying to kill one another and the next we were chatting as friends.

I was given seventeen weeks' leave and returned to 36, Stockwell Park Road; our home at number 83 had been 'blitzed'. My elder sister had lost five children when a V2 had landed on Ilford Broadway in November 1944.

Clive Ridge:- Near the end of the war we operated with the 2nd SAS commanded by Lieut Col Franks DSO, MC, cord trousers, silk scarf and a revolver tied to his leg Gary Cooper style. His unit consisted of a dozen or so armed jeeps with twin K guns in the back ration boxes, and the three crew all in silk top hats! They would form up outside a village, six down one side, six down the other, one behind the other. One section would go to the left outside the village, one to the right and then join up and roar down the centre, what a sight! Several members of 15th Recce believe that it was whilst operating with 2nd SAS that they were amongst the first to encounter the horrific camp at Belsen. Lieut Harry Green entered the camp on 12 April and had seen the inmates in desperate circumstances. Some troops did enter the camp but Len Watson volunteered to stay with the vehicles; even at a distance he recalls that the stench from the site was over-powering.

A great advantage in my role as 'Rover 15' was that I always knew what was happening in front of us and was aware of the latest situation. We changed the batteries for the 19 set each evening and put the newly-charged ones on for the next day. I never experienced a breakdown with the 19 set from start to finish of the campaign. Punctures were our main problem, we suffered lots! Fortunately I did not have to change the wheels, the Light Aid Detachment did it promptly for the Colonel, and on we went.

Ernest Jellinek:- 'Old men forget; yet all shall be forgot, But he'll remember, with advantages, What deeds he did that day' - King Henry V. Retrospection after more than sixty years is very liable to Shakespeare's 'advantages' which I hope to avoid by use of old letters and a diary of the last three months of the German war. A few days before the launch of 'Operation Veritable' in early February 1945, to clear the left bank of the Rhine, I had written home, optimistically, 'I expect the Russians will cross the Oder fairly soon and I shall not be at all surprised if that led to a repetition of the events of July 1944 – the Generals at least will have enough sense to give up when there is something to be given up, though Hitler probably fancies himself fighting a battle of extermination.' I was wrong, and the Regiment was to suffer a third of all its casualties in the coming battles of Cleve, the Reichswald and then east of the Rhine; twenty-four killed and many more wounded.

After an interval in Belgium when we changed from Humber to Daimler armoured cars, we resumed action in April, looking for gaps and drawing fire, reconnoitring initially for the 6th Airborne Division in the river crossings from the Weser to the Leine. On 8 and 9 April I was liaison officer with 5 Parachute Brigade, commanded by Brigadier (later General Sir Nigel) Poett, and I was greatly impressed by their expertise and dash, having led the advance from the Weser bridgehead where they had dropped on 24 March.

On 11 April we were again reconnoitring, leading our own Division toward the river Aller at Celle, thirty miles on. My own troop was down to a scout car and my own heavy Daimler and in unpleasant close wooded country. A west-bound French straggler (ex-prisoner) warned of trouble ahead at the Ehlerhausen road and rail junction. At the edge of the village I quizzed a German civilian and was suddenly faced by a man with a bazooka (panzerfaust), a few yards away in a ditch, and then bang! I recall asking Tpr Moffatt, my excellent gunner, for a hand grenade, and throwing it out of the turret, before passing out. I had not been aware of a similar concurrent attack on the scout car in front which had killed Cpl Harry Rogal and Tpr Leonard Ward MM. My next memory is being in an American field hospital in France, and hearing that President Roosevelt was no more; he had died on 12 April.

Apparently our driver had baled out when we were hit, and Moffatt got into his seat from the turret, managed to turn the car, drove back to Squadron HQ and first aid. Evacuation and surgery was by US medical services on our right. Jock Browne with his Bren gun carriers had been close behind me at Ehlerhausen. He wrote to me later about 'our combined ops in the wood. The whole thing was chaotic; after you were hit one of my carriers had a near miss, we got quite a packet of MG fire which caught two of my lads. We then pulled back out of the wood. The infantry (9th Bn Cameronians) arrived ten hours later and put in a battalion attack with artillery support and a squadron of tanks. Two of the tanks were knocked out – the infantry had a rough time of it.'

John Boynton wrote on 24 April about the Ehlerhausen affair. 'On the whole we have been lucky, only fourteen fatal casualties in the Regiment since the Rhine. Our tanks (I believe from 6 Guards Armoured Brigade) were a long time coming up but eventually got to Celle that night. We saw a concentration camp at Celle and at last I have no more doubts whether what one has read is propaganda.' The even greater horrors of Belsen were ten miles north of Celle.

I reached the military hospital for head injuries in St Hugh's College at Oxford about a week after I was wounded. This was a super-specialised and highly successful unit set up by Sir Hugh Cairns, the dynamic Australian professor of surgery at Oxford, half a bicycle ride between his beds at the Radcliffe Infirmary and his home in North Oxford. It was staffed by a medical elite, some of whom were my teachers when I became a medical student at the end of 1945. (Ernest lost his left eye and was readily identified by his black eye patch).

At St Hugh's I first encountered Tony Babington, one of the most impressive men I ever met. He had been an infantry officer in the Arnhem aftermath when shrapnel caused damage to much of the left half of his brain, with loss of speech (aphasia) for weeks and months, and a right hemiplegia (paralysis). Despite contrary advice he became a student of law, using scribes, rising to become a judge and the author of eight influential books on historical topics, shell-shock, the reform of courts martial etc. He allowed me to publish his medical history, a triumph of mind over matter, in the 'Journal of the Royal Society of Medicine' in 2003; he died in 2004.

A comparable - wounded but not disabled - infantry officer who became a Judge is W.A.Elliott who served with 2nd Scots Guards. He became a friend when I moved to Edinburgh twenty years after the war, his splendid *Esprit de Corps* (Norwich 1996) ends with a moving account of his experience with the Guards Armoured Division from the Rhine to the North Sea, to the left of our own line of advance. They suffered even more heavily, and he was at the end the only subaltern left who had joined in North Africa. The many small but lethal islands of resistance were armed with panzerfausts, and were tackled by the infantry riding on the tanks.

The Guards Recce was provided by Household Cavalry armoured cars; they have a silent memorial in the 'Robin Chapel' in Edinburgh. Robin Tudsbery and the crew of his Daimler armoured car were blown to pieces as late as 30 April near the North Sea coast, days before the surrender. His grieving parents built a beautiful interdenominational chapel in 1950 in the Thistle Foundation, a residence for the war disabled, which they endowed as a memorial to their son. I functioned there sometimes as a doctor. The other memorial in Edinburgh of some relevance is a display of papers, pictures and books in the entrance hall of Napier University in the old Hydropathic Establishment at Craiglockhart, which had served as a shell-shock hospital in the 14-18 war. Wilfred Owen MC and Siegfried Sassoon MC had been patients there together, and wrote some of their best poetry there, before returning to the front. Owen was killed in France on 4 November 1918. He has been immortalised by Benjamin Britten's setting of some of the poems in the War Requiem of 1962.

By April 1945 we all wished to avoid Owen's fate, when victory in Germany was assured, and there may have been a tendency to use sledge-hammers (artillery and tanks) to crush single fanatics with Panzerfausts etc. to limit our own casualties. This critique of relative sluggishness by the Second Army towards the end is made by Sir Max Hastings in his powerful overview *Armageddon* (Macmillan 2004). But it needs to be read for the horrifying termination of the war in Europe, with its hundreds of thousands of deaths, military and civilian.

Duff Cooper, *Sergeant Shakespeare 1949* may have been right in his surmise that the Bard had experienced sixteenth century warfare in the Low Countries. In April 1945 'The better part of valour is discretion' (Henry IV/2) became more and more valid than the Germans' obedience until death, and earlier surrender would have saved increasingly pointless casualties.

*   *   *   *   *

Near Neetze B Squadron veterans clearly remember the mirth that Tpr McManus caused when he came wandering down the street with a mangy half-starved lion on a rope lead. The animals had been evacuated from the zoo at Hamburg and were clearly in need of care and attention.

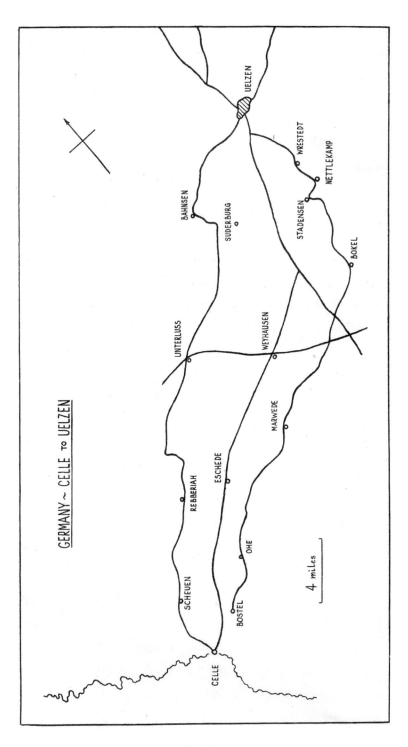

GERMANY ~ CELLE TO UELZEN

Map 18

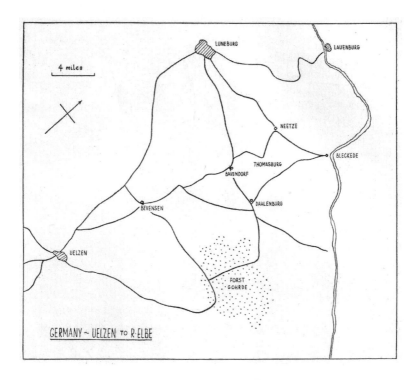

Map 19

Bill Liddell

Arthur Lawrence and Alan Westby at
R.G. Gurney's graveside

Teddy Cudmore

Teddy Cudmore's grave

Graham Nicklin and Gordon Nursaw

Tpr Jackson's grave

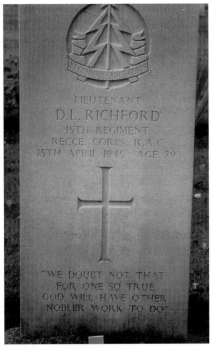

Lt Richford's grave

CHAPTER XXI

OVER THE ELBE TO BATTLE'S END
Map 20

The Elbe was crossed on 29 April. Before then there was much to be done. Owing to the losses of the last two or three weeks, it was impossible to send into action three complete reconnaissance squadrons, so it was decided to work with only two until the regiment was brought up to full strength again. The decision was made before the colonel departed on 23 April for a course and his leave, leaving Major MacDiarmid to command the regiment. A Squadron and C Squadron—the latter once more led by Major Mills, who had returned from England—were reinforced from B Squadron, and what remained of B Squadron was to follow the rest of the regiment like a led lame horse.

The reorganization kept everybody busy, but that was not all. There were the problems of the German people, who were bewildered and cautious. They did not know what they were allowed to do, and they were not taking any chances, so they took their troubles to anything which resembled headquarters. They were happier if they had a form which looked official. Given a piece of 'Army Form Blank' bearing a scribbled nursery rhyme and the stamp of the quartermaster's stores, they would depart contented. There were also the informers. Frau Schmidt would come, full of virtue and tales of the Nazi activities of Frau Tutz. Then Frau Tutz, with tales of Frau Schmidt. But it was from Polish displaced persons that the regiment learned that the Germans had buried documents in a wood outside Neetze. The RSM superintended two days' digging which uncovered more than thirty large steel filing cabinets containing records of the Reich Arbeitsdienst (Labour Battalions); twenty typewriters; and much stationery. The records included personal histories of members of the Nazi Party over a wide area. They were not the Field Security Section's highest priority, but were put in a safe place for future reference.

Meanwhile everything was being rapidly prepared for VIII Corps, the 15th Scottish Division and 1 Commando Brigade to begin Operation Enterprise— the assault on the Elbe line and the advance to the Baltic coast. The plan was that VIII Corps should make the bridgehead and strike north into Schleswig-Holstein, that XII Corps should cross into the bridgehead and branch left to Hamburg, and that the American XVIII Corps should cross east of VIII Corps and protect its right flank. There were now four divisions and two brigades under Lieut General Barker's command—the 11th Armoured Division, the 5th Division (brought from Italy), the 15th Scottish, the 6th Airborne, 6

Guards Armoured Brigade and 1 Commando Brigade. The job of making the bridgehead was given to the Scottish Division and the Commando Brigade, and the Scottish Division thus became the only one in the Second Army to assault all the three great river barriers, the Seine, the Rhine and the Elbe. The war correspondents, with their flair for the picturesque, named it 'the crossing sweepers'.

Preparations for the crossing were difficult because the flat, open country south of the river was overlooked by the wooded cliffs on the other side, and all movement within four miles of the south bank had to be by night. So that the infantry could be ready for the attack, A Squadron relieved 46 Brigade by the river north of Neetze on 28 April, and on the evening of the same day Capt Gray's force, drawn from the regiment's headquarters and what was left of B Squadron, took over from parts of 227 Brigade between the villages of Avendorf and Tespe, three miles west of Artlenburg. At midnight the artillery began a tremendous pounding of the enemy defences on the far side of the river. Two hours later the first Buffaloes carried the assaulting infantry across the three hundred yards of water. There were two brigades in the assault. The Lowlanders crossed at Artlenburg, and the Commando Brigade stormed the cliffs at Lauenburg while the 7th Seaforth, under its command, crossed farther east to envelop the town from the rear. The Commando Brigade also had the regiment's anti-tank battery, and the 6-pounders and their crews were ferried across in Buffaloes early in the assault. By dawn both brigades had substantial bridgeheads.

The enemy shelled and bombed the crossings, and C Squadron patrols suffered casualties from air attack while waiting to be ferried across the river. Lieut Falloon was wounded for the second time in the campaign. Sgt Kirrage, who had served the squadron cheerfully and well in both 54th and 15th Divisions, was wounded badly. The patrols and the squadron's tactical headquarters landed in the bridgehead in the afternoon, and patrols working with the SAS went more than six miles from the river to Kollow, where an SAS jeep crew engaged a battery of 75 mm guns at close range with a 2-inch mortar. They hit one of the guns, whereupon the other gunners surrendered or withdrew. At dusk the patrols were pulled back, but the bridgehead was seven miles wide and up to five miles deep. Although opposition round the perimeter had stiffened, some objectives had been gained two days ahead of schedule.

Around the bridgehead was a country of field and farm, deer forests and lakes, lonely castles, villages and little country towns, and west, along the Elbe, the outcrop of the sprawling, mangled port of Hamburg. The only civilian traffic on the cobbled streets of the country places was the waggons drawn by short, long-bodied, unblinkered horses. Storks nested on the high roofs of the long farmhouses. Into this country A Squadron and C Squadron were jabbed on 30 April—fingers from the expanding palm of the bridgehead. A Squadron went west to Hamwarde and found the enemy strong enough to delay it until 227 Brigade cleared the way. C Squadron went north to Kollow again and to Schwartzenbek, a railway and road junction on the main Hamburg-Berlin road. Leaving the rest of their patrol on the edge of the woods near this small town, Lieut McFall and Cpl Lavery walked into it and found it looking so unwarlike that they had the impression that people were shopping. Then a German staff car came from the west, so they shot it up. The two occupants took to their heels. The troop took up positions round the road junction; captured an SS officer who arrived by motor cycle combination; and had bacon and eggs at a very good public house, not greatly troubled by the Germans holding the railway station.

On the eastern edge of the bridgehead 46 Brigade was having to fight hard at Lutau and Dalldorf, and to draw off some of the enemy pressure Lieut Gillings took a C Squadron patrol south-east of Schwartzenbek. Meeting SS troops about a mile from the town, he talked to them and persuaded some to surrender. It was apparent that more could be achieved by somebody with fluent German, so the intelligence officer of the SAS was sent, and he disappeared in a German staff car to negotiate the surrender of 1,800 SS at the German headquarters. This was not accomplished, in its entirety, but a large number, including officers, gave themselves up. The intelligence officer returned at night.

Next day A Squadron patrols from Hamwarde encountered the enemy on approaching the great Sachsenwald, about five miles away, and C Squadron went out from Kollow and took Brunstorf. The 5th Division had by then occupied the eastern part of the bridgehead, and there the 11th Armoured Division was gathering, ready to break out. On the opposite flank the Welsh Division, old friend of so many engagements, was moving into position for its thrust towards Hamburg, so the Scottish Division was left with only the north-west section of the perimeter, which included the Sachsenwald. During the day there were minor truces and negotiations, and the munitions factory spread over many acres above the Elbe at Geesthacht, where Nobel invented dynamite, was surrendered. It was 1 May. In the afternoon the news of Hitler's death was broadcast. In the regiment Cpl G. West translated the statement of Admiral Dönitz, a toast was drunk and the musical items in the programme were thoroughly enjoyed.

On 2 May the 11th Armoured Division, in the last of its splendid advances, crashed through to the cobbled towns of Bad Oldesloe and Reinfeld and the teeming Baltic port of Lubeck, while the Scottish Division cleared the Sachsenwald and found the Prince and Princess Von Bismarck in a castle at Friedrichsruh. A Squadron patrolled towards Bergedorf and Hamburg, and Sgt Tiny Kirman became the first link in the chain of negotiations which resulted in the surrender of Hamburg and, ultimately, of the German armies in North-West Europe. This is his story of what happened:

> My car patrol going towards Hamburg came under heavy fire, and we pulled back to allow the Argyll and Sutherland Highlanders and the Coldstream Guards' tanks to attack. The battle was at its height when I noticed two German officers walking forward with a white flag. Thinking that they wanted to surrender, I drove up to them with a sergeant major of the Highlanders, and the senior officer, a major, immediately asked to be taken to an officer.
>
> I told them we would have to blindfold them to take them through our lines. The major fussed about this, but in the end they were blindfolded and taken back. They returned, and later two staff cars full of Germans were brought through. By now the rumour of peace negotiations had got around, but the battle continued, although people were coming and going all the time. After the infantry and tanks had cleared the way we made a short advance. Then we received orders not to go farther.

Commenting on this incident six days later, when fighting in Europe had ended, 'The Scotsman' stated: 'The outcome of the negotiations started in the lines of the 15th Scottish Division is now common knowledge. It is a fitting tribute to this famous formation, the only one to have included in its triumphant career from the Normandy beaches assault crossings of the three major river obstacles... that it was to the 'Fighting Fifteenth' that the surrender overtures were first made.'

On 2 May, with the German envoys newly in his lines, Brigadier Colville, commanding 227 Brigade, went to his wireless and explained excitedly to divisional headquarters that this was something really big.

Sgt Kirman's enterprise in his patrolling on the road to Hamburg that day was one of the reasons why he was awarded the Military Medal. He outflanked German positions, eliminated machine-gun posts and gave valuable support to the attacking infantry.

On 3 May it was obvious that the end must be very near. Both squadrons advanced rapidly north-west to the Hamburg-Lubeck autobahn against a confused enemy, who hardly resisted at all. There seemed to be no end to the stream of prisoners. Speeding through Grande and Trittau, A Squadron had reached the lovely Lutjensee by ten o'clock and the autobahn at Hammoor an hour and a half later. There was some opposition from SS posts. The squadron captured a train at Gros Handsdorf and occupied its objective for the day— Bargteheide, one of the straggling, cobbled villages just off the autobahn.

On the left C Squadron's patrols, which had made swift progress to the villages of Papendorf and Langelohe were continuing to their objective on the autobahn when German staff officers approached and informed them that they could go no farther before two o'clock. It seemed odd, but it was right. Hamburg was being surrendered. So the squadron avoided the demarcation line around Hamburg and went on to capture the small town of Ahrensburg, whose castle, surrounded by a tranquil moat, was to be the headquarters of the Scottish Division for many months. The patrols which went ten miles from Ahrensburg and Bargteheide met no opposition, and Major MacDiarmid and the commander of the SAS drove all the way along the autobahn to Lubeck unimpeded.

That evening a patrol was sent from C Squadron to Friedrichsruh to be a guard for the Swiss ambassador and his family, who were in a public house. The C Squadron men found an excellent billet in Max Schmelling's training quarters, and the patrol commander put on a tie and had dinner with the ambassador, then went out in the dark to take turn in the guard.

Next day the Lowland Brigade took over at Bargteheide and 227 Brigade at Ahrensburg, and all the regiment had to do was to move peacefully to Elmenhorst, between Bargteheide and Bad Oldesloe. It was at 6.20 that evening, 4 May, that Field Marshal Busch signed the surrender at Field Marshal Montgomery's headquarters on Luneburg Heath. The 'cease fire' was to be at eight o'clock the following morning. It was the news for which everyone had been waiting for nearly six years, the goal towards which the regiment had fought in four countries. There was no wild excitement, but a great satisfaction and overwhelming relief, mixed oddly with a feeling of emptiness, because the breaking of camp in the chill darkness before dawn, the long drives, the patrols, the hasty meals and the poring over maps—all the things which were to end—had become so completely the pattern of life. That night the tracer from the Bofors rose lazily to make V signs in the sky.

But for the regiment there were soon postscripts to the campaign. At midnight Lieut Colonel Franks came to RHQ with the information that one of his jeeps had been ambushed at Heiderfeld by SS troops. The burgomaster of Heiderfeld had brought the news by bicycle to the SAS harbour at Borstel, and had said that the SS intended to ignore the surrender orders. So armoured cars, mortars and anti-tank guns under the command of Major MacDiarmid joined two squadrons of the SAS early in the morning and set out for Heiderfeld. Patrols found the jeep, abandoned and damaged, but the SS, about sixty of them, had left the village two hours earlier. The armoured cars went farther north, and at Bark captured ten SS, who said that the main force had withdrawn into the Forest of Segeberg, where it intended to hold out. It was nearly eight o'clock, so Major MacDiarmid's force and the SAS returned and reported the situation to divisional headquarters.

The sequel was that on 8 May, the day on which Britain was celebrating Victory in Europe, the regiment was taking part—as umpire and longstop—in its last action of the war. The British command had decided that the Wehrmacht should itself deal with its recalcitrants in the forest, and on the evening of 7 May the following order was received:

'GO 493. RESTRICTED. By permission of 8 Corps fighting will take place tomorrow morning MAY 8 between SS unit holding FORST SEGEBERG and units of the WEHRMACHT under gen ZOUBERZUIG. area involved is . . . details NOT known but believed fighting starts first light with WEHRMACHT clearing forest from EAST to WEST. 15 Recce Regt will provide stops along line of rly to prevent SS escaping to NE. infm concerning this op should be passed all ranks so that no question of BRITISH tps being involved and when firing is heard they know what is taking place. Wide margin has been given to avoid cas from overs although still possibility of overs in vicinity this area. all infm.'

The regiment sent a force from B Squadron, under the command of Major Dove, to carry out these orders. General Zouberzuig's men, alert and well armed, drove up in lorries and disappeared into the forest, where the situation was complicated by the presence of armed displaced persons, some of whom managed to get themselves shot by German sentries. No SS tried to get past B Squadron's posts, and the Wehrmacht carried out its task without any battle. Nobody seemed to know quite what happened to the SS, but after two days the forest was reported clear. There were no B Squadron casualties.

Meanwhile, at Elmenhorst, the regiment had been checking the amazing procession of the defeated German forces along the Hamburg road. They were coming from the east and the north. There were men on foot, men on bicycles and men in carts. There were wheezing, massive, dilapidated lorries dragging three or four or five trailers, all piled high with passengers and baggage. When stopped, some of the lorries managed to start again. Many did not. Looking at this motley collection, one wondered how the German Army had managed to resist so long. In some of the lorries men had girls with them.

On 7 May the regiment was given two other jobs to do. A Squadron was placed under the command of 46 Brigade Group for what proved to be a peaceful occupation of the scarred port of Kiel, where the squadron seized bridges in the harbour area without interference. C Squadron established posts on the bridges over the Kiel Canal to control the Germans moving south from Denmark to surrender. Thus on the day of the celebration of victory the regiment found itself variously engaged and widely scattered—with A Squadron at Kiel, and C Squadron at Brunsbuttel, about sixty-five miles apart and both about sixty miles from RHQ, still at Elmenhorst, while B Squadron kept watch on the Forest of Segeberg. Having maintained communications in four countries in action, the signallers (now commanded by Capt Jennings) were determined not to be defeated by these immediate demands of peace, and the lofty aerials with which they kept up the wireless links were displayed to all visitors with pardonable pride.

Major General Barber issued a Special Order of the Day on 7 May, thanking a 'gallant Division' for 'all your great achievements'. He mentioned that so far the division had taken 24,500 prisoners, and the count was continuing. He mentioned, too, the cost: casualties of 669 officers and 11,422 other ranks, including 181 officers and 2,793 other ranks dead or missing.

In the absence of Lieut Col Smith, Major MacDiarmid issued a Special Order of the Day on 8 May, congratulating all ranks in the regiment on a 'job well and gallantly done'.

Since splashing on to the beaches near Arromanches the regiment had travelled about 1500 miles—by the route of RHQ—in 316 days. It had fought many battles, suffered many discomforts, led many advances and shared in many triumphs. Along those 1,500 miles it had left the graves of most of the seven officers and sixty-six other ranks who had lost their lives. To their memory our story is dedicated.

Alan Westby:- Another outfit, which asked for our support, was the Special Air Service. It is well known the effect the SAS had on the enemy and we found it disconcerting to operate with them. The approach to an enemy village was halted whilst incendiary rounds were fired at the buildings. Anyone emerging to escape the flames was shot and then we moved quickly on to the next farm or hamlet. All this, without, it seemed to us who were not familiar with these tactics, any precautions against counter-attacks. I understood the reality behind their motto 'Who Dares Wins'.

Gordon Nursaw:- We were down near the river preparing to reverse onto a Buffalo when I heard the scream of a German dive-bomber. I looked up and saw a bomb leave the aircraft seemingly heading straight for me. I jumped out of the carrier just as the bomb landed a few feet away. I was thrown into the air and landed on my back, I got to my feet and ran across a field to a house. I ran my fingers through my hair and they were wet with blood, I realised that I was wounded. When I tried to walk I almost fell, my left leg was damaged. Someone came along and took me to the first aid post. Later I found out that Sgt Kirrage had been really cut to pieces but survived.

I was taken to Osnabruck, no one helped me in, I had to hop on one leg, waited in a room, then into theatre. After two weeks in hospital I was sent to a holding unit in Lubeck. During this time my war trophy of a pearl-handled revolver which I had found in a house disappeared! After a few days in Lubeck I saw a truck with the Scottish Lion on the number 41; I stopped the driver and asked if he would take me back to the Regiment. I reported back to Lieut John Wheeler who was pleased that I had made the effort to return.

Lieut Arthur Buck MC of B Squadron entered a small village and dismounted from his vehicle. He spotted two German soldiers in a house, one armed with a panzerfaust. As he posed the more serious threat, Arthur shot him first. The other soldier was young and his rifle was wobbling around, Arthur claimed he could see the bullet in the barrel, they both fired simultaneously, the German dropped. Unfortunately the enemy bullet hit Arthur's shoulder and shattered humerus and clavicle, damaging his scapula, a wound that would cause pain for the rest of his life. Arthur was furious that he missed the celebrations marking the end of the war! All soldiers adjust and adapt their equipment to suit battle conditions and Arthur improved the attack capability of his boots by simply adding an additional sole. When split seconds could mean the difference between living or dying the extra strength and weight ensured fast access to houses and dazed soldiers did not recover from a well aimed boot!

Clive Ridge:- On the last day of the war, it came over the wireless that we could not advance any further and we were forbidden to cross a main road, my job was over! Fortunately I was soon posted to the wireless school at Bovington as a Sergeant Instructor.

Len Watson:- We were sleeping in a school which was great as we normally slept alongside our carriers or armoured cars with tarpaulin sheets over us. Sgt Major Franks said, 'The war is over, there will be no reveille in the morning'. At 0400 hrs on 8 May we were awakened and instructed to prepare for a patrol. It appeared that some SS units intended to ignore the ceasefire. We went to an old railway station, it was a nerve racking situation for two days. We had battled all the way from Normandy and the war was supposed to be over. We seemed like sitting ducks with our vehicles, when German tanks, fully armed, could so easily have destroyed us; we prayed that they had been informed that the war was indeed over. That night in the distance an artillery unit produced a spectacular firework display with their Bofors firing V signs in the sky and wonderful tracers; it was a memorable sight as they discharged their star shells and ammunition. I have never bothered with fireworks since!

After the armistice we were in Northern Germany and our duties were to collect firearms from villages and farms. On one occasion we had collected a number of weapons and I came across a really good 16-bore shotgun with an underneath rifle barrel, quite an unusual piece. At the time we were smashing up all the confiscated weapons and disposing of them in the river. At a later stage it became illegal to possess a rifle-barrelled firearm as there were a number of accidents, some fatal, with soldiers examining and not being familiar with automatic weapons. On returning home on demob, I brought the 16-bore with me, I put the barrel in one part of my overcoat and the stock in the other, folded my greatcoat over my arm and walked through customs. It served me well game shooting for many years and I eventually sold it at auction a few years ago.

Alan Westby:- One day, around noon, a rumour was circulated that an armistice was to be signed at 1100 hours the following morning. After thanks had been expressed, the serious business of celebrating was addressed. All manner of bottles were unearthed and their contents disposed of in workmanlike manner. The two sergeants did an excellent job as minders and nursemaids, eventually putting the lads to bed to sleep off the effects. Alas, the effects were not wholly slept off for 'Reveille' was very early the following morning, quickly followed by orders to move. Not even time for the 'hair of the dog', and we were off with gear changing and steering proving particularly difficult! The problem was a group of Waffen SS who were rumoured to be in a wood some distance away. Our friends the SAS had orders to find and dispose of these men before 1100 hours, the time of the signing of the surrender, and they wanted our support. Neither the wood nor the SS were found but a concentration camp was discovered and liberated. The camp guards were rounded up and handed over to the inmates and their tender mercies but they were too frail to seek retribution. The SAS soon found an answer. Each of the seven or eight guards were lined up, given a spade and ordered to dig a hole six feet long by eighteen inches wide. Having guessed the significance of this exercise, some of the guards displayed a certain arrogance and demanded their rights as POWs, others knelt and asked for mercy, some wept but most obeyed orders and dug. When all the holes had reached a satisfactory depth, the guards were again lined up behind them. A jeep with twin 'K' guns was driven round to face the men and starting at one end of the line, the guns were traversed down its length, aiming just over the heads of the Germans. As they were escorted away to the POW cages one could only speculate on how this close brush with death was to affect their later lives.

John Kay:- While in Kiel, the regiment undertook two quite unlikely tasks. The first was to accept the surrender of the German Kriegsmarine. Three reconnaissance cars, each carrying an officer, were despatched to an enormous concrete blockhouse in the middle of town. The officers' job was to go in and collect signed documents, the rest to await their return. As they went in, one said, 'If we don't come out in forty-five minutes, you come and get us out.' Luckily, no action was needed. After a tense half-hour, all returned safely.

The second was even odder. 'Go to the Kiel Canal and see whether there are any prisoners on board the merchant ships in the Canal' was the order. Like good soldiers, HQ unit of A squadron went to the Canal, took some rowboats and went to the ships anchored in the Canal. Climbing some thirty feet up the rope ladders thrown down by the sailors was quite scary. We were not foolish enough to go inside. Conversations with ships' officers took place on deck. They in turn denied having prisoners and begged for food. (Who did not?). No prisoners were found and the landsmen (us) returned to shore. Six or seven ships were inspected in this way.

This item is quite personal, it has not been told before by me. I guarantee it is 100 per cent true.

One day, as we were occupying Kreis Stormarn, the chap I was billeted with returned from a night out looking pale. 'Was he OK?'. Unfortunately, it was his turn to collect the unit's pay from about fifty miles away. 'Would I do it for him?' OK.

There was only one downside to the fifty-mile drive in each direction: the turret on the Humbers gave the steering so much torque that if the driver did not let go at once after a corner, his arms got a lashing. Moreover, at that time, our headgear had given my forehead a rash and the unit medic had treated it with gentian blue. When I arrived at the other unit (5th UK Division if I remember right), the doc took one look at me and asked what was wrong. I explained. He was horrified and applied something in place of the gentian. In three days my rash was gone.

After lunch, I was shown the unit's lines. They were neat and extensive. At the end of the tour, my guide asked casually if I would like to meet the members of their brothel. It turned out that the Division, which had gone as far as the boundaries of Iran, had had one for some time. As they told their story, they had full approval for it -- about five or six ladies stored in a 3-tonner. Their health was maintained to a high standard, safeguarding both the ladies and their eager clients.

The return journey was slowed by German families fleeing their homes ahead of the Russians.

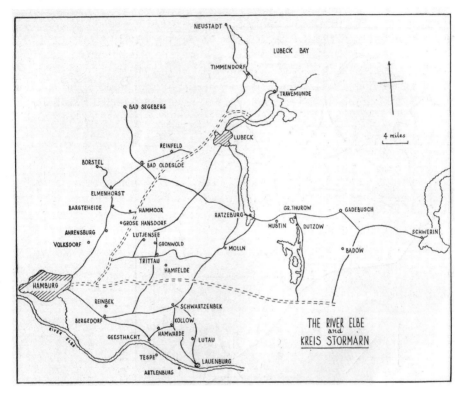

Map 20

Sgt 'Tiny' Kirman MM

Lieut Ken Pearce

Tommy Thomson with mug. Captured bus + POWs

Daimler crew
Staff Sergt W. McClellan standing; Tpr Forfar driver in turret; Tpr Parker, w/op gunner standing on vehicle

W. Coburn; unknown; Len Watson
Daimler scout car, 1945

A Squadron - Kiel May 1945
Top: Tommy Webster
Standing (L to R): 'Ditcher' Jones, Freddy Andrews, Lieut Green, 'Holy' Cole, 'Snips' Parry
Front (L to R): Jimmy Conner, Terry Casey, 'Barney' Shushter

Overture for the surrender of German forces

On 2 May, 1945, the Chief of Staff to Field Marshal Busch, accompanied by his staff officer, approached the British Lines held by 227 (H) Inf Bde (2A&SH and Troops of the 15 (S) Recce Regt) with an overture for the surrender of the German armed forces; he was to arrange an interview between his Commander and Field Marshal Montgomery with a view to an Armistice.

Picture shows Lt Col. Russel Morgan CO 2A&SH back to the photographer, discussing with the GOC's ADC (Lt V. Sadgrove in beret) the GOC's instructions. Meanwhile the C of S and his staff officer, having returned from an interview at Corps HQ, wait for a safe pass to return to their own lines.

British Official Photograph. Crown Copyright Reserved

Left to right: Major General C.M. Barber, CB, DSO; Lieutenant General Sir Evelyn Barker, KBE, CB, DSO, MC;
Brigadier L. Bolton, DSO; Brigadier E.C. Coalville, DSO.

One of the 'liberated' typewriters was used by Sgt Bill Ponting for the rest of the war and served him faithfully
for many years afterwards

CHAPTER XXII

INTO HISTORY

One almost feels that the story should end there—early in that sunny May of 1945, with the long battle newly over. For that was the end to which everything had been the means ever since the first gathering of the motley and the raw at Felton Hall—the clay for Peterkin the Potter. But to finish thus would be to leave the regiment in a state akin to what the Army loved to call suspended animation. That would not do. The regiment did not leave any of its jobs unfinished, and this its story must try to be worthy of its tradition. In this book the regiment has been born, and since among the lakes and woods and cobbled streets and storks' nests of Northern Germany the regiment died, so too in these pages it must die.

The partings began early, even before the bittersweet process of demobilization daily thinned the ranks. Adam Gordon went, posted to be second-in-command of the 2nd Reconnaissance Regiment in the Far East. Adam Gordon, who had commanded—and, indeed, nursed—B Squadron throughout, who had made sure, with infinite patience and quiet good humour, that his squadron suffered nothing from lack of attention to detail, even in the weariest hours of action. The squadron and the regiment were glad at his promotion, and sorry to say 'Goodbye'. His sergeant major, SSM Franks, left soon afterwards, also for promotion well deserved. And Major MacDiarmid, Major Mac, Peter Mac, whose twinkling eye and trim moustache would have been out of place on anyone not a cavalry officer. He had commanded Headquarter Squadron and A Squadron, had been second-in-command of the regiment, and had commanded it in the colonel's absence, all with a great calm and an impish humour which even the gloomy woods of Best could not prevent from gently hoaxing a duty officer who really felt certain, but could not be quite, that Churchill tanks did not patrol woodland paths by searchlight at night. Major Mac went off to command the 49th Reconnaissance Regiment. Did he, one wonders, ever dance a highland measure there in spurs?

Captain Kemsley joined Public Relations to follow, as observer officer at divisional headquarters, his old occupation of newspaper reporter. Jean Wahl, the delightful Frenchman, returned to his France—Jean Wahl who had been so surprised when his jeep refused to run without oil, and when a corps commander complete with outriders and priority flags, had made fierce gestures in the wake of the muddy reconnaissance car which had blithely overtaken him. Captain Gray, the regiment's first MC and Stinker (affectionately) ever since he became an officer in the Royal Fusiliers, left to become a policeman in his old country, Malaya. Gerry Harvey, another old Fusilier and first commander of B Squadron's assault troop, entered Military Government. Gillie, Captain Gillings, succeeded Harry Whitham as the man who ran the division's Red Lion Club in those pleasant houses in Lubeck.

On 28 September 1945, the regiment said 'Goodbye' to the tall Lancer, the self-styled 'poor bloody regular', who had done so much as second-in-command to polish up its final training before D Day, and who led it from the Belgian-Dutch border to the Baltic. Lieut Col K. C. C. Smith, DSO, 12 Lancers—Col Ken—was ordered to join the 1st Indian Armoured Division as G.S.O. 1.

With 'whip outs' and 'crack on', he had coaxed and driven the regiment through the mud of Holland and the floods of Cleve, and he had seen the achievement of his ideals in the swiftly-covered miles between the Rhine and the Elbe. Wherever there was a 'scrap', in whatever place seemed to the average mortal best avoided, there would appear the jeep with the gleaming crest and Corporal Ridge; out would step the familiar broad-shouldered figure of the colonel, muffled in that colossal padded jacket. He would just be keeping himself 'in the picture' so that he could give a personal 'sitrep' of the battle to his divisional commander.

He could be blunt—a spade was a spade. If, however, the regiment sometimes smarted under his tongue, it was probably not without cause. He demanded the best of, and for, his regiment and himself; foolishness got short shrift from him in battle, where mistakes cost lives. The regiment trusted his judgement and was encouraged by his example. These, and his charm, his determination to see that his regiment got the best of everything that was going, and his sympathy for other people's troubles, made him a respected commander. The regiment had lost a good friend.

On 29 September Lieut Col R. Heathcoat-Amory, MC, of the 1st Royal Dragoons, took command, and the regiment soon decided that, by sending him, the Royals had atoned for their destruction of the sports kit. The new commanding officer guarded the regiment's interests and directed its activities with a quietness, a pleasantness and a firmness that won him its liking and respect. And when the time came for the funeral rites, he was a charming and considerate undertaker. The regiment was almost disbanded when, on 24 March 1946, he departed to command the 53rd Reconnaissance Regiment.

In the previous July the regiment had begun to miss other familiar faces as the calls of civilian life were answered, though at first the effect of demobilization was slight, except where it claimed one of the great characters such as Sgt Piney, whose 'duff' was always 'just the job'. One of the first to go was old Q, Captain H. E. Hughes, who had reigned over B Echelon as a king over what was to the rest of the regiment a rather remote kingdom flowing with milk and honey and rum. Those going back to B Echelon to scrounge a new battledress, or with work for the scissors and needle of Nordensvard, could discard their maps for the last mile and find their way by the mighty gusts of the quartermaster's laughter. His due is the plain statement that the regiment never lacked anything—and what more could a quartermaster wish?

In the story of a unit in action it is so easy to do less than justice to those whose jobs were not the most dangerous but not the least arduous and certainly not the least important—RQMS Dobbin and the quartermaster's other henchmen; the squadron quartermaster-sergeants, Waddell, Piper, Reeder and Leadbetter; the lorry drivers such as Creasey and Megan; Sgt Ponting in the MI room; Sgt Gilbert and his orderly room staff; the squadron clerks, Mills, Hook, Knight and Pickard, the quiet and smiling Pickard who put down his pen and picked up his Bren at Nettelkamp; Sgt Budd and his MT staff; Sgt Bob Davidson with his maps; Sgt Hine, commanding the regimental police with the soft voice of Devon; Sgt Harrison, of the Royal Corps of Signals, who kept the regiment always in wireless communication with divisional headquarters; Cpl Raven and Richardson with their loads of charged batteries and batteries for charging; the 'dog rogers' such as Hudson, Hartshorne, Greatrix, Shipton and Robinson. The unnamed must be many. Their very anonymity is the highest praise which can be bestowed upon them. For in a regiment in action it is a great thing to be taken for granted. And away from the regiment, at GHQ, 2nd Echelon, S/Sgt Coton was always looking after its welfare.

RSM Eardley was granted an immediate commission, and he became the regiment's new quartermaster, SSM Ward succeeding him as regimental sergeant-major. There were other promotions to compensate for other departures. Captain Davies, who had twice commanded A Squadron in moments of crisis when his squadron leader had been wounded, became major in command of B Squadron, with Captain Jackson as his second-in-command. Major Mills succeeded Major MacDiarmid as second-in-command of the regiment, and C Squadron was commanded successively by Major Liddell and Major R. H. Fleet, who had been one of B Squadron's troop leaders and a quietly efficient administrator at A Echelon. Major Kemp resumed his old command—Headquarter Squadron. Captain Riesco succeeded the genial Mac Blount, most thorough of adjutants, and Captain Shirley became technical adjutant in succession to George Pearce, whose bald head had shone through the haze of battle wherever a vehicle had been stricken. Sgt MacLellan was promoted to be sergeant major of A Squadron, Sgt Campbell to be sergeant-major of B Squadron, Sgt Jennings to be sergeant major of C Squadron and Sgt Budd to be sergeant-major of Headquarter Squadron.

North of the Elbe when the fighting ended, the regiment remained in that part of Germany until its disbanding followed swiftly upon the disbanding of the division which it had served. It was stationed by the Baltic at Timmendorfer Strand—a place of hotels, temporary hospitals and comfortable houses which looked out on the sunken ships in Neustadt Bay. It was stationed in Mecklenburg. But most of the time it was scattered over Kreis Stormarn, between Hamburg and Lubeck.

And what a mixture life was!

There were the ceremonial guards at Copenhagen and at divisional and corps headquarters at Ahrensburg and Plon; there were training cadres; the regimental school run by Capt Boynton, Capt Isaac, Sgt Kay and Sgt Arthur; the division's Games and drill and rugby football championships, in all of which the regiment gained second place, beaten only by the King's Own Scottish Borderers or the Lowland Brigade team.

There were the pastimes of riding, sailing and swimming in the Baltic or the many lovely lakes, and visiting Hamburg, where clubs, canteens, cinemas, theatres, the Philharmonic Orchestra and the Opera flourished among the ruins.

Guards were provided for trains, and escorts for displaced persons going back to Poland. A census of accommodation had to be taken so that German refugees from the east could be absorbed. The watch on the displaced persons' camps never ceased, for these were a source of many troubles. In them were law-abiding people—of many walks of life and many talents—who had no desire to return to their old countries in the east because their views were at variance with Russian ways; they were grateful for what was done for them. But there were also men who shot and robbed and kept illicit stills.

Between 19 May and 31 May 1945, 275,619 prisoners of war, being sent from the American Zone to the Oldenburg Peninsula in the north, passed through the staging camp which the regiment organised in the woods above Timmendorfer Strand or through the detraining point which the regiment supervised at Neustadt.

In June the Scottish Division took over the province of Mecklenburg, soon to be passed to Russian control under the Yalta agreement. Across Mecklenburg flowed a tide of refugees from the east—German families with all that was left of their possessions piled on their wagons. There were great camps of them, living in whatever shelter they could throw up against the wheels of their carts. They were pathetic, just as the refugees in France and Belgium had been pathetic early in the war. In Mecklenburg, too, there were still people of other nations whom the war had driven or drawn to Germany. They were scattered among the farms and villages where they had worked. Before the Russians came the regiment had to scour the countryside to find out who these people were, where they were and if they were to be sent to the west or left.

After many Russian delays, the province was handed over on 1 July. Before then the German movement to the west had been halted, and at the time of handing over the Germans were confined to their homes in order to prevent any last-minute exodus. Watched from behind many curtains, armoured cars from A and B Squadrons patrolled the area to send by wireless details of the progress of the change of control from one army to the other. C Squadron manned posts on the new boundary between the zones—at Mustin, Thurow and Dutzow. The Russians came with lorries, self-propelled guns, and the smallest armoured car that the regiment had ever seen, and some impressively uniformed officers in staff cars. The difficulty of language curbed the regiment's efforts to be friendly, and after each side had regarded the other briefly and with curiosity the armoured car patrols withdrew.

The zone boundary had been drawn without regard for local problems, and Thurow, where RHQ occupied a lakeside mansion, was almost an island in the Russian area. The Russians had control of four hundred yards of the main road from Ratzeburg, and since all efforts to obtain permission to use this stretch were unsuccessful the only way to RHQ was by several miles of sandy tracks. The corps commander wished to hold a conference with the Russian Army commander to sort out frontier problems and discuss the evacuation of German wounded from Schwerin, so a meeting, to be accompanied by luncheon, was arranged for 4 July at RHQ. After the many preparations had been completed, the conference was postponed at the last minute until 7 July. By that date a garden had been made at the approaches to RHQ, and it was amid surroundings of impressive smartness that the guard of honour waited. Armoured cars were drawn up at the main gates, while a guard of three officers and fifty other ranks, under the command of Capt Blount, stood on the front lawn, where the flags of Great Britain and the USSR were broken when the generals arrived. The problem had been to find a red flag. Major MacDiarmid had solved it by standing over some German seamstresses in Lubeck until they had made one. Both the Russian Army commander and General Barker praised the arrangements.

On 19 July the regiment handed over its frontier posts to the 119th LAA Regiment and took up its quarters in Kreis Stormarn.

At the beginning of March 1946, the colonel received the following letter from Field Marshal Montgomery:

'To meet the effects of the release scheme, it has become necessary to reduce the number of units in this theatre. It is with the greatest regret that I have now to inform you that I have decided to disperse the regiment under your command. I know that this will be a great disappointment to you all, but I am sure that you and all your officers and men will realise that I would not have taken this step had it not been essential.'

General Barber inspected the regiment and said 'Goodbye' on 4 March, and a few days later the colonel and the adjutant went to GHQ 2nd Echelon in Brussels and the headquarters of the British Army of the Rhine to arrange postings. The largest drafts were to the 13th/18th Hussars and the 14th/20th Hussars.

On 1 April 1946, the 15th Scottish Reconnaissance Regiment was history— three years six weeks and three days after Peterkin the Potter first looked at his clay.

Michael Riesco:- Memories from Regimental Headquarters.
The end of the road from Normandy ended for RHQ in the Baltic coastal resort of Timmendorfer Strand (a few miles north of Lubeck), where we began to learn our new 'occupational' role.

The immediate problem was to provide escorts for the seemingly endless stream of German prisoners through various staging camps, which themselves had to be guarded. Although hostilities had ended, there was little chance of experiencing any feeling of anti-climax or boredom for the foreseeable future. Most of the tasks centred round assisting the newly created Military Government, which was set up to bring some form of order to the post-hostility civil authority chaos. Their task was considerably aggravated by the influx of thousands of refugees from the east, who had to be housed and fed. Amongst these were a considerable number of 'undesirables', trying to escape internment or prison camps. There was also a large number of Displaced Persons Camps, where most inmates from many nationalities had no intention of returning to their eastern home countries. These camps had to be closely monitored, as they were becoming a law unto themselves. Consideration also had to be given beyond this foreseeable future, when hopefully these tasks would diminish and thought had to be given to keeping everyone gainfully and constructively occupied until demobilization. However there was still time to enjoy and appreciate long forgotten leisure activities in the pleasant summer resort of Timmendorfer Strand.

Our next move was to Thurow on the proposed new borders between West and East Germany (Schleswig-Holstein and Mecklenburg). We took over an impressive lakeside mansion, together with its German staff. This proved quite a shock to the system after the past months of wartime conditions. We were even served afternoon tea in the lounge on a silver tea service by white coated staff! Attached to the main house was a superbly fitted-out stable block, with about fifteen stables and staff accommodation for both house and stable staff. This set up was immaculately run by the 'Master of Horse', a seemingly delightful ex-cavalry man of the old school. As can be imagined this was Ken Smith's pride and joy. We used to ride out nearly every day on magnificent horses with the Master of Horse, who Ken Smith used to invite into the mess for drinks from time to time! A temporary Russian border post had been set up just a few minutes down the road from RHQ. It was manned by a somewhat motley collection of dishevelled, sullen looking soldiers. We looked at each other with mild curiosity, but none of them understood English and we certainly didn't understand Russian. Due to our proximity to the Russian border, RHQ was chosen to host a meeting of top brass from the British and Russian forces to formalise the area border lines and to try and come to some agreement concerning the continuing stream of refugees who were still appearing out of nearby woods before the border officially closed. In view of the forthcoming meeting, security became paramount. I was sent to Divisional HQ to see Sandy Rosdol, the Divisional Intelligence Officer. I returned with a large pile of 'Fragebogen' (questionnaires), which I was to hand out to all German personnel in the vicinity. An official German interpreter was sent from

Divisional HQ to assist in the interviews when the completed questionnaires were handed in. The Master of Horse (unfortunately I have forgotten his name) was last to be interviewed, and to our utter amazement, he freely admitted to have held a senior position in the Nazi SS several years earlier, before the war. He actually seemed very proud of the fact, although he knew the reason why the forms had been handed out. I duly returned to Divisional HQ with the interpreter and Sandy Rosdol was equally amazed. He immediately sent a guard over to RHQ to collect the Master of Horse, together with one or two others he was suspicious about. They had already gone by the time I returned to RHQ! I was never able to find out what happened to them. As can be imagined, I was not the most popular person in the mess; I don't think Ken Smith spoke to me for days!

The top brass meeting went off without a hitch and was a most impressive affair. Every stone in sight was whitewashed and the Regiment supplied a very impressive Guard of Honour of both personnel and armoured cars. The third and last location for RHQ was at Lutjensee, with its picturesque lakeside setting and a number of very high quality homes with gardens going down to the lakeside. Here there was a choice of rowing, motor or sailing boats and swimming in the lake. It was here that Ken Smith left us and there was a short gap before Lieut-Col Roddy Amory appeared on the scene. Peter MacDiarmid and Harry Mills thought this was an ideal opportunity to throw a big party. It was quite something, even by their standards! Few of us could last the course and went to bed. The devastation that greeted us the following morning was beyond belief and our first reaction was that we would have to move house! However, Peter and Harry were shamed into commandeering a number of locals, who managed to restore some semblance of order so that RHQ could at least continue to function.

The legendary Cyril Kemp was always noted for being able to produce anything from out of a hat. During this period of occupation he really came into his own. I think if Harry had wanted an elephant at his party, I am sure Cyril would have produced one from somewhere. We often wonder whether he did not actually do so! Cyril's Headquarters were at Grossensee just south of Lutjensee, another beautiful lakeside setting. His HQ became a veritable Aladdin's cave! By this time, I had taken over from the very efficient Blount as Adjutant, a difficult act to follow. The amount of paperwork that had to be dealt with was prodigious. Without Alf Gilbert and his staff it would have been nigh on impossible. The last task proved the saddest and hardest of all - the process of disbanding the Regiment. Alf and I had the perfect boss for the job - Roddy Amory. He treated the whole task with the utmost care and consideration, as if he was doing it for a Regiment he had commanded for years instead of only a few months. There were endless meetings with Squadron Commanders to decide who was going where and the dispersal of equipment. I wonder what happened to Cyril's Aladdin's cave! At the very end, Alf and I were left to sort out the Regimental Archives.

Over the past few months, whenever I had to go to Divisional H.Q., I always visited Capt Charles Lawton, who had been given the task of drafting the

Divisional History (*The Path of the Lion*), before the mass of archival material was either dispersed or destroyed. He had asked me to check the parts relative to our Regiment. This I gladly did and it taught me the way round our own archives. That really sowed the seed for our ultimate decision. No way could we possibly destroy them as instructed. We packed all the important archives into a large packing case and I eventually took them home with me. We planned to meet up as often as possible after our demob, and put together some kind of record of the Regiment's history. Fortunately I had a small room set up for the purpose, with the walls covered in maps and of course the vital war diary. The ever faithful Alf came over as often as he could, and after many months, ended up with a very large pile of foolscap sheets all written in longhand. By some miracle, Walter Kemsley managed to translate our efforts into readable English and the result was *The Scottish Lion on Patrol*.

Len Watson:- We played a lot of cricket for the regiment, one match was against 'Danish Old Boys' in Copenhagen when we mounted a special guard at the Palace. We were treated to a superb meal in a hotel and the cherry brandy flowed copiously. Many of the Danes had previously played football at Wembley. Unfortunately a return fixture planned for the following Sunday was cancelled, much to our disappointment, because of bad weather. Arthur and I claim we played cricket for England in an international!

Arthur Watkins recalls that the regimental messing facilities were not available in Copenhagen so food was taken at NAAFIs; he really enjoyed mid-morning breaks which were hardboiled eggs and a glass of cognac. Less fun was when some exuberant comrades pushed him into the monkey pit at the zoo! On disbandment Arthur Watkins went into the Royal Scots Greys and learnt to ride a horse; I was transferred to the 13th/18th Hussars.

I remember an incident during the campaign when one of our men trod on a mine in a wood and was badly injured; sadly I cannot recall his name but he said 'Thank God it's not so and so, he goes on leave tomorrow.' Brave, brave men.

Arthur Watkins:- Near Lubeck we used German prisoners to load up some of the latest captured tanks with special sights that were being sent to the UK for evaluation. The prisoners seemed to really enjoy marching particularly to music so we encouraged them to sing 'We march against England'; the irony of the situation seem to be lost on them!

Alan Westby:- Some time after the end of the war we learnt that we were to be transferred to the 13th/18th Hussars or the 17th/21st Lancers. I did not relish the thought of spit and polish for its own sake and sought an alternative occupation. Squadron Orders requested volunteers for a clerks' course. Typing formal and informal letters, command structures and communications were more or less mastered and the final exam miraculously passed. I had put down a 6-pounder and picked up a pen; a job was required. The Darlington Hotel, Cuxhaven, was an Officers' Transit Centre through which all officers travelling to Hull passed and they needed a reception clerk. A 'cushy' number indeed; all that was needed was the year 1947 and Release Group 52. Whilst at Cuxhaven I witnessed the destruction of the military installations on the island of Heligoland. The detonation was reputed to be equivalent to one sixth of an atomic bomb; it was a mighty explosion, windows rattled and I could see a huge mushroom cloud from forty miles away.

* * * * *

Reunions

Veterans' Reunion   by Walter Kemsley

They come to London once each year-
These men with grey and thinning hair,
Long pants to keep out autumn cold,
And cheap rail tickets for the old.
They meet. They shake arthritic hands,
And wince. They tell of prostate glands,
But to each other make quite clear
That looks have fooled another year.

In conversation when they dine
They mention battles near the Rhine,
But in this talk interpolate
New details of their families' state.

Grandchildren's welfare means much more
Than fading memories of war
To these whose fellowship began
In hiding fear and fighting man.

Thus men who dashed from Orne to Seine
Past reddened hulks and bloated slain,
And watched the shadows' menace pass
From bitter nights beside the Maas

Leave early for the homeward train.

The men who formed the Regiment were of a type that could demonstrate initiative, intelligence and courage; their opponents acknowledged their battle skills. Each vehicle operating as a unit with a three- or four-man crew could identify a crucial element, feature or secure information which could prove decisive in moving the battle forward to our advantage. With the war won most of the men left the Army and returned to Civvy Street. Officers held regular re-unions and then an association was formed to include all who had served. There were many annual May lunches at the Army and Navy Club in London. As the members aged there was a desire to revisit some of the sites of past actions. Some of the more notable re-union visits have been detailed. There have been many more in all parts of the UK. Time has inevitably reduced the numbers but whenever they meet the bond of extended 'family' is still clearly in evidence. Many have clear recollections of their time with the Regiment and what for many was the most intense experience of their lives.

Helmond Holland 31st May-2nd June 1985

A party of twenty-eight members and wives attended a reception at the Kasteel Raadhuis where they were received by the Burgemeester. Adam Gordon presented a crystal bowl magnificently carved by Michael McFall. Many of the villages well known to the men during the war were visited, completely unrecognisable from the desolation of forty years before. Asten and Deurne were visited and the Royal British Legion in Eindhoven. At the Hout Blerick church (Squadron HQ during the winter of 44/45) a piper in full-dress uniform led the group into a packed church behind the RBL Standard. The piper played the 'Lament' which was most moving, heightened by the spontaneous applause of the congregation when the group marched out. Although much had changed, the house of Mrs Kersemakers-Moll remained unaltered in Helmond. Many officers had taken a bath there, the plumbing had not changed in forty years and Mrs Kersemakers-Moll at eighty-six showed Adam Gordon and John Boynton her visitors' book they had signed so long ago. The visit was remembered for the overwhelming kindness and enthusiasm shown by the Dutch guides and hosts.

Paris June 1987 Twenty-seven members and wives visited Paris and areas familiar to the Regiment. Herqueville, Muids, Fretteville and le Thuit were visited. There was a ceremony at the 'Monument aux Morts' followed by a reception in les Andelys.

Berlin July 1990 organised by Ken Sadler who was resident in the city. A party of thirty-two members and wives visited both east and west sectors of the city. Highlight was a visit to the 14th/18th Hussars who allowed them to drive or command their Challenger tanks over an assault course.

Normandy 14–18 June 1991

A party of forty-three members and wives returned to France with their base at Caen. All squadrons of the regiment were involved in Operation Bluecoat and Hervieux crossroads, Lutain woods, St Pierre Tarentaine and le Beny Bocage were visited and a service with French veterans was held at the Scottish Divisional memorial at Tourville-sur-Odon.

Several formal lunches and dinners were enjoyed and Jean Wahl, the French liason officer attached to the regiment during the war, was an invaluable asset in preparing appropriate toasts and speeches. Fallen comrades lying in Bayeux cemetery were visited. The Regimental dinner was held at Chateau Creully which had been Monty's HQ for a time. It was on this trip that four former officers of the regiment, John Boynton. Arthur Buck, Bill Liddell and Doug Peterson, handed over the Regimental flag to Monsieur Jean Noel for display at the Arromanches Museum. The friendliness of the reception, the goodwill and generosity which was encountered everywhere meant a lot to all the visitors.

Stirling October 1992 A party of forty-nine members and wives visited the area. Bryan White and Ken Jenkins, two Dunkirk veterans, were pleased to see the Skylark at Loch Lomond, one of the famous 'little ships'. It was at this reunion that the leather-bound Regimental scrap book was lodged with the military museum at Edinburgh Castle.

Netherlands 25-30 October 1994 Fifty-eight association members and wives returned to Tilburg to participate in the fiftieth anniversary commemorations of the area's liberation from the Nazis. Students were keen to interview the veterans and to form a picture of life at a critical time fifty years ago.

Cemeteries with Regimental dead were visited and Major Reg Fleet laid wreaths on the graves of three of his former Troop members, Fred Eaton, Edwin Taylor and Fred Behling in Mierlo. It was noted that Tpr Dodd's headstone was engraved 1st Recce and it was hoped to rectify this error. At Oirschot Barracks we met Captain Hans Steenmetz who proved to be an authority on the Regiment's activities in the area during the war. Best and Helmond were visited and so too was Moergestel with its famous bridge. The marching party arrived a little late for the 'Keep them Rolling' parade on Saturday, so we formed up in a side street and quite rightly assumed the lead position as the column approached. The genuine appreciation and outpouring of goodwill for the veterans from the Dutch people was something that will never be forgotten.

Bruges-Arnhem September 1995 Thirty-nine members and wives visited Bruges and Ypres and scenes of the Regiment's actions in Ooike and Deerlyck. Arnhem, Gheel and Moll stirred memories of action there in the Autumn of 1944. Schloss Calbeck had been the HQ for B and C Squadrons during the fierce fighting in the Reichswald forest. The brick fabric of the building bore witness to the intense artillery and mortar fire, which had been endured by many of the party. Comrades lying in the Reichswald Forest and Venray cemeteries were visited.

Newcastle September 1997 Forty Members and wives attended. Felton Hall was revisited at the kind invitation of the owner, Major Dennis Burton. It was here in early 1943 that three independent reconnaissance companies became the 15th Scottish Recce Regiment. The area around was familiar from the numerous exercises that had been undertaken during the intensive training period. A live firing of mortars was observed at Otterburn Camp.

Lubeck September 1998 Thirty-one association members travelled across Holland to Lubeck. The ancient Hanseatic port of Lubeck had received some attention from the might of Bomber Command but had been spared from really destructive raids because it became a centre for Red Cross activity and exchanges during the war and its status was recognised by the Allies. Old haunts and previous HQs were sought out and everywhere we received a courteous welcome. We visited Luneberg Heath where the locals had quickly demolished the plaque marking the site of the German surrender once we had ceased to protect it. It was an emotional moment when the men lost at Nettelkamp were visited where they lie in Becklingen cemetery. We visited the site of Belsen, a terrible place and a telling testimony to those we fought against and, thank goodness, vanquished.

Normandy October 2002   Thirty-four association members returned to Normandy staying at Bayeux. A splendidly dressed piper accompanied us down to the cross of remembrance for a service in the beautiful maintained cemetery at Bayeux. Michael McFall presented a plaque carved by Edwin Reetham to the Mayor of Arromanches. Places familiar to the group were visited and the veterans were pleased to receive a commemorative plaque from the museum at Pegasus Bridge. A splendid gourmet dinner was enjoyed in the Lion d'Or, Bayeux. Bryan White reminded the group that he had stayed in the hotel with three other former officers in 1949.

Pontefract September 2003   B and C Squadrons were based at the racecourse in September 1943. A framed copy of the photograph of the Officers in front of the Grandstand was presented for display.

Netherlands October 2004   A Grant from 'Heroes Return' enabled 50 members of the association to visit for the sixtieth anniversary of the liberation of Tilburg. The Reichswald and all other cemeteries in the area where comrades lie were visited. Services of remembrance were held in Tilburg, Best and Helmond. A service was held in Moergestel and dominating the bridge is a fine statue of Major General C.M. Barber CB, DSO. The 15th Scottish Division, was commanded by the General from the 4 August 1944 until disbandment. At 6 foot 8 inches tall Sir Colin was the tallest General in the British Army and was inevitably nicknamed 'Tiny Barber', the longest and leanest 'SUNRAY' of them all.

Hans Steenmetz, a former officer in the Dutch army, had planned a surprise for our group. As the coach approached Helmond castle a Dingo and a Humber armoured car provided close escort. After the reception at the castle 'Gilly' (Capt A. Gillings) rode proudly in the turret of the Humber to Mierlo cemetery.

Most of the veterans were able to secure rides in the parade of vintage army vehicles on the final day of commemorations. The kindness and generosity of the Dutch people was quite overwhelming and it touched the veterans who had made a real effort to attend.

Scarborough October 2006   A group of veterans re-visited the town where, during the war, the regiment were based at the Esplanade Hotel.

Army & Navy Club London May 2007   This was a special occasion attended by Major General Peter Grant Peterkin CB, OBE who after a distinguished military career was now the Serjeant at Arms at the House of Commons. The regiment had been created by Peter's father Lieut Colonel J.A. Grant Peterkin DSO. It was most appropriate that, at this, the last of the formal gatherings, the toast to the 15th Scottish Reconnaissance Regiment was proposed by someone with a real understanding of its outstanding achievements.

Netherlands October 2009 The Orange Committee of Tilburg invited members of the association to the city to commemorate the sixty-fifth Anniversary of its liberation. A party including six veterans attended. The former Sgt John Kay at the age of ninety made the journey over from the United States. There were many moving services, and places well known to the regiment were visited. The genuine appreciation and hospitality of the Dutch people was overwhelming. The final parade where the veterans were driven round the city in vintage military vehicles was most moving.

Reconnaissance Reborn

The Army's first new regiment in more than three decades began operations on 6 April 2005. The Special Reconnaissance Regiment is highly trained and will operate alongside the SAS. The badge has a Corinthian style helmet a sword and the scroll reads 'Reconnaissance'. The helmet faces forward and suggests the viewer is being watched while the wearer behind the mask is anonymous. We wish all members of the newly formed unit every success in pursuit of the Queen's enemies.

15th Scottish Division Memorial Tourville Sur Odon.

Michael Riesco wrote:

The memorial was unveiled on Sunday 26 of June 1949 by General Sir Richard O'Connor GCB, DSO, MC. The Regiment was represented by Major C.K. Kemp, E.A. Royle, B.H. White and M.R. Riesco. The monument itself was designed by General Barber, who was unfortunately not able to be present. It is a most worthy memorial to the deeds and more especially to the heavy casualties of the Division. Round the base of the simple but imposing stone pillar are bronze plaques depicting the dedication and the Battle Honours. On the main pillar are a further four bronze plaques listing all the units of the Division by Brigades. Twenty feet above the base stone stands the bronze Lion Rampant facing across the famous Odon valley.

The unveiling and Service of Dedication were very moving and remained long in the memory of those who were fortunate enough to be present. There were approximately eighty members of the Division and Next of Kin present together with the populations of all the surrounding villages. After the unveiling by General O'Connor, a piper in full-dress uniform, standing at the foot of the Memorial, played the Lament 'Lochaber No More'. In the minute's silence which followed, one could not help but wonder at the complete quiet and stillness of the scene, which still bore marks of the devastation of five years ago. In the valley below the trees are still deformed and many of the buildings still rubble, the burning sun still shone from a cloudless sky on the dusty tracks and hedgerows. It seemed a little unreal that the countryside should look so much the same but the circumstances of our presence there so different. Then, to the familiar strains of the Divisional March, the Piper stirred our minds back to the present. After the Prayers of Dedication, the Mayor of Tourville accepted the Memorial for safe keeping. The ceremony was closed with the laying of wreaths. One was laid at the foot of the Memorial by representatives from each Brigade, we being included with Divisional Troops. We had, however, brought our own wreath of fresh flowers which we placed on the Memorial after the ceremony had ended.

Amongst my souvenirs!

On our return to 'Blighty' on the coach from Holland after the 2004 pilgrimage to Tilburg, we had to vacate the vehicle at the Customs whilst a search was conducted. We thought it was a bloody cheek and that their time could have been better spent preventing the flow of illegal immigrants.

However... Perhaps they had good reason. 'The Times' of 7 April 2005 carried the headline. 'War veterans' coach had £12.5m cocaine onboard'. The coach carrying veterans from a pilgrimage to France the previous October was on the same route as ourselves. The driver used the veterans as an unwitting but respectable front for his activities, placing three holdalls of the class 'A' drugs amongst the pensioners' luggage. The fifty-three year old driver was jailed for twelve years. So well done to those plucky Customs' chappies for achieving a result!

At many venues where we have held reunions, much amusement was caused by our group being referred to as the 15th Scottish 'Renaissance' Regiment; old soldiers they might be, but Leonardo Da Vinci never served with them!

15th (Scottish) Infantry Division   1939-1946

A Drumhead service was held at the Cavalry Barracks, Edinburgh on 14 September 1996, the fiftieth anniversary of the disbandment of the Division. The courage, service and devotion to duty of all those who served during the years 1939-46 was acknowledged with pride.

National Memorial Arboretum, Alrewas, Staffs

From donations and Regimental funds, £300 was raised for the planting of a Scots Pine Tree. Commander David Childs RN was Director of the project and he was most helpful in ensuring our service and planting ceremony on the 29 September 2000 was efficiently executed despite difficult site conditions. A plaque bearing the Regimental badge carved by Edwin Reetham was sited in the memorial chapel. Over the years Edwin has skillfully carved additional plaques which have been presented to All Hallows' Church, London, the Mayors of Tilburg and Helmond and the museums at Arromanches and Pegasus Bridge. The Regimental flag proudly hangs near to the entrance in the D.Day Museum, Arromanches. It was presented in June 1991 for safe keeping and display.

A Book of Remembrance to all those who lost their lives serving with the Reconnaissance Corps was deposited in the Church of All Hallows by the Tower in 1950 and a stained glass window of the Corps badge was dedicated in 1985. In the Memorial Hall at Bovington the Reconnaissance Corps is included in the list of regiments commemorated.

Appendix B Honours and Awards (Addition)

At a May reunion lunch, one of the authors of *Scottish Lion on Patrol*, Walter Kemsley was presented with a specially-bound copy of the book. He pointed out that there was an omission in this section and that Victor Sadgrove had been awarded a Mention in Despatches. This was a deserved recognition of his valuable service as General Barber's ADC and right hand man in many situations, after being seconded to Divisional HQ as the Regimental Liaison Officer.

Armistice Day by Walter Kemsley

We take them out and make them shine-
Our medals and our memories-
Just once each year, and you in line
March out from long closed histories
Who were unlucky or just brave.
You dug the latrines, you cleaned the Bren,
Patrolled, were mortared, found your grave.
Now we patrol with you again
But draw back from a distant war
And shut the turret top once more.

Odd Ode No. V by Charles Millway

Charles Millway never claimed to be a poet in the classic sense but his 'ODE' clearly demonstrates fierce loyalty to his Troop and the Regiment. It is a worthy record of the campaign.

ODD ODE NO: V
or
FIVE TROOP

Now gentlemen of Five Troop, please get on parade,
And listen to this latest ode about yourselves I've made.
It tells, how back in Normandy, where shells were not on t'shore,
How we, who were then Three Troop, were introduced to war.
And later, of those great events, which we helped to unfold,
But this was not our worry, we just did as we were told.
Enough of this preamble! Let's get on with this ode,
About those gallant gentlemen, who to fame and glory rode.

Dedicated to 5 Troop, A Squadron,
15th Scottish Reconnaissance Regiment.

How well that first engagement will be remembered by us all,
When first we heard the mortars and their shells around us fall.
How well that night at Rauray, our first in action spent,
When little did we know or guess the enemy's intent.
To surround us was his aim, he didn't quite succeed,
'Twas the infantry who pushed him back, in that our hour of need.
Next evening on the BBC we heard about our plight,
Of how we were surrounded on that memorable night.

Having thus been 'Blooded' and to Sequeville withdrawn,
Before the next encounter on a fateful Monday morn.
The day dawned grey and dreary with intermittent rain,
As through a hail of mortar shells we reached the field of grain,
Where Panzers lay in waiting, for such an easy prey
As those two cars we lost at Eterville that day.
The cars we lost were nothing, but the lives we lost were dear,
Our Commander and his driver, who had never learnt to fear.

With 'tails between our legs' we departed from that scene,
Aware that when in action, we still were very green.
Pursued by countless mortar shells, we fell back to Verson,
To reckon up our losses, a third of us had gone,
And this was our first recce in our fourth week of war!
God! How could we survive if we had to do much more?
With our morale thus lowered, to Sequeville once again,
To get some new equipment, and some vehicles to maintain.

When the next attack was made, we had a different role,
The carriers brought in wounded, the car was 'Gap Control'.
The rest of us at echelon, were commissioning two cars,
Amidst the thunderous roar of an Alamein barrage.
At night their bombers overhead sought the offending guns
Which had caused so much discomfort to the 'poor bewildered Huns'
The plane above us dropped its flares, then circled round about
To select the gun position which he thought that he'd knock out.

We crowded in our dug outs, the atmosphere was tense,
The drone above continued and held us in suspense.
And then a different noise was carried to our ears,
An awe inspiring scream, which seemed to last for years,
And then a sickening thud, a rending crash, a livid roar,
Everything went black, we thought we'd see no more.
The darkness turned to dusk, the dusk into a haze,
And all around, it seemed, were vehicles ablaze.

Pandemonium reigned, we scattered far and wide,
In undress uniform - which must have hurt our pride,
We ran, we crawled, we ran again, and often had to duck,
To dodge the flying missiles from the blazing ammo truck.
At last, we re-assembled, at a new found rendezvous,
Where all reported present,- all excepting two.
Next morning we were cheered to see not only the sunrise,
But British bombers overhead, just like so many flies.

We left the bloody fields of Caen to rest at Balleroy,
Where several days of peace and quite, we were able to enjoy.
Then the news was given that the 'Yanks' had broken through,
And we knew that soon for us as well there'd be some work to do.
So from Caumont we set forth to smash the German line,
Supported by our bombers, the drive was going fine.
There were, however, snipers who tried to check our pace,
But our terrific weight of armour was more than they could face.

'Twas on this great advance that we had a big surprise,
When several Jerry fighters swooped from out the clouded skies.
We thought at first that they were ours, till from their wings burst flames,
They'd let their rockets off at us, the dirty 'wot's their names'
I was with the carriers, but we didn't stay inside -
We left the 'blasted' things to give themselves a ride.
We never will forget the sound which those few rockets made,
We knew then how Jerry felt in a Typhoon's cannonade.

As the trap began to form, resistance got more tough:
And we were soon to learn that they hadn't had enough.
The scene was set at Drouet, and there we were to spend
A day unmatched in fury, - which never seemed to end.
The job was flank protection to a company of Guards,
And the way they stood the strain would have stirred the ancient bards.
In the next few lines I'll try, as simply as a I can,
To tell of how we passed that day, and hardly lost a man.

'Twas quiet when we got there, but this did not last for long,
Our new acquaintance 'Minnie' commenced her moaning song.
It was obvious to us that we'd gone a bit too far,
As shells burst by the dozen, around our armoured car.
We then drew back a little: we stopped, and there dug in,
To take what might come to us - squarely on the chin.
It was when our tanks arrived that things got rather hot,
As one by one they 'brewed up' when they reached a certain spot.

Then one, pursued by 'eighty eight', came crashing through at speed,
The hedge, which was our cover, behind which stood our steed.
She took it like a 'lady' as it mounted on her back,
But we didn't stay there watching that rending, grinding track.
No, Sir! When the crew saw what happened, they got out mighty quick,
Their nerves were rather shattered, they were feeling kind-er sick.
The car looked rather battered, but the wheels still went round,
So as a fighting vehicle, she yet was pretty sound.

We settled down once more, to watch the flank again,
To listen to the battle, and that terrible refrain
Of barking guns and bursting shells, but by far the worst of all
The rattle of those burning tanks, beneath a thick black pall.
The day wore on, it got more quiet, 'till shortly after tea
His most desperate attack was made.- Oh! For eternity!
What we had been through all that day, compared with this was nought.
Did we waver? No, not us! But we gave it just a thought.

Then, while the din was at its height, we were told by those that knew,
That our job was nearly finished, so forthwith our car withdrew,
For we were nigh disabled and grave risks we had to run,
To cross that dreaded valley, pin-pointed by the 'Hun'.
This we did, without mishap, and crawling up the hill
Saw spread before us and below, a sight which gave a thrill,
We saw the battle being fought, a sea of stabbing flames.
Yes, this was modern man and youth, having fun and games!

Covered by two Vickers, we turned left and to the rear,
Where the ghastly noise of battle was more tolerable to bear.
It was not long before we found our harbour of that morn,
We had a meal and bedded down to wait another dawn.
Our comrades joined us soon, they were more at ease
As we lived again that day, in our 'bivvy' 'neath the trees.
And I lay awake and wondered, as I looked up at the stars,
If this was war on Earth, what was it like on Mars?

The 'Gap' was nearly closed, and so for several days
We were pulled out of the battle 'til the breakthrough at Falaise.
Everything was checked, and checked as ne'er before,
For our job was so important, we were 'Recce' for a Corps.
Provisions for a month, or as much as could go on,
Oil and petrol too, for one tremendous 'Swan'.
I cannot say we welcomed it, this facing the unknown,
But whatever were our thoughts, there was very little shown.

'The Day' arrived, we started up, proceeded on our way
To witness scenes we'll never forget until our dying day.
The wreckage of an army, packed tight in country lanes,
Mangled men and horses, guns and tanks, and even planes.
And yet amidst this carnage, the worst in any wars,
Stood country people waving, beside their cottage doors.
And this was but the start of a long triumphant ride,
Yes, the tears of liberation were difficult to hide.

Thro' villages beflagged and thronged with joyous crowds,
And fitting weather too, unmarred by any clouds.
Yes, this was one good recce I'd like to do again,
Opening up those roads from Falaise to the Seine.
Where all we had to do, was to ask the folk around,
When they'd last seen 'Jerry' and whither he was bound.
Of tanks and guns we had no fear we'd find around a bend:
'But would it be like this,' we thought, 'right to the bitter end?'

Then came the Seine, which checked our pace
'Till a bridgehead was formed, to renew the chase
Of the beaten 'Hun', whom we didn't contend
Would have enough men, for that line to defend.
So keen were our leaders to get us across,
That we dashed off at speed regardless of loss,
Which occurred, when a car drove into the back
Of the one just in front, 'cos the night was so black.

Now we, in the cars, crossed first on a ferry,
On the following morn', so fateful for 'Jerry'
Passing through Muids, we had on us bestowed
Plenty of fruit, and 'one for the road'
Then through a large wood, and beyond it we found
That our opposite number was on the high ground.
ATTACK! was our mood, so attack him we did.
We wanted revenge, so revenge was our bid.

By stooks of corn he'd dug himself in,
It was difficult to know just where to begin.
Then 'Taff' opened up from the light car ahead:
I saw my first target, and shot the man dead.
The second I ranged on was a 'biggish affair'
I squeezed the wrong trigger, it went up in the air.
While 'Tommy' was nursing his elbow inside
The bloke(s) in the target had gone for a ride.

By this time two more cars had joined in the scrap,
And 'Jerry' was getting 'in a bit of a flap',
His fire was scant, his mortars were few:
While our Troop Commander knew just what to do.
With grenades in his hands he stepped to the ground
And dropped them in trenches where a 'Jerry' was found.
While the notorious 'Terry', to everyone's glee,
Chased a poor prisoner who'd hid in a tree.

Our Infantry came, they resisted no more,
We collected our prisoners and counted the score:
Two dozen captured and as many killed
We'd had our revenge for that other field:
Where we'd been the losers, and we'd had to pay
With the blood of our comrades, as they did that day.
The job thus completed, once more cross the Seine,
We were ferried, to contact the Squadron again.

A 'brew' and a 'kip'. And then on once more
To cross that broad river, but not as before,
Instead of by ferry, by bridge: (I must say,
That the Sappers as well, had worked hard that day)
And so into 'Harbour', until it got light,
With the coming of dawn, a day not so bright
We were called out again to go forward and see
What help we could give them at les Andelys.

The way to this town was clear it was found,
The FFI held the hills all around.
With his own equipment they'd beaten the 'Hun',
Of course, it was true that we'd made them run.
But even so, their help was immense,
For threatened within he had no defence,
And we were enabled to keep up the pace,
To maintain the rout, and continue the chase.

Flat out we were, when we tore into Lille,
Like conquering heroes it made us feel.
That this should be, I don't know why:
But 'twas as easy to live as it was to die!
Our mates in the carriers, we almost despised,
'They were miles behind!' That's what we surmised.
But they all arrived in an hour or two,
One had to give credit where credit was due!

And so into Belgium: we hadn't the chance
To get to know properly much about France.
But this didn't apply quite so much to me,
For seven more days of it I was to see.
And now it seems I'll have to relate
Our next encounter with 'The Sons of Hate':
And how it was they caused me to spend
A week away from you, - my friend.

We got to Bercham, just over the border,
On our way to Ostend, for that was the order.
A pocket had formed, he was trying at least
To make a break out away to the East.
We recced to Kaster, and there we were checked
By a counter attack which we didn't expect.
Our leading patrol were proud to relate
How they'd looked down the barrel of an 'Eighty-eight'

We took up positions until it was found
He was trying his damnedest our troops to surround.
Our position was 'deadly', 'twas no 'ruddy good',
We asked to pull out, - and were told that we could.
This brought on the climax, this started the fun,
For while we'd been waiting, he'd brought up a gun.
A 'twenty-milli' it seemed that he had
By the size of the hole which it made in our 'rad'

Our strength, it seemed, was known to the Hun,
For he showed no intention to 'up sticks and run'.
Instead it was us, who were forced to withdraw,
Less a six-pounder and carrier withal,
An anti-tank gunner, of whom it is said,
Had been slightly wounded, was later found dead.
Our car, which was crippled, was taken in tow
As back to Bercham, we had to go.

Next morning a battle raged where we had been,
'Twas then that our infantry came on the scene.
We knew that the 'Flat-feet' would put matters right,
It was always the same when they joined the fight.
A 'Scammel' arrived to take back our bus,
We guessed how the others would murmur and cuss,
'Their infernal luck!' that's what they would say
Aye, and we'd been the same if they'd gone away.

For ten short days we had nothing to do
But enjoy ourselves at Wattrelos.
Our consciences pricked us oft' at night,
'Why should you rest, while others fight?'
We needn't have worried if only we'd known
That in having pleasure we weren't alone,
The Troop we discovered encamped at Meerhout,
With every man jack of 'em 'walking out'.

For a few days more we rested there,
Till the invasion of Holland, - mainly by air.
Once more came the order to 'Pack up and move!'
'Twas the west of the salient we had to improve.
So over the border! We didn't think much
Of our first impressions of the doughty Dutch.
But nothing daunted, we gave them a fill
Of side splitting laughter, - they saw us at drill.

One day of this nonsense, then off to war,
s'Hertogenbosch at noon, if not before!
Yet that live long day we spent at rest
Two 'kilos' from a place called – Best.
There we stayed till the following morn,
When, as per usual, we were off at dawn
To recce 'that road' in pouring rain,
But 'twas no use, we were stopped again.

Yes, stopped indeed, for we saw the flash
Of the gun which was fired, - we awaited the crash:
But lucky for us, it never came,
We'd gone far enough if that was his game.
For a week near Best we made our abode,
At a place further north called St Odenrode.
We were heavily shelled whilst moving here,
Which cost us two casualties, both very severe.

It happened so quickly, we were caught unaware,
We didn't expect it on 'peace time' affairs.
Our second car was stopped, we guessed what was wrong-
It was 'Tommy' and 'Jack', 'Tommy' didn't live long.
A few more days of the country round Best,
Then back for ten days, to Helmond for rest.
And gosh! What a rest! They treated us grand.
We paid them with 'Bully', and turned out the band.

Like all good things, this came to an end,
As once more to war we'd our efforts to bend.
First, a rehearsal, for the next operation,
Flank protection, we heard with elation:
Somehow, this job, it never seemed bad,
At least, not so much as some that we'd had.
But soon our morale was put to the test,
When they broke the news gently, 'You're going to Best'

'An infantry job for a week or more'
The very suggestion made us feel sore.
To make matters worse, we relieved a brigade,
And we couldn't help feeling the gaps that were made.
The guards, the patrols, the shelling too,
'Browned us off' quickly, but what could we do?
An attack was put in, then a silence serene,
We found nothing but mines where Jerry had been.

Our Troop was unlucky, we couldn't get through,
We'd to follow the tracks of Troop No.2.
Almost to Boxtel we followed the Hun,
All things considered a day's work well done.
Our spirits were high, on returning that night,
Down the road we'd been given, with hardly a fight.
We proudly stood by, as the convoys sped on
O'er that broad strip of concrete which we'd held so long.

As last we turned our backs on Best,
The thrust had changed from North to West,
Tilburg, the prize before us lay,
But we did not get there, sad to say,
To enjoy ourselves as they said we would,
We were called to where we'd do more good.
Away to the east we'd change our tack,
Where 'Jerry' was driving our allies back.

The Div took over, the Yankees went,
The Huns were absorbed, their drive was spent.
Our Troop was employed and was doing fine
Till we lost a patrol on a 'ruddy' mine.
The rest of us were truly amazed
When the crews turned up no worse than dazed.
Our 'Recces' then ceased for a little while,
Once more we'd to fight in the infantry style.

Our job near Liesel was to man the line,
In weather which was far from fine.
We did this turn and turn about
And 'twas lucky we were not flooded out.
An attack went in, so we manned our cars
And headed now for the river Maas.
O'er flooded tracks, o'er marshy ground,
We wondered how our wheels went round.

For miles it seemed, we floundered on,
O'er open country till we came upon
A concrete road, where we guessed we'd find
A present from Jerry, so thoughtful, so kind.
Out in the open, whilst approaching a wood,
Three sitting targets, his luck ne'er so good.
A flash and a bang, near our leading car
'You've 'ad it, Jerry!' 'We know where you are!'
We opened up with all that we'd got,
Whoever was there must have wished they were not.
Then we made a model withdrawal
To form a firm base and await our recall.
It was not long before it came,
We returned once more to our recent 'haeme'.

And so for awhile, some hours, too few,
We were left without a job to do.
The 'O' Group came, we feared the worst,
We'd to concentrate near Horst at first.
From there, through woods, we'd take to our cars
To clear the Hun from the west of Maas.
Those woods gave us the 'creeps' and 'willies',
Why, they'd have us in the bag, like gillies!

Our fears of course, were reck'd as nought,
We'd do the job as we'd been taught.
And luck was with us too, that day,
As through those woods we made our way.
Of paratroops we saw no trace
Till we came to a village, a little place.
Here the locals told us where we'd find
The Jerries we sought and the places they'd mined.

Prisoners were taken, some three or four,
Then we moved up the street to look for more.
Till some Dutchmen cautioned us to stay,

'There's mines', they said 'up yonder way!'
Beyond the mines a 'castile' stood,
As strongly held as Jerry could.
How we tackled this, on that fine day
The BBC had a word to say.

With our 'heavies' drawn up two abreast,
We entered on this strange contest.
With shot and shell and Besa too,
The best we had to make a 'brew'.
But that staunch old 'castile' wouldn't play,
However hard we blazed away.
The answer to this brazen act
Was quite negligible, - in fact.

But while our 'stonk' was going on,
We were slowly being crept upon.
A shot was heard, from not so far,
A shout went up, from near my car.
The shout was followed by an oath,
And laughter mingled loud with both.
'Our Troop Commander sounded merry?'
That rifle shot had nicked his beret!

This impudence could not go on,
It really must be frowned upon!
I traversed left to seek the Hun,
A Besa burst soon made him run.
And we were left quite 'cock a hoop',
A lucky and successful troop.
Which was more than what the rest of 'A'
Could say about their luck that day.

Our recces for the year were ended,
With a river line to be defended,
An outlook really grim and drear,
When victory once seemed so near.
The sector which to us seemed worst
Was the area just east of Horst,
Where things did not turn out so well,
About which, without pride, I'll tell.

The first spell in the line was good,
Things which happened, were things that should.
Occasional shells and mortars too,
But even these were very few.

The 'stags' at night were 'deadly' tho',
Patrols were too, but much more so,
When every unfamiliar sound
Was another Jerry prowling round.

Then came relief, 'A bit of cake!'
Was the only report that we could make.
Yet whilst at rest, forgetting our cares,
Rundstedt was taking the Yanks unawares.
The Ardennes offensive was well under way,
But on the banks of the Maas our Div had to stay
Where patrolling increased by day and by night,
Perhaps in our next spell we may have to fight.

To make matters worse there were cadre courses
Which sadly depleted our available forces,
In this way we lost an officer too,
One whom we trusted, respected and knew.
To take his place a freshman was sent,
A substitution we were soon to repent.
For in events which occurred, experience was needed,
Orders we knew and orders we heeded.

And so for the line our turn came again,
That trouble was brewing was increasingly plain.
On the second night out 'he' brought off a coup.
By capturing nine men from our No.2 Troop.
The following night all guards were doubled
But in point of fact we needn't have troubled,
We couldn't expect him to come on a raid
To try out the traps we'd so carefully laid.

For that live long night we kept awake,
Fearful lest a noise we'd make.
Then, crack! A trip-flare burst with light,
Making day of that dark night.
We strained our eyes to see what we
Sought vainly for, but could not see.
Nothing happened, now't was heard,
Must have been a blooming bird!

Then came the dawn, so chill and foggy,
Through lack of sleep we all felt groggy.
Half our forces then withdrew,
The rest of us must wait till Two.
By which time it was believed

Our Squadron would have been relieved.
But when the hour had come and passed,
Our morale was falling very fast.

It must have been sometime near three
When they brought us sandwiches and tea.
To prepare us better for the shock,
Of being relieved near six o'clock.
For all that day did the fog persist,
Although at times 'twas just a mist
When Jerry must have looked around
At our positions on the ground.

Throughout that day, so tired we'd been,
That our weapons we'd not cared to clean,
Of their true sad state we wouldn't know
Unless we had to 'have a go'.
And that chance now seemed so remote
Against it happening we could dote.
But hardly had this dream been dreamed,
When overhead a mortar screamed.

That shook our shattered nerves still more,
Tho' even worse was yet instore!
Our positions here, it seemed, were found,
By the way he pinned us to the ground,
With mortar and machine-gun fire,
We couldn't advance, we couldn't retire.
It was obvious he'd make a raid,
With such a barrage being laid.

Our only answer, now and then,
An occasional shot from a 'bunged up' Bren.
Then 'Sheldrake' and our 4.2s
Aspired to dispel the blues.
Yet even this plan went aglae,
When our line to base was blown away,
And the 'stonk' intended for the Hun,
Fell on us and made us run.

'Every man for himself!' the officer said,
For we'd do no good alive or dead.
But the time was late, it was getting dark
And our retreat made some Bren gun bark,
Guess they thought we were Jerries who'd got across.
So they peppered us in case we were,
Regardless of losses they might incur.

We fell back then to the 'Middlesex'
Feeling ought but bloody wrecks,
Tired, weary, exhausted, ill,
Dying almost, for a meal.
Then shelling started on our right,
Gosh! Have we yet to stand and fight?
Machine guns chattered. Were they through?
At least we now knew what to do.

Contact established once again,
The picture clear, it now was plain
Those positions we must occupy,
There to stand, to do, or die.
We staggered once more to our feet,
Retraced the ground of our retreat
And stumbled once more to our places,
Dead beat, but with more determined faces.

Peace reigned at last and now we knew
The cause of all the late 'to do'.
Jerry had planned an extensive raid,
But thanks to the part our artillery played,
Only a few had managed to cross,
The rest of 'em suffered considerable loss.
For us it was lucky he didn't succeed,
Dire then, would have been our need.

Midnight it was 'ere the infantry came!
'Where the 'ell 'ave yer been' But we couldn't well blame
Those lads who'd to march wherever they went,
But they knew what was said was not what was meant.
We picked up our weapons and 'got off our knees',
And headed for food, and comfort, and ease.
For this moment we'd waited, and knew it was here!
Yes, those thirty long hours had seemed like a year.

Christmas came, we were out for a rest
Near the town of all towns we had come to like best,
Helmond of course, where our Xmas cheer
Was greatly enjoyed, with English beer.
Here we were too on New Year's day,
When Jerry planes gave a mad display
Of low level strafing, it didn't succeed.
But losses on both sides were heavy indeed.

Our revelling over and feeling fine,
We prepared once more to man the line.
The Venlo sector now we had,
By all reports, 'twas not so bad.
The worst we suffered was the snow,
'Cos out in it we had to go
From dawn till dark, in positions where
All movements made were made with care.

Two tours of duty in these parts
Sufficed to chill the stoutest hearts.
The time for rest was in the day,
At night we chased the patrols away.
But once a slight mistake was made,
When our 'listening post' had warned 'A Raid'.
The sergeant leading back his band,
Was neatly shot, right through his hand!

Mid January came at last,
When the holding of the line was passed
From our Div. to the 'Airborne' boys,
Who, lightly armed, made up with noise
For the heavier weapons we possessed.
We left them there and then for a rest
In a monastery so bleak and cold
That a fire was worth its weight in gold.

Her new ideas were put in hand,
And thus was formed that worthy band
Called 'Five Troop', who once used to be
The armoured cars of good old 'Three'.
Our Troop Commander, young and keen,
Was inaptly named Lieutenant Green,
Whilst with us, we were pleased to see,
He got a well deserved MC.

For several days we shivered here,
Then news was given which raised a cheer,
To Tilburg for a week or more!
Of course, we guessed what that was for.
But as we lived from day to day,
We enjoyed each moment, come what may.
Tho' to remind us of the war,
Oft! Overhead V1s would roar.

The purpose of our sojourn here
Was never really very clear,
And none of us could guess at all
Where the next blow in the west would fall.
The first to learn the reason why
My driver, Harry, he and I
Were detailed for a special role,
Which robbed the Troop of one patrol.

Our job, liaison with old 'Pete',
Made our good fortune quite complete.
At least that's what we thought we'd have
With the RHQ of the 'Household Cav',
To Nijmegen then, we made our way
For a concentration, which they say,
Was heavier than there'd ever been,
'For the final act and the final scene'

The biggest barrage of the war
Followed bombers, which had gone before
To blast the towns 'twixt Maas and Rhine,
The outposts of the Siegfried Line.
Then five divisions forged ahead,
And ours, of course, the one which led.
In front of that, and by your leave,
Our 'Recce' was the first in Cleve.

And while this 'fun' was going on
We waited for the Guards to 'swan',
Until at last they had to say,
The 'swan' we had has gone astray!
For by flooding and resistance grim
The Hun had well nigh made us swim
And so our job had come to nought,
We weren't so lucky as we thought.

Our orders came, which of course we knew,
To report back to our own HQ
And there, of course, we guessed they'd say,
'On the next patrol you'll lead the way!'
With heavy hearts we took our leave
And 'waded' down the road to Cleve.
We looked all around, all eyes, to see
'Der Vaterland' - or, Germany!

We passed through Cleve, whilst overhead,
Jet planes dropped their bombs and fled.
Thus 'homeward bound' our way we made,
Our job, - liaison at Brigade,
Where we were pleased, no end, to find,
The Troop, at last, we'd left behind.
Alas, our job here soon was ended
When forward movement was suspended.

At Bedburg, with the Troop again
We heard about their great campaign,
Stirring tales of the 'fun' we'd missed
Above all others, one would persist
Of a recce they had done at night!
This was great indeed, if they were right.
Whilst we were here, and the weather fine,
We hung our 'smalls' on the Siegfried Line.

For recces we were not required,
When Goch was taken, the Div, retired.
Once more to Tilburg, and so elated
At having the billets which we'd vacated.
This lasted for a week or so,
When further back we had to go,
To Belgium, to Bourg Leopold,
Where they gave us new cars for our old.

Three weeks here on Daimler courses,
Seemed to us like changing horses.
So lucky had our Humbers been,
To lose them, we weren't over keen.
Especially as you soon shall see
How Five Troop were to lose all three.
But in convoy, like a cavalcade,
They put the Humbers in the shade.

Our conversion over, we were told the design
Of the grand assault on the River Rhine.
And later, of the part we'd play
As o'er the Reich we'd blaze our way.
The two Divisions for the task,
The 51st, and need you ask?
The 15th, fighting side by side,
With 'Airborne' troops, as well supplied.

The land assault was made at night,
Then came the dawn, and what a sight
As countless planes swarmed overhead.
But 'Five Troop?' - They were still in bed,
And in them too, we might have stayed
Until a Bailey bridge was made.
But two days later we were there
And, all too soon, had done our share.

With our Troop Commander sent away,
We were in reserve for that fatal day,
When orders were given for us to see
If a certain road was entirely free.
With information very vague,
The Troop set out with Sgt Craig,
Then to get more news of what we sought
At an infantry post he called a halt.

All four cars drawn up in line,
Of the enemy we saw no sign,
Till suddenly, with a puff of smoke,
A well concealed SP gun spoke.
Our first car got it in the wing,
But he was turning and could swing
And speeding up got safe away,
To take the tidings back to 'A'.

The second turned to follow suit,
But that 'Eighty-Eight' in swift pursuit,
And quicker than the eye could see
Claimed Les and Rex, - for eternity.
In our car, as the engine stalled
The sergeant from without had called,
'Get out! As quickly as you like!'
We did: and scrambled in a dyke.

Hardly had we reached the ground,
When we heard once more that rending sound
Which 'Eighty-Eights' alone can make.
Our car above was seen to shake,
Then up she went in smoke and flames,
The recording angel had missed our names.
But Jerry was not yet content.
To get the crew was his intent.

With air- bursts and with rifle shot
He pinned us neatly to the spot,
Whilst we unarmed, could not reply,
But to get back, we had to try.
At length, by crawling on our bellies,
From ditch to ditch, - and o'er dead Jerries,
That we'd reached safety, seemed quite clear
When we bumped into a Brigadier.

The Troop now mustered one patrol
To battle on and reach the goal
Which even now seemed far away,
Despite the progress made that day.
The 'Airborne Div', their Recce gone,
Our services were called upon,
The regiment, I mean, of course,
Which, at that time, was quite a force.

From Osnabruck to Minden, cross the Weser, nigh to Celle,
We led the 'sons' of Pegasus, yet they took the praise as well.
Then 'our lads' took over, for the town they had to fight,
Which so delayed our progress that we stayed there for the night.
The day before this happened our Dingo had a scoop,
When, colliding with a Jerry car, it claimed it for the Troop
To carry car less members, excepting poor ol' me,
Who soldiered on with Six Troop, bags of action there to see.

Next morning, bright and early, we started off again
Through country where his gas troops often used to train.
And here was left the Dingo, 'knocked out' by 'Panzer fist',
Fired from so short a range, it couldn't well have missed.
The crew, however, got away and joined a civvy car
Its amazing, when yer come to think, how lucky some folks are.
And so we came near Uelzen, where C Squadron took the rap,
When the Clausewitz Division came, and wiped them off the map.

With Uelzen in the bag, the 'swan' was on once more,
Supported by the SAS into Bevensen we tore.
Then on again to Neetze, the Elbe before us lay,
And over it the beaten Hun, well and truly now at bay.
Yet 'ere we drove them all across,
We suffered from them one more loss,
When a 'Panzer-fist' had found its mark
On our Troop Commanders heavy 'Arc'.

Of the five cars which had crossed the Rhine, four of them were lost,
In material alone, of course, this was quite a heavy cost.
The Regiment as well, had had its losses - true,
Its Squadrons, which had numbered three, now mustered less than two.
So while at Neetze we weren't surprised,
When the Regiment reorganised.
And A was once more made complete
With armoured cars, instead of feet.

For the crossing of the Elbe, the 15th Div was taken,
And the role we had to play, left us not a little shaken.
Once more to hold the line while the grand assault was made.
Once more our little Squadron relieved a whole brigade.
The old familiar barrage, the scream of many shells,
The 'crumps' as some fell short, kindly sent us by our pals.
And then when daylight came, the air as well was filled
As many planes of both sides zoomed, and banked, and wheeled.

With the bridgehead firmly held, from the river we withdrew,
For on the other side there was recceing to do.
Yes, recceing indeed! And little did we guess
That our partners in these exploits would be the SAS
It puzzled us a little, when they looked on us as tanks,
We surveyed our 'matchbox' armour and didn't murmur - 'Thanks'
Despite our grave misgivings, everything went well,
Although an SP gun nearly 'blasted us to hell'.

Our recces for that day had brought us on to Wurth,
And near here, on the morrow, Dönitz's delegates set forth,
To meet, not us, but Three Troop, for we were in reserve,
But speaking for the Squadron, a reward we did deserve.
The war was not yet over, once more 'swanning' must be done.
We set a course for Denmark, and we had them on the run.
Then came the final recce, the grandest of them all,
The atmosphere of which, I'll try on paper, to recall.

We set out for the autobahn 'twixt Hamburg and Lubeck,
Where SS men, 'twas rumoured, might hold us all in check.
We approached this road with caution, blasted houses on its side.
And waited for an answer, - but not a shot replied.
With SAS patrols, we scoured the ground in vain,
Then crossed the autobahn, to push on north again.
Soon, coming to a café, near dinner time as well,
We gave them food to cook for us, and they did it, really swell.

And while we sat there eating a phone began to ring.
Up jumped our Troop Commander, 'Don't touch that - thing!'
He changed his mind, and told the girl 'Be careful what you say!'
When suddenly, a bright idea seemed to have come his way.
He questioned her, then told her to put a phone call through,
To an English-speaking doctor, whom she said she knew.
In strident tones he threatened, almost burning up the wire,
If the place was not surrendered he would set the town on fire.

Orders quickly followed. 'Start up!' the sergeant cried.
We scrambled on our vehicles en route for Beteheide.
On the outskirts of the town a delegation waited.
The bluff had worked! We'd pulled it off! And gosh, weren't we elated!
Prisoners came in quietly, a hundred, maybe more,
With little fight left in them, they'd had enough of war.
The SAS were with us, and they'd soon 'laid on' a meal,
In a civvy's house of course, quite at home it made us feel.

Thus ended our last recce, our last battle fought and won.
We'd had our ups and downs and also had our fun.
Of those fifteen men who'd started, in June of Forty Four,
Only Terry and myself remained of that old armoured core
Which once the cars of 'Three Troop', was later known as 'Five',
But although we two alone, were left, there are others who survive.
The front at last was 'frozen'. Surrender terms were signed,
Then came the shabby grey-green hordes, all to their fate resigned.

Two days before VE Day the Squadron left for Kiel.
As I watched them leave without me, quite depressed it made me feel.
But then I recollected, I was due to go on leave,
Then that moment had arrived, 'twas so hard to believe.
The future still was clouded, the Japs were still at war,
But surely we had done our bit, they couldn't ask for more.
My future was decided, a clerk they thought I'd make,
So instead of guns, a fountain pen! Cor blimey! What a break!

The Russians sent their tallest General but he could not match 'Tiny' Barber

Even senior officers occasionally
are 'wrong footed'

7 July 1945

'Tiny' Barber shows how a Highland Reel should be danced

Entertainment

'Grip and Grin'

That's where the line should be!

7 July 1945

RHQ entrance Lutjensee
July 1945

C Squadron Divisional Guard, June 1945 Reinfeld

Sgts Dove, Southall and Lavery

Sgt Bill Ponting (Medical Section) and Sgt Jimmy Hine (Regimental Police)
1945

MEMBERS PRESENT

S. S. M.	Mc Lellan	S. Q. M S.	Hodges
Sgt.	Carmichael	Sgt.	Machin
"	Carr	"	Mc Kean
"	Cattanach	"	Munton
"	Craig	"	Murphy
"	Daurnhime	"	Morters
"	James	"	Robinson
"	Johnstone	"	Smith
"	John	"	Webster
"	Kirman	"	Williams

GUESTS

Sgt.	Dullaway	Sgt.	Shaff
"	Holland	"	Tavener
	Sgt. Webber.		

GUEST OF HONOUR

Tommy Hanlon.

OUT OF STATION

Sgt.	Gillespie	Sgt.	McGimpsey
"	Jamieson	"	Wilshaw

Menu

HORS D'OEUVRES VARIOUS

CREAM OF PEA SOUP

SALMON MORNAY

ROAST GOOSE WITH STUFFING
AND BREAD SAUCE

BAKED AND BOILED POTATOES - GREEN PEAS

CHRISTMAS PUDDING
BRANDY SAUCE

MINCE PIES

BISCUITS AND CHEESE

COFFEE

GIN - CHAMPAGNE - LIQUEURS

CIGARS

'The Last Supper'
A Squadron Sergeants' Mess, Christmas 1945
Beats rationing in the UK

Officers of the 15th Scottish Reconnaissance Regiment, Pontefract Racecourse - March 1944

From Left to Right

Back row: 2/Lt D.A. Clarke; 2/Lt J.B. Finney; Lt J.A. Isaac; Lt B.H. White; Lt M.R. Riesco Lt F. Sharman (REME); 2 Lt H.E. Whitham; Lt A.R. Rencher; Lt W. Falloon; Lt P.C. Kerridge; Lt R.W. Parker; Capt W. Kemsley; Lt R.H. Fleet; Lt M.H. Leppard; Lt G.H. Carey; Lt J.M. Blair

Centre row: Lt A.V. Sadgrove; Lt K.W. Gray; Lt J.M. Pooley (RAMC); Revd. E. Bradbrooke; Lt W.H. Rogers; Lt D.L. Richford; Lt K.B.M. Shirley; Lt G.J. Harvey; Lt J.M. Arundel; Lt K.G. Jenkins; Capt T.J. Bryson; Lt H.A. Green; Lt R.D. Martin; Lt A.E. Gillings; Lt G.R. Blount.

Front row: Capt T.G. Fordyce; Capt G.E. Pearce; Capt A.C. Davies; Major W.R. Rowlands; Major L.H. Mills; Major K.C.C. Smith; Lt Col J.A. Grant Peterkin; Major P.T.I. McDiarmid; Major A. Gordon; Capt W.B. Liddell; Capt C.K. Kemp; Capt J.E.F. Lane; Lt H.E. Hughes (QM)

PERSONAL MESSAGE
FROM THE C-IN-C

Christmas 1945

1. On the first Christmas Day since the war in Europe and the Far East has been won, let us look back with gratitude on the great victories and achievements which have been granted to the Allied arms.

The evil which we set out to destroy has been destroyed; the world is at peace once more. Let us give thanks to

"The Lord mighty in battle"

for sustaining us during the past six years.

2. Christmastide has always been the festival of

"peace, goodwill towards men".

Today we join with our families and friends all over the world to give thanks for the gift of peace which has been given to us. And today we all sing the old carols we love so well : and which have a fuller meaning now that the war is ended.

3. But Christmastide is also the festival of the family. We in Germany cannot just yet be reunited with our families; this must be a great sadness to one and all.

In your name I would like to send them a message from all of us in Germany. I should like to wish them

"Good luck, and a Happy Christmas".

4. We must also remember today all those who have given their lives in the winning of this war. They have paid the heaviest price of all: which was not asked of us who remain. They leave behind many for whom the joys of Christmas are full of sadness and the sense of loss. We will remember them: always. And we will be determined to build a future which shall be worthy of those who fell.

5. And so I should like to wish all of you who are with me in Germany today

"A MERRY CHRISTMAS"

and best wishes for the New Year that will shortly be on us. Let us pray that our efforts to build a fair and lasting peace will be crowned with as great success as was granted to our arms in war.

B. L. Montgomery

Field-Marshal,
Berlin.
Christmas 1945.

Military Governor and C-in-C,
British Army of the Rhine.

APPENDIX A

15TH SCOTTISH RECONNAISSANCE REGIMENT (RAC)

ROLL OF HONOUR

OFFICERS
Killed in Action

Lt J. M. Arundel
Lt G. H. L. Carey
Lt N. R. Kenneford

Lt D. L Richford
Lt E. Goodrich

Died of Wounds

Lt J. M. Blair

Maj G. A. Gaddum

OTHER RANKS
Killed in Action

Tpr C. H. G. Ballard
Tpr R. T. Bates
L/Cpl F. Behling
Tpr R. Bodsworth
Tpr G. T. Border
Tpr J. Burke
Sgt A. G. Cameron
Tpr T. F. Cross
Tpr E. T. Cudmore
Tpr A. A. D. Davies
Tpr R. Dodd
Cpl F. C. L. Eaton
Sgt E. Fielding
Tpr R. Forster
Tpr G. J. Grant
Tpr H. W. Greig
Tpr D. Griffiths
Sgt H. W. Hanby
Cpl A. J. Hartley
Cpl C. W. J. Haynes

Tpr R. R. Johnson
Tpr D. Machen
Tpr J. D. Meadows
Tpr B. T. Miggins
Tpr R. M. Miller
L/Sgt K. A. Mosgrove
Tpr F. McNeil
Tpr J. C. Neville
Tpr W. J. Pugh
Tpr A. Richardson
Tpr H. L. Roberts
Tpr J. D. Roebuck
Cpl H. Rogal
Tpr R. J. Slaughter
Tpr I. T. M. Stewart
Tpr F. Taylor
L/Sgt E. P. Thompson
Tpr G. H. Thompson
Tpr P. C. Walker
Cpl H. A. Ward

Cpl H. J. Higginson
Tpr H. Hoyle
L/Cpl J. R. Hutchinson
Tpr L. S. Jackson
Tpr W. L. James

Tpr L. A. Ward, MM
Tpr M. A. West
Sgt F. W. Whiting, DCM
Sgt W. C. Young

Died of Wounds

Cpl D. L. Atkin
Tpr F. W. Beard
L/Cpl L. Cole
Tpr N. P. Ellis
Tpr F. L. Griffiths
Tpr R. G. Gurney

Cpl J. Innes
L/Cpl J. Maxwell
Tpr S. D. Robertshaw
Tpr F. Strand
Tpr E. W. Taylor
Tpr D. B. Torrance

Died on Active Service

Cpl E. A. Hunt (Missing, presumed killed)
Tpr M. H. Lawn (Missing, presumed killed in action at sea. Tpr Lawn was wounded and on board the hospital ship *Amsterdam* when she was sunk.)
Tpr J. H. Gray (Died of accidental wound)
Tpr R. J. G. Packman (Died of accidental wound)
Tpr J. Rushton (Died from injury in battle accident)

APPENDIX B

15TH SCOTTISH RECONNAISSANCE REGIMENT (RAC)

HONOURS AND AWARDS

DISTINGUISHED SERVICE ORDER
Lt Col J. A. Grant Peterkin   Lt Col K. C. C. Smith

MILITARY CROSS
Capt G. R. Blount   Lieut P. C. Kerridge
Capt J. K. Boynton   Lieut M. H. Leppard
Lieut A. Buck   Maj W. B. Liddell
Maj A. Gordon   Maj P. T. I. MacDiarmid
Capt K. W. Gray   Lieut M. Morris
Lieut H. A. Green   Capt E. A. Royle

CROIX DE GUERRE (SILVER STAR)
Lieut A. E. Gillings

MENTIONED IN DESPATCHES
Capt J. K. Boynton   Maj W. B. Liddell
Lieut G. T. B. Dalton   Maj L. H. Mills
Maj R. H. Fleet   Capt G. E. Pearce
Maj L. T. Ford   Capt M. R. Riesco
Lieut H. A. Green   Lieut J. Wheeler

COMMANDER-IN-CHIEF'S CERTIFICATE (GALLANTRY)
Lieut J. L. Bosch   Lieut M. B. McFall

COMMANDER-IN-CHIEF'S CERTIFICATE (GOOD SERVICE)
Maj C. K. Kemp

OTHER RANKS

DISTINGUISHED CONDUCT MEDAL
Sgt R. Millroy   Sgt F. Whiting

MILITARY MEDAL
Tpr J. Bolton   Cpl J. MacDonald
Tpr J. Bunker   Sgt W. McMinn

Tpr W. Coburn
Sgt T. Craig
Sgt D. Daurnhime
WO2 (MQMS) H. Gartland
L/Sgt F. Grice

Sgt F. Short
Sgt R. Trim
WO1. A. Ward
Tpr L. Ward
Sgt K. Kirman

CROIX DE GUERRE (BRONZE STAR)
L/Sgt F. Grice

CROIX DE GUERRE (1940 WITH PALM)
Sgt S. Kirrage

MENTIONED IN DESPATCHES
Sgt J. Arthur
Sgt R. Gillespie
Sgt F. Jennings
Sgt D. Ladds

Tpr C. Parry
L/Sgt W. Sheppard
Cpl P. Lavery

COMMANDER-IN-CHIEF'S CERTIFICATE (GALLANTRY)
Tpr W. Charlton
L/Sgt T. Fraser
Tpr H. Holmden
Sgt A. Litton

Tpr R. Mellers
Sgt C. Moss
L/Cpl E. Wade

COMMANDER-IN-CHIEF'S CERTIFICATE (GOOD SERVICE)
AQMS G. Baldwin, REME
SQMS A. Budd
Sgt P. Carmichael
L/Cpl E. Clarke
Cpl P. Dobson
L/Sgt W. Dutch
WO1 W. Eardley
Cpl R. Hansen, REME
L/Cpl J. Holderness

Cpl S. Hook
Sgt S. Kirrage
Sgt G. McCullock
L/Sgt S. Mills
Sgt S. Pliskin
L/Sgt W. Ponting
Sgt R. Trim
WO1 A. Ward
Cpl J. Webster

GOC CERTIFICATE
L/Cpl W. M. Anderson
Tpr A. N. Ash
Tpr B. C. Booty
Sgt V. R. Bradley
L/Cpl F. J. Butterfield
Sgt A. H. R. Davidson

Sgt G. Johnstone
Sgt J. A. Kay
Cpl J. R. Knight
Tpr R. W. Lawson
L/Cpl N. Long
Tpr T. F. Marshall

Cpl A. P. Field
L/Cpl C. Franklin
Tpr R. C. I. Geddes
S/Sgt A. J. Gilbert
Tpr J. A. Hillman
Sgt J. H. Hine
Tpr H. R. Holmden
Sgt R. J. D. James

SSM W. W. McLellan
Tpr C. H. Merriman
L/Cpl W. Murray
Cpl R. C. Penfold
Tpr A. A. H. Phillips
Tpr D. Ross
Tpr A. Sinclair
L/Cpl A. G. Webb

APPENDIX C

MAPS

APPENDIX D

OBITUARIES

Lieutenant General Sir Colin Muir Barber CB, DSO 27 June 1897 – 5 May 1964. Served on the Western Front in the Great War with the Liverpool Scottish and the Cameron Highlanders. Served in France with the BEF in 1940. Commanded the 15th Scottish Division from August 1944 to disbandment. At 6 foot 8inches he was the tallest General in the British Army, hence his soubriquet 'Tiny'.

Captain Kingsley W. Gray MC. Died 1973 at the early age of fifty-three. Served with 'C' Squadron. Worked in Malaya after the war and later was a Lieut Col commanding the Gendarmerie Company protecting Shell Oil installations in Oman.

Brigadier J.A. Grant Peterkin DSO. Died 1981. The first CO of the Regiment, responsible for its creation and ensuring it achieved the highest standards of efficiency during training which enabled it to operate with confidence, skill and success in action. Only forty-eight hours before his death, had taken part in a very successful shoot at which he was in his finest form with the gun.

Lieut. Arthur Buck MC. Died 1992, he served in B Squadron and was badly wounded almost at war's end. Served with Command Staff Inspection Team at HQ Far East Land Forces Singapore and Malaya until 1973.

Tpr Bill Coburn MM. Died 1995, a member of 10 Troop C Squadron. At the end of October 1944 under very heavy fire he stayed on the radio set, and subsequently jumped into the driver's seat and brought the carrier back safely after a fragment of shrapnel had severed the aerial base.

Captain Tony Royle MC. Died 1997, he served in C Squadron throughout the active part of the campaign as a Troop Commander. He was a solid, fearless type and it was no surprise when he was one of the first to be awarded the MC in France.

Tpr Charles Millway. Died 1997, emigrated to Australia but attended several reunions through the nineties. Served throughout the campaign with A Squadron. Wrote 'Ode' to 5 Troop.

Brigadier Roderick Heathcoat-Amory MC. Died 1998 aged ninety-one. Had the melancholy task of disbanding the Regiment which he achieved with tact and efficiency.

Lieut Peter Kerridge MC. Died 1998, joined the Regiment in 1943 and served with A Squadron through to disbandment. Married to a Dutch lady he mastered the language and at the fiftieth Victory Celebrations in Tilburg made a never to be forgotten speech half in Dutch and half in English, intermittently!

Captain Michael Riesco. Died 1998, aged seventy-eight. Joined the 54th Independent Recce Company at Orford in 1942. Served with the Regiment throughout the campaign and was the last Adjutant. Played a key role in preparing the regimental history of which he was the co-author. He was the secretary for the old comrades association for forty-five years.

Lt Col Adam Gordon MC. Died on 28 November 1999, aged eighty-eight. A regular soldier and highly respected commander of B Squadron. He was commissioned from Sandhurst in 1931 and served for twenty-eight years as an officer of the Highland Light Infantry.

Major Reg Fleet. Died on 5 December 2000, aged eighty-two. Commanded 7 Troop B Squadron and awarded a MID. Emigrated to Canada in 1947.

Sergeant Alfred 'Ace' Gilbert. Died 2000. An enormously efficient RHQ member, survived working under three COs and it was said that he 'ran the Regiment'. Brought home the Regimental records after the war, which made possible the writing of the history.

Sergeant Austen Knibb. Died 2000. Wounded on his birthday in August 1944, a courageous member of B Squadron. A great lover of donkeys he did much for their welfare, post war.

Sergeant Jack Short. Died 2000, aged seventy-nine. Served in C squadron during training, was selected for a commission and joined another Recce regiment for the campaign. Stalwart of the 'All Ranks Association' of the Regiment after the war.

Captain Ken Jenkins. Died on 4 April 2001, aged eighty-three. Went to France in 1940 with the 1/6th Bn Staffordshire Regiment, saw action there and was evacuated from the beaches of Dunkirk. Commissioned from Sandhurst in 1943, he became responsible for 6 Troop B Squadron together with Lieut Nick Carey.

Cpl James Ferrier. Died 2001, aged seventy-six. Wounded in March 1945 when his fellow crew members were killed, Troopers W. James and R. Miller of 5 Troop A Squadron.

Tpr Reginald Jones. Died 2001, aged seventy-six. C Squadron member throughout the campaign. A proud Welshman, he was a stalwart supporter of the association.

Sergeant Charlie Royce. Died 2002. Commanded a carrier section in 10 Troop C Squadron. He was a gem of a man, a fine soldier and a great wit.

Lieut Bryan White. Died on 1 November 2002, aged eighty-two the day after celebrating sixty years of marriage to Betty. He led 10 Troop C Squadron to a high level of efficiency. Their positions were heavily mortared early on 1 July 1944, Bryan was severely wounded, losing his left leg and a large part of his right hand.

Bryan's enthusiasm and dedication inspired all those who served with him. He was a most capable and courageous man who bore his incapacity with such great fortitude and was an example to all who knew him both during and after the war.

Major Bill Liddell MC. Died 2002, aged eighty-seven. A Staff Officer at Div HQ in England and later took command of C Squadron. A fine all round sportsman, particularly keen golfer in later life. Was a successful solicitor in Oban after the war.

Lieut Doug Peterson. Died 2003, aged eighty-six. Wounded whilst attempting to extricate crew from a disabled vehicle. Chief Superintendent in the West Midlands Police and was awarded the Queen's Police Medal in 1974. Was awarded a MID which was omitted from the honours list.

Major Victor Sadgrove. Died 2003, aged eighty-four. Born Armistice Day 1918. Served with the regiment in Normandy but in August 1944 became ADC to General Barber where he remained for the rest of the war. Awarded a MID Victor always said that it was for keeping the General adequately supplied with gin throughout the campaign!

Lieut Michael"Alfie" McFall. Died 2003, aged seventy-nine. Served in Palestine after the end of the war. Writer, broadcaster, illustrator, farmer and charity fund raiser.

Tpr John Arnold. Died 2003, aged eighty-one. He was one of the group that rescued a crew of a Beaufighter that crashed in flames in Northumberland. Whilst serving with Lieut Peter Kerridge in the area Waereghem-Kerkhove of Belgium, he suffered severe head injuries. Married a Pontefract girl, Audrey.

Cpl Bob Knight. Died 2003, aged seventy-nine. Medical orderly with B Squadron; slightly wounded when approaching a section of 'friendly' troops. CEO of the Kettering Co-op Society.

Captain Graham Fordyce. Died 2004, aged eighty-six. Served with the regiment from its early days, wounded in Normandy and injured in traffic accident shortly after his return. Worked in banking and was a County Councillor for many years.

Cpl Bert Bonner. Died 2005, aged ninety-one. A B Squadron stalwart he is fifth from the right in the front row of the photograph which shows Field Marshal Montgomery inspecting a guard of honour.

Captain Ken Pearce. Died 2006, aged seventy-nine. Landed in Normandy with the 59th Staffordshire Division. Casualties were higher than anticipated and as the junior division the 59th was disbanded to feed other units as reinforcements. Ken joined the regiment and served with it to the end of the war.

Tpr Alan Westby. Died 2006, aged eighty-two only a few days after attending a re-union in Scarborough. A Yorkshireman, he worked in the mining industry and was a lifelong Methodist.

Tpr Oscar Thomas. Died 2006, aged eighty-two. Passionately fond of classical music with an impish sense of fun, a devout Catholic.

Lieut Harry Green MC. Died 2006, aged eighty-seven. A fine sportsman, Harry commanded a section of Bren carriers in A Squadron. He travelled widely in his career with the World Health Organisation and his fluent French was a great help in pilgrimages to Normandy.

Cpl Ken Sadler. Died 2006, aged eighty-two. Wounded in Normandy, he returned to the Regiment in time for the Rhine crossing. Worked for the Control Commission after the war in Germany. A fluent German speaker he organised a remarkable re-union in Berlin July 1990.

Sergeant Bill Rees. Died 2006, aged ninety-two. A popular and professional sergeant, fiercely proud of his Welsh origins.

Lieut Gordon Dalton. Died 2006. Married a Dutch girl and lived in Helmond, Holland and joined the group for the visit to the castle in 2004.

Sir John Boynton MC. Died 2007, aged eighty-nine. A lawyer, John retired as Chief Executive of Cheshire C.C. He supervised, in his role as Election Commissioner Southern Rhodesia, voting in that country in 1980. He was a stalwart of the regimental association. His younger brother Lieut William Boynton of the Royal Engineers was killed at Enfidaville, North Africa on 22 March 1943 aged twenty-three.

Cpl Clive Ridge. Died 2007, aged eighty-three. Skilled with the wireless he was appointed driver to the two Colonels of the regiment throughout the campaign.

Tpr George Bunn. Died 2007, aged eighty-three. Driver of armoured cars in 6 Troop B Squadron. He was involved in the action at Moll.

Tpr Arthur Watkins. Died 2008, aged eighty-four. Gunner/wireless operator with George. Joined the Army at fifteen to avoid a life down the mines in the Forest of Dean; a tall man and frequently selected to lead parades.

Captain Walter Kemsley. Died 2008, aged ninety-three. A talented artist and poet. He was co-author of the Regimental history and a stalwart of the association. He was signals officer with RHQ.

Tpr Ben Howe. Died 2008, aged eighty-four. A Londoner who worked in the newspaper industry. A C Squadron assault troop member he was captured at Nettelkamp.

Tpr Gordon Nursaw. Died 2009, aged eighty-four. A member of 9 Troop C Squadron.

Tpr Len Watson. Died 2009, aged eighty-five. A member of 6 Troop B Squadron. Served with the regiment from beginning to end and actively supported all reunions. Owned a successful country club in Nottinghamshire for over twenty years.

Sgt Bill Ponting. Died 2009, aged eighty-nine. Sergeant in charge of the Regimental Aid Post for over three years. A kind and capable man he maintained contact with the regimental association to the end.

Sgt Thomas Fraser. Died 2009, aged eighty-eight. Badly wounded in Normandy. After the war he became a petrol-tanker driver.

Cpl Stan Hook. Died 2009, aged ninety. A meticulous clerk in RHQ with a terrific memory for names and addresses with outstanding recall even after fifty years.

Bryan White was fond of this Scottish soldier's toast which seems an appropriate end:

"Here's to us. Who is like us?
Damn few and they are all dead"

APPENDIX E

15th Scottish Reconnaissance Regiment - Roll of Honour

Lists eighty-one men who lost their lives whilst serving with the Regiment.

Name	Rank	Number	Date of Death	Age	Location	Country
ARUNDEL, John Michael	Lieut	245224	13 July 1944	33	BANNEVILLE-LA-CAMPAGNE war cemetery, Normandy. Plot 9, Row B, Grave 22.	France
ATKIN, Denis Law	Cpl	4972652	29 September 1944	34	VALKENSWAARD war cemetery. Plot 2, Row C, Grave 19	Netherlands
BALLARD, Charles Herbert George	Tpr	6351646	10 July 1944	31	BANNEVILLE-LA-CAMPAGNE war cemetery, Normandy. Plot 12, Row B, Grave 21.	France
BATES, Robert Thomas	Tpr	14505792	7 April 1945	20	HANOVER war cemetery, Plot 15, Row J, Grave 2	Germany
BEARD, Frank William	Tpr	6352586	1 July 1944	24	BAYEUX war cemetery, Normandy. Plot 18, Row E, Grave 3	France
BECK, Edward Faraday	Tpr	3657756	14 May 1945	27	ALL SAINTS CHURCHYARD, Orton, Cumbria.	England
BEHLING, Frederick Henry Squire	L/Cpl	14392571	31 October 1944	20	MIERLO war cemetery, Plot 7, Row D, Grave 9	Netherlands
BLAIR, James Michael	Lieut	240066	16 July 1944	21	RYES war cemetery, Normandy, Plot 6, Row C, Grave 7	France

Name	Rank	Number	Date of Death	Age	Location	Country
BODSWORTH, Ronald	Tpr	14569422	23 February 1945	24	REICHSWALD FOREST war cemetery, Plot 58, Row D, Grave 8	Germany
BORDER, George Thomas	Tpr	14636940	22 February 1945	34	REICHSWALD FOREST war cemetery, Plot 58, Row D, Grave 2	Germany
BURKE, Joseph	Tpr	14504171	10 August 1944	20	BAYEUX war cemetery, Normandy. Plot 20, Row A, Grave 7	France
CAMERON, Alexander George	Sgt	3321195	1 July 1944	27	BAYEUX war cemetery, Normandy. Plot 16, Row D, Grave 20	France
CAREY, George Henry Leonard	Lieut	245269	2 August 1944		BAYEUX war cemetery, Normandy. Plot 19, Row D, Grave 7	France
COLE, Lionel	L/Cpl	10603043	9 September 1944	28	BETHUNE TOWN CEMETERY, Plot 3, Row L, Grave 1	France
COX, George Thomas	Sgt	795828	1 October 1941	30	WOOLWICH (PLUMSTEAD) cemetery, London. Sec. Q, Grave 1040	England
CROSS, Thomas Frank	Tpr	5954385	26 September 1944	28	UDEN war cemetery, Plot 1, Row F, Grave 4	Netherlands
CUDMORE, Edwin Thomas	Tpr	14506460	15 April 1945	21	BECKLINGEN war cemetery, Soltau, Plot 10, Row H, Grave 6	Germany
DAVIES, Austin Arthur Desmond	Tpr	14511023	7 September 1944	22	OOIKE CHURCHYARD, Grave 1	Belgium
DODD, Ralph	Tpr	4268798	20 October 1944	31	MIERLO war cemetery, Plot 4,	Netherlands

Name	Rank	Number	Date of Death	Age	Location	Country
					Row A, Grave 9	
EATON, Frederick Charles Lindsay	Cpl	5953991	1 November 1944	28	MIERLO war cemetery, Plot 7, Row D, Grave 7	Netherlands
ELLIS, Norman Peter	Tpr	14371310	2 September 1944	20	SAINT DESIR war cemetery, Plot 2, Row D, Grave 5	France
EMERY, Edward Charles Steven	Tpr	14509883	3 February 1944	20	SANDY cemetery, Bedfordshire. Sec. G Grave 109	England
FORSTER, Robert	Tpr	14331106	17 July 1944	20	SAINT MANVIEU war cemetery, Cheux, Calvados, Plot 6, Row B, Grave 17	France
FIELDING, Edward	Sgt	4543973	15 April 1945	30	GROESBEEK MEMORIAL, Nijmegen, Panel 1	Netherlands
GADDUM, Geoffrey Alfred	Major	130982	24 October 1944	34	EINDHOVEN (WOENSAL) General cemetery, Plot KK, Grave 171	Netherlands
GOODRICH, Edwin William	Lieut	300881	9 October 1944	27	GROESBEEK MEMORIAL, Nijmegen, Panel 1	Netherlands
GRANT, Cyril James	Tpr	6354349	16 July 1944	21	BANNEVILLE-LA-CAMPAGNE war cemetery, Nomandy. Plot 10, Row B, Grave 24.	France
GRAY, James Henry	Tpr	14508525	5 May 1945	21	KIEL war cemetery, Plot 5, Row J, Grave 2	Germany
GREIG, Henry William	Tpr	14508009	30 October 1944	20	NEDERWEART war cemetery, Plot 2,	Netherlands

Name	Rank	Number	Date of Death	Age	Location	Country
GRIFFITHS, David Leslie	Tpr	14504757	10 July 1944	32	BANNEVILLE-LA-CAMPAGNE war cemetery, Normandy. Plot 9, Row B, Grave 21. Row F, Grave 13	France
GRIFFITHS, Frederick Lawrence	Tpr	14201758	30 September 1944	21	VALKENSWAARD war cemetery. Plot 2, Row C, Grave 17	Netherlands
GURNEY, Robert George	Tpr	14505287	15 April 1945	32	BECKLINGEN war cemetery, Soltau, Plot 10, Row H, Grave 8	Germany
HANBY, Herbert William	Sgt	4384083	6 September 1944	37	DEERLIJK COMMUNAL CEMETERY. Grave 4	Belgium
HANCOX, Charles Leslie	Tpr	10603597	27 May 1944	21	NETHERTON (ST ANDREW) CHURCHYARD, Dudley, W Midlands. Sec 2 Grave 1195	England
HARTLEY, Albert James	Cpl	5342579	30 October 1944	24	MIERLO war cemetery, Plot 4, Row A, Grave 9	Netherlands
HAYNES, Charles Joseph William	Cpl	6475059	22 February 1945	30	REICHSWALD FOREST war cemetery, Plot 58, Row D, Grave 5	Germany
HIGGINSON, Henry Joseph	Cpl	3601829	6 August 1944	28	SAINT CHARLES de PERCY war cemetery, Normandy, Plot 5, Row C, Grave 3	France
HOYLE, Harold	Tpr	14503055	6 September 1944	20	CEMENT HOUSE CEMETERY, Langemarck, Plot 17, Row B, Grave 6	Belgium
HUNT, Edmund Arthur	Cpl	14508039	22 February 1945	32	REICHSWALD FOREST war	Germany

Name	Rank	Number	Date of Death	Age	Location	Country
					cemetery, Plot 58, Row D, Grave 3	
HUTCHINSON, James Reginald	L/Cpl	10603292	10 July 1944	29	BANNEVILLE-LA-CAMPAGNE war cemetery, Normandy. Plot 11, Row B, Grave 24.	France
INNES, Johnston	Cpl	3059489	24 July 1944	30	PORTOBELLO CEMETERY, Edinburgh, Grave 246	Scotland
JACKSON, Leonard Sidney	Tpr	5340500	15 April 1945	27	BECKLINGEN war cemetery, Soltau, Plot 10, Row H, Grave 7	Germany
JAMES, Walter Leslie	Tpr	14333225	27 March 1945	20	REICHSWALD FOREST war cemetery, Plot 58, Row C, Grave 11	Germany
JOHNSON, Randolph Ridley	Tpr	14658685	14 April 1945	20	GROESBEEK MEMORIAL, Nijmegen, Panel 1	Netherlands
KENNEFORD, Norman Roland	Lieut	311626	26 November 1944	24	VENRAY war cemetery, Plot 6, Row F, Grave 8	Netherlands
LAWN, Maurice Herbert	Tpr	14238841	7 August 1944	20	BAYEUX MEMORIAL, Normandy. Panel 2, Column 3	France
MACHEM, Derrick	Tpr	14636112	3 August 1944	19	SAINT CHARLES de PERCY war cemetery, Normandy, Plot 9, Row A, Grave 5	France
MAXWELL, John	L/Cpl	14315113	21 April 1945	24	KILDOWIE CEMETERY, Old Kilpatrick, Renfrew, Section F, Grave 32	Scotland

Name	Rank	Number	Date of Death	Age	Location	Country
MEADOWS, James Dixon	Tpr	14242761	23 February 1945	21	REICHSWALD FOREST war cemetery, Plot 58, Row D, Grave 7	Germany
MIGGINS, Brinley Thomas	Tpr	14308355	7 September 1944	21	OOIKE CHURCHYARD, Grave 2	Belgium
MILLER, Ronald Mortimer	Tpr	14440738	27 March 1945	19	REICHSWALD FOREST war cemetery, Plot 58, Row C, Grave 10	Germany
MITCHELL, George Ernest	Tpr	14505252	7 April 1943	18	HENLEY-ON-THAMES cemetery, Oxfordshire. Sec 16 Grave 99	England
MORRIS, Robert	Tpr	5116317	8 May 1946	29	BISHOP'S CASTLE (ST. JOHN THE BAPTIST) CHURCHYARD, Chyd, Shropshire, S.E. of the church.	England
MOSGROVE, Kenneth Angus	L/Sgt	3191549	15 April 1945	26	HANOVER war cemetery, Plot 7, Row E, Grave 2	Germany
McNEIL, Frederick	Tpr	14260678	3 August 1944	32	SAINT CHARLES de PERCY war cemetery, Normandy, Plot 13, Row C, Grave 4	France
NEVILLE, James Charles	Tpr	6352354	6 September 1944	33	DEERLIJK COMMUNAL CEMETERY. Grave 3	Belgium
PACKMAN, Roland James George	Tpr	6922292	17 August 1944	21	BANNEVILLE-LA-CAMPAGNE war cemetery, Nomandy. Plot 11, Row F, Grave 9.	France
PUGH, William James	Tpr	14505033	22 July 1944	20	BAYEUX MEMORIAL, Normandy. Panel 2, Column 3	France
RICHARDSON, Archibald	Tpr	14504109	20 July 1944	19	SAINT CHARLES de PERCY war	France

Name	Rank	Number	Date of Death	Age	Location	Country
					cemetery, Normandy, Plot 13, Row G, Grave 15	
RICHFORD, David Lincoln	Lieut	251917	15 April 1945	29	BECKLINGEN war cemetery, Soltau, Plot 10, Row H, Grave 5	Germany
ROBERTS, Hesketh Lloyd	Tpr	14572154	6 August 1944	19	SAINT CHARLES de PERCY war cemetery, Normandy, Plot 5, Row C, Grave 4	France
ROEBUCK, Joseph Denis	Tpr	14218951	29 August 1944	20	SAUSSAY-LA-CAMPAGNE CHURCHYARD, Normandy, North of the Church.	France
ROBERTSHAW, Stanley Dawson	Tpr	14660580	12 December 1944	35	EINDHOVEN (WOENSAL) General cemetery, Plot KK, Grave 239	Netherlands
ROGAL, Harry	Cpl	6898415	11 April 1945	29	HANOVER war cemetery, Plot 15, Row C, Grave 16	Germany
RUSHTON, Jack	Tpr	14509687	9 April 1945	20	HANOVER war cemetery, Plot 15, Row D, Grave 15	Germany
SLAUGHTER, Richard Jack	Tpr	7952257	10 February 1945	21	REICHSWALD FOREST war cemetery, Plot 58, Row D, Grave 9	Germany
SIMMONS, Ronald George Edward	Tpr	14233945	27 May 1944	N/K	CHESSINGTON (ST MARY) CHURCHYARD, Surrey. Grave C 54	England
STEWART, Ian Thomas McPherson	Tpr	14624756	26 September 1944	29	UDEN war cemetery, Plot 1, Row H, Grave 12	Netherlands

Name	Rank	Number	Date of Death	Age	Location	Country
STRAND, Frederick	Tpr	1465 8743	15 April 1945	23	HAMBURG CEMETERY, Ohlsdorf, Plot 1A, Row J, Grave 3	Germany
TAYLOR, Frank	Tpr	14380875	24 October 1944	20	VALKENSWAARD war cemetery. Plot 1, Row D, Grave 15	Netherlands
TAYLOR, Edwin W.	Tpr	10603505	1 November 1944	21	MIERLO war cemetery, Plot 5, Row B, Grave 10	Netherlands
THOMPSON, Eric Percy	L/Sgt	5954251	2 August 1944	27	BAYEUX war cemetery, Normandy. Plot 19, Row D, Grave 6	France
THOMPSON, George Henry	Tpr	14655160	31 October 1944	19	NEDERWEERT war cemetery, Plot 1, Row F, Grave 44	Netherlands
TORRANCE, Donovan Brown	Tpr	14306325	15 July 1944	20	SEQUEVILLE-en-BESSIN war cemetery, Cheux, Calvados, Plot 2, Row C, Grave 3	France
WALKER, Peter Cracknall	Tpr	14509759	30 July 1944	20	SAINT CHARLES de PERCY war cemetery, Normandy, Plot 15, Row G, Grave 6	France
WARD, Harry Alan	Cpl	10602994	17 July 1944	24	SAINT MANVIEU war cemetery, Cheux, Calvados, Plot 6, Row B, Grave 18	France
WARD, Leonard Albert MM	Tpr	14267627	11 April 1945	21	HANOVER war cemetery, Plot 15, Row D, Grave 2	Germany

Name	Rank	Number	Date of Death	Age	Location	Country
WEST, Maurice Alfred	Tpr	4540333	5 April 1945	25	HANOVER war cemetery, Plot 15, Row J, Grave 18	Germany
WHITING, Frederick William DCM	L/Sgt	5623972	5 April 1945	25	HANOVER war cemetery, Plot 15, Row J, Grave 9	Germany
WILLIAMS, David Garfield	Tpr	14203384	9 April 1943	N/K	BISCOT (HOLY TRINITY) CHURCHYARD, Bedfordshire. Sec F, Row 5, Grave 13	England
YOUNG, William	Sgt	6475016	29 August 1944	31	SAUSSAY-LA-CAMPAGNE CHURCHYARD, Normandy, North of the Church.	France

15th Scottish Reconnaissance Regiment
Roll of Honour - Location of war grave cemeteries & memorials by country

Lists eighty-one men who lost their lives whilst serving with the Regiment.

Name	Rank	Number	Date of Death	Age	Location	Country
HOYLE, Harold	Tpr	14503055	6 September 1944	20	CEMENT HOUSE CEMETERY, Langemarck, Plot 17, Row B, Grave 6	Belgium
NEVILLE, James Charles	Tpr	6352354	6 September 1944	33	DEERLIJK COMMUNAL CEMETERY. Grave 3	Belgium
HANBY, Herbert William	Sgt	4384083	6 September 1944	37	DEERLIJK COMMUNAL CEMETERY. Grave 4	Belgium
DAVIES, Austin Arthur Desmond	Tpr	14511023	7 September 1944	22	OOIKE CHURCHYARD, Grave 1	Belgium
MIGGINS, Brinley Thomas	Tpr	14308355	7 September 1944	21	OOIKE CHURCHYARD, Grave 2	Belgium
GRANT, Cyril James	Tpr	6354349	16 July 1944	21	BANNEVILLE-LA-CAMPAGNE war cemetery, Nomandy. Plot 10, Row B, Grave 24.	France
HUTCHINSON, James Reginald	L/Cpl	10603292	10 July 1944	29	BANNEVILLE-LA-CAMPAGNE war cemetery, Nomandy. Plot 11, Row B, Grave 24.	France
PACKMAN, Roland James George	Tpr	6922292	17 August 1944	21	BANNEVILLE-LA-CAMPAGNE war cemetery, Nomandy. Plot 11, Row F, Grave 9.	France

Name	Rank	Number	Date of Death	Age	Location	Country
BALLARD, Charles Herbert George	Tpr	6351646	10 July 1944	31	BANNEVILLE-LA-CAMPAGNE war cemetery, Nomandy. Plot 12, Row B, Grave 21.	France
GRIFFITHS, David Leslie	Tpr	14504757	10 July 1944	32	BANNEVILLE-LA-CAMPAGNE war cemetery, Nomandy. Plot 9, Row B, Grave 21.	France
ARUNDEL, John Michael	Lieut	245224	13 July 1944	33	BANNEVILLE-LA-CAMPAGNE war cemetery, Nomandy. Plot 9, Row B, Grave 22.	France
PUGH, William James	Tpr	14505033	22 July 1944	20	BAYEUX MEMORIAL, Normandy. Panel 2, Column 3	France
LAWN, Maurice Herbert	Tpr	14238841	7 August 1944	20	BAYEUX MEMORIAL, Normandy. Panel 2, Column 3	France
CAMERON, Alexander George	Sgt	3321195	1 July 1944	27	BAYEUX war cemetery, Normandy. Plot 16, Row D, Grave 20	France
BEARD, Frank William	Tpr	6352586	1 July 1944	24	BAYEUX war cemetery, Normandy. Plot 18, Row E, Grave 3	France
THOMPSON, Eric Percy	L/Sgt	5954251	2 August 1944	27	BAYEUX war cemetery, Normandy. Plot 19, Row D, Grave 6	France
CAREY, George Henry Leonard	Lieut	245269	2 August 1944		BAYEUX war cemetery, Normandy. Plot 19, Row D, Grave 7	France
BURKE, Joseph	Tpr	14504171	10 August 1944	20	BAYEUX war cemetery, Normandy. Plot 20, Row A, Grave 7	France

Name	Rank	Number	Date of Death	Age	Location	Country
COLE, Lionel	L/Cpl	10603043	9 September 1944	28	BETHUNE TOWN CEMETERY, Plot 3, Row L, Grave 1	France
BLAIR, James Michael	Lieut	240066	16 July 1944	21	RYES war cemetery, Normandy, Plot 6, Row C, Grave 7	France
McNEIL, Frederick	Tpr	14260678	3 August 1944	32	SAINT CHARLES de PERCY war cemetery, Normandy, Plot 13, Row C, Grave 4	France
RICHARDSON, Archibald	Tpr	14504109	20 July 1944	19	SAINT CHARLES de PERCY war cemetery, Normandy, Plot 13, Row G, Grave 15	France
WALKER, Peter Cracknall	Tpr	14509759	30 July 1944	20	SAINT CHARLES de PERCY war cemetery, Normandy, Plot 15, Row G, Grave 6	France
HIGGINSON, Henry Joseph	Cpl	3601829	6 August 1944	28	SAINT CHARLES de PERCY war cemetery, Normandy, Plot 5, Row C, Grave 3	France
ROBERTS, Hesketh Lloyd	Tpr	14572154	6 August 1944	19	SAINT CHARLES de PERCY war cemetery, Normandy, Plot 5, Row C, Grave 4	France
MACHEM, Derrick	Tpr	14636112	3 August 1944	19	SAINT CHARLES de PERCY war cemetery, Normandy, Plot 9, Row A, Grave 5	France

Name	Rank	Number	Date of Death	Age	Location	Country
ELLIS, Norman Peter	Tpr	14371310	2 September 1944	20	SAINT DESIR war cemetery, Plot 2, Row D, Grave 5	France
FORSTER, Robert	Tpr	14331106	17 July 1944	20	SAINT MANVIEU war cemetery, Cheux, Calvados, Plot 6, Row B, Grave 17	France
WARD, Harry Alan	Cpl	10602994	17 July 1944	24	SAINT MANVIEU war cemetery, Cheux, Calvados, Plot 6, Row B, Grave 18	France
ROEBUCK, Joseph Denis	Tpr	14218951	29 August 1944	20	SAUSSAY-LA-CAMPAGNE CHURCHYARD, Normandy, North of the Church.	France
YOUNG, William	Sgt	6475016	29 August 1944	31	SAUSSAY-LA-CAMPAGNE CHURCHYARD, Normandy, North of the Church.	France
TORRANCE, Donovan Brown	Tpr	14306325	15 July 1944	20	SEQUEVILLE-en-BESSIN war cemetery, Cheux, Calvados, Plot 2, Row C, Grave 3	France
RICHFORD, David Lincoln	Lieut	251917	15 April 1945	29	BECKLINGEN war cemetery, Soltau, Plot 10, Row H, Grave 5	Germany
CUDMORE, Edwin Thomas	Tpr	14506460	15 April 1945	21	BECKLINGEN war cemetery, Soltau, Plot 10, Row H, Grave 6	Germany
JACKSON, Leonard Sidney	Tpr	5340500	15 April 1945	27	BECKLINGEN war cemetery, Soltau, Plot 10, Row H, Grave 7	Germany

Name	Rank	Number	Date of Death	Age	Location	Country
GURNEY, Robert George	Tpr	14505287	15 April 1945	32	BECKLINGEN war cemetery, Soltau, Plot 10, Row H, Grave 8	Germany
STRAND, Frederick	Tpr	14658743	15 April 1945	23	HAMBURG CEMETERY, Ohlsdorf, Plot 1A, Row J, Grave 3	Germany
ROGAL, Harry	Cpl	6898415	11 April 1945	29	HANOVER war cemetery, Plot 15, Row C, Grave 16	Germany
RUSHTON, Jack	Tpr	14509687	9 April 1945	20	HANOVER war cemetery, Plot 15, Row D, Grave 15	Germany
WARD, Leonard Albert MM	Tpr	14267627	11 April 1945	21	HANOVER war cemetery, Plot 15, Row D, Grave 2	Germany
WEST, Maurice Alfred	Tpr	4540333	5 April 1945	25	HANOVER war cemetery, Plot 15, Row J, Grave 18	Germany
BATES, Robert Thomas	Tpr	14505792	7 April 1945	20	HANOVER war cemetery, Plot 15, Row J, Grave 2	Germany
WHITING, Frederick William DCM	L/Sgt	5623972	5 April 1945	25	HANOVER war cemetery, Plot 15, Row J, Grave 9	Germany
MOSGROVE, Kenneth Angus	L/Sgt	3191549	15 April 1945	26	HANOVER war cemetery, Plot 7, Row E, Grave 2	Germany
GRAY, James Henry	Tpr	14508525	5 May 1945	21	KIEL war cemetery, Plot 5, Row J, Grave 2	Germany
MILLER, Ronald Mortimer	Tpr	14440738	27 March 1945	19	REICHSWALD FOREST war cemetery, Plot 58, Row C, Grave 10	Germany

Name	Rank	Number	Date of Death	Age	Location	Country
JAMES, Walter Leslie	Tpr	14333225	27 March 1945	20	REICHSWALD FOREST war cemetery, Plot 58, Row C, Grave 11	Germany
BORDER, George Thomas	Tpr	14636940	22 February 1945	34	REICHSWALD FOREST war cemetery, Plot 58, Row D, Grave 2	Germany
HUNT, Edmund Arthur	Cpl	14508039	22 February 1945	32	REICHSWALD FOREST war cemetery, Plot 58, Row D, Grave 3	Germany
HAYNES, Charles Joseph William	Cpl	6475059	22 February 1945	30	REICHSWALD FOREST war cemetery, Plot 58, Row D, Grave 5	Germany
MEADOWS, James Dixon	Tpr	14242761	23 February 1945	21	REICHSWALD FOREST war cemetery, Plot 58, Row D, Grave 7	Germany
BODSWORTH, Ronald	Tpr	14569422	23 February 1945	24	REICHSWALD FOREST war cemetery, Plot 58, Row D, Grave 8	Germany
SLAUGHTER, Richard Jack	Tpr	7952257	10 February 1945	21	REICHSWALD FOREST war cemetery, Plot 58, Row D, Grave 9	Germany
GADDUM, Geoffrey Alfred	Major	130982	24 October 1944	34	EINDHOVEN (WOENSAL) General cemetery, Plot KK, Grave 171	Netherlands
ROBERTSHAW, Stanley Dawson	Tpr	14660580	12 December 1944	35	EINDHOVEN (WOENSAL) General cemetery, Plot KK, Grave 239	Netherlands
JOHNSON, Randolph Ridley	Tpr	14658685	14 April 1945	20	GROESBEEK MEMORIAL, Nijmegen, Panel 1	Netherlands
FIELDING, Edward	Sgt	4543973	15 April 1945	30	GROESBEEK MEMORIAL, Nijmegen, Panel 1	Netherlands

Name	Rank	Number	Date of Death	Age	Location	Country
GOODRICH, Edwin William	Lieut	300881	9 October 1944	27	GROESBEEK MEMORIAL, Nijmegen, Panel 1	Netherlands
DODD, Ralph	Tpr	4268798	20 October 1944	31	MIERLO war cemetery, Plot 4, Row A, Grave 9	Netherlands
HARTLEY, Albert James	Cpl	5342579	30 October 1944	24	MIERLO war cemetery, Plot 4, Row A, Grave 9	Netherlands
TAYLOR, Edwin W.	Tpr	10603505	1 November 1944	21	MIERLO war cemetery, Plot 5, Row B, Grave 10	Netherlands
EATON, Frederick Charles Lindsay	Cpl	5953991	1 November 1944	28	MIERLO war cemetery, Plot 7, Row D, Grave 7	Netherlands
BEHLING, Frederick Henry Squire	L/Cpl	14392571	31 October 1944	20	MIERLO war cemetery, Plot 7, Row D, Grave 9	Netherlands
GREIG, Henry William	Tpr	14508009	30 October 1944	20	NEDERWEART war cemetery, Plot 2, Row F, Grave 13	Netherlands
THOMPSON, George Henry	Tpr	14655160	31 October 1944	19	NEDERWEERT war cemetery, Plot 1, Row F, Grave 44	Netherlands
CROSS, Thomas Frank	Tpr	5954385	26 September 1944	28	UDEN war cemetery, Plot 1, Row F, Grave 4	Netherlands
STEWART, Ian Thomas McPherson	Tpr	14624756	26 September 1944	29	UDEN war cemetery, Plot 1, Row H, Grave 12	Netherlands

Name	Rank	Number	Date of Death	Age	Location	Country
TAYLOR, Frank	Tpr	14380875	24 October 1944	20	VALKENSWAARD war cemetery. Plot 1, Row D, Grave 15	Netherlands
GRIFFITHS, Frederick Lawrence	Tpr	14201758	30 September 1944	21	VALKENSWAARD war cemetery. Plot 2, Row C, Grave 17	Netherlands
ATKIN, Denis Law	Cpl	4972652	29 September 1944	34	VALKENSWAARD war cemetery. Plot 2, Row C, Grave 19	Netherlands
KENNEFORD, Norman Roland	Lieut	311626	26 November 1944	24	VENRAY war cemetery, Plot 6, Row F, Grave 8	Netherlands
BECK, Edward Faraday	Tpr	3657756	14 May 1945	27	ALL SAINTS CHURCHYARD, Orton, Cumbria.	England
WILLIAMS, David Garfield	Tpr	14203384	9 April 1943	N/K	BISCOT (HOLY TRINITY) CHURCHYARD, Bedfordshire. Sec F, Row 5, Grave 13	England
MORRIS, Robert	Tpr	5116317	8 May 1946	29	BISHOP'S CASTLE (ST. JOHN THE BAPTIST) CHURCHYARD, Chyd, Shropshire. S.E. of the church.	England
SIMMONS, Ronald George Edward	Tpr	14233945	27 May 1944	N/K	CHESSINGTON (ST. MARY) CHURCHYARD, Surrey. Grave C 54	England
MITCHELL, George Ernest	Tpr	14505252	7 April 1943	18	HENLEY-ON-THAMES cemetery, Oxfordshire. Sec 16 Grave 99	England
HANCOX, Charles Leslie	Tpr	10603597	27 May 1944	21	NETHERTON (ST ANDREW) CHURCHYARD Dudley, W Midlands. Sec 2 Grave 1195	England

Name	Rank	Number	Date of Death	Age	Location	Country
EMERY, Edward Charles Steven	Tpr	14509883	3 February 1944	20	SANDY cemetery, Bedfordshire. Sec. G Grave 109	England
COX, George Thomas	Sgt	795828	1 October 1941	30	WOOLWICH (PLUMSTEAD) cemetery, London. Sec. Q, Grave 1040	England
MAXWELL, John	L/Cpl	14315113	21 April 1945	24	KILDOWIE CEMETERY, Old Kilpatrick, Renfrew, Section F, Grave 32	Scotland
INNES, Johnston	Cpl	3059489	24 July 1944	30	PORTOBELLO CEMETERY, Edinburgh, Grave 246	Scotland

APPENDIX F

15TH SCOTTISH RECONNAISSANCE REGIMENT OFFICERS

OLD COMRADES' ASSOCIATION 1946

Adcock, Howard W.
Ambler, Peter C. H.
Amswych, Basil A.
Ansley, William H. G.
Ashworth, R.
Atkins, W. J.

Barber, Cecil G.
Bays, Marcel A.
Bishop, Gerald H.
Blount, George R.
Bosch, John L.
Boynton, John K.
Bradbrooke, Rev. E.
Brasier, H. J.
Bray, Leonard
Browne, George S.
Bryson, Thomas J.
Buck Arthur
Byron, E. A.

Cartwright, Gordon H.
Chalmers, Thomas S.
Cockburn, R. H. A.
Collins, P. B.
Corner, Thomas W.
Crowder, Brian.

Dalton, Gordon T. B.
Davies, Christopher A.
Davis, John D.
Day, J.
Dove, Cecil R. T.
Dunning, I.

Eardley, William H.
Ellacott, Royston W.

Falloon, William.
Favell, K. W.
Fenwick, W. H.
Fleet, Reginald H.
Ford, Lawrence T.
Fordyce, Graham T.
Fox, R

Gillings, Albert E.
Gordon, Adam
Grant Peterkin, J. A.
Gray, Kingsley W.
Green, Henry A.

Halford, M. C. K.
Hart, Richard A.
Harvey, Gerald J.
Heathcoat-Amory, R.
Higgs, Royston
Hughes, Henry E.
Hutchings, E. A.

Isaac, Jack A.

Jackson, Douglas E.
Jellinek Ernest H.
Jenkins, Kenneth G.
Jennings, Joseph W.
Johnson V. G.

Kemp, Cyril K.
Kemsley, Walter

Kerridge, Peter C.
Killacky, D.
Kirkpatric, H. D.

Lane, John E. F.
Lawson, N. C.
Leeming, John W.
Leppard, Martyn H.
Liddell, William B.

Martin, Donald R.
McCathie, Colin
McCord, John
MacDiarmid, Peter T. L.
MacDonald, Duncan
McEwan, Ian C.
McFall, Michael B.
McJannett, F.
Millar, D
Mills, Leslie H.
Morris, Michael.
Morrison, E. R.

Nelson-Keys, M.
Noakes, John R.
Norton, Gerald W. T.

O'Brian, Tippett Michael
Orr, John H.

Parker, Raymond W.
Paton, George M.
Pearce, George E.
Pearce, Kenneth A.
Pederson, R. A.
Perkin, L.
Peterson, Peter D,
Pooley, Michael J.

Randall, Rev. W. R.
Rencher, Ronald A.
Riesco, Michael R.
Rogers, William H.
Rowlands, Leslie W.
Royle, Anthony E.

Sadgrove, Victor A.
Salmon, George B.
Sharman, Frederick
Shirley, Kenneth B. M.
Smith, K. C. C.
Sole, Eric A. S.

Tamblyn, A. L.
Tierney, D. F.

Vroome, Pierre G.

Wahl, Jean
Wain, Eric S.
Watson, John
Watts, B. W. H.
Weller, Wilfred L.
Wheeler, John
White, Bryan H.
Whitham, Henry E.
Whyte, A. R.

117 Officers
   5 Killed in Action
   2 Died of Wounds
124 Total

REUNIONS

15 SCOTTISH RECONNAISSANCE REGIMENT

Re-Union Dinner - 5th October, 1946

.....................A. V. SADGROVE.................

Formation. Enemy. None To-night.

Own Tps. A list of members who have accepted the invitation will be found on the back.

Intention. This Dinner WILL be kept as informal and as friendly as possible, but the following Rules of Procedure will help to keep some semblance of order.

Method. *Phase 1.* You are now in the Ante Room where drinks may be obtained from the Bar on payment. A plan of the seating accomodation in the Dining Room will be found in a prominent position. The Records and Accounts of the Association will be found on a table. Please treat them with care and do not take them away from the table.

Phase 2. At 8 o'clock (or when announced) you will be called to the Dining Room, adjoining the Ante Room. A card bearing your name will mark your place, corresponding with the plan in the Ante Room. A photograph will be taken, primarily to be sent to members who are still serving abroad. You may order one for yourself if you wish.

Phase 3. Dinner. Drinks (2 beers *gin cup* and 1 Port) will be supplied by the Fund.

Phase 4. As seating accomodation at table is unavoidably crowded, you are encouraged to circulate within the two rooms after dinner. A Bar will be available in the Ante Room for drinks on payment. There is no fixed time limit to the proceedings.

Eat, drink and be merry, for it's rare that we meet

ADCOCK, H. W.	KENNINGTON, F. W.
AMSWYCH, B. A.	KERRIDGE, P. C.
BOYNTON, J. K.	LIDDELL, W. B.
BUCK, A.	McCATHIE, C.
DALTON, G. T. B.	MARTIN, R. D.
DAVIES, A. C.	MILLS, L. H.
DAVIS, J. D.	MORRIS, M.
DOVE, C. R. T.	PARKER, R. W.
FALLOON, W.	PEARCE, G. E.
FLEET, R. H.	PEARCE, K. A.
FORDYCE, T. G.	PETERSON, P. D.
GILLINGS, A. E.	RENCHER, A. R.
GREEN, H. A.	RIESCO, M. R.
GRAY, K. W.	SADGROVE, A. V.
HARTER, R. J.	SALMON, G. B.
HEATHCOAT-AMORY (M.C.),	SHIRLEY, K. B. M.
Lt. Col. R.	SMITH, D.S.O.,
HIGGS, R.	Lt. Col. K. C. C.
JACKSON, D. E.	WAHL, JEAN
JENKINS, K. G.	WAIN, E. S.
JELLINEK, E. H.	WELLER, W. L.
JENNINGS, W. J.	WHITE, B. H.
KEMSLEY, W.	WHITHAM, H. E.
	CROWDER B.

15 SCOTTISH RECONNAISSANCE REGIMENT

FIRST

Officers' Re-Union Dinner

THE CONNAUGHT HOTEL
CARLOS PLACE, LONDON, W.1

Saturday, 5th October, 1946

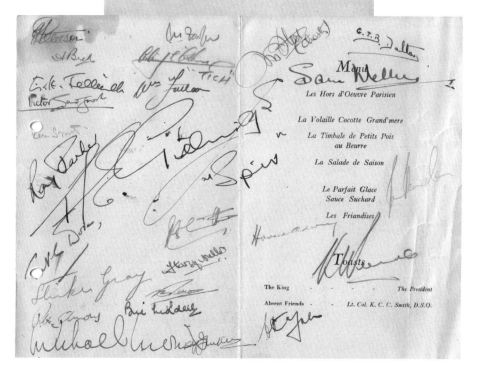

Menu

Les Hors d'Oeuvre Parisien

La Volaille Cocotte Grand'mere

La Timbale de Petits Pois
au Beurre

La Salade de Saison

Le Parfait Glace
Sauce Suchard

Les Friandises

Toasts

The King   The President

Absent Friends   -   Lt. Col. K. C. C. Smith, D.S.O.

First Re-Union Dinner 5 October 1946 Connaught Hotel (41 attendees)

1: Fordyce; 2: X; 3: Jenkins; 4: Peterson; 5: X; 6: Riesco; 7: Sadgrove; 8: Jellinek; 9: Boynton; 10: Dove; 11: X; 12: Gray; 13: Gillings; 14: McCathie; 15: Falloon; 16: Mills; 17: Heathcoat-Amory; 18: Smith; 19: Liddell; 20: Fleet; 21: X; 22: X; 23: X; 24: X; 25: Dalton; 26: X; 27: X; 28: Davies; 29: X; 30: Pearce; 31: Green; 32: Buck; 33: X; 34: Shirley; 35: Kemsley; 36: Wahl; 37: Pearce; 38: X; 39: Amswych; 40: White

X = unknown

Please read NOW.

15 SCOTTISH RECONNAISSANCE REGIMENT.

Fourth Re-Union Dinner   -   16th October, 1948

Information. Enemy. Haven't seen any for 3½ years.
Own Tps. Appear more frequently and a list of probable starters will be found overleaf.

Intention. Although some semblance of order must prevail, this Dinner WILL be kept as informal as possible.

Method. *Phase 1.* Assemble for drinks in the Ante Room as from 18.15 hrs. Association Records and Accounts are available. Please treat them with care and do not take them away from the table.

Phase 2. At 19.00 hrs. (or when announced) adjourn to the Dining Room. A card bearing your name marks your place. A photograph will be taken, primarily to be sent to members unable to be present.

Phase 3. Dinner. Drinks supplied by Club Funds.

Phase 4. After Dinner the following move will take place in an orderly fashion : S.P. Connaught Hotel. *Route :* Out of front door—Right—five yards—Right again along Mount Street to within ten yards of X Rds—Stop—D.P. will be on your Right—The Audley Hotel where the All Ranks Reunion will be in full swing.

Phase 5. Unpredictable (any control over the assembled company which have might been evident prior to this phase is now expected to disappear).

Sunday, 17 October. Anyone who is able to assemble (with wife attached) at the Cafe Royal bar at 12.30 prior to having some lunch, please inform M.R.R. during Phase 1.

First Old Comrades Association re-union took place in London on Friday October 3 1947.

63 attendees: A Squadron 13; B Squadron 17; C Squadron 20; HQ Squadron 13

Eat, drink and be merry, for it's rare that we meet.

15 SCOTTISH RECONNAISSANCE REGIMENT.

Fourth Re-Union Dinner   -   16th October, 1948

Lieut. P. C. H. AMBLER.	Capt. C. G. LAWTON.
Capt. B. A. AMSWYCH.	Major W. B. LIDDELL, M.C.
Capt. W. H. G. ANSLEY.	Capt. C. McCATHIE.
Capt. G. R. BLOUNT, M.C.	Lieut. M. B. McFALL.
Capt. J. K. BOYNTON, M.C.	Lieut. J. R. NOAKES.
Major B. CROWDER.	Lieut. M. O'BRIEN TIPPETT.
Lieut. G. T. B. DALTON.	Capt. G. E. PEARCE.
~~Major C. R. T. DOVE.~~	Lieut. K. A. PEARCE.
Capt. T. G. FORDYCE.	Lieut. P. D. PETERSON.
Capt. A. E. GILLINGS.	Capt. E. A. ROYLE, M.C.
Col. J. A. GRANT-PETERKIN, D.S.O.	Capt. M. R. RIESCO.
	Capt. A. V. SADGROVE.
~~Lieut. R. HIGGS.~~	~~Capt. O. B. SALMON.~~
Capt. D. E. JACKSON.	~~Capt. K. B. M. SHIRLEY.~~
Capt. K. G. JENKINS.	Lt.-Col K. C. C. SMITH, D.S.O.
Lieut. E. H. JELLINEK.	
Major C. J. KEMP.	Capt. E. A. S. SOLE.
Capt. W. KEMSLEY.	~~Lieut. C. P. VROOME.~~
~~Lieut. P. C. KERRIDGE, M.C.~~	Capt. B. H. WHITE.
	Capt. J. WAHL.

Re-Union Dinner October 1948 Connaught Hotel

Standing back row (L to R): X; X; Ansley; K Pearce; Dalton; Sadgrove; Fordyce; McCathie; Kemp; Kemsley; Lawton; Sole

Seated back row (L to R): X; X; Jenkins; Gillings; Boynton; GE Pearce; Riesco; Blount; Smith; Grant Peterkin

Seated second row (L to R): Jellinek; Peterson

Seated third row (L to R): Liddell; McFall; Royle; Wahl

Seated front (L to R) White; Amswych

X = unknown

6th Officers' Reunion Dinner Connaught Hotel, London, October 1950

Officers Dinner Club.

6th Reunion Dinner,

14th October 1950.

Headquarters 15th Scottish Division.

Major General C.M. Barber, C.B.,D.S.O.
Major J.F. Marnan, M.B.E.
Captain C.B. Lawton.

15th Scottish Reconnaissance Regiment (R.A.C.)

Colonel J. A. Grant Peterkin, D.S.O.
Lieut. Colonel K.C.C. Smith, D.S.O.

Lieut. P.C.H. Ambler
Captain B.A. Amswych
Captain J.K. Boynton,M.C.
Lieut. A. Buck, M.C.
Lieut. G.T.B. Dalton,
Major, C.R.T. Dove.
Captain L.T. Ford.
Captain T.G. Fordyce.
Captain A.E. Gillings.
Captain K.W. Gray, M.C.
Captain D.E. Jackson.
Major C.K. Kemp.
Captain W. Kemsley.
Captain J.W. Leeming.
Major W.B. Liddell, M.C.
Captain C. McCathie.
Lieut. M.B. McFall.
Lieut, R.D. Martin.
Major L.H. Mills.
Lieut. P.D. Peterson.
Captain M.R. Riesco.
Captain E.A. Royle,M.C.
Captain A.V. Sadgrove.

Captain E.A.S.Sole
Lieut. W.L. Weller.
Captain B.H. White.
Lieut. J. Wahl.
Sgt. A. Gilbert.

O.R. Reunion

E.S. Waine.
J. Bosch.

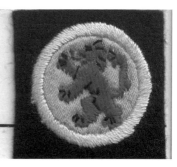

M.R. RIESCO

Back (L to R): Capt C.G. Lawton; Major C.R.T. Dove; Lt Col K.C.C. Smith DSO; General Barber CB DSO; Col Grant Peterkin DSO; Major J.F. Marnan MBE; Major L.H. Mills; Captain W. Kemsley; Sgt A. Gilbert

Front left (front to back): Captain J.W. Leeming; Captain C. McCathie; Captain E.A. Royle MC

Front right (front to back): Captain B.A. Amswych; Captain B.H. White; Captain K.W. Gray MC; Captain E.A.S. Sole

14th October 1950.   6th Officers Dinner.

Diner Normande

Crème de Tomate ··· TOURVILLE

Caneton D'Aylesbury Roti ST GABRIEL

Petits Pois au Beurre ··· DU BOSQ

Chouxfleur Polonaise ···· ST PIERRE

Pommes Fondantes ··· BOCAGE

Poire Dame Blanche AU BON REPOS

Palmiers Dôre ··· EN BESSIN

Café ···· AU CAVARIE

Calvados ··· NORMANDE

The Helmond Bowl

This crystal has been engraved by Michael McFall, a former officer of the 15th Scottish Reconnaissance Regiment. Its inscription 'To the people of Helmond from the 15th Scottish Reconnaissance Regiment - with gratitude' reflects the close ties which existed between the town and the Regiment in the winter of 1944/1945. Indeed the Oost Brabant newspaper in its issue of 29 November 1945 was moved to say:

All British elite troops have been stationed at Helmond between November and December 1944, including the 15th Scottish Recce Regiment (whom the Helmond people called 'their own army')

The motifs on the bowl include armoured cars and the badges of the Reconnaissance and Royal Armoured Corps with, representing the Helmond link, drawings of Helmond Castle and swans.

Major Adam Gordon MC B Squadron C.O.
in conversation with Captan Hans Steenmetz,
Dutch Army
Helmond Castle 1995

Jack Robinson with Mark Worthington at
Arromanches Museum, 7 June 1998

Felton Hall, September 1997

Corps window - All Hallows by the
Tower Church

Tree planting, September 2000

Doug Peterson plants the
Regiment's tree

Edwin Reetham with the plaque he had carved
which is in the Chapel at The National Arboretum

Edwin and Gwen Reetham with the plaque in All Hallows' Church

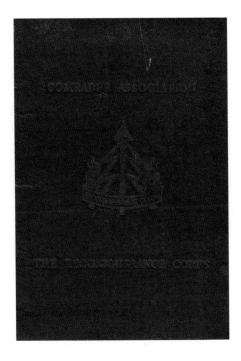

Normany 2002 - Bayeux Cemetery
David Reetham; Edwin Reetham; Richard Theobald; Len Watson; Tim Chamberlin; Michael McFall; 'Gilly'; Bill
Howlett; Bill Rees; Alan Westby; Stan Hook; French Piper
Seated - Bryan White

Normandy 2002

Michael Blair's grave centre

Pegasus Bridge

Former members of 7 Troop B Squadron, May 2002
L to R: Cyril Coomber; Doug Peterson; Bert Bonner; Ernest Jellinek

Pontefract September 2003
From row (L to R): J. Boynton; G. Blount*; A. Gillings*; G. Fordyce*; R. Knight
Middle row (L to R): W. Howlett; W. Mincedorf; K. Sadler; S. Hook; B. Higham; O. Thomas
Back row (L to R): B. Howe; G. Nicklin; G. Nursaw; R. Benson; A. Westby; L. Watson; E. Reetham

*Appear on March 1944 photo

= BREAKING OFF THE RECONNAISSANCE =

= I HAVE NOTHING TO REPORT - YET =

= ONE PRISONER WAS TAKEN =

= THE APPROACH TO CONTACT =

John Boynton was running the Regimental school in a little village called Hoisdorf not far from Ahrensburg and Bad Oldesloe. They were drawn by a German artist, Kurti Geffers who had attached himself to the school after walking back from the Russian front. John provided the captions and basic ideas and Kurti did the rest - he had been involved in cartoon work in his professional career.

Tilburg 2004

'Gilly' in command of a Humber

Not quite as agile as sixty years previously

Leading the parade

Bernie Higham lays our wreath at Best

Len Watson with his grandson, Oliver Stubbs, at the graveside of his great friend 'Tod' Slaughter

Bernie and Kath Higham; Oliver Stubbs

Ben Howe

Helmond Castle
L to R: Oscar Thomas; Len Watson; Bill Thomas; Ben Howe; Alan Westby; Richard Theobald; George Young;
Stan Hook; Ernie Clarke; Edwin Reetham; Bill Howlett; Ken Sadler; Gordon Nursaw; Clive Ridge; George
Turner; Bernie Highham
Seated: Bill Rees; Gordon Dalton. Turret: 'Gilly'

Miniature clogs carved as souvenirs from the people of Best for the veterans' 50th and 60th anniversaries
of their liberation (1994/2004)

Gilly's 85th - July 2004
L to R: George Bunn; 'Gilly'; Arthur Watkins; Len Watson; Bill Rees
Seated: Sir John Boynton

The final luncheon, Army/Navy Club, London, May 2007
L to R: R. Theobald; B. Howlett; Des Warner (Phantom Recce); A. Gillings; Revd E. Clarke; S. Hook; E. Jellinek; B. Ponting; W. Jamieson; A. Mason; B. Howe; G. Turner; E. Reetham; W. Mincedorf; G. Young; G. West (56 Recce); W. Thomas; L. Watson; B. Higham; P. Grant Peterkin; C. Ridge; T. Chamberlin

Lincoln, September 2008
L to Ri: Len Watson; 'Gilly'; Richard Theobald; Stan Hook; Ernie Clarke; Ricky Coomber*; John Kay*
*Travelled over from their homes in the US

Tilburg 2009

15th (S) Division Veterans at Gilze-Rijen Air Force Base

Dora and Ernie Clarke with
Gail Chamberlin

George Turner has a good vantage point

John Kay 'Ready to Go'

Bernie Higham lays our wreath at the Princess Irene Brigade Memorial

Tiny Barber memorial, Moergestel. John Kay lays the wreath

Tourville-sur-Odon (Calvados)

Le Monument de la 15th Division Ecossaise
(Champ de Bataille de L'Odon - 1944)

"In honoured memory of all ranks of the 15th Scottish Division who laid down their lives in the North-West
Europe Campaign 26th June 1944 - 5th May 1945"

Memorial unveiled 26 June 1949

More than sixty years later the lion rampant
still stands proudly.

From 1950 original:

The Regimental Association would like to place on record their gratitude
to the advertisers who appear on the following pages.

The generosity shown both by them and by certain members of our
Association has helped appreciably towards the production of this book.

INDEX

Military Formations & Units